WHAT MATTERS
INVESTING
IN RESULTS
TO BUILD STRONG, VIBRANT COMMUNITIES

Federal Reserve Bank of San Francisco
& Nonprofit Finance Fund

FEDERAL RESERVE BANK OF SAN FRANCISCO

101 Market Street
San Francisco, CA 94105

NONPROFIT FINANCE FUND

5 Hanover Square, 9th Floor
New York, NY 10004

Editors

Valerie Bartlett
Antony Bugg-Levine
David Erickson
Ian Galloway
Janet Genser
Jennifer Talansky

ISBN 978-0-692-87808-8

Printed in the United States of America

S. LEONARD SYME

This book is dedicated to UC Berkeley Professor **Len Syme**. He is considered by many to be the father of social epidemiology. His insights on the social determinants of health have been instrumental in helping many of us in the community development field better understand how our efforts to improve neighborhoods also improve health and wellbeing.

Len once said that after 60 years of studying the statistical and epidemiological models that predicted health, he noticed something unmistakable: Healthy children had brighter eyes. In other words, bright eyes were as powerful a predictor of future health as all his high-powered science; only when faced with mounting callenges did the brightness fade and disease creep in.

This book is dedicated to the idea that all children are born with bright eyes and that the ultimate "outcome" is keeping their eyes bright for a lifetime. That outcome requires new ways of orienting our social systems, including new business models and new financing techniques, which are described in detail in the following pages.

ACKNOWLEDGMENTS

Completing a project of this size and scope requires the commitment of many partners. First and foremost, we must thank the 80 authors who worked hard to communicate their ideas, experiences, and insights in these pages. Without them there would be no book. We were guided by a first-rate advisory committee, and we would like to call out Andrea Levere's great work in synthesizing the many themes of our authors in her chapter.

The Nonprofit Finance Fund team wishes to thank all their philanthropic partners for the support they received to work on this project, particularly Bank of America Charitable Foundation for its core support of this work. They are also grateful to: Ford Foundation, The Kresge Foundation, John D. and Catherine T. MacArthur Foundation, Omidyar Network, The Robin Hood Foundation, and The Rockefeller Foundation.

The Federal Reserve Bank of San Francisco team would like to thank John Williams, Adrian Rodriquez, and Scott Turner; their commitment to rigor, intellectual honesty, and innovation are woven through this book and have created a culture at the bank that makes a project like this possible. We're also grateful to the bank's print shop, which makes every copy of this book to the highest industry standard.

We also want to thank our skillful copy editor, Kelly Kramer, who kept this book readable, consistent, and accurate. Early in the process, Barbara Ray of Hired Pen also provided editing; she has been an editor on all four *What Works* books and we appreciate her ongoing guidance.

Our designers, C&G Partners, have crafted the look for all the *What Works* books. They have successfully interpreted the themes of this book and represent them here in an artful way.

ADVISORY COMMITTEE

Nancy O. Andrews
Low Income Investment Fund

Gordon Berlin
MDRC

Dash Boyer-Olson
Merrill Lynch

Xavier de Souza Briggs
Ford Foundation

John Cassidy
Monitor Deloitte

Kimberlee Cornett
The Kresge Foundation

Michele Jolin
Results for America

Jeremy Keele
Sorenson Impact Center

Zia Khan
The Rockefeller Foundation

Jitinder Kohli
Monitor Deloitte

Terri Ludwig
Enterprise Community Partners, Inc.

Andy McMahon
CSH

Tyler Norris
Well Being Trust

George Overholser
Third Sector Capital Partners, Inc.

Tracy Palandjian
Social Finance Inc.

Sonal Shah
Georgetown University

Kathy Stack
Laura and John Arnold Foundation

Kerry Sullivan
Bank of America Charitable Foundation

David Wilkinson
The White House

TABLE OF CONTENTS

Why is This Important?

2 HOW THIS WORKS

Prototypes

Better Results for Vulnerable Communities

Field and Sector Implications

Reasons for Caution and Optimism

3 SYNTHESIS AND WAY FORWARD

FOREWORD

Deval Patrick
Managing Director, Bain Capital Double Impact
Former Governor of Massachusetts

The American social sector is unique in its scope and scale. Our foundations, community and faith-based organizations, and other nonprofits mobilize substantial effort and resources to respond to a dizzying array of social challenges in virtually every corner of the country. Much of this relies on America's celebrated private philanthropy, which last year contributed a record $400 billion. A range of taxpayer-sponsored services supported by municipal, state, and federal governments contributes significantly as well. Despite heroic work and undeniable progress on many fronts, social challenges persist. Indeed, many economists view social challenges like income inequality, low educational achievement, job scarcity, homelessness, and opioid addiction not just as social problems but drags on broad economic growth and prosperity.

Although addressing social ills serves the common good, the business sector generally has not viewed itself as a partner in this work. Indeed, solutions to many social ills involve goods and services that help address social challenges or improved means of production. The time is ripe for a new kind of collaboration. Business has a role—and a profitable one at that.

Fortunately, a new generation of leaders in business, government, and the social sector are bringing precisely that spirit of collaboration into play. I've seen impact investing in the private sector and social impact bonds on the public side begin to address our most pressing social challenges collaboratively and effectively across sectors.

As governor of Massachusetts, I supported the nation's first state-level social impact bond. This Pay for Success contract mobilized private investors to fund the expansion of the nonprofit Roca, using flexible funding to transform the prospects of hundreds of young people in some of the Bay State's most marginalized neighborhoods. We supported an innovative way to address youth recidivism, trying a new approach to public policy but with private funds at risk. The investors get paid based on the savings produced by preventing recidivist behavior.

A similar kind of collaboration happens with impact investing. I launched an impact investing business at Bain Capital, where we invest in scaling private companies whose products or services create impact in sustainability, health and wellness, or community building. I am privileged to meet inspiring entrepreneurs and investors eager and able to build world-class businesses that not only create wealth for investors but also intentionally deliver social or environmental good.

What connects the social workers at Roca and the entrepreneurs and investors we work with at Bain Capital is a common motivation to improve outcomes in our communities. Although that sounds like an obvious focal point for organizing our social sector, as this book makes clear, that is not how our system is currently organized. But it can be. And a system organized around outcomes and results can substantially and affordably address our most vexing social challenges.

Reorienting our social system around outcomes is not going to be easy. This type of change never is. And it will require building trust and collaboration between leaders in the private and public sectors unused to working together. But it offers a way out of the cycle of exhausting effort, disappointing results, and eroding political support that too often characterize our efforts to address our most pressing social challenges.

We can all play a role in spurring this new way of working. Government officials and donors can collaborate with the social service organizations they fund to set clear expectations and then give these organizations the flexibility and data they need to reach them. Nonprofit leaders and social entrepreneurs can take the risk of embracing results-based funding that will pay only if programs work. Investors can help provide the upfront financing to enable this collaboration. And business leaders can go to market recognizing the long-term value of sustainable practices.

This is not the easiest path forward. But the examples in this book point to its potential. And the clear-eyed examination of the hurdles gives me confidence we will get over them. Reorienting our social system around outcomes could finally honor the generosity of donors and the effort of nonprofit workers with the results they deserve and that our communities sorely need.

DEVAL PATRICK *is a managing director of Bain Capital Double Impact, where he focuses on investments that deliver both a competitive financial return and significant positive social impact. In 2006, in his first bid for public office after a successful career in law and business, he became the first African-American governor of the Commonwealth of Massachusetts. He is a Rockefeller Fellow, a Crown Fellow of the Aspen Institute, and the author of two books,* A Reason to Believe: Lessons from an Improbable Life *and* Faith in the Dream: A Call to the Nation to Reclaim American Values.

SO, WHY ALL THIS FUSS ABOUT RESULTS AND OUTCOMES?

Antony Bugg-Levine
Nonprofit Finance Fund

You are likely not alone if you are wondering why we have written a book about the potential to orient our social system around results and outcomes. Because isn't that what it's already about? Don't we already provide funding to hospitals to keep people healthy, to homeless shelters to end homelessness, to childcare centers to prepare children for a fruitful life, and to job training programs to find people permanent employment?

Unfortunately not. We know that the deepest aspirations of the people who work in and run these organizations, and the government officials and private donors who fund them, is to make long-term and sustained positive impact on the clients and communities they serve. But that's not the way the social sector works.

Instead, we live in a system oriented around activities and outputs. Almost all the funding for our social system is allocated by activities, rather than long-term results. Payment flows to the hospital for providing treatments, to the homeless shelter based on the number of shelter beds occupied, to the early childcare center for keeping the classroom filled, and to the job training program for providing training.

Many organizations do amazing work and provide essential services that make an important, positive impact on the people they serve. But this output orientation forces too many to spend too much time and effort complying with the red tape that comes from contracts that release funds only when an organization proves it undertook a prescribed set of activities. And they do not have the flexibility to innovate and figure out what works in pursuit of results we all seek. For example, the homeless shelter paid by the number of beds it fills will not be in a position to provide additional therapy services that could help its clients address the root cause of their homelessness and more quickly transition out of the emergency shelter.

Despite our real progress on a range of social issues, over 45 million Americans still live in poverty,[1] more than half-a-million remain homeless according to the latest HUD point-in-time count,[2] unemployment among young African American men stubbornly persists around 30 percent in many cities,[3] an opioid abuse epidemic is sweeping across our country,[4] and, while the United States has five percent of the world's people, we hold 25 percent of the world's prisoners in a system that tends to warehouse rather than rehabilitate.[5]

Fortunately, we can do better. Orienting programs and funding around outcomes fundamentally changes this dynamic. In an outcomes-oriented system, service providers and funders partner to effect lasting outcomes they both seek. And the flow of money falls in line with the deepest motivations and moral commitments of the people providing and using it. An outcomes-oriented system has the potential to spur productive innovation by enabling service providers and government agencies to mobilize flexible funding and focus on delivering services that produce lasting change. Orienting programs around outcomes compensates the hardworking service providers for the impact they have achieved instead of the paperwork they file, allowing them to prioritize the work and delivery of services over short-term widget counting. And it could reinvigorate political support for social service funding as a worthy endeavor rather

---

1 Carmen DeNavas-Walt and Bernadette D. Proctor, "Income and Poverty in the United States: 2013," U.S. Census Bureau (September 2014), available at https://www.census.gov/content/dam/Census/library/publications/2014/demo/p60-249.pdf.

2 Alan Taylor, "America's Tent Cities for the Homeless," *The Atlantic* (February 11, 2016), available at https://www.theatlantic.com/photo/2016/02/americas-tent-cities-for-the-homeless/462450/.

3 Teresa L. Córdova, Matthew D. Wilson, and Jackson C. Morsey, "Lost: The Crisis Of Jobless and Out Of School Teens and Young Adults In Chicago, Illinois and the U.S.," Great Cities Institute, University of Illinois at Chicago (January 2016), available at https://greatcities.uic.edu/wp-content/uploads/2016/02/ASN-Report-v5.1.pdf.

4 American Society of Addiction Medicine, "Opioid Addiction: 2016 Facts & Figures," available at http://www.asam.org/docs/default-source/advocacy/opioid-addiction-disease-facts-figures.pdf.

5 Michelle Ye Hee Lee, "Does the United States Really Have 5 Percent of the World's Population and One Quarter of the World's Prisoners?" *Washington Post* (April 30, 2015), available at https://www.washingtonpost.com/news/fact-checker/wp/2015/04/30/does-the-united-states-really-have-five-percent-of-worlds-population-and-one-quarter-of-the-worlds-prisoners.

than a waste of taxpayer resources. Success might restore faith that we can make a difference and improve lives.

This movement toward an outcomes orientation is gaining widespread support across the country and across the political spectrum. The Republican governor of South Carolina and her Democratic counterparts in Colorado, Massachusetts, and New York have all publicly supported outcomes-oriented programs, as have mayors in places as diverse as New York City, Salt Lake County, and Denver. Congressional bills to support this work have received bipartisan co-sponsors in the House and Senate. Why does this outcomes orientation have such potential widespread appeal? Because it represents something we all can love: government spending on programs that work to address persistent social challenges, particularly upstream, and to avoid more expensive, inefficient, emergency treatment that happens downstream. It encourages government spending on programs organized to unlock innovation and improvement, and to free people providing services from the red tape that currently occupies so much of their attention. In these divided times, we cannot think of many other concepts that have received endorsements from such a wide range of leaders, from Republican and Democratic governors and mayors to nonprofit leaders and investment bankers.

But, to realize the potential of this new approach, we need to be clear about how this contrasts with business-as-usual and focus on the hard work ahead. Reorienting our system around outcomes and results requires a new social contract between those who deliver social services and those who pay for them. In this new contract, taxpayers and private donors will enjoy the benefits of knowing their funding is paying for demonstrable results. In return, they will need to free the organizations delivering these services from the red tape that comes with current funding tied to compliance to preset activities and agree to pay the full cost of sustaining this work.

Our legacy systems have not prepared us well to operate in this new way. Finding data to determine if results are met is difficult. So is aligning data systems across various government agencies and private databases. And even when the data are in place, agreeing on results necessitates new analytical skills.

Orienting around results also necessitates breaking down silos. For example, reducing the number of children in foster care can best be achieved through a coordinated program that includes support for parents to access housing, drug rehabilitation, and employment placements. Currently, these services exist in separate agencies funding different organizations to deliver a set of disconnected activities. And coordinating across agencies is only one step. Often, the most promising outcomes-oriented solutions involve similar silo-busting between government and foundation donors, and the recruitment of private investors working through large financial services institutions and private companies offering technology and other solutions. Beyond just setting new financial incentives, we will need to commit resources to enable organizations to invest in adapting to this new way of working, including new data infrastructure and personnel who can build and manage novel coalitions.

TOWARD A NEW FUNDING MODEL

Both the new social contract promoters and its skeptics are represented in *What Matters*. The organizations and agencies delivering social programs have learned to be skeptical about new funding approaches that historically have been the harbinger for budget cuts and unfunded mandates. Those of us who want to see the system improved will need to acknowledge the skepticism that the current broken system has conditioned so many reasonable people to feel and to advocate for the full costs of orienting toward outcomes.

We will also need to be clear about how the movement to popularize this new social contract fits in an increasingly crowded constellation of people and organizations promoting government and governance reform. Closest is the push for "evidence-based policy." As some of its leading proponents describe in this book, this movement seeks to channel government funding to programs that are proven to work. Often, outcomes-oriented approaches rely on this type of evidence. But after evidence identifies what works, funding can still flow to pay for activities the evidence suggests will lead to long-term results rather than those results themselves. The new social contract calls for a deeper transformation in not only what we fund but also how we align funding with the results we all seek. In an outcomes-oriented system, funding will also allow for flexibility, continuous improvement, and tracking of results.

Another source of both momentum and confusion for this systems shift is the explosion of innovation in social-sector financing. Chapters in this book explore a range of new, and some tried and tested, ways in which financial innovation can support organizations and agencies operating in an outcomes-oriented system. Terms and concepts, such as "Pay for Success," "social impact bonds," "advance market commitments," "rate cards," and "social impact insurance," can sometimes overwhelm the non-finance experts who typically make funding decisions and implement social programs. And they sometimes lead people to mistake financial innovation as an end in itself, rather than a means to ensuring that great organizations get to do great work that makes a lasting, positive difference for more people.

You do not need to be a finance expert to understand this book or act on its insights. Just remember that ultimately, organizations and agencies require *funding* that will eventually pay for the outcomes they generate, while *financing* can provide money upfront to support the work that is required to achieve them.

This may all sound a bit wonky and technical. But in communities across the country, everyday people in government agencies, community-based service organizations, and charitable foundations are already showing how orienting around outcomes and results is practical and powerful. They are making the extraordinary routine.

The chapters in this book capture some of their experiences. In our daily work, we are privileged to hear many more. And we have spared you long debates about language and terms or dispositions on logic models and theories of change. We use the words "results" and "outcomes" interchangeably to describe a system oriented around the ultimate good we seek to generate, in contrast with the activities or outputs we undertake to get there.

Reorienting around outcomes has the potential to substantially improve the results that social-sector funding generates. And it has the potential to liberate us from a system that frustrates all its participants: the taxpayer who wonders what she's getting for her money, the nonprofit service provider burdened by compliance rules that force attention and activity in areas she is not convinced will make a difference, and the people left without jobs, or health, or hope when the compliance-based system fails to deliver results.

Realizing this potential will require all of us to honestly acknowledge how many of our cherished practices and assumptions are accommodations to a broken system rather than necessary or beneficial. We will need to meet each other with empathy, understanding the constraints we all face that sometimes mask the unity of our purpose. And we will need to honor the lessons of people working on the ground and the insights they uncover about how this world actually works, even when those insights conflict with compelling theory.

By making clear why reorienting around outcomes is disruptive, better, and feasible, we hope this book provides a useful starting point and accelerant for action.

———

ANTONY BUGG-LEVINE *is chief executive officer of Nonprofit Finance Fund (NFF), a national nonprofit and financial intermediary that advances missions and social progress through financing, consulting, partnerships, and knowledge-sharing that empowers leaders, organizations, and ideas. A leading community development financial institution (CDFI), NFF has $250 million in assets under management and has provided $620 million in financing and access to additional capital in support of over $2.3 billion in projects for thousands of organizations nationwide. Bugg-Levine is the co-author of* Impact Investing: Transforming How We Make Money While Making a Difference. *Prior to joining NFF in 2011, he designed and led The Rockefeller Foundation's impact investing initiative and oversaw its program-related investments portfolio. He was the founding board chair of the Global Impact Investing Network and convened the 2007 meeting that coined the phrase "impact investing." A former consultant with McKinsey & Company, he also taught at Columbia Business School.*

1

SHIFT TO
OUTCOMES

Shift to Outcomes
HOW DID WE GET HERE?

THE MARCH TOWARD OUTCOMES-BASED FUNDING

David J. Erickson
Federal Reserve Bank of San Francisco

C reating social welfare systems that care for those who are struggling is a relatively recent phenomenon. Over the past 130 years, we have tried many different approaches to helping people improve their chances to live healthy and productive lives. The following essay sketches out how some of those programs have evolved over the years and lands us at today's debate over how we should organize our social services sector and pay for it in the most effective way possible. We are hungry for innovation and a breakthrough. Too many individuals and families are suffering and not living up to their potential. It is both a moral issue and an economic one. The status quo is expensive in terms of paying for the negative effects of failure in the social sector (e.g., incarceration, chronic disease, underemployment, and remedial education). In this book, we ask a number of questions about the status quo: Could social service resources be spent more effectively? Might one important strategy be paying specifically for the outcomes we want? Is that even possible? This essay, and the essays in this book, are an effort to explore how we might pay directly for the outcomes we want as a strategy to achieve the breakthrough that is overdue.

THE EVOLUTION OF SOCIAL POLICY IN THE UNITED STATES

Historians bristle when people say that the Civil War (1861–65) was a battle between the Industrial North and the Agricultural South. The North did have more factories than the South, but to say it was an industrial economy is wrong. Almost half of workers in the North had ties to agriculture, and although the percentage was higher (80 percent) in the South, both societies were overwhelmingly agricultural.[1] In 1860, only

---

Thanks to my Federal Reserve colleague Ian Galloway for his assistance with this chapter. The views expressed are my own and may not reflect those of the Federal Reserve Bank of San Francisco or the Federal Reserve System.

1 Library of Congress, *Civil War Desk Reference* (New York: Simon & Schuster, 2002), p. 74.

one in five Americans lived in a city (defined as 2,500 or more inhabitants), and the country was overwhelmingly rural.[2]

Americans, attracted by factory jobs and growing urban economies, did not start moving into cities in big numbers until the 1880s. This shift in our society set three powerful trends in motion:

1 Competition for industrial jobs drove down wages in many industries.

2 Competition for places to live near those jobs drove up rents.

3 Leaving home for the city cut social ties that were traditionally provided by families and small, tight-knit communities.

A significant result of these three trends was the creation of slums or ghettos, where struggling low-income Americans concentrated.

For some, the distance traveled from farms to ghettos was short, and others crossed oceans and continents. Many of the new arrivals thrived, but for those who didn't there was not much of a social safety net. Churches and charities provided some relief, as did local governments, but these efforts were small in comparison with the growing problem.

There were many waves of this phenomenon: Southern and Eastern Europeans in the late 1800s and early 1900s; poor Southern whites and blacks during the Great Migration to Northern cities starting after 1915; dramatic increases in immigration from Latin America after 1965; and, of course, it continues today in many cities worldwide as rural populations flock to cities seeking opportunity. The United States became a majority-urban nation by 1920,[3] while the worldwide population did not reach majority-urban until 2008.[4]

There were early coordinated efforts to help stabilize new arrivals to the cities. Pioneers, such as Jane Addams in the late 1800s, addressed these issues through the Settlement House movement, which might be

---

2 U.S. Census, "The Urban Population as a Percentage of the Total Population by U.S. Region and State (1790–1990)," available at https://www.census.gov/population/censusdata/table-4.pdf.

3 Ibid.

4 United Nations Population Fund, *State of World Population 2007: Unleashing the Potential of Urban Growth* (New York: United Nations Population Fund, 2007), p. 1.

considered the first place-based/cross-sector intervention for low-income communities. And tight-knit immigrant communities were able to provide for many of the needs of new arrivals. These efforts, however, were small and local.

Source: "The White Angel Bread Line" by Dorothea Lange, San Francisco, CA, 1933; Records of the Social Security Administration; Record Group 47; National Archives.

With the arrival of the Great Depression in the 1930s, local interventions were no longer a match for that era's mass unemployment and mass misery. By that time, American society was urban and industrial, and downturns in the economy were more than a "cold shower," in Joseph Schumpeter's famous phrase; they were moments of widespread suffering and political instability. By 1933, the gross national product had dropped in half from the 1929 level, and one in four workers was without a job.[5] Relief systems for the poor were beyond their breaking points, as epitomized by the ubiquitous sight of breadlines in American cities. During the

5 David M. Kennedy, *The American People in the Great Depression: Freedom from Fear, Part One* (New York: Oxford University Press, 1999), p. 163.

Figure 1. Poverty Rate and Number in Poverty: 1959 to 2015

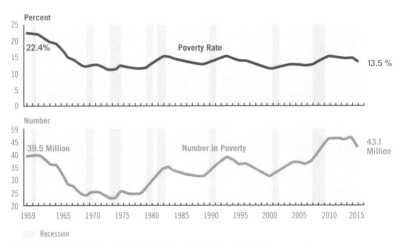

Note: The data for 2013 and beyond reflect the implementation of the redesigned income questions.
Source: U.S. Census Bureau, Current Population Survey, 1960 to 2016 Annual Social and Economic Supplements.

New Deal, the federal government had two choices, according to Chicago Mayor Anton Cermak in his congressional testimony: It could send relief to Chicago; if not, it would have to send troops.[6]

The economic development and jobs programs of the New Deal—and later, the massive spending to mobilize for the Second World War—got the country working again. After the war, a combination of successful public policies and economic growth drastically reduced the percentage of Americans living in poverty. Between the 1940s and the early 1970s, the U.S. poverty rate was estimated to drop from 33 percent to a low of 11 percent in 1973.[7] In real terms, family income grew almost 75 percent from the end of the Second World War to the mid-1960s.[8] In the 50 years since then, however, the poverty rate has been stubbornly persistent between 12 and 15 percent (see Figure 1 above). Meanwhile, the absolute

---

6 Ibid, p. 88.

7 Robert D. Plotnick et al., "The Twentieth-Century Record of Inequality and Poverty in the United States," Institute for Research on Poverty (Discussion Paper no. 1166–98: July 1998), p. 21, available at http://www.irp.wisc.edu/publications/dps/pdfs/dp116698.pdf.

8 Andrew Glyn et al., *The Rise and Fall of the Golden Age of Capitalism: Reinterpreting the Postwar Experience* (New York: Oxford University Press, 1990).

number of Americans living in poverty has risen with the nation's population growth.

EXPERIMENTS IN THE 1960s: THE WAR ON POVERTY AND THE BIRTH OF COMMUNITY DEVELOPMENT

Even in the midst of the postwar economic boom, it was clear that poverty still had a hold on American life. Writers such as Michael Harrington, in his book *The Other America* (1962), put a spotlight on lingering urban and rural poverty in the United States. Thanks to powerful allies (e.g., organized labor and the civil rights movement), the federal government launched an effort to eradicate poverty in 1964. President Johnson announced that his administration had "declared a war on poverty in all its forms, in all its causes, and we intend to drive it underground and win that war."[9]

The historian James Patterson observed that President "Johnson, [Sargent] Shriver, and the others who developed the war on poverty...were not radicals. They were optimists who reflected the confidence of contemporary American liberal thought." According to Patterson, "They were not so much concerned about inequality. They focused instead on programs to promote greater opportunity—a politically attractive goal."[10]

True to that vision, the war on poverty would not be a radical program of income redistribution. The programs would focus on creating opportunity. The lead agency for the war on poverty was the Office of Economic Opportunity, which was responsible for multiple programs in health, employment, education, and housing.[11] There were efforts to eliminate hunger through the Food Stamp Program; reduce education disparities through Head Start and additional funding through the Elementary and Secondary Education Act; provide access to legal advice (Neighborhood Legal Services); and create opportunities to participate in improving communities as a volunteer (VISTA) and as a community

---

9 Lyndon Johnson, Remarks at the Johnson County Courthouse, Painstville, KY, 1964. The American Presidency Project at the University of California, Santa Barbara, available at http://www.presidency.ucsb.edu/ws/?pid=26190.

10 James T. Patterson, *Grand Expectations: The United States, 1945–1974* (New York: Oxford University Press, 1996), p. 538.

11 Alan Brinkley, *The Unfinished Nation: A Concise History of the American People*, 4th ed. (New York: McGraw Hill, 2004).

member (Community Action).[12] The Department of Housing and Urban Development (HUD) was created in 1965, and in the words of its first secretary, Robert Weaver: "We are involved in the exciting and creative business of bringing all our resources and energies to bear in solving the problems of your cities."[13]

One important legacy from the war on poverty in the 1960s is an approach to revitalizing low-income areas that grew out of the Gray Areas Program of the Ford Foundation. The idea was to fund local corporations that were rooted in and rooting for struggling communities. It was the first attempt, according to Robert F. Kennedy, to not treat single issues contributing to poverty, but to "grab the web [of urban poverty] whole."[14]

These community development corporations (CDCs) got their start with the Bedford Stuyvesant Restoration Corporation in New York City in the mid-1960s. CDCs were nonprofit but subject to market discipline in their pursuit of better local social outcomes and a stronger local economy. "These groups were born of the activist spirit of the '60s—products of the War on Poverty and the civil rights movement, and reactions to the negative effects of the federal urban renewal program," according to housing scholar Avis Vidal, who noted that "these groups often began as community service or community action agencies and later moved into community economic development."[15] Today, there are over 4,000 CDCs working in communities in all 50 states.[16]

CDCs and social service providers were often constrained by lack of capital, and their projects and initiatives often required extra help to underwrite financially. Loans, initially from the pension dollars of nuns and churches, were the first into this financial breach. Those loans

---

12 Patterson, *Grand Expectations* (1996), pp. 539–40.

13 Address to a convention of the National League of Cities by HUD Secretary Robert Weaver, March 30, 1966. Record Group 207, Federal Archives, College Park, MD.

14 Scott Kohler, "Bedford-Stuyvesant and the Rise of the Community Development Corporation," Duke University Sanford School of Public Policy, Center for Strategic Philanthropy and Society (Case Study 33: 1966), available at https://cspcs.sanford.duke.edu/sites/default/files/descriptive/bedford-stuyvesant.pdf.

15 Avis Vidal, *Rebuilding Communities: A National Study of Urban Community Development Corporations* (New York: New School for Social Research, 1992), p. 2.

16 National Congress for Community Economic Development (NCCED), "Reaching New Heights" (June 2006), p. 4, available at http://community-wealth.org/content/reaching-new-heights-trends-and-achievements-community-based-development-organizations.

spawned a new type of institution to meet the credit needs of low-income neighborhoods, the community loan fund. The loan funds were the precursors to community development financial institutions (CDFIs) that got federal funding in the early 1990s.

CDFIs were partners to the creative new transactions that were financing the revitalization of communities around the country; they took more risks, and their patient capital often brought about the innovative transactions that harmonized multiple sources of capital (private, public, and philanthropic). Over time, these transactions became more routine, and more likely to be funded by traditional banks. Today, there are over 1,000 CDFIs[17] with over $35 billion in assets.[18]

The government funding programs that grew this small network of CDCs and CDFIs came from federal block grants (Community Development Block Grants and HOME Investment Partnership for affordable housing) and tax incentives in the form of investment tax credits (Low Income Housing Tax Credit and New Markets Tax Credit). There were private-sector sources of funding as well. Many banks were motivated to engage CDCs and CDFIs as a way to meet their requirements under the Community Reinvestment Act (CRA) of 1977. The CRA was an explicit policy to end "redlining," a practice where banks would take deposits from a community but not lend back to it because it was low-income and considered too risky. This practice stripped wealth out of communities and was particularly devastating to African American neighborhoods.

Philanthropy also played an important part in building this new system. In addition to the work of the Ford Foundation mentioned earlier, many leading philanthropies invested in the creation and growth of the community development network. This extended beyond grantmaking as well; many foundations experimented with new ways to finance community development work through program-related investments (PRIs), which provided a below-market rate of return for their investment in exchange for funding activities that promoted the foundations' missions. And

---

17 CDFI Fund, U.S. Treasury. Exact numbers available at https://www.cdfifund.gov/programs-training/certification/cdfi/Pages/default.aspx.

18 Luis G. Dopico, "20 Years of CDFI Banks and Credit Unions: 1996–2015: An Analysis of Trends and Growth," Opportunity Finance Network (January 31, 2017), available at http://ofn.org/sites/default/files/OFN_CDFI_CreditUnion_LongStudy_FINAL.pdf.

another development were mission-related investments (MRIs), which were similar in promoting a social outcome but with a market-rate return.

This new network of players, funded by public and private sources, created something that operated like a market. This quasi-market had many advantages over the older, top-down, Washington-based approach to community revitalization. Different players would come together to develop a particular property or project. They could then disassemble and recombine with new partners for new projects, providing greater flexibility and nimbleness as times and needs changed.[19]

The glue keeping these different groups working together was the funding from the many sources of community development finance. This funding provided the effective "demand" that created a market for community revitalization. CDCs and CDFIs were the first into this marketplace, but other for-profit real estate developers and banks followed. In the end, this system was successful in creating tens of billions of dollars of investments into low-income neighborhoods.

Overwhelmingly, these investments were in real estate. In the early years, most of the investing was in affordable housing (often with social services embedded in them). Later, however, there was more investment in clinics, charter schools, homeless shelters, and grocery stores in food deserts. There were practical reasons for this; lending against property is easier for banks since there is collateral against the loan. But the theory behind the community development strategy was that if you could improve the physical place—the disinvested neighborhood—then you would create new opportunities for the people who lived there. As Nancy Andrews, chief executive of the Low Income Investment Fund, once said, "We thought if we got the buildings right, everything else would take care of itself." The challenge of creating opportunity in low-income communities proved to be harder than that theory of change anticipated.

---

19 The process of coalescing and then disbanding to join again in a new configuration with new partners provides the opportunity to learn from mistakes. It guards against turf battles and the sclerosis that can set into traditional bureaucratic institutions. It allows flexibility in the response to a problem, so that if the need arises for more expertise in a particular area, such as education, health, or crime prevention, other groups or institutions with those skills or knowledge can join the network. (David J. Erickson, *Housing Policy Revolution: Networks and Neighborhoods* [Washington, DC: Urban Institute Press, 2009], p. 157.)

Community development finance is not to blame for the lack of success in the fight against poverty over the past 50 years. There were many headwinds in this fight; chief among them was a dramatically changing economy—thanks to globalization and technology—that reduced the need for low-skilled workers. As a strategy to overcome poverty, improved real estate may be a necessary condition. However, it is insufficient to dramatically improve the lives of people who live in those neighborhoods. All communities need both place- and people-oriented strategies to improve health, increase incomes, and reduce the incidence of poverty.

Poverty overwhelms narrow interventions because it results from a culmination of causes. Put another way, social exclusion is the product of many overlapping and reinforcing social exclusions. These overlapping obstacles include disinvestment in neighborhoods, deteriorating buildings and substandard housing, and lack of transportation and other amenities—parks, good schools, access to affordable fresh food. But there are human-capital contributions to poverty as well—poor physical and mental health, lack of competitive job skills, and insufficient support from one's family and community.

In other words, barriers to economic success require physical- as well as human-capital solutions. Paul Grogan, president of the Boston Foundation and one of the founders of the Local Initiative Support Corporation (LISC), tackled this question in *Investing in What Works for America's Communities* (2012). In looking to the future of community development, he wrote:

> It lies in turning the architecture of community development to meet urgent challenges of human development. How to turn a successful community organizing and real estate development system toward the goal of increasing educational outcomes, employment success, family asset building, individual and community resilience to weather setbacks? As an industry, we need new strategies to face these challenges.[20]

---

20 Paul Grogan, "The Future of Community Development," *Investing in What Works for America's Communities: Essays on People, Place & Purpose*, edited by Nancy O. Andrews and David J. Erickson (San Francisco: Federal Reserve Bank of San Francisco and Low Income Investment Fund, 2012), p. 188.

Terri Ludwig's chapter in this book tackles this question squarely: Can a system that has been built to invest many billions of dollars annually in places also be configured to invest in people?

EXPERIMENTS IN THE 1990s AND 2000s: EFFORTS TO COORDINATE MULTIPLE INTERVENTIONS FOR COMMUNITIES

[A]n argument can be made that the essential ingredients of improved public performance in the twenty-first century are not so much strengthened internal workings of agencies. Rather, they are improvements in how agencies collaborate and interact with other organizations through networks to achieve results. To ignore this dimension is to miss much of what is important in public management today.[21]

—J. Christopher Mihm

Our current policy era is one that prizes the need to be "comprehensive" and to coordinate services among multiple service providers. The drive to coordination has flown many banners—Comprehensive Community Initiative, Comprehensive Community Development, Neighborhood Improvement Initiative, Comprehensive Community Revitalization Program, Neighborhood and Family Initiative, Rebuilding Communities Initiative, New Futures, and Sustainable Communities (and the many other Obama-era federal initiatives).

These many efforts have had mixed results, but it is safe to say they are all in the rearview mirror; today the focus for coordinated social interventions is on the concept that FSG Consulting calls Collective Impact. In the Collective Impact model, there are five fundamental aspects to achieving better outcomes: 1) a common agenda, 2) shared measurement, 3) mutually reinforcing activities, 4) continuous communication, and 5) leadership and coordination from a backbone organization (see Figure 2).

However, in addition to these five conditions, the FSG authors suggested that there were three preconditions to get an effort like this started: "*an influential champion, adequate financial resources,* and a sense of *urgency*

---

21 J. Christopher Mihm, "Managing Successful Organizational Change in the Public Sector," *Debating Public Administration: Management Challenges, Choices, and Opportunities*, edited by Robert F. Durant and Jennifer R.S. Durant (Boca Raton, FL: CRC Press, 2013), p. 24.

Figure 2. The Five Conditions of Collective Impact

COMMON AGENDA	All participants have a shared vision for change including a common understanding of the problem and a joint approach to solving it through agreed upon actions.
SHARED MEASUREMENT	Collecting data and measuring results consistently across all participants ensures efforts remain aligned and participants hold each other accountable.
MUTUALLY REINFORCING ACTIVITIES	Participant activities must be differentiated while still being coordinated through a mutually reinforcing plan of action.
CONTINUOUS COMMUNICATION	Consistent and open communication is needed across the many players to build trust, assure mutual objectives, and create common motivation.
BACKBONE SUPPORT	Creating and managing collective impact requires a separate organization(s) with staff and a specific set of skills to serve as the backbone for the entire initiative and coordinate participating organizations and agencies.

Source: Fay Hanleybrown, John Kania, and Mark Kramer, "Channeling Change: Making Collective Impact Work," *Stanford Social Innovation Review* (January 26, 2012).

for change [emphasis in original]."[22] (For an interesting critique of Collective Impact, see Tom Wolff's essay, "Collaborating for Equity and Justice: Moving Beyond Collective Impact," in *Nonprofit Quarterly*.)[23]

Around the same time, in an essay in *Investing in What Works for America's Communities*, my co-authors and I proposed a similar better-coordination model to social interventions. Based on many of the same examples that FSG examined—the Harlem Children's Zone, Strive Partnership, Purpose Built Communities, etc.—we found that successful cross-sectoral interventions had five common characteristics: 1) trust from the community they serve, 2) cross-sector (health, education,

---

22 Fay Hanleybrown, John Kania, and Mark Kramer, "Channeling Change: Making Collective Impact Work," *Stanford Social Innovation Review* (January 26, 2012), available at https://ssir.org/articles/entry/channeling_change_making_collective_impact_work. The original article on this topic was written by John Kania and Mark Kramer, "Collective Impact," *Stanford Social Innovation Review* (Winter 2011), available at https://ssir.org/articles/entry/collective_impact.

23 Tom Wolff et al., "Collaborating for Equity and Justice: Moving Beyond Collective Impact," *Nonprofit Quarterly* (January 9, 2017), available at https://nonprofitquarterly.org/2017/01/09/collaborating-equity-justice-moving-beyond-collective-impact/.

housing, etc.), 3) place-based, 4) data-driven, and 5) led by a "community quarterback," an organization that has as its main objective the overall managing and coordinating of the intervention. Of course, we had preconditions, too: Each successful intervention seemed to be spearheaded by a charismatic super-genius with a close friend who was a billionaire.[24]

That is not scalable or replicable. The lesson, it seems to me, is to find a way to reverse-engineer the genius (or "influential champion" in the FSG framework) and the billionaire (or "adequate financial resources," according to FSG). The premise of this book is that the billionaire is replaced by the wiser use of public and private dollars to create a quasi-market for social outcomes that employs both people- and place-based strategies. Put differently, this transition to the market does not require new public dollars. Rather, it requires a rearranging of the many tens of billions of public dollars that are already being spent on expensive but not value-producing activities or things, such as treatment of chronic disease, incarceration, enhanced policing of poor neighborhoods, special education resources spent on children who are not ready to learn when they arrive at kindergarten.

This new market is likely to behave similarly to the quasi-market that was created by community development finance for community-enhancing real estate development in the 1980s and 1990s. There will be new institutions, like CDCs and CDFIs—or new activities within existing institutions—to develop projects and finance them. There may be some private-sector players entering this market as well. But the essential element of this new marketplace will be a cadre of community entrepreneurs who will combine their deep knowledge of their particular neighborhood's and population's needs with their problem-solving and bridge-building skills. Community entrepreneurs are the CDCs of the twenty-first century, and they will be the ones to play the role of the super-geniuses in community change.

Similar to entrepreneurs in the general economy, community entrepreneurs can come in many stripes. Perhaps the ur-example, however, is

---

24 David Erickson, Ian Galloway, and Naomi Cytron, "Routinizing the Extraordinary," *Investing in What Works for America's Communities: Essays on People, Place & Purpose*, edited by Nancy O. Andrews and David J. Erickson (San Francisco: Federal Reserve Bank of San Francisco and Low Income Investment Fund, 2012), pp. 377–406. I should note that my co-editor who co-created the idea for the community quarterback, Nancy O. Andrews, and I disagree on this point. We agree to disagree.

Geoffrey Canada, who started the Harlem Children's Zone. I have been struck by how many people I have met over the years who could play the role Canada invented. It helps that Canada had the support of high-net-worth people in New York City. But I know someone like Chris Krehmeyer, chief executive of Beyond Housing in St. Louis, is able to orchestrate new affordable housing construction, maintain a health-oriented grocery store in a food desert, and connect his residents to high-quality services they need—from child care to job training to substance abuse treatment.[25] Krehmeyer, a cross between a community organizer and a riverboat gambler, could be just as effective as Canada with the right financial backing. If we organized a market that valued better health, for example, and there were a cash flow for achieving that goal, there is no doubt that community entrepreneurs would rise to the challenge. And, once this role is more established, I suspect elite MBA programs would start training the next generation of community entrepreneurs.

FUTURE EXPERIMENTS: PAYING FOR OUTCOMES

The nineteenth-century department store magnate John Wannamaker is supposed to have said, "Half the money I spend on advertising is wasted; the trouble is, I don't know which half." We spend a lot of money in the United States (as do governments and charities around the world) to solve social problems, but we don't know exactly which half (or more) is working. According to former White House officials John Bridgeland and Peter Orszag, "less than $1 out of every $100 of [U.S.] government spending is backed by even the most basic evidence."[26]

What we are trying to capture in this book is not just that we think that programs should have a deeper evidence base to know whether they work. They should. But what we are proposing here is more than that. It is an effort to create a new way of doing business that allows us to create clusters of programs that work in concert to achieve better outcomes than any one program could achieve alone. We hope for an ecosystem—or market—that creates the right incentives to collect, analyze, and be

---

25 For more on Beyond Housing, see http://www.beyondhousing.org/our-leadership.

26 John Bridgeland and Peter Orszag, "Can Government Play Moneyball?" *The Atlantic* (July 2013), available at https://www.theatlantic.com/magazine/archive/2013/07/can-government-play-moneyball/309389/.

guided by data. This market also incentivizes better cooperation among multiple players from multiple sectors.

To that end, this book proposes that paying for outcomes—the actual desired outcomes, not simply the programs or infrastructure we "think" will get us there—will generate new business models to achieve better social outcomes. In some ways, it is a follow-on book to two books in the *What Works* series: *Investing in What Works for America's Communities*, which focused on new place-based/cross-sector interventions to improve low-income communities that incorporated both people- and place-based investing strategies, and *What Counts: Harnessing Data to Improve America's Communities*, which focused on how the appropriate use of data could better align multiple sectors to achieve better outcomes. This book, *What Matters*, is an effort to find new ways to finance these new business models by focusing on outcomes. All three books tell parts of the story of the march toward outcomes-based funding, and the ultimate creation of a market that values social outcomes.

POVERTY AS A COMPLEX ADAPTIVE SYSTEM

Poverty, as stated previously, is a product of overlapping and reinforcing phenomena. Another way to describe that reality is to say that poverty is a complex adaptive system. Each issue—housing, jobs, structural racism, transportation, education—has ways in which it can make the problem worse or better. Guiding a response that provides the right intervention, with the right partners, at the right time, and at the right scale, is very hard.

Sometimes the term "complex adaptive system" can put off readers because it signals something "too complex" to tackle, but there can be simplicity in this concept. In essence, complex systems are ones that have no central planner, and yet they achieve amazing results. There are examples in many varied settings. In nature, army ants basically do three things: 1) find food, 2) build and maintain a nest, and 3) protect the queen. One army ant alone would simply die. But hundreds of thousands of ants working together create elaborate communities and thrive. Similarly, T-cells in our bodies basically are able to do only three things: 1) determine if a cell in our bodies is "us" or "not us," 2) if it is "not us", take notes on its details, and 3) help other parts of the immune system create neutralizers for the "not us" intruder. With those simple rules, T-cells protect our bodies from billions of harmful intruders every day. Similarly, consumers in a market make purchasing decisions based on perceived quality and price. Those simple decisions drive trillions of dollars of investment, production, and sales every day. All three examples are complex adaptive systems, and yet they rest on fairly simple decision rules.[27]

The relevance here is that we could build a complex adaptive system by inventing an end goal—a child ready to learn at kindergarten, a student graduating from high school, a formerly homeless person who is stably housed, a retrained worker who holds a steady job, etc.—that has the potential to help align the many organizations to work together more effectively across sectors and silos to achieve these outcomes without a central planner.

At times, we think of this as an ecosystem that allows for multiple players to use their strengths (operational abilities, knowledge of local conditions and the population they are working with, trust from years of providing good service to the community, etc.) to act on newly emerging information (new data analyses, changing characteristics of a population, new partners, new business models, etc.) to find ways to improve their results. But another way to think of this is as a market for social outcomes.

USING MARKET MECHANISMS TO ACHIEVE IMPROVED SOCIAL OUTCOMES

When we use outcomes-based financing to create a quasi-market for improved social outcomes, we create incentives for comprehensive and coordinated social service interventions. These incentives create a market dynamic where independent actors are responding to market mechanisms (i.e., simple decision rules) to achieve a desired outcome.

In this marketplace, there will be community entrepreneurs who will lead us through potential breakthroughs or innovations. Those community entrepreneurs will need funding (and the existence of funding creates more community entrepreneurs). They will need data and analysis. They will need partners who can deliver on certain aspects of an outcomes-oriented business plan. Consider the analogy of a general contractor

---

27 For a good overview of complex adaptive systems, see Melanie Mitchell, *Complexity: A Guided Tour* (New York: Oxford University Press, 2009).

building a house. A general contractor has to coordinate subcontractors, such as the carpenter, plumber, electrician, and painter. Similarly, the community entrepreneur will have to assemble a team of "social subcontractors"—teachers, affordable-housing builders, household financial stability coaches, nurses—to meet the needs of his or her community. In many ways, the community entrepreneurs resemble the community quarterbacks from the *What Works* book, but it is intended to be a larger concept that allows for coordination of more than a cross-sector intervention; it would be the entity that owns the outcomes risk and might be the one to employ several community quarterbacks to achieve the desired result.

This combination of general contractors and subcontractors will be different in every place; no one size fits all. This is why so often policies and programs emanating from Washington, DC, or state capitals, don't work. In some places, issues around racial justice and healing might be the first priority. In other places, the highest-order concerns may have more to do with a deadly scourge of opioid addiction, requiring a public health intervention to stabilize the community. A third community might be struggling with the loss of low-skill/middle-wage jobs at a factory, mill, or rural regional hospital. In this third case, the first intervention might be to focus on the stability of families in economic transition (especially their children), with a tighter focus on job retraining and optional relocation to higher-opportunity communities. Still other interventions might first focus on the celebration of local culture—of Native Hawaiians or Mexican Americans in the colonias along the Texas border, for instance—as a first building block toward building stronger community cohesion and a foundation on which to brainstorm plans to lift the community.

In all cases, the community entrepreneurs will have to use their knowledge of the community to guide their strategies. Of course, that strategy will constantly be challenged or reinforced by using real-time data to measure progress. Hitting the appropriate milestones along the path to the ultimate outcome will be critical. And the strategy will have to evolve constantly. What worked in the first time period will not work in subsequent time periods. Solving one problem (e.g., crime) often triggers another problem that will require new types of interventions (e.g., gentrification and displacement).

A MARKET THAT VALUES HEALTH[28]

In many ways, focusing on health is the ultimate silo-busting strategy to help coordinate multiple interventions for a community. Health is often confused with medical care, but, at root, it is a reflection of wellbeing. Another way to think about health is that your body is the sum record of your challenges and opportunities.[29] Because opportunities often cluster in places, it is not a surprise that your ZIP Code is more important than your genetic code for influencing your health over a lifetime.[30] This understanding about health has been around for a long time—and has deep roots outside of the United States—but has only recently been gaining traction outside of medical and public health circles, thanks mostly to the work of the Robert Wood Johnson Foundation. But as far back as 1948, the World Health Organization defined health as "a state of complete physical, mental, and social wellbeing and not merely the absence of disease or infirmity."[31]

Creating the conditions that allow all Americans to achieve complete physical, mental, and social wellbeing is an elegant concept. Other concepts, such as "improved social outcomes" or "ecosystem" or "complex adaptive system," are clumsier because they are too vague or imprecise about the effort to improve the life chances of low-income Americans. For the remainder of this essay, I will lump all of those overlapping concepts under the simplified idea of a "market that values health."

Not only does a market that values health help focus our concept of an improved multisector and place-based intervention, but it also connects to the largest potential funding source for this new market. The scale of spending on medical care is mindboggling. And much of it would be unnecessary if we made appropriate investments upstream in people's lives to head off the development of avoidable chronic disease.

---

28 This phrase was first coined by Kevin Jones, co-founder of the Social Capital Markets (SOCAP) conference.

29 We are all in debt to Clyde Hertzman for this powerful idea. For more, see his paper titled "The Biological Embedding of Early Experience and Its Effects on Health in Adulthood," *Annals of the New York Academy of Sciences* 896 (1) (December 1999): 85–95.

30 Robert Wood Johnson Foundation Commission to Build a Healthier America, *Beyond Health Care: New Directions to a Healthier America* (Princeton, NJ: Robert Wood Johnson Foundation Commission to Build a Healthier America, 2009).

31 World Health Organization, "Constitution of the World Health Organization: Principles" (July 22, 1946), available at http://www.who.int/about/mission/en/.

Consider the observation in a recent speech by Federal Reserve Bank of San Francisco president John Williams, who said: "Health care accounts for a large share of the U.S. economy, and treatment of chronic disease is a big part of that."[32] The numbers Williams is referring to are stark: 1) more than $3 trillion is spent annually on medical care; 2) 86 percent of that is spent on patients with chronic diseases;[33] 3) most chronic disease is avoidable; and 4) most avoidable chronic disease is generated in low-income neighborhoods.[34]

And the numbers are getting worse: By 2024, the United States is projected to spend $5.5 trillion on medical care.[35] There are no medical breakthroughs that will bend this cost curve. But there may be a great opportunity in avoiding illnesses before they start by creating opportunities for low-income families and in low-income neighborhoods. Improving wellbeing is the fair thing to do, but it also could be an enormous cost-saving strategy. For two very compelling discussions on this theme, see essays by Peter Long, and Tyler Norris and Jme McLean, in this book.

So if medical care is not a sufficient strategy to improve health, what other levers are there? One is education. A college graduate will live, on average, nearly a decade longer than a high school dropout when their life expectancies are measured at age 25.[36] Income is another lever. For adults reporting poor health, 31 percent live below the federal poverty line, and only seven percent earn four times the poverty rate income.[37] Health issues like chronic disease, obesity, violence, and other ailments melt away as people overcome the layered causes of poverty.

32 John Williams, "The Health of Nations," Presentation to the National Interagency Community Reinvestment Conference, Los Angeles (February 10, 2016), available at http://www.frbsf.org/our-district/press/presidents-speeches/williams-speeches/2016/february/health-of-nations-interagency-community-reinvestment-conference/.

33 Centers for Disease Control and Prevention, available at https://www.cdc.gov/chronicdisease/.

34 Jessie Gerteis et al., "Multiple Chronic Conditions Chartbook: 2010 Medical Expenditure Panel Survey Data," Agency for Healthcare Research and Quality (Publication 14–0038: 2014).

35 Sean P. Keehan et al., "National Health Expenditure Projections, 2016–25: Price Increases, Aging Push Sector to 20 Percent of Economy," *Health Affairs* 36 (3) (2017): 553–63.

36 Elaine Arkin et al., "Time to Act: Investing in the Health of Our Children and Communities," Robert Wood Johnson Foundation Commission to Build a Healthier America (2014), p. 34.

37 The Center of Social Disparities of Health at the University of California, San Francisco, "Health Varies by Income and Across Racial or Ethnic Groups," Robert Wood Johnson Foundation (2008), available at http://www.commissiononhealth.org/PDF/hlth_inceg.pdf.

Although we do not call out health specifically in the title of this book, many of its essays focus on improving health. And the book itself is dedicated to S. Leonard Syme, a UC Berkeley social epidemiologist who helped us down the path toward outcomes-based funding by pushing us to think of the needs of the whole person rather than siloed focuses on medical care, or housing, or jobs, or education.

HOW DOES A MARKET THAT VALUES HEALTH WORK? BUYERS, SELLERS, AND CONNECTORS[38]

There are a number of entities that are interested in paying for better health outcomes, and for the purposes of this essay, I will call them buyers. Some of them are obvious: The federal government, through its Medicare, Medicaid, and Veterans Administration health programs, is the 800-pound gorilla in that category. But there are others, too: health insurance companies, employers who self-insure their employees, hospital systems who are concerned about the costs associated with readmitting patients without the ability to bill for additional procedures, foundations that care about health (e.g., Robert Wood Johnson, Kresge, and health conversion foundations like the Colorado Health Foundation or the California Endowment). And of course, as we get more comfortable with the expanded concept of health as wellbeing, there are many other funders who pay for the building blocks for good health: affordable housing (HUD and the Low Income Housing Tax Credit), jobs (Small Business Administration and the New Markets Tax Credit), transportation (infrastructure spending), and schools (Department of Education and state governments).

A seller of health is any person or entity that promotes wellbeing. As was mentioned earlier, education is a driver of better health outcomes. Therefore, teachers are sellers of health. Reading at grade level is a more powerful predictor of lifelong health than any medical measurement for kids, such as body mass index.[39] We saw how income is a driver of health.

---

38 The typology of this market into "buyers of health," "sellers," and "connectors" was developed by Ian Galloway, Federal Reserve Bank of San Francisco, for the SOCAP Health conference in 2013. For more details on that conference, see the agenda and other content at http://www.frbsf.org/community-development/events/2013/september/socap-social-capital-markets-health/.

39 George C. Halvorson, *Three Key Years: Talk — Read — Play — Sing to Support & Help Every Child in America*, (Sausalito, CA: Institute for InterGroup Understanding, 2014). See chapter six on reading, educational success and other factors, available at https://www.intergroupinstitute.org/userfiles/books/chapters/15/Chapter-6-Three-Key-Years.pdf.

Therefore, anyone who provides a living-wage job is a seller of health. There are many other factors that help kids succeed, and one demonstrated example is having an adult outside your immediate family who cares about you. A study following generations of children growing up in Kauai found that children with a nonparent caretaker, such as an aunt, a babysitter, a teacher, or a coach were much more likely to thrive later in life.[40] Therefore, Big Brothers Big Sisters is a seller of health. The list here could go on, but in the end, anyone who helps low-income people take control over their own lives, or anyone who helps impart a sense of agency and control over one's destiny, is a seller of health.[41]

In this system, there are also connectors who play an important role in making this market work, and several of the pioneers are authors in this book. These connectors are often Pay for Success strategies and vehicles, like the Strong Families Fund described by Kimberlee Cornett. Or the Equity-with-a-Twist tool developed by the Low Income Investment Fund and described here by Nancy Andrews. The tool that Maggie Super Church's essay discusses, the Healthy Neighborhood Equity Fund, is a connector. She was motivated by a simple question: Why can we invest in a pill that lowers blood pressure but we can't invest in a neighborhood that does the same thing? Her fund has an interesting mix of "buyers of health" that are investing in neighborhoods to make them more salutogenic: banks, hospitals, and insurance companies (in addition to many government and philanthropic sources). We are at the very beginning of developing the connector tools and vehicles to marry buyers to sellers, but once we have more than a few pilots, the potential here to create a large and vibrant market is enormous.

Of course, the best possible connector is a health entity that is either an organization that is both an insurance company and a medical care provider (e.g., Kaiser Permanente; see Tyler Norris and Jme McLean's essay) or an insurer that owns the majority or all of the downstream medical-care cost risk for a population that is relatively contained (e.g., a large, self-insured corporation or a rural county with one health insurer).

---

40 Emmy E. Werner and Ruth S. Smith, *Journeys from Childhood to Midlife: Risk, Resilience, and Recovery* (New York: Cornell University Press, 2001).

41 For an extensive discussion of how "control of destiny" can improve health, see the following interview with S. Leonard Syme available at https://www.youtube.com/watch?v=eU8xTOumoQc.

These entities would be on the vanguard of the "population health" business model, where they are paid per person/per year to keep someone healthy. Unlike the largely fee-for-service medical system as a whole, their business incentives are aligned with health rather than illness. The healthier their members, policyholders, employees, or residents, the better off they are. That arrangement is the ultimate connector, since it has a significant motivation to work upstream to improve the social determinants of health to save on downstream medical-care cost risk. That insurer, leading a coalition of other buyers of health, would create pockets where a market that valued health could take root.

In many ways, this evolution parallels the birth of the modern capitalist economy, as Adam Smith explained in *The Wealth of Nations* (1776); he described early modern economies emerging in cities in northern Europe as "islands in a feudal sea." Of course, I recognize that today's medical care system remains overwhelmingly oriented toward fee-for-service, but that may well be changing. What we might start seeing are islands of population-health business models in a sea of pay-for-service medical care.[42]

BENEFITS OF A MARKET THAT VALUES HEALTH

This market does not overthrow old approaches to fighting poverty; it incorporates them into a new whole. Strategies that exist today—Head Start, affordable housing, Meals on Wheels, job training, etc.—are elements of the intervention that improve the social determinants of health. In other words, they are sellers of health, and this new market will create more demand for that work. And as Avis Vidal noted about the quasi-market created by community development finance, institutions from the prior era (e.g., community action agencies) morphed into players in the new quasi-market regime (CDCs). It is true that some programs and efforts that are not as effective in delivering improved health may lose funding over time. But that winnowing of ineffective programs is good stewardship of limited resources. CDCs compete for resources to do their work, and that has created a more professional and capable nonprofit sector. Competition in the market that values health would do something similar. (The worry here is that the sector focuses too much

---

42 The Commonwealth Fund, "In Focus: Reimagining Rural Health Care" (March 30, 2017), available at http://www.commonwealthfund.org/publications/newsletters/transforming-care/2017/march/in-focus.

on what services can be commodified. For a smart analysis of this risk, see Jodi Halpern and Doug Jutte's essay, "The Ethics of Outcomes-Based Funding Models," and Megan Golden, Jitinder Kholi, and Samantha Mignotte's essay, "A Focus on Cost Savings May Undermine the Influence of Outcomes-Based Funding Mechanisms," in this book.)

The market helps facilitate many players who are working on a particular neighborhood through better coordination, but an even more interesting aspect of this mechanism is the capability of expanding beyond traditional areas of doing business. In the past, we have concentrated our efforts on low-income people in low-income neighborhoods. There were good reasons to do this because these were the areas of highest need. It allowed for better coordination of services. But a new mechanism could cast a wider net to identify those in need who are living in middle-income or affluent geographies. The concentrations would be less (ten to 20 percent of the residents perhaps), but the total opportunity may be greater because there are more of those communities. This wider net could apply the same market for better social outcomes as will exist in low-income areas.

Expanding this market to cover wider geographies solves a problem identified by Elizabeth Kneebone and Emily Garr at the Brookings Institution, where they found that "by 2008, suburbs were home to the largest and fastest-growing poor population in the country."[43] It would be a new tool to reach into those areas with less of a history of poverty, and thus fewer institutions to address it. The market would help organize social service networks that don't have the benefit of longstanding relationships and geographic density, as exists in older urban centers. And, of course, having a more universal system in place to catch all those in need would encourage a more stable political base of support.

The market that values health will build a demand for community entrepreneurs, and the selection process for those leaders has equity baked in. The people most likely to be successful in this job must have both problem-solving skills and a deep understanding of the community in need. This combination almost guarantees that the teams that the community entrepreneur builds will also reflect the racial, ethnic,

---

43 Elizabeth Kneebone and Emily Garr, "Suburbanization of Poverty: Trends in Metropolitan America, 2000 to 2008," Brookings Institution (2010), available at http://media.timesfreepress.com/docs/2010/02/Brookings_report_on_poverty_0208.pdf.

language, cultural, gender, sexual identity, and other characteristics of the community they serve.

In addition, this new market will create new job ladders for community entrepreneurs and their social subcontractors in their communities. We saw something like this happen in community development finance, where local residents got their first jobs at the neighborhood CDC. Over time, they developed skills that were valuable to other employers, and many went into government or the private sector. This created a new job ladder in communities that lacked the connections to gain experience and advance professionally.

As this market develops, it will create a need for new technology to serve the needs of the new business models. Caroline Whistler and Matt Gee, along with Emily Gustafsson-Wright discuss the need to develop new information technology tools to make cross-sector and place-based interventions work more effectively. It will require ways of tracking financing to help community entrepreneurs decide where to best spend limited resources on the margin for better outcomes.

The market will also create a demand for more and better data. Community entrepreneurs will need a "sense-and-respond system that has at its core reliable, frequently updated data that are consistently assembled and aligned from myriad sources." We describe how this might work in our essay "Routinizing the Extraordinary" in the first *What Works* book. In that essay, we describe the role of data in the work of the community quarterback, but it could apply to the community entrepreneur as well.[44]

An abundance of data will create an explosion of academic and policy research, which could bring about an atmosphere of innovation and sharing of knowledge. All the transactions in the market that values health will leave a trace of data on what was tried and what worked. In the way that financial markets rely on millions and billions of transactions to build financial models and measure risk, we will finally have that number of data points to develop much more sophisticated interventions in the social sector. This could trigger nothing short of a paradigm shift in how we think about poverty, as Jacob Harold describes in his essay.

---

44 Erickson et al., *Investing in What Works* (2012). p. 392.

Of course, data do more than simply guide more effective interventions. They are a language, as Cassidy explains in his essay: "An important step to leveraging this growing body of evidence will be to develop a common language in describing outcomes and measuring performance." And when we all speak the same language (interoperable data systems) and all focus on the same target (outcomes), then we have the ability to coordinate across institutions. This was the never-realized dream of the many comprehensive community development initiatives mentioned eariler.

Shifts in understanding (paradigms), combined with changes in language and the advent of new catalyzing players (community entrepreneurs) and new business models, will begin to do something even more powerful: change culture. As Zia Khan explains in his chapter, you must reorient an army of individuals working for social change. Khan reminds us that we must focus on whether the "emotional dynamics of what it takes for people to change behaviors are factored into the change strategy."

When all of these incentives and forces are pointed in a new direction, Whistler and Gee in their essay predict something revolutionary:

> There is a structural inertia that makes a culture of innovation both elusive and incredibly scalable if we are able to drive that inertia toward outcomes for the largest organization in service of humanity.... We have the opportunity to ignite a public-sector innovation revolution in our lifetime.

RISKS ASSOCIATED WITH A MARKET THAT VALUES HEALTH

We recognize that this approach to funding social change has risks. It will be disruptive and create winners and losers. Many organizations that have long track records of helping communities might not be able to participate in this new outcomes marketplace. We need to build in the ability for legacy organizations to transition to new funding realities or find compassionate ways to wind them down.

Many early critics of the quasi market for community revitalization—using block grants and tax credits—argued that it was also too complicated. The question was why should we create a convoluted system that rewards too many lawyers and accountants to structure complicated financing deals? (There are still critics of this system.) But for anyone who had an organization languish under the earlier regime dominated by direct funding from Washington bureaucracies would attest, the new system, although complicated, was better.[45]

Some critics also say that understanding what allows people to thrive, the dynamics of a neighborhood, or the complex adaptive problem of poverty are all too complicated to research and understand. As Jack Shonkoff said recently at a Federal Reserve Community Development Research Conference, "Cancer is complicated. Because something is complicated is not an excuse for not tackling the problem."[46]

CONCLUSION

At the end of the day, we want to see a shift where governments and others pay for what outcomes they want rather than paying someone to follow a recipe that often does not work. Paying for outcomes creates a demand that begins to reshape institutions, behaviors, relationships, and culture. An open structure, like a market, will permit problem-solving ideas to come from every direction. It is inherently anti-monopoly, pro-local, and community-empowering. It may create the breakthrough we so desperately need.

Fork in the Road: Who Owns Improved Outcomes? The Community Itself

In the 1890s, most of America's large cities were building power generation and distribution systems. Some argued that this new technology should be owned by the community at the neighborhood level and held as a local asset. The production costs might be higher than at a larger, regional power plant, but the distribution costs were less. In contrast, the cost-per-kilowatt advantage of the regional plant was offset by higher distribution costs. It was a wash. But the regional system won out. Why? According to Stanford professor Mark Granovetter, the reason was that elites preferred to have the option of investing in the new utility.[47] The

---

45 Erickson, *Housing Policy Revolution* (2009).

46 This was a comment onstage by Shonkoff at the Federal Reserve System Community Development Research Conference (Washington, DC, March 23–24, 2017). More information is available at https://minneapolisfed.org/community/tenth-biennial-federal-reserve-system-community-development-research-conference/agenda.

47 Mark Granovetter and Patrick McGuire, "The Making of an Industry: Electricity in the United States," *The Laws of the Markets*, edited by Michel Callon (Malden, MA: Blackwell, 1998), pp. 147–73.

final outcome was not determined by the technology; it was a process determined by power. Elites wanted to invest in this new value stream.

Soon communities will be creating value by improving wellbeing using the incentives and tools of outcomes-based funding. The evolution of the market that values health could follow a similar path to electrical genera-tion. As we transition to this revolutionary approach to creating and paying for better social outcomes—complete physical, mental, and social wellbeing for all Americans—let's be mindful that it is the communities themselves who are creating increased value and should share in its rewards.

—————

DAVID J. ERICKSON *is director of community development at the Federal Reserve Bank of San Francisco. In this role, he leads the community development team in its mission to advance economic opportunity for lower-income Americans. Erickson's book on the history of community development,* The Housing Policy Revolution: Networks and Neighborhoods, *was published in 2009 by the Urban Institute Press. He also co-edited all four books in the* What Works *series. He has a PhD in history from the University of California, Berkeley, and an undergraduate degree from Dartmouth College.*

PERFORMANCE-BASED CONTRACTING CAN PROVIDE FLEXIBILITY, DRIVE EFFICIENCY, AND FOCUS RESOURCES ON WHAT WORKS IN SOCIAL SERVICES

Emily Gustafsson-Wright
Brookings Institution

Courtney arrived at Frontline Services, a nonprofit organization that helps citizens in Cleveland, Ohio, when she was 28 years old. She was living in a shelter for homeless women, struggling with mental health and substance abuse issues, and parenting three young children who were in custody of the county.[1] Courtney had just about given up hope that she would ever be able to care for her children on her own. Until then, the county caseworker assigned to her family had little incentive to reunite mother and children, as the caseworker's primary job was to protect the children. Living with a birth parent is almost always better for a child's development than foster care, as long as the home environment is safe and healthy. However, before entering Frontline Services, Courtney had few options to change the trajectory of her children's lives. What Courtney didn't know when she arrived at Frontline that day (and likely will never know) was that she was walking into a social services experiment—one of only seven other similar experiments across the country at the time.[2]

In this experiment, a type of performance-based contract called Pay for Success, the county government had pledged to repay private investors for the successful reduction of out-of-home placements of children whose primary caregiver was homeless. What did this

---

The author would like to thank Sophie Gardiner and Katie Smith for their research assistance.

1 Name has been changed to protect the identity of the beneficiary.

2 Emily Gustafsson-Wright, Sophie Gardiner, and Vidya Putcha, "The Potential and Limitations of Impact Bonds: Lessons Learned from the First Five Years of Experience Worldwide," Brookings Institution (2015), available at http://www.brookings.edu/research/reports/2015/07/social-impact-bonds-potential-limitations.

mean for Courtney? It meant that she was assigned a caseworker dedicated to her, someone who would look at her particular circumstances and who would set out a tailored plan to help her turn her life around with the end goal of reuniting her with her children. It meant that her caseworker could work across the county service providers to identify the right mix of services for Courtney. It also meant that a dedicated group of stakeholders was meeting regularly across government and nongovernment entities to focus on one thing: Reuniting Courtney and her children (and other families in similar circumstances) as quickly as possible.

By focusing on outcomes, Pay for Success contracts encourage service providers to tailor their interventions according to what works for their target population. For this reason, they may be particularly suitable for addressing the needs of historically marginalized individuals, like Courtney and her family, who have a complex range of needs. With a combination of assistance in addressing existing debts, classes in financial management, and family counseling, Courtney was able to reunite with her children, enroll them in supportive school environments, and stop the cycle of dependency on the foster care system. The result was not only a better family outcome, but also a reduction in the enormous direct costs to the county that would otherwise have been incurred had Courtney's children remained in county care.

Government plays a critical role in ensuring that all citizens, regardless of privilege or circumstance, receive the basic services necessary to live safe, healthy, and productive lives. Beyond public goods, such as street lights and basic education, the government also provides social services that address market failures, particularly as they impact marginalized populations. Given limited budgets, government is continually searching for ways to deliver these services in the most efficient and effective manner.

The way that government funds and delivers social services takes varied forms and has had shifting patterns over time. For instance, government funding often reaches beneficiary populations via nonprofits responsible for delivering services—in fact, it is estimated that over half of social services are provided through this type of public-private partnership.[3] In fiscal year 2014, for example, the U.S. Department of Health and Human

---

3 Elizabeth Boris et al., "Human Service Nonprofits and Government Collaboration: Findings from the 2010 National Survey of Nonprofit Government Contracting and Grants," Urban Institute (2010), available at http://www.urban.org/sites/default/files/alfresco/publication-pdfs/412228-Human-Service-Nonprofits-and-Government-Collaboration-Findings-from-the-National-Survey-of-Nonprofit-Government-Contracting-and-Grants.pdf.

Services contracted for $21 billion worth of services.[4] Such funding can sometimes be in the form of grants; however, most often the government contracts with the nonprofit sector using fee-for-service, fixed-cost, and performance-based contracts.

Performance-based contracts, an umbrella term used to describe contracts that make compensations partially or fully contingent upon performance achievement, have become increasingly used to incentivize service providers to deliver results. The past two decades have seen a further push under the umbrella of performance-based contracts toward contracts that provide incentives to deliver measurable results in the form of outcomes, as opposed to outputs. Pay for Success, also known as a social impact bond, is the most recent iteration of such outcomes-based funding. Outcomes-based funding has enormous potential to help achieve equitable access to quality social services. The greater focus on outcomes can lead to flexibility, innovation, and adaptive learning in service delivery, and an emphasis on evaluation can enhance transparency in social spending and facilitate funding what works.

FROM INPUT-BASED CONTRACTING TO PERFORMANCE-BASED CONTRACTING

The U.S. government began to contract for social services in the late 1960s. At the time, high demand for skilled workers resulted in several pieces of legislation that allowed for service delivery contracts with nongovernmental organizations.[5] In 1972, this was further formalized through the Comprehensive Employment and Training Act, which "paved the way for community-based organizations to occupy a major role in delivering services in the human services field."[6] Ever since this contracting

---

4 National Contract Management Association and Bloomberg Government, "Annual Review of Government Contracting: 2015 Edition" (2015), available at http://www.ncmahq.org/docs/default-source/default-document-library/pdfs/exec15---ncma-annual-review-of-government-contracting-2015-edition.

5 Paul Terrell, "Private Alternatives to Human Services Administration," *Social Services Review* 53 (1) (1979): 56–74.

6 Shabu Varghese, "A Paradigm Shift in Human Service Delivery in the United States: A Change in Approach from the Government to the Governance Model," *Journal of Public Policy* (2015), available at http://jpublicpolicy.com/2015/11/29/a-paradigm-shift-in-human-services-delivery-in-the-united-states-a-change-in-approach-from-the-government-to-the-governance-model/.

model was established, policymakers have been trying to improve the contracting process and optimize government's role as a contract manager.

Initially, the primary form of payment method was either cost reimbursement (reimbursing approved expenses), fixed cost (paying a set price for a set of services, regardless of expenses), or fee-for-service (payments per time unit spent delivering the service or per beneficiary served). In other words, government contracting focused on inputs delivered, such as the number of staff, facilities, equipment, and supplies used (see Figure 1). In this type of design-focused contracting, there could also be contracts around the process of delivery, such as those based on statements of work or on service definitions.

Figure 1. Spectrum of Service: Inputs to Outcomes

INPUTS	PROCESS	OUTPUTS	QUALITY	OUTCOMES
• Staff	• Service definitions	• Measures of service volume	• Timeliness	• Results
• Facilities	• Statements of work	• Units of service	• Reliability	• Impacts
• Equipment			• Conformity	• Accomplishments
• Supplies			• Tangibles	
• Material			• Other dimensions	
• Funding				
• Service recipients				

DESIGN SPECIFICATIONS   PERFORMANCE SPECIFICATIONS

Source: Lawrence Martin, "Performance-Based Contracting for Human Services: Does It Work?" Center for Community Partnerships, College of Health and Public Affairs, University of Central Florida (2005).

However, input-based contracts often did not produce desired results and highly restricted service providers. Consequently, in the 1980s, government contracting began to shift from input-based to performance-based. Broadly, performance-based contracting (PBC) refers to contracts where compensations (such as payment, extension, or contract renewal) are either partially or fully dependent on the achievement of some performance metrics, which can include outputs, the quality of those outputs, or outcomes (or some combination thereof). Output measures include, for example, the number of beneficiaries reached or the volume of services delivered. Outcomes, on the other hand, include measures of impact on the beneficiary, such as improved health indicators or entry into sustained employment. It is important to note that definitions of PBC vary greatly, from statements of work based on performance outputs, to contract renewal based on outcomes, to a payment scale tied to degrees of performance.

PBC was primarily driven, to begin with at least, by contracts within the defense sector.[7] For example, contracts were issued to build airplanes with certain specifications in a given time period. This expanded to include human services at the federal level, with state and local governments subsequently growing their use of PBC for both human services and nonhuman services.[8] Several legislative acts set standards, guidance, and targets for this expansion (see Figure 2). At the federal level, the Government Performance and Results Act of 1993 required federal agencies to set goals, measure results, and report on progress toward those goals. Also at the federal level, the Office of Management and Budget established a target to make 20 percent of all service contracts over $25,000 performance-based by the end of fiscal year 2002. In a similar vein, the Federal Procurement Executive Council set a target for half of all service contracts to be performance-based by fiscal year 2005. This type of contracting marked a major shift away from dictating how nonprofit providers should design and deliver services toward telling nonprofit providers what the end result of those service provisions should be. Legislation beyond 2005 marks a transition to contracts more closely tied to outcomes.[9]

Although PBC has been strongly supported by policy, its use is still relatively rare, compared with input-based contracting, as a 2012 survey of nonprofit-government contracts revealed (see Figure 3).

---

7   U.S. Government Accountability Office, "Contract Management: Trends and Challenges in Acquiring Services," Statement of David E. Cooper, director of acquisition and sourcing management before the Subcommittee on Technology and Procurement Policy, Committee on Government Reform, U.S. House of Representatives (2001), available at http://www.gao.gov/assets/110/108858.pdf.

8   Lawrence Martin, "Performance-Based Contracting for Human Services: Does It Work?" Center for Community Partnerships, College of Health and Public Affairs, University of Central Florida (2005), available at http://www.cdss.ca.gov/ccr/res/pdf/performance/3.%20PBC_Does_it_Work.pdf.

9   Ibid.

Figure 2. Federal Government Policy Related to Results-Based Funding

YEAR	POLICY
1960s	**Manpower Development and Training Act**, the **Economic Opportunity Act**, and the **Emergency Employment Act** for employment training allow the government to contract with nongovernmental organizations at large scale for the first time.[10]
1972	**Comprehensive Employment and Training Act** passed, which further increases the role of "community-based organizations" in delivering human services.[11]
1977	**Community Reinvestment Act** passed, incentivizes depository institutions to invest in low-income communities where they do business.[12]
1986	**Low Income Housing Tax Credit** passed, providing tax credits for investment in low-income housing.[13]
1993	**Government Performance and Results Act** passed, requiring federal agencies to set goals, measure results, and report on progress toward those goals. However, there was little emphasis on addressing unsatisfactory outcomes.[14]
2000	**New Markets Tax Credit** passed, providing a tax incentive for private investment in low-income communities.[15]
2001	**Office of Management and Budget set a target** for 20 percent of all service contracts over $25,000 to be performance-based by the end of fiscal year 2002.[16]
2004	**Office of Management and Budget set a target** for 40 percent of service contracts over $25,000 to be performance-based by 2005.[17]
2010	**Government Performance and Results Modernization Act** passed, introducing an interagency Performance Improvement Council to improve performance management.[18]
2013	The appropriations bills from 2013 to 2016 **authorized the U.S. Department of Labor, U.S. Department of Justice, and Corporation for National and Community Service to provide outcomes-based funding** for Pay for Success.[19]
2014	The 2014 and 2015 appropriations bills authorized the Corporation for National and Community Service's **Social Innovation Fund** to use up to 20 percent of grant funds to support the development of Pay for Success.[20]
2014	**Workforce Innovation and Opportunity Act** signed into law, allowing local workforce investment boards to direct up to ten percent of their federal dollars to Pay for Sucess contracts.[21]
2015	**Social Impact Partnership Acts** introduced in U.S. House of Representatives and Senate.[22]
2015	**Every Student Succeeds Act** passed, allowing for Pay for Success funding in education.[23]
2016	**Evidence-Based Policymaking Commission Act** established a commission to improve federal government use of data and evaluation.[24]
2016	Social Impact Partnership Act reintroduced in the House of Representatives as **Social Impact Partnerships to Pay for Results Act** and passed Ways and Means Committee.[25]

In this sample, only nine percent of small organizations used performance-based payments alone, while less than a quarter of large nonprofit organizations ($1 million or more in annual expenses) reported contracts with performance-based payments. Slightly more, 28 percent, reported contracts with a combination of unit cost payments and performance-based payments. Among grants to nonprofits, between 14 and 18 percent used performance-based payments alone, and between nine and 16 percent used a combination of the two. One clear trend: The larger the organization, the more likely it is to use PBC.

10 Varghese, "A Paradigm Shift" (2015).

11 Ibid.

12 Gustafsson-Wright, "The Potential and Limitations of Impact Bonds" (2015).

13 Office of Policy Development and Research, "Low Income Housing Tax Credits," U.S. Department of Housing and Urban Development (2016), available at https://www.huduser.gov/portal/datasets/lihtc.html.

14 Sithara Kodali, "The Movement Towards Government Performance," Third Sector Capital Partners (2016), available at http://www.thirdsectorcap.org/blog/the-movement-towards-government-performance/.

15 New Markets Tax Credit Coalition, "New Markets Tax Credit Fact Sheet" (2016), available at http://nmtccoalition.org/fact-sheet/.

16 Martin, "Performance-Based Contracting" (2005).

17 U.S. Office of Management and Budget, "Memorandum for Chief Acquisition Officers Senior Procurement Executives," Executive Office of the President (2004), available at http://georgewbush-whitehouse.archives.gov/omb/procurement/pbsa/pbsc_increasing_070704.pdf.

18 Kodali, "The Movement Towards Government Performance" (2016).

19 Nicole Truhe, "How the Every Student Succeeds Act Rewards Results Through Evidence-Based Programming," America Forward (2015), available at http://www.americaforward.org/blog/the-every-student-succeeds-act-paying-for-success-in-education.

20 Corporation for National and Community Service, "SIF Pay for Success" (2016), available at http://www.nationalservice.gov/programs/social-innovation-fund/our-programs/pay-success.

21 Gustafsson-Wright, "The Potential and Limitations of Impact Bonds" (2015).

22 U.S. Congressional Record, "H.R.1336 and S.1089, 114th Congress" (2015), available at https://www.congress.gov/search?q=%7B%22source%22%3A%22legislation%22%2C%22congress%22%3A114%7D.

23 Truhe, "How the Every Student Succeeds Act" (2015).

24 Justin Milner, "Everything You Need to Know About the Commission on Evidence-Based Policymaking," Urban Institute (2016), available at http://www.urban.org/urban-wire/everything-you-need-know-about-commission-evidence-based-policymaking.

25 Committee on Ways and Means, "Markup of Bills to Improve TANF," U.S. House of Representatives (2016), available at http://waysandmeans.house.gov/event/39841647/.

TYPE OF PAYMENT METHOD	PERCENTAGE OF ORGANIZATIONS BY SIZE		
	$100,000 TO 249,999	$250,000 TO 999,999	$1 MILLION OR MORE
Contracts			
Fixed cost (flat amount)	52%	51%	58%
Cost reimbursable payments	45%	60%	68%
Unit cost payments/fee-for-service ($ per time unit)	36%	39%	58%
Unit cost payments/fee-for-service ($ per individual/family)	27%	33%	42%
Performance-based payments	9%	20%	22%
Combination of unit cost payments/fee-for-service and performance-based	11%	20%	28%
Grants			
Fixed cost (flat amount)	63%	62%	62%
Cost reimbursable payments	55%	62%	69%
Unit cost payments/fee-for-service ($ per time unit)	13%	18%	26%
Unit cost payments/fee-for-service ($ per individual/family)	9%	14%	23%
Performance-based payments	14%	18%	18%
Combination of unit cost payments/fee-for-service and performance-based	9%	12%	16%

Notes: Figures are based on nonprofit organizations included in the sampling frame. Missing or non-applicable answers were excluded. Respondents were allowed to provide multiple responses to the question related to the main services provided by their organization. Thus, survey responses will not total 100 percent.

Source: Sarah L Pettijohn et al., "Nonprofit-Government Contracts and Grants: Findings from the 2013 National Survey," Urban Institute (2013), available at http://www.urban.org/sites/default/files/publication/24231/412962-Nonprofit-Government-Contracts-and-Grants-Findings-from-the-National-Survey.pdf.

A FURTHER SHIFT TOWARD OUTCOME MEASUREMENT: FUNDING SOCIAL SERVICES BASED ON OUTCOMES

Most PBCs to date have provided compensation for the delivery of outputs, and few have provided compensation for outcomes. Further, many PBC contracts have only a small portion of payment (such as ten percent) tied to outputs or outcomes, or simply contract renewal, while the remainder is tied to prescribed inputs. This may not allow providers the flexibility required to improve service quality.

Social impact bonds or Pay for Success contracts are a form of PBC that explicitly focuses on outcome achievement and almost always tie 100 percent of government payments to outcomes.[26] They differ from traditional PBC in that private investors provide upfront capital to service providers. The private investors, often a combination of senior and subordinate investors, are repaid by an outcome funder (usually government) contingent on outcome achievement.[27] In this model, the investors absorb the financial risk that would normally be held by the service provider and government. The idea of social impact bonds originated in the United Kingdom in 2010. The aim of the first social impact bond was to reduce the high rates of prison recidivism among short-term male prisoners. In 2012, this model came to the shores of the United States at the Rikers Island jail in New York City. Since then, there have been an additional 13 Pay for Success transactions introduced across the country for a range of social issues, including child welfare, homelessness, and early childhood education.

The expansion of Pay for Success has been supported by several pieces of federal and state legislation (see Figure 2). At the federal level, for example, appropriations bills from 2013 to 2016 authorize the U.S. Department of Labor, U.S. Department of Justice, and Corporation for National and Community Service (CNCS) to provide outcome funding

---

26 In some social impact bonds, outputs rather than outcomes are chosen as metrics, though the general idea is to focus on outcomes.

27 For clarity, impact bonds, despite the name, are not bonds in the traditional sense. The term "social impact bond" in this chapter is defined as an arrangement where payments to investors are dependent on, and positively correlated with, positive outcomes. For a number of uses of the term that do not fit the commonly used definition, see Emma Tomkinson, "When Is a Social Impact Bond (SIB) Not a SIB, and Why Should We Care?" Personal Blog (2015), available at http://emmatomkinson.com/2015/05/28/when-is-a-social-impact-bond-sib-not-a-sib-should-we-care/.

for Pay for Success.[28] In 2014 and 2015, CNCS's Social Innovation Fund was authorized to use up to 20 percent of grant funds to support the development of Pay for Success programs.[29] In 2015, the Social Impact Partnership Acts were introduced in the U.S. House of Representatives and Senate; they passed as the Social Impact Partnerships to Pay for Results Act in the House Ways and Means Committee in May 2016.[30] Additionally, at least 18 states have passed legislation specific to the use of social impact bonds.[31]

Why do outcomes-based contracts matter? Outcomes-based contracts provide greater flexibility to service providers, which may increase the quality of their services. They also require outcome evaluation, which allows government to direct its funds most efficiently. In the example from Ohio, the various service providers working with Courtney would have each had separate goals and no incentive to coordinate under input-based contracting. She may never have been encouraged and supported to meet all of the requirements for family reunification. Frontline Services was able to provide higher-quality services under the outcomes-based contracting model because it spent far less time reporting on a govern-ment-issued laundry list of performance indicators that had little relevancy. Rather, Frontline was contracted to do whatever was necessary to achieve the outcome of utmost importance: family reunification.

However, outcomes-based contracts are not without their risks and chal-lenges. Firstly, setting them up can be a very complex and costly process, requiring considerable time to negotiate between actors and finalize the technical aspects of the deals.[32] While the nature of an outcomes-based contract involves a shift of financial risk from the government to the investors, they may also be a risky undertaking for governments and service providers, who take on more reputational risk in the face of the heightened scrutiny of the outcomes-based structure. In particular, for governments, paying large returns to private investors may be damaging

28 Truhe, "How the Every Student Succeeds Act" (2015).

29 Corporation for National and Community Service, "SIF Pay for Success" (2016).

30 Committee on Ways and Means, "Markup of Bills to Improve TANF" (2016).

31 Gustafsson-Wright, "The Potential and Limitations of Impact Bonds" (2015).

32 Ibid.

to their public image if the nature of the outcomes-based contract is not effectively communicated. The government will also continue to face the risk that they must bear responsibility for the consequences of the contract: For example, if the contract allows service providers to "cherry pick" the beneficiaries served, and thus avoid the neediest individuals.[33] This aspect emphasizes the importance of tightly defining the target population and impact metrics, to ensure the results of interest closely align with the government's goals and that meaningful outcomes are achieved.

THE FUTURE OF RESULTS-BASED FUNDING

The trend to measure results and link them to compensation is not limited to the United States. In health, for example, results-based funding is being used in countries such as Spain, Sweden, and the United Kingdom.[34] Additionally, as of this publishing, social impact bonds were contracted across 12 high-income countries. The landscape has also shifted over the past five to ten years in developing country contexts. Increasingly, institutions such as the World Bank,[35] the U.S. Agency for International Development, and the U.K. Department for International Development[36] are using results-based contracts to address some of the most intractable challenges facing the developing world, including maternal and child health and schooling outcomes.

For the United States and globally, PBC provides a tremendous opportunity to ensure not only more effective government spending but also broader systemic change. At its best, PBC—particularly that which focuses on outcomes—has the potential to increase collaboration across stakeholders, strengthen monitoring and evaluation systems, and drive performance management to allow for adaptive learning. However, PBC is not without costs and risks: Arranging outcomes-based contracts

---

33 Ibid.

34 William Savedoff, "Basic Economics of Results-Based Financing in Health," Social Insight (2010), available at https://rbfhealth.org/sites/rbf/files/RBF%20Economics_0.pdf.

35 Results-Based Financing for Health, "Mission," World Bank (2016), available at https://www.rbfhealth.org/mission; World Bank, "Results-Based Financing and Results in Education for All Children" (2016), available at http://www.worldbank.org/en/programs/reach#2.

36 United Kingdom Department for International Development, "Payment by Results Strategy: Sharpening Incentives to Perform" (June 26, 2014), available at https://www.gov.uk/government/publications/dfids-strategy-for-payment-by-results-sharpening-incentives-to-perform/payment-by-results-strategy-sharpening-incentives-to-perform.

may be more costly and, relative to input-based contracting, may be more risky. The highest priorities for the field moving forward will be to identify which services would benefit most from outcomes-based funding, to establish protocols on procuring outcomes-based contracts to reduce transaction costs, and to determine appropriate guidelines to ensure quality while allowing for service flexibility. The task may sound abstruse, but in Courtney's case and in many others, the opportunity for an improved system is overwhelmingly clear.

─────

EMILY GUSTAFSSON-WRIGHT *is a fellow in the global economy and development program at the Brookings Institution. She specializes in applied microeconomic research within the fields of education and health globally with a primary focus on developing countries. As part of this work, she conducts research on innovative financing mechanisms including public-private partnerships, social impact investing, results-based financing, and impact bonds. Most recently she published the most comprehensive global study to date on social and development impact bonds and a study analyzing the potential applications of impact bonds for early childhood development in low- and middle-income countries. Her previous professional experience includes working at the Amsterdam Institute for International Development, the World Bank, and UNICEF's Innocenti Research Center. Gustafsson-Wright holds a PhD in economics from the Tinbergen Institute at the University of Amsterdam, and an MS in applied economics and finance and BA in economics from the University of California at Santa Cruz. She has published numerous articles in peer-reviewed journals as well as contributed to several books in her field.*

PAYING FOR RESULTS
Reforming How the Public Sector Funds Social Services

Daniel Barker, John Cassidy and Winny Chen
Monitor Deloitte

A quiet revolution is taking hold across the United States. Faced with diminishing budgets and a rising demand for social services, governments at every level are adopting innovative funding models to protect against waste and ineffective programs while improving outcomes for the people they serve.

In the wake of a child welfare crisis in 2006, Tennessee adopted a new model to reduce the amount of time it takes to place children in permanent homes. Research indicated that reducing the time a child spends in a temporary home would not only lead to better outcomes for the child but also decrease costs in services and their administration later on. With this in mind, Tennessee implemented a new contract that sought to transform its child welfare system. The terms were relatively straightforward: Providers that improved on baseline performance received a share of the state's savings, and those that performed worse than the baseline reimbursed the state for cost overages. Once fully implemented in 2010, Tennessee's new model nearly cut in half the average time a child spends in temporary care, from more than 22 months to 14.[1]

Tennessee is part of a wave of governments and other funders looking for new and better ways to have an impact with increasingly scarce resources. By re-engineering the way it traditionally delivered services, the state was able to improve the lives of some of its most vulnerable populations while saving taxpayer dollars. The state employed just one of a growing number of outcomes-based funding models that hold immense promise for transforming the way governments deliver services and improve the lives of their citizens.

---

1 Beeck Center for Social Impact & Innovation, "Funding for Results: A Review of Government Outcomes-Based Agreements," Georgetown University (November 2014).

This chapter outlines the challenges of traditional funding models and how results-based funding improves on them. It also covers different types of results-based funding mechanisms and considerations for selecting and designing these mechanisms. It reviews the benefits, weaknesses, and challenges to using results-based funding models as well as the potential for widespread adoption of these innovations.

MISDIRECTED INCENTIVES OF TRADITIONAL FUNDING MODELS

In traditional funding models, governments and the social sector primarily focus on providing a prescribed set of services or activities. For different reasons, these efforts often fall short of delivering on the outcomes that funders want, and they do not always help the beneficiaries. One potential reason for this is that traditional funding models do not lend themselves to knowing which programs work and which do not. Instead, the model focuses on compliance and performing prescribed activities. Bureaucratic inertia can compound the problem. Organizational or legislative resistance to change leads to programs getting funded the same way year after year, regardless of impact.

The second hurdle centers on rigid and misaligned funding streams, or what some call the "wrong pockets" problem. Sometimes, the entity that fronts the cost of implementing a program does not receive commensurate benefit.[2] For example, one government entity may know of a cost-efficient, evidence-based intervention or program that produces better outcomes. However, the majority of the resulting savings may accrue to different government entities. Therefore, the first government entity would bear the cost of implementation and have little incentive to pursue the program. This challenge dissuades that entity from carrying out a program that would improve lives and save money.

However, change is coming. With a growing emphasis on evidence-based practices, data-driven decision-making, and fiscal accountability, governments and the social sector are redoubling efforts to identify and support programs that work. Funders, too, are devising new and creative ways to get around the wrong pocket problem. For example, the U.S. Department of Education, as part of its Performance Partnerships Pilots, has launched

2 John Roman, "Solving the Wrong Pockets Problem: How Pay for Success Promotes Investment in Evidence-Based Best Practices," Urban Institute (September 2015).

initiales to "braid" (strategically coordinate separate programs and funding streams) and "blend" (consolidate funding streams from separate programs) funding to increase the success of disconnected youth in achieving educational, employment, wellbeing, and other key outcomes.

IDENTIFYING, MEASURING, AND PAYING FOR RESULTS

No longer interested in paying for compliance, governments and other funders are shifting the focus to identifying, measuring, and evaluating success. Funders also now have many distinct tools to deploy based on the unique circumstances of the challenge or social policy to be addressed. We focus on three of the most promising models: 1) incentive prizes and challenges, 2) outcomes-based grants and contracts, and 3) Pay for Success. (See Figure 1 for a summary of the models.)

Incentive Prizes and Challenges

Incentive prizes and challenges are competitions among individuals, groups, or other entities designed to achieve clear, defined goals in a defined time frame. In a challenge, the funding organization identifies a problem, creates and publicizes a prize-based challenge for solving that problem, signs up diverse participants, and offers a reward to the winner. The funding organization awards the prize funds to the solver(s) with the best solution that achieves the desired outcome.

Outcomes-Based Grant or Contract

Outcomes-based grants or contracts are bilateral agreements between a payer and service provider(s). Under the arrangement, service providers receive some funding from the payer to operate the program, and they receive additional performance payments if they achieve agreed-on outcomes. (The proportion of total funding that additional payments make up can vary significantly.)

Pay for Success

Pay for Success projects, also known as social impact bonds, are contracts that enable a funder, typically government, to pay only when the program achieves desired outcomes. An external organization assumes responsibility for delivering outcomes. If (and only if) the outcomes are achieved, the funder releases an agreed upon amount of money to the external

Figure 1. Three Models for Outcomes-based Funding

	INCENTIVE PRIZES AND CHALLENGES	OUTCOMES-BASED GRANTS OR CONTRACTS	PAY FOR SUCCESS
PROBLEMS ADDRESSED	Social and scientific	Social	Social, often issues conducive to preventative solutions
KNOWLEDGE OF SOLUTION	Unclear, ineffective, unknown or multiple solutions	May have a known or promising solution	May range from a strong track record to some early evidence of success
TYPICAL TIMEFRAME FOR ACHIEVING OUTCOMES AND MAKING PAYMENTS	Varies from a few months to many years	1–3 years	3–8 years
TYPICAL LEVEL OF OUTSIDE RESOURCES LEVERAGED	Significant time, money, and effort from solvers	Low to non-existent	Significant financial resources from external organizations
PARTNER ORGANIZATIONS TYPICALLY BEARING MOST OF THE FINANCIAL RISK	Solvers — those coming up with the solution and expending money and time	Service providers — those providing the direct service, at partial funding risk	Often investors — those putting up the money

organization. Often, external organizations raise money from investors to fund service providers who work to achieve the outcome.

CHOOSING A RESULTS-BASED FUNDING OPTION

Not all results-based funding mechanisms are suited for all social policy objectives. When considering which innovation to use, governments and funders should closely examine the challenge they wish to address and consider several factors before selecting a specific instrument. We recommend considering four factors: 1) the nature of the problem, 2) the track record of solutions or potential solutions, 3) the time frame for achieving outcomes and making payments, and 4) the typical level of outside resources and partner organizations involved. Each of these considerations is important to identifying the most effective tool.

Nature of the Problem

Nearly every results-based funding mechanism is designed to address social problems. However, within the social arena, some tools are better suited for certain types of social problems, and a few can be used for non-social issues. For example, incentive prizes and challenges, which seek to galvanize people outside the funding organization to develop innovative solutions to vexing challenges, tend to be more flexible in that they can be used for social and scientific challenges. In contrast, Pay for Success and outcomes-based grants or contracts tend to focus exclusively on social problems, with the former placing a greater emphasis on preventive interventions and solutions.

Knowledge of Solution

Whether effective solutions have already been identified and tested affects the tool selection process. Some tools are suited for discovering or devising new solutions, while others encourage and reward the implementation of proven or promising interventions. Many fall somewhere in between testing and scaling. The incentive structure of prizes and challenges allows for multiple solvers and multiple answers to a challenge. Given that prizes and challenges are meant to devise solutions for particularly complex and intractable problems, no previous solution or intervention need exist. In contrast, Pay for Success is made practical (and practicable) by the existence of a solution, the track record of which may range from promising to proven. Because the financial risk of Pay for Success projects is high, external organizations and investors tend to want or require interventions that have a high likelihood of achieving results.

Outcomes-based grants or contracts tend to require something between prizes and challenges' "white space" and the effective interventions of Pay for Success. In outcomes-based grants or contracts, a known or promising solution may not exist, although having an existing promising solution tends to lead to better results. In the Tennessee example above, service providers could have either implemented a promising or proven intervention to achieve the performance targets or devised their own approach in hopes of meeting the targets. Similarly, managed care and outcomes-based contracts are designed to encourage practitioners and service providers to adopt activities and behaviors that are shown to lead to certain outcomes but leave room for service providers to innovate and test new interventions.

Time Frame for Achieving Outcomes and Making Payments

Another consideration is the timeline. On one end of the spectrum is incentive prizes and challenges, which can take as little as a few months to structure, implement, and pay out (although they can take years to complete). Loan incentives, investment tax credits, and performance-based contracting also tend to be quicker to structure and lead to change on shorter timelines.

Outcomes-based grants or contracts typically last between one and three years. Because they are often modifications to existing government grants that provide base funding and incentives based on performance, the timeline of outcomes-based grants and contracts tends to mirror that of traditional funding models and government contracts.

Meanwhile, Pay for Success arrangements typically last between three and eight years, although there are exceptions, such as the Chicago early childhood education project, which is slated to run 17 years. The typical three-to-eight-year timeline is driven largely by financial considerations; Pay for Success must balance the time needed to prove or disprove the efficacy of an intervention (and achieve results) and the time that investors and funders are willing to tie up money before receiving payment.

Outside Resources and Partnerships

Another important distinction between the various types of results-based funding is the degree to which external partners are engaged in the process. For funders, it is critical to determine to what extent outside resources are needed and desired to solve the problem. Although collaboration across levels of government and sectors is almost always necessary, the degree to which external partners contribute resources and are involved in program implementation will vary. Given the significant investment required for creating and managing partnerships, funders must weigh the benefits, limitations, and appropriateness of engaging external resources to meet their objectives. In addition, the specific ways that funders (particularly government agencies) can leverage external resources may vary by state on the basis of legislation and other regulations.

On one end of the spectrum are Pay for Success projects, which require a high degree of resources from external stakeholders. The most obvious resource requirement is the external financial resources typically used to pay the implementation partner conducting the intervention. In the United States, private investors, philanthropies, and even nonprofit organizations have all contributed financial resources to Pay for Success deals. For many funders, one or more partners are required to fill knowledge gaps related to innovative finance, monitoring and evaluation, stakeholder management, or other issues.

Perhaps even more important than the financial commitment is the investment of time required from all stakeholders. Pay for Success is still a fairly new concept, and each deal requires a highly tailored agreement that aligns the objectives of each group. The deals can take from several months to more than a year to craft, and they require a high level of commitment and coordination from all stakeholders.

As mentioned earlier, the very nature of the problems that incentive prizes and challenges are best at tackling lends itself to involving multiple stakeholders. The problem solvers in particular must invest significant time and potentially money in developing solutions. In addition, funders may work with other organizations to identify potential solvers and promote participation. They may also seek out partner organizations to provide financial and advisory resources for the planning and design phase of a challenge as well as contributions to the award.

The external resources required for outcomes-based grants or contracts are comparatively low. As discussed above, the social issues addressed by this type of results-based funding are more clearly defined. As such, funders may only need to engage an implementation partner who will be paid on the basis of his or her success.

SHARED CHARACTERISTICS OF FUNDING MODELS
Delivering Greater Impact

Although the considerations in determining the most suitable tool for a given challenge vary, the benefits of these tools are similar. The most important is, of course, the impact on a given population or issue area. One of the principal benefits of outcomes-based funding is that it allows government and other funders to differentiate between programs that are providing value to beneficiaries and those that are not. By requiring programs to meet established outcomes for a target population and then rigorously testing programs' abilities to achieve those goals, funders have

ISSUE AREAS IN OUTCOMES-BASED FUNDING

Outcomes-based funding mechanisms have already covered a range of issues, including but not limited to:

- Early childhood education
- Recidivism
- Public health
- Healthcare
- Job skills and employment

- Green energy infrastructure
- Homelessness
- International development
- Scientific innovation

the data to make decisions about where to channel resources for the highest impact.

Sharing and Shifting Risk

The structure of many results-based funding mechanisms offers funders the opportunity to share or even shift financial risk. In the case of outcomes-based contracts, government or foundations are able to share the risk of success or failure with the service provider. If a provider does not successfully meet the objectives of the contract, the provider may forfeit a bonus or may not receive a portion of the agreed upon contract value. In the case of Pay for Success projects, the government does not incur any costs should a program not meet the outlined objectives and targets. For incentive prizes, government shifts the costs of developing innovative solutions to the problem solvers (although there may be some sunk program management costs). When choosing between mechanisms, funders should consider their appetite for taking on financial risk.

The "failure" of the first Pay for Success initiative in the United States, New York City's Adolescent Behavioral Learning Experience (ABLE) intervention, demonstrates the success of outcomes-based funding. The ABLE project did not meet the targets established by the city of New York and agreed on by the investors, philanthropic partners, and the service provider. As a result, government paid nothing for the intervention. This left the city with the ability to channel resources to more proven interventions or to experiment with another innovative solution.

Greater Financial Stewardship of Scarce Dollars

A focus on results also means that government and philanthropic resources are spent in a more responsible and meaningful way. In an era of tighter budgets, results-based contracts and other "pay for results" tools allow funders to ensure greater social value for every dollar spent. In the case of services that prevent a more costly intervention, paying for outcomes may actually mean paying less in the long run.

Reduced Administrative Burdens

A results approach also lowers administrative costs. As discussed, the current model of grant or contract management focuses heavily on monitoring who does what and how, rather than on what they achieve. This focus requires funders to spend a great deal of time monitoring various activities and arbitrary indicators of compliance, placing a significant administrative burden on agencies.

CHALLENGES TO TRANSFORMING THE STATUS QUO FUNDING MODEL

To make this transition possible, funders must invest significantly in developing the capacity to monitor and evaluate the programs. This will require not only training, the creation of new tools, and the development of new business processes, but also a fundamental shift in the way administrators think about funding. For government, this would require both steps taken at the executive level and the alignment of other powerful actors, including the legislature and government administrators. Despite the significant investment in resources and time, a shift from an administrative to an outcomes focus would pay significant dividends for both funders and beneficiaries.

Additionally, as with any system that awards funding, there is the potential for manipulation of programs or data to give the appearance of meeting outcomes. It is possible that some programs may seek to channel services only to those most likely to succeed, leaving out those who are most at-risk and often have the most need. This would be a perverse incentive that lowers the social value of funding. In addition, without the ability to substantively monitor and evaluate programs, it is possible that results could be manipulated to demonstrate outcomes that have not been achieved.

SCALING RESULTS-BASED FUNDING

Despite the challenges, outcomes-based funding is once again the focus of governments and philanthropic funders across the country. Several Pay for Success initiatives have been launched. (See Figure 2 for a map of Pay for Success activity in the United States.) Large philanthropic funders like the Annie E. Casey, Laura and John Arnold, and Bill & Melinda Gates foundations (to name only a few) have also changed how they think about grant making, with a renewed focus on demonstrated outcomes for continued funding.

Figure 2. United States Pay for Success Activity Map

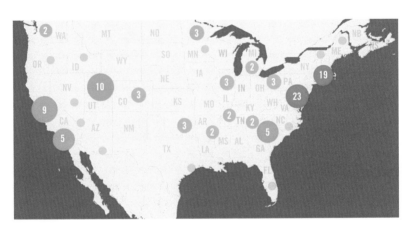

Source: Nonprofit Finance Fund Pay for Success Learning Hub, available at http://www.payforsuccess.org/pay-success-deals-united-states. Note: Activity includes projects, legislation, and opportunities to support Pay for Success efforts.

Most important, the infrastructure required to scale up outcomes-based funding is improving. The body of evidenced-based interventions is growing. Organizations such as the Washington State Institute for Public Policy (WSIPP) have created databases of evidence-based interventions, which funders can use to determine which issue areas might be ripe for scaling their outcomes-based funding portfolios.

An important step to leveraging this growing body of evidence will be to develop a common language for describing outcomes and measuring performance. In the impact investing field, initiatives such as IRIS and the Sustainable Accounting Standards Board are attempting to codify what impact means for investors. Similar initiatives would offer funders the opportunity to speak with one voice and reduce the monitoring and evaluation burden for all parties.

———

DANIEL BARKER *is a senior consultant at Monitor Deloitte where he focuses on social finance, public sector innovation, and sustainable development. Prior to Monitor Deloitte, Barker was a program coordinator at Columbia University's Earth Institute where he managed a number of the organization's global health partnerships. Barker also served as a research associate within the Global Health Program at the Council on Foreign Relations. He holds an MA in international finance and economic policy from Columbia University and a BA in international relations from New York University.*

JOHN CASSIDY *is a senior manager in Monitor Deloitte's public sector strategy practice based in Washington, DC. His work focuses on helping governments and public sector foundations use innovative finance and market-based solutions to improve program design and outcomes. Cassidy has an MPP from Harvard University.*

WINNY CHEN *is a manager in Monitor Deloitte's federal practice where she consults to government agencies and commercial entities on strategy, innovation, communications, and performance management. Prior to Monitor Deloitte, Chen was a senior associate at Human Rights First, where she developed and advocated U.S. policies on prevention of and intervention in genocide and other mass atrocities. Before that, she was manager of China studies and a policy analyst on the Center for American Progress' national security team. Chen holds an MA and a BA from Georgetown University.*

Shift to Outcomes
WHY IS THIS IMPORTANT?

CREATING A SUSTAINABLE OUTCOMES MOVEMENT
Federal Policies to Build an Enabling Infrastructure

David Wilkinson
Former Director of the White House Office of Social Innovation

We've applied data and evidence to social policy—to find out what works, scale up when it works, and stop funding things that don't—thereby fostering a new era of social innovation.[1]

—President Barack Obama

The movement to create a more outcomes-driven government and social sector has advanced considerably over the past eight years. We've developed new ways to align resources with results, used data as never before to help us achieve them, and built more evidence than we've ever had about what works. Results-driven, collaborative, person-centered approaches are all part of what we've referred to as social innovation. These approaches are proving they can move the needle for vulnerable communities. And, by gaining bipartisan support, they have the potential to survive and even expand despite shifts in the executive branch.

Eight years ago, much of this work was in a concept phase or the early stages. Today, we've achieved proof of concept. It is still early days, to be sure, but we've come a long way, further and faster than many expected. Through legislation and federal funding, regulations and guidance, convenings and spotlight, President Obama's White House Office of Social Innovation sought to support this movement. As we consider how to grow from proof of concept to widespread adoption, this essay addresses the challenges and opportunities, especially at the federal level.

---

1 Remarks by President Barack Obama at The White House Frontier's Conference on October 13, 2016.

It suggests promising next steps in federal policy that can put the movement on the path to scale.

THE OUTCOMES MOVEMENT'S EXISTENTIAL THREAT

In most communities and most of the time, introducing outcomes-centered solutions is a herculean task. They require uncommon commitment involving creative workarounds, hard-to-attain waivers, and active engagement from leaders at the highest levels, among other special circumstances. This is neither scalable nor sustainable. Three core challenges inhibit adoption of outcomes-focused approaches:

Lack of incentives — The funding systems into which supporters introduce outcomes-driven solutions were not designed to prioritize outcomes. Evidence is rarely valued; funding of service providers typically focuses on compliance and outputs rather than outcomes. In a funding environment that does not incentivize outcomes, proven, high-impact approaches have little comparative advantage to receive funding. For example, a Social Innovation Fund grantee took the courageous step of exposing its afterschool program to rigorous evaluation. But most school district procurement officers valued the grantee's compelling evidence of impact, as the program's director put it, "about as much as a glossy picture of a kid on a slide" — which is to say, very little. Until procurement rules value evidence, we are less likely to build it. Until they value impact, we are less likely to get it.

Systemic barriers — This absence of incentives for social service providers to engage in what works is compounded by the presence of systemic obstacles. Those bold organizations seeking to implement results-driven approaches face pervasive barriers, including tightly prescribed limitations on reimbursable activities, costly reporting requirements unrelated to outcomes, and, critically, restrictions on cross-silo collaboration, data sharing, and co-funding. For example, a workforce training program alone is less likely to help an at-risk mom get a steady job if her housing situation is unstable and if she does not have reliable child care. But siloed funding disincentivizes the coordination that increases the likelihood of family success. By inhibiting collaboration while also distracting from outcomes due to overemphasis on process compliance, the current system discourages innovation and favors those who stick to business as usual.[2]

Lack of capacity—Government staff and service providers themselves have adapted to the systems in which they operate. In particular, funding systems that are primarily built around compliance and outputs shape the priorities, activities and expertise of the public and social sectors. As a result, even where the will emerges to adopt results-driven approaches, the tools to track outcomes and the capacity to deliver them are rarely in place. Under-resourced and overstretched in significant part by procedural demands unrelated to results, few social services agencies or providers can develop necessary capacity in data analytics, evaluation, and outcomes tracking and delivery.

BUILDING AN ENABLING INFRASTRUCTURE

For results-driven approaches to expand and scale, the current, underlying systems must be upgraded and transformed. In their place, we must build an enabling infrastructure in which outcomes-based solutions are a natural fit rather than a square peg in a round hole. The policy recommendations here are a selection of concrete and practical next steps to advance systems infrastructure that incentivizes the achievement of outcomes, removes systemic barriers, and enhances the capacity of government and service providers to be more results-driven.

Incentivizing Outcomes

At every level of government, laws, regulations, guidance, contracts, and grant agreements can be shaped to reward the achievement of outcomes. Through these mechanisms, we can introduce a spectrum of results-oriented policies that permit, encourage, or, when appropriate, require outcomes-focused approaches.

Permitting outcomes-focused approaches—A major barrier to outcomes-focused approaches is that most federally funded programs do not clearly authorize them. Working with Congress, the Obama administration introduced hundreds of millions of dollars in annual federal, state, and local authority to engage in outcomes contracting in workforce training

---

2 Such barriers tend to reinforce one another at every level of government. A state seeking to take on these challenges, for instance, may find limits on its authority to do so federally and resistance from municipal program administrators who may lack the will, capacity, or resources for systems change.

and education, among other programs. There are much greater opportunities to provide similar authority in block grants, formula funds, and discretionary funds, which together represent the bulk of social services funding in America.

Encouraging evidence and outcomes—Low- and no-cost policies can accelerate a shift to outcomes. With bipartisan support, we incentivized adoption of outcomes contracting by launching Pay for Success grant programs at eight agencies, spurring $160 million in new funding and helping to develop the Pay for Success sector. This has leveraged hundreds of millions more in state and local funding to pay for outcomes rather than process, while seeding an outcomes mindset in communities and states. We also encouraged a shift toward outcomes by making evidence of effectiveness a meaningful scoring factor in multiple grant programs. These approaches have shown promise and should be expanded. In addition to Pay for Success approaches that involve financing, there is great promise in a broader array of funding models that attach payment to outcomes, including partial outcomes and bonus payments, tracking outcomes and rewarding successful providers in subsequent funding rounds, and rate cards.

Requiring outcomes-focused approaches—Making outcomes accountability the rule rather than the exception is understandably rare and, for the most part, premature. Infrastructure and capacity have a long way to go before this would be widely appropriate. However, relevant early steps have been made in this direction. For instance, the new federal education law requires inclusion of evidence-based practices to improve low-performing schools.[3] New results-driven contracting approaches in multiple jurisdictions, from Rhode Island to Seattle, also indicate progress.[4]

Removing Barriers
As noted above, systemic barriers to cross-silo collaboration reduce service providers' ability to deliver results-driven, person-centered approaches. As a result, we too often provide those in need with fragmented services and

---

3 U.S. Department of Education, "Every Student Succeeds Act (ESSA)," available at https://www.ed.gov/essa?src=rn.

4 Harvard Kennedy School Government Performance Lab, "Results-Driven Contracting: An Overview," available at http://govlab.hks.harvard.edu/files/siblab/files/results-driven_contracting_an_overview_0.pdf?m=1456763365.

uncoordinated care. We've found promising approaches that effectively remove obstacles to results-driven collaboration:

Removing barriers to pooled funding when outcomes are tracked— Exchanging individual grant compliance for outcomes tracking and accountability across grant programs has promise. It also has bipartisan support and precedent upon which we can build. For example, Performance Partnership Pilots (P3) give communities flexibility to combine funds across multiple federal funding streams to advance outcomes-driven strategies for at-risk youth. This pooling approach should be applied to other populations.[5]

Building coalitions of the willing—Through the White House Data-Driven Justice initiative, we organized a bipartisan coalition of 140 state and local leaders to facilitate collaboration to reduce unnecessary incarceration and provide better care to high-cost super-utilizers. With the right leadership and spotlight, the coalition-of-the-willing model could apply to other issue areas where success calls for communities to advance cross-silo solutions by cutting through red tape.

Promising Solutions

To better understand the barriers to implementing results-driven approaches, we engaged with hundreds of grantees through our federal grantee experience initiative. There are promising solutions to address the most common and frustrating challenges grantees cited, including:

Simplifying reporting while finding ways for it to add value— Reporting requirements of federal grantees are often time-consuming, costly, and redundant, distracting service providers from focusing on outcomes. There is great opportunity for new technology to reduce reporting redundancy. We launched a technology pilot to simplify reporting while finding ways for it to add value rather than distract. Such models should be studied and, if effective, expanded.

Shifting focus to what's needed rather than what's prescribed—Federal programs often seek certain outcomes but tightly prescribe the activities a grantee may undertake to achieve them. A common complaint among

---

5 Increased outcomes accountability should be accompanied by reduced reporting and compliance burden unrelated to outcomes, as it does with P3.

grantees is that they are often unable to provide the appropriate service to meet a client's needs because the service is not reimbursable under a grant award. Outcomes contracting models, like Pay for Success, can give additional latitude to service providers, providing grantees a great deal of flexibility by shifting the focus from activities to results.

Broadly speaking, governments at all levels should work with grantees to reduce reporting and compliance burden in exchange for outcomes accountability. There are new opportunities to do so. Recently published federal Uniform Guidance introduces several authorities that remove barriers and can waive restrictions that get in the way of cross-silo and outcomes-focused approaches.[6]

Building Capacity

In the social services sector, both government administrators and nonprofit practitioners have built their operations around the current, compliance-focused system. There will be understandable trepidation around systemic shifts. That said, when programs focus on outcomes, they better honor the mission and dedication of the public- and social-sector employees who deliver services. No one should expect the sector, often under-resourced and overworked, to turn on a dime. It will need help getting there. Key areas of pursuit include:

Public-sector and service-provider data access and capacity — Access to reliable and recent data is critical for successful implementation of outcomes-oriented approaches at scale. Among other things, this is essential if we are to reduce reporting burden for outcomes accountability; it is foundational for informed cross-silo collaboration; it is needed for low-cost, rapid evaluation; and it is the basis of planning and executing outcomes contracting models. The Obama administration took a variety of steps to advance local data capacity, from Data-Driven Justice and new HIPAA guidance to the Commission on Evidence-Based Policymaking, which holds hope to increase responsible data access, not just for researchers but also for local practitioners. Through the Social Innovation

---

6   Agencies at all levels of government may seek to use these new authorities as appropriate. Just one such promising authority is federal agencies' ability to offer "fixed-amount awards." Through such awards, federal agencies and their grantees can eschew the typical model of cost reimbursement for prescribed activities in favor of payment for results. This broad authority has been rarely used in connection with social programs but holds great promise. For more information please see https://www.gpo.gov/fdsys/pkg/CFR-2014-title2-vol1/pdf/CFR-2014-title2-vol1-sec200-201.pdf.

Fund's administrative data pilot and data readiness grant programs, communities will be better able to access and interpret data that will help them target services to those most in need and assess outcomes.

Outcomes-focused technical assistance—Each year, governments spend billions on technical assistance (TA). There is significant unrealized potential to deploy TA resources to help government and service providers use data and evidence to achieve measurably better results. In particular, outcomes-focused TA builds capacity of service providers to: 1) Identify the most important outcomes that service providers are trying to achieve, and measure them; 2) Implement evidence-based practices most likely to achieve target outcomes in local communities by meeting service providers where they are and help them adapt evidence-based programming to their current efforts; and 3) Use data to inform service delivery by identifying and targeting populations in need of services, as well as to assess real-time outcomes with the objective of enabling service providers to learn, course correct where necessary, and continuously improve.[7]

Funding overhead costs to enhance capacity and performance— Reorienting programs around outcomes will require nonprofit service providers to increase investment in capacity, talent, data, and evaluation. Too often, however, nonprofits have very limited overhead and administrative resources. The Obama administration introduced new federal guidance enabling service providers to access greater funding for administrative overhead or indirect costs.[8] Uptake by nonprofits has been slow in a cost-competitive environment. Governments should see this mandate as an opportunity rather than a cost. Philanthropies, which often contribute overhead funding, are well-positioned to advocate for adoption.

THE PATH AHEAD

Many are daunted by the road ahead. I am among them. In this constrained budget environment, worthy programs may find themselves fighting for limited resources. But, several of the advances described here

---

7   For more information about outcomes-focused TA see David Wilkinson, "Outcomes-Focused Technical Assistance: Enabling Greater Impact Through Data and Evidence," The White House Office of Social Innovation (December 15, 2016), available at https://obamawhitehouse.archives.gov/blog/2016/12/15/ outcomes-focused-technical-assistance-enabling-greater-impact-through-data-and.

8   U.S. Government Printing Office, "OMB Guidance § 200.414 Indirect (F&A) Costs," available at https:// www.gpo.gov/fdsys/pkg/CFR-2014-title2-vol1/pdf/CFR-2014-title2-vol1-sec200-414.pdf.

have gained bipartisan congressional support. Helpfully for the outcomes movement, the most important steps Congress can take, including most proposals noted above, involve little or no cost and would increase the effectiveness of federal funds.

Advocacy will be critical. Elected leaders must see that there is a constituency for evidence and impact that offers concrete, practical, actionable proposals.

Thankfully, the outcomes movement has already begun to show that by using data and evidence to do things smarter, by collaborating across silos, and by doing so with a clear-eyed focus on results, we can measurably move the needle for communities in need. By more effectively deploying taxpayer dollars for verifiable results, we can build trust in government. Most important, these tools and approaches can help us build a country that is more just, a society that is more equal, and communities that are stronger.

———

DAVID WILKINSON *is the former director of the White House Office of Social Innovation. Prior to his work at the White House, Wilkinson served as executive director of City First Enterprises, a federally regulated nonprofit bank holding company and incubator of social finance solutions. Wilkinson is a graduate of the University of Virginia and Yale Law School.*

THE FUTURE OF EFFECTIVE GOVERNMENT
Use Evidence, Build Evidence, Repeat

Erica Brown, Josh McGee, and Kathy Stack
Laura and John Arnold Foundation

At the beginning of President Obama's first term, Congress created a $650 million grant program for the U.S. Department of Education (DOE) known as Investing in Innovation (I3).[1] This program offered an unprecedented opportunity to re-imagine how federal funding competitions could promote the use of existing evidence to improve important student outcomes (including achievement or student growth, high school graduation rates, and college enrollment and completion rates) while simultaneously generating new knowledge about how to move the needle in K-12 education.[2] The brief statute stipulated that funds must flow to entities with a track record of closing the achievement gap for disadvantaged students. However, it left the executive branch considerable flexibility to design a program that would advance evidence-based decision-making at multiple government levels.

To design the new program, the Office of Management and Budget worked with two DOE offices that had limited experience collaborating with each other: the program office, which was responsible for administering new grants, and the Institute of Education Sciences (IES), which includes research experts who manage impact evaluations. Together, these teams created a three-tiered program with evidence built into its DNA. Under the tiered structure, the largest grants supported strategies that were backed by the strongest evidence of impact—including from large-sample, multi-site randomized controlled trials (RCTs)—and were considered ready for scale-up. Medium-sized grants were awarded

---

1 U.S. Department of Education, "U.S. Secretary of Education Announces National Competition to Invest in Innovation" (2009), available at https://www.ed.gov/news/press-releases/us-secretary-education-announces-national-competition-invest-innovation.

2 U.S. Department of Education, "Programs, Investing in Innovation Fund i3," available at https://www2.ed.gov/programs/innovation/index.html?exp=0.

to support validation of promising strategies that were backed by less rigorous evidence from quasi-experimental evaluations, and small grants were awarded to evaluate innovative or untested strategies with a strong theory of change. In every tier, applicants were required to demonstrate how they used relevant research to inform program design and to provide a plan for rigorously evaluating the impact of their interventions.

The I3 program became a blueprint for other tiered-evidence initiatives launched by the Obama administration in education, in workforce training, and through the Social Innovation Fund. It also served as a guide for evidence-based initiatives launched at the state and local levels. Many of these recent initiatives embody the same characteristics as the I3 program: They are co-created by government and researchers; they focus on using and building evidence of effectiveness in real-world settings; and they employ rigorous evaluation to determine a program's impact.

The growing enthusiasm for data-driven, outcomes-focused public policies is promising. However, to make meaningful progress in addressing society's biggest challenges—things like joblessness, health disparities, and recidivism—the process for learning about which strategies measurably improve people's lives must be accelerated. We believe this will occur only if federal, state, and local governments commit to an iterative, evidence-building approach like the one I3 embodies. This must include program designs that are informed by research, ongoing randomized experimentation, and a commitment to drive resources toward solutions that demonstrate results.

This highlights an important, yet often overlooked, feature of evidence-based policymaking: It is a dynamic, long-term pursuit of outcomes that requires sustained focus on using data and evaluation to learn and continuously improve approaches that address important problems. Put another way, employing evidence-based policy goes beyond simply using prior evidence to figure out what to do next. Making informed decisions based on the best evidence available at the time is important, but without a commitment to generating new knowledge, progress will be unacceptably slow and episodic. Instead, when governments try new programs, they should incorporate rigorous evaluation to monitor whether they deliver the intended results. A commitment to doing so is the only way to ensure that good ideas are adopted and scaled and that we can learn from and improve upon less successful efforts.

Unfortunately, I3's incorporation of evidence building is the exception rather than the rule among government programs. Engaging in evidence-based decision-making will require time, resources, and a culture shift in the public sector, as many real and perceived challenges prevent government officials from routinely implementing this approach. However, there are also a number of solutions that can help governments overcome these obstacles.

One of the most frequently cited challenges is that data can be expensive, messy, and difficult to access. Although collecting new data can certainly be costly, governments already collect a wide range of data, referred to as "administrative data." These data can be an excellent source of information for performance management, observational research, and impact evaluation.[3] And while administrative records can be messy and not always aligned with government's policy interests, the investment required to clean these data and align collection with outcomes of interest is minimal relative to the total amount spent on the delivery of government programs. It can also pay huge dividends for many years to come. Research-practice partnerships, including the Houston Education Research Consortium, have been successful in combining local, state, and national data and analyzing that data to inform policymakers about important decisions, including whether to continue teacher incentive and supplementary reading programs.[4]

A second set of challenges stems from the fact that administrative data are often disjointed, housed in multiple agencies, and protected by important privacy laws. Given that individuals often enroll in multiple government

---

3 J-PAL North America Resources on How to Obtain and Use Nonpublic Administrative Data, "Using Administrative Data for Randomized Evaluations," available at https://www.povertyactionlab.org/admindata.

4 Dara Shifrer, "Houston Independent School District's Aspire Program: Estimated Effects of Receiving Financial Awards 2009–10 Aspire Program," The Houston Education Research Consortium (HERC) Kinder Institute for Urban Research Rice University (2013), available at https://kinder.rice.edu/uploadedFiles/Kinder_Institute_for_Urban_Research/Programs/HERC/ASPIRE%202009-10.pdf; Daniel Bowen, "An Evaluation of the Houston Independent School District's Secondary Reading Initiative: First Year Student Effects," The Houston Education Research Consortium (HERC) Kinder Institute for Urban Research at Rice University (2014), available at https://kinder.rice.edu/uploadedFiles/Kinder_Institute_for_Urban_Research/Programs/HERC/2014V2I2.BOWEN_SRI1[3].pdf.

programs, data sets must be linked together to allow researchers and policymakers to track outcomes across programs and identify comprehensive solutions to challenging social problems. While collecting and linking data is often time-consuming and generally done on an ad-hoc basis, the development of Integrated Data Systems (IDS) has helped governments overcome these challenges by routinely linking databases, streamlining data access, and protecting privacy.[5] The state of South Carolina is leveraging its IDS, which links multiple-state data sets, to conduct a large-scale, low-cost, randomized evaluation of a home visitation program as it is expanded to serve more families across the state. Policymakers will use the evaluation findings to determine the program's cost-effectiveness and make future programmatic adjustments or improvements.

Governments also face difficulties in identifying evidence-based solutions for the problems they are trying to solve. In many areas of public policy, we simply don't know much about what works, for whom, and under what circumstances. But this only underscores the need for the approach outlined above. Governments must build evidence rather than simply consume it. Although a small number of interventions have promising prior research evidence, including programs like those found in IES's What Works Clearinghouse and those funded by I3's large grants, we don't know how effective those solutions will be when they are scaled and replicated in different settings. Sometimes the hoped-for effect is achieved, as occurred when KIPP expanded its network of middle schools and improved reading and math achievement among students.[6] Other times, however, the result differs from what is expected. Recent findings from a randomized evaluation of Success for All, a promising schoolwide reform program for high-poverty schools, showed that the program did not improve reading fluency or comprehension among students.[7] These results were considerably weaker than those reported in an earlier randomized

5   Actionable Intelligence for Social Policy, "Establishing an IDS," available at http://www.aisp.upenn.edu/integrated-data-systems/establishing-an-ids/.

6   Christina Clark Tuttle et al., "Understanding the Effect of KIPP as it Scales: Volume I, Impacts on Achievement and Other Outcomes (Executive Summary)," Mathematica Policy Research (2015), available at https://www.mathematica-mpr.com/our-publications-and-findings/publications/executive-summary-understanding-the-effect-of-kipp-as-it-scales-volume-i-impacts-on-achievement.

7   Janet Quint et al., "Scaling Up the Success for All Model of School Reform: Final Report from the Investing in Innovation (i3) Evaluation," MDRC (2015), available at http://www.mdrc.org/publication/scaling-success-all-model-school-reform.

evaluation, which found significant positive impacts.[8] This example shows that there is no guarantee of success when programs that initially demonstrate promising results are replicated on a larger scale, with new target populations, or in a different context. So although governments should use research and evidence to design programs and policies to ensure the best chance of success, they must also rigorously evaluate those programs in order to build additional evidence and advance our knowledge of "what works" over time.

Yet another challenge is the fact that employing evidence-based policy requires, among other things, technical capacity to collect, store, and manage large amounts of data; the ability to rigorously analyze that data; and the social-science expertise to set up and execute prospective randomized program evaluations. In addition to using existing resources, including administrative data, evidence repositories, and natural opportunities for experimentation (i.e., oversubscribed programs), governments must pursue partnerships with organizations that can provide these essential knowledge-building skills. One of the most promising models is a strategic partnership with a university which can help governments develop robust data systems, embed rigorous evaluation into the policymaking process, and support innovation. Examples include the Government Performance Lab at the Harvard Kennedy School, which deploys teams of highly qualified fellows to state and local government agencies to help them develop results-driven contracting processes and tie spending to outcomes; the Rhode Island Innovative Policy Lab at Brown University, which helps the state design policy experiments; and JPAL North America, which helps governments implement randomized evaluations.

To make real, measurable progress in solving today's big social problems, we must embrace a culture of innovation and learning. We should be humble about what we know and hungry for more evidence about approaches that will deliver better outcomes for those in need. The pace of learning and discovery dramatically increased when we began to apply scientific method in such fields as medicine and the hard sciences; the social sciences are long overdue to follow suit. By focusing on both the

---

8 Geoffrey D. Borman et al., "Final Reading Outcomes of the National Randomized Field Trial of Success for All," *American Educational Research Journal* (2007), available at http://aer.sagepub.com/content/44/3/701.

use and generation of evidence, we believe that the public sector is poised to rapidly accelerate the pace at which we learn what solutions work, for whom, and why.

————

ERICA BROWN *is director of public accountability at the Laura and John Arnold Foundation where she is responsible for identifying high-leverage philanthropic opportunities that improve outcomes in the public sector. She leads the foundation's efforts on Pay for Success and manages a portfolio of grants focused on evidence-based policy and results-driven government.*

JOSH MCGEE *is a vice president at the Laura and John Arnold Foundation and a senior fellow at the Manhattan Institute. McGee is an economist whose work at the foundation focuses on evidence-based policy and public finance. His personal research investigates issues related to retirement policy, K-12 education, and economic development and has been published in popular media outlets and scholarly journals.*

KATHY STACK *is vice president of evidence-based innovation at the Laura and John Arnold Foundation. Previously she was a senior executive at the White House Office of Management and Budget, where she oversaw education, labor, and social services programs under five presidents. During the George W. Bush and Barack Obama administrations, she helped federal agencies design and implement innovative grant-making models that allocate funding based on evidence and evaluation quality.*

RULES AND RITUALS
How to Drive Change

Zia Khan
The Rockefeller Foundation

Recently I was fortunate to join a meeting in India with economists, political scientists, politicians, and civil servants to explore big questions on how to drive major change in the way government works. The conversations were confidential and thus very candid. One senior official told a story of a well-intended change that never took hold. There was a particular department that was aiming to improve its service levels. For every citizen who requested the service, it would log the request, go through the usual processes to provide the service, and log the completion. This was all done with pen and paper. But management wanted to get the data digitally to inspect and hopefully improve performance. So it implemented a computer-based logging system and a sophisticated dashboard to help monitor performance. Knowing that process completion times would be monitored, government workers were expected to accelerate their work. All sorts of benefits were imagined—identifying best practices, motivating bottom-up process improvement, etc. However, after implementation, there was no improvement, and there were even anecdotes of increased processing time. It turned out that the government workers simply maintained a "shadow" logging system. They would record each start time in a separate book, and when they felt reasonably sure that the work would be completed, they would enter a delayed start time in the system, thus creating two very different realities: what people actually experienced and what the dashboard was calculating.

The point of this story isn't that the government workers were bad or lazy. They were actually quite well-intentioned and proud of their work. The challenge was that the rational computer-based system was implemented without properly accounting for the fact that it was asking people to change—people with pride in what they do, knowledge of subtle details about how things worked, and personal relationships with colleagues who helped them solve problems that arose. Any new way of working will naturally disrupt these informal systems. Most often, people will resist and reject ill-conceived changes, particularly those designed with rational logic but overlook emotional motivators. This is why any new set of "rules" has to be balanced with a shift in an organization's underlying "rituals."

Results-based funding is an exciting movement that could dramatically improve efficiency and effectiveness in the delivery of key programs. More important, clearer framing of desired goals with more flexibility for how those goals can be achieved will unlock entrepreneurial energy and lead to important innovations. However, the need for change is implicit in realizing the promise of results-based funding.

Our work at the The Rockefeller Foundation often revolves around scaling compelling innovations to catalyze broader system changes and realize big, sustainable impact. In the years that I've overseen many diverse initiatives around the globe, and based on my former life as a private-sector strategy consultant, I would argue that one of the biggest differentiators between success and failure in driving system change is whether the emotional dynamics of what it takes for people to change behaviors are factored into the change strategy.

Any system that guides how groups of people get things done can be thought of as a combination of "rules" and "rituals." The rules are the formal part of the system: goals, strategies, processes, etc. They're the things that can often be written on paper. Leaders like to work with the formal system because it's rational and easy to communicate. The rituals are the informal part of the system: values, personal networks, and sources of pride. Rules speak to the head, and rituals speak to the heart. Our behaviors are driven by both.

Most of the current conversation about driving results-based funding focuses on rules. The people driving this conversation are very smart, produce thoughtful reports, and have worked out the logic of incentives, financial flows, etc. This probably has a lot to do with their backgrounds in policy, finance, and strategy—all of which tend to be very "head-driven" fields. However, if we were to pull in other leaders from more "heart-driven" fields, where one has to speak to people's emotions to create commitment and motivate behaviors—people like marine drill sergeants, call center managers, and school teachers—we'd hear a lot more questions about which people need to drive results-based funding, what matters to them, and how they'll be motivated (or not) by proposed changes.

A paradigm shift toward results-based funding is a major analytical breakthrough. But its benefits can be realized only if we look at the number of rituals that need to change and make sure we balance strategy with culture in thinking about how to make those changes. To achieve this balance, there are a few general factors that we should keep in mind.

The first factor is to gain a deeper understanding of the current situation and the change that's necessary. It's easy for innovators to dismiss how people currently do things. "Status quo," "not-invented-here resistance," and "silos" have a negative and dismissive connotation. But there are often good reasons why people do the things they do. No one shows up to work seeking to be old-fashioned, change-resistant, and inefficient.

For example, a results-based funding approach may require a government team to shift from funding long-standing partners toward a process where different partners are invited to submit bids to achieve a specific goal. This is generally one of the strategic benefits of results-based funding—a shift from funding activities to funding outcomes. However, you would want to deeply explore some questions before implementing such a strategy:

- How strong are the personal relationships between the government team and the long-standing partners?

- Are there benefits to the established relationship that haven't been fully considered—for example, the ability to have trust-based conversations about what is or isn't working?

- Does the government team develop expertise and knowledge from the long-standing partner that is respected internally and that may be threatened with a change in partners? Will that threaten the team's adoption of and commitment to a new partner?

You would need to ask similar questions of investors, solution implementers, and all the other actors who will need to change their own rituals to make the overall partnership work.

It's important to note that the existing rituals do not always impede change. In fact, they can be harnessed to drive change, which leads to the second factor: how rituals can be channeled to drive the change instead of being a barrier. Despite the many leadership books that have been written about culture change, the unfortunate reality is that culture is extremely hard to change. What you're better off doing is identifying existing sources of pride and seeing how those can be reframed to motivate the behaviors you want in a results-based funding approach. For example, as difficult as implementing innovative models can be, particularly across different sectors, everyone is generally motivated by the same outcome — improving service for people. And what better way to animate that source of pride than to capture meaningful stories early and frequently and to ensure that they are part of the communications approach? While lots of thought is given to monitoring metrics to track the rational strategy, what's often overlooked is the ability to capture the human stories that will keep motivating people who are trying something new and operating in unfamiliar territory. If the innovative model works, there should be ample successes to share that tap into pride in what is being accomplished to keep people motivated along the journey and driving toward the ultimate goal.

This need to keep people motivated links to the third factor: ongoing investment in building trust and informal relationships across the community that is expected to work together. Results-based funding approaches will involve government, investors, social service organizations, and local communities. While the leaders of the different organizations and teams might quickly align to common objectives, it's the teams themselves who have to deal with day-to-day implementation. Too often collaboration is thought to be driven by alignment to formal project plans, investment memos, and success metrics. What's also needed is the informal sense of shared values, common language, and trust in others' intentions to tackle the issues and problems that emerge "off-plan." Spending time upfront discussing personal drivers, doing real work together to deeply understand each other's culture and language, and believing in people's positive intentions even while fiercely debating approaches is often the secret to making cross-sector collaborations work. It builds the team's resilience in working toward the goal. This is an important asset to draw upon in the future, when unknown challenges are guaranteed to arise.

CONCLUSION

Results-based funding is a powerful concept that could transform how we fund programs and what results they achieve. Realizing that potential will take lots of hard work and change. Let's be sure to capture the opportunity by matching brilliantly designed rules with thoughtful treatment of less obvious rituals.

———

ZIA KHAN *is vice president of initiatives and strategy at The Rockefeller Foundation where he leads the global program team. Khan writes and speaks frequently on strategy, innovation, and cross-sector partnerships. Prior to joining the foundation, he was a management consultant advising senior leaders on strategy and organizational performance. Khan is the co-author of* Leading Outside the Lines *published by Jossey-Bass in 2010. He has a PhD in fluid dynamics from Stanford University.*

INVESTING IN LEADERSHIP TO BUILD A SUSTAINABLE NONPROFIT SECTOR

Kerry Sullivan
Bank of America Charitable Foundation

Today, across the United States, we face enormous challenges that require extraordinary leadership to solve. One in seven families in America is at risk of hunger, youth unemployment is double the national average, and poverty and income inequality rates have risen over the past five years. It's clear that strong, collaborative leadership across the public, private and nonprofit sectors is essential to help address these pressing concerns and help individuals and families from vulnerable communities gain economic mobility. A great example is how Houston leaders, including a range of nonprofits and public officials, joined forces to work on the issue of homelessness in a new and innovative way that helped reduce chronic homelessness by nearly 60 percent. However, in order to help leaders do more, we need to expand opportunities to bring more capital into the equation and encourage honest dialogue about true costs, intended impact and sustainability. An evidence-based approach to funding provides promise. But to realize the true potential of this approach, we need to consider investing in nonprofit leadership so they are ready to meet this change.

New technologies and innovations are changing dynamics across industries, and the nonprofit sector is no different. The sector's leadership must be able to anticipate and navigate economic, societal, and sector-wide changes if they are to support the most vulnerable people in our society. The nonprofit landscape has undergone significant changes in the last decade, and the way organizations operate now is very different today than it was ten or 15 years ago. The pace of change shows no sign of subsiding. Since the recession, nonprofit leaders have faced a huge increase in demand for their services. In fact, Nonprofit Finance Fund's 2015 State of the Sector survey found that 76 percent of nonprofits reported an increase in demand for services—the seventh year that a majority reported increases. To cope with overwhelming demand, nonprofits have had to learn to do more with less to survive and try to meet needs. However, the reality is that traditional financing from government and philanthropic funders cannot cover the extensive financial needs of our communities, and we're called upon to look at the full spectrum of how we invest in communities in order to advance social change.

OPPORTUNITIES TO BUILD A STRONGER NONPROFIT SECTOR THAT CAN MEET COMMUNITY NEEDS

Expanding the tent of investors that support nonprofits' work. Results-based funding, impact investing in particular, has fundamentally changed the dialogue within the system and how government, private, and nonprofits sectors intersect. Nonprofit leaders must begin to rethink their business model in order to deal with the reality of today's funding experience. While the move to results-based funding is still nascent, we are seeing it shake up the way that nonprofits do business. It's a welcome change to how we deliver resources to address the intractable issues we face, but we must empower nonprofit leaders to deliver the necessary metrics through more informed dialogue with investors. In addition to answering the age-old questions of how they can create positive change in their community, take their model to scale, and make it sustainable, we need to have a more comprehensive conversation around their business model and long-term sustainability. All of this requires leadership from our nonprofit trailblazers, as well as a deeper understanding by funders and investors of the fundamental issues at stake.

Structuring and measuring programs to demonstrate outcomes. Under traditional financing models, government and funders want to see monitoring and evaluation of the programs, but they often do not provide the funding to cover this work. In many cases, nonprofits use their own capital, or dollars not included in the grant, to cover the cost of evaluation. Results-based funding turns this on its head. Investors focus on the outcome, not the model that establishes how you're going to get there. Monitoring and evaluation are at the very heart of an outcome-focused approach, and nonprofits can ask to be compensated to cover this work. While many large funders are increasingly willing to pay for evaluation to cover their investment, this alone is not a sustainable model. Nonprofits also need to embrace a different operating model that leverages technology and data so that they can build and oversee systems to track outcomes. This often requires new managerial skills as well as additional capital investment.

HOW INVESTMENTS IN LEADERSHIP SUPPORT TODAY'S RESULTS-BASED MODEL

In any situation, nonprofit leaders must have a clear vision for how their organizations will create change in their communities, and this is pivotal in a results-based model. To help investors believe enough to invest in them, nonprofit leaders have to demonstrate that they are well-integrated in their local community and can work with government to create change at scale. Additional coaching and support, can be instrumental in helping nonprofit leaders create the networks and integrated partnerships needed for success.

I've seen from more than 13 years of Bank of America's Neighborhood Builders program that investments in nonprofit leadership deliver significant return for our communities. For example, Pine Street Inn in Boston has supported homeless people with emergency shelter for many decades. After being recognized as a Bank of America Neighborhood Builder—an award that enables high-performing nonprofits to advance their strategic planning by investing in their leadership in conjunction with flexible funding—Pine Street Inn conducted a study of their clients and found that a majority of those seeking emergency shelter were actually repeat guests who had numerous challenges. Pine Street Inn's leadership evolved their services to more effectively work on ending homelessness by no longer focusing solely on providing emergency shelter services, but rather working to move people into supportive housing—and they are expanding their services on that front. It's a longer-term solution in partnership with the city, offering a full range of supportive services that address the underlying issues at the heart of homelessness. Examples like this show that nonprofits can adapt their model to deliver an even deeper community impact when their leadership is supported to make change.

Put simply, valuing and investing in nonprofit leadership is critical to the success of the sector and how we will make the shift to focusing on outcomes. Results-based funding offers a tremendous opportunity to deliver meaningful change in our communities. And it can be achieved if we invest in the people who will oversee this change—nonprofit leaders. By supporting nonprofit leadership, we can actually help create more effective nonprofits that can deliver the vital services, track outcomes and effectively work across sectors to achieve the ultimate goal of changing the lives of individuals and families to put them on a path toward economic progress and shared success.

———

KERRY HERLIHY SULLIVAN *is president of the Bank of America Charitable Foundation, whose mission is to help advance economic mobility for individuals, families and communities in order to create thriving communities across the company's global footprint. In this role, Sullivan leads a team responsible for philanthropic strategy in support of the company's commitment to responsible growth through a focus on environmental, social and governance factors. The foundation is delivering on a ten-year $2 billion philanthropic giving goal, with a particular focus of serving low-income communities and vulnerable populations.*

UNDERWRITING INNOVATION
How Information Technology and Pay for Success Contracting Can Transform Public-Sector Outcomes

Caroline Whistler
Third Sector Capital Partners, Inc.

Matt Gee
BrightHive Inc.

The San Diego Workforce Partnership (SDWP) had a problem. As a recent recipient of a Pay for Success demonstration grant to increase employment outcomes for youth involved in the justice system, SDWP was excited to work with Third Sector Capital Partners, Inc. (Third Sector) to develop an innovative, outcomes-based service model for its hardest-to-serve youth. The problem was not the intervention, partnership, or SDWP's willingness to pay for results. It was their data. Measuring success meant knowing how youth in the program avoided jail, got jobs, and earned good, living wages years after. But SDWP had no access to justice data or wage data to see if their programs resulted in increased wage growth for youth over time. Worse still, the data SDWP needed were marbled throughout various state databases, provider Excel spreadsheets, and balkanized case management systems, and none of the organizations in that information network had the funding or strong incentive to change or improve their own data infrastructure to support SDWP's, new programmatic model. Without access to quality data across a fractured ecosystem of stakeholders, how could SDWP procure outcomes and ensure they were delivered for these young people?

San Diego is not alone. Across the country, nonprofit and government service providers are experiencing a wave of interest in moving from funding programs to funding outcomes. But many of these jurisdictions are facing the same chicken-and-egg problem: To enable outcomes contracting, you need data and information technology (IT) infrastructure that yields meaningful metrics across information silos; but to develop and support the appropriate data and IT infrastructure, you need new contract structures and revenue sources that can justify the added cost across a distributed information network.

For government to achieve outcomes, it needs to solve the dual problem of how it procures information technology and how it contracts for services. Our two organizations, BrightHive (focused on digital infrastructure) and Third Sector (focused on social services contracting), have spent the past half-decade helping organizations become outcomes-oriented. When we began working together, we realized that the principles of outcomes-oriented IT infrastructure and Pay for Success contracting are incredibly similar and highly complementary. They are both fundamentally about shifting government procurement processes from focusing on cost and compliance to delivering value. This chapter offers a guidebook for how to think about integrating these reforms as part of a comprehensive strategy to drive public-sector outcomes.

PRINCIPLES OF OUTCOMES-ORIENTED INFORMATION TECHNOLOGY PROCUREMENT

IT procurement is a dark art, and every state and locality has its own byzantine navigation rules that complicate the picture. These rules, more often than not, get in the way of procuring technology that supports improved outcomes in services. But there has been a sea change in recent years in the thinking and practice of government IT procurement. This change is most apparent in guidance provided by U.S. Digital Service, Code for America, and the U.K. government's Digital Service Standard.[1] At its heart, smarter IT procurement focuses on ensuring that technology is helping, not hindering, the delivery of better services. Some of these principles are discussed below.

People are the most important part of your digital infrastructure. Good people, not fancy technology, are your greatest asset in the hard work of creating outcomes-oriented digital infrastructure. Over the years, BrightHive has found that motivated, empowered, and properly trained data engineers can work around just about any technical hurdle if they are given the tools and leadership support they need to build workarounds. These unsung data superheroes have been at the heart of every data-driven organization we've worked with. So if you are deciding between signing

---

1 U.K. Government, "Digital Service Standard," Government Service Manual, available at https://www.gov.uk/service-manual/service-standard; Code for America, "How We Do It," available at https://www.codeforamerica.org/how/#principles; U.S. Digital Service, "Digital Services Playbook," available at https://playbook.cio.gov/.

a new $300,000 licensing contract with an enterprise vendor and hiring a technologist looking to make a difference, choose the new hire over the new tool every time.

Make it smaller; make it modular. An important lesson from the Healthcare.gov fiasco was that the general contractor model of government IT procurement is broken. Instead of a massive RFP issued to a single vendor for a system that does everything, break up your procurement of digital services into pieces made up of simple, well-contained services. This "microservices" approach to IT procurement may require a bit more upfront thinking and coordination, but it pays off in making government IT infrastructure more flexible and resilient.[2]

Insist on interoperability. A majority of existing government IT systems, by design, don't have a way to communicate with systems and services outside the walled garden of their product suite. This is good for the vendors, but bad for governance. Outcomes-oriented governance relies heavily on integration of data across systems and service providers. Government agencies must use their purchasing power to enforce data interoperability. Procure only systems that have well-documented application programming interfaces, or APIs.

Default to open-source software. Open-source software, historically the pariah of government IT procurement, is quickly becoming the darling. This makes a lot of sense. It's philosophically aligned: Public digital infrastructure investment should both benefit from and contribute to the public good. But it also makes for better technology. Open-source software is a more secure, more interoperable infrastructure that empowers technical staff to build on and improve the system directly and has a robust community of developers who offer and support solutions built on top of it. Because the software is open, it is often easier for other software vendors to integrate with it.

Ban black boxes. As more IT systems and data services come with integrated analytics, algorithmic transparency is increasingly important. Avoid

---

2   The state of California, with the help of Code for America and 18F, just demonstrated how to do this right with a major RFP overhaul of the child welfare system: Amanda Ziadeh, "California's Step-by-Step Solution for Its New Child Welfare System," *GCN Magazine* (February 2, 2016), available at https://gcn.com/articles/2016/02/02/california-agile-procurement.aspx.

the words "proprietary algorithm" like the plague. Machine-learning algorithms can have inherent biases that can lead to disastrous consequences for the people they are meant to serve. Imagine if SDWP used a proprietary algorithm to identify youth for whom to provide employment supports and unintentionally racially profiled individuals. If you can't open up the hood to know how a targeting algorithm is working, you can't guarantee that the processes being informed by those algorithms aren't inherently biased. Insist on algorithmic transparency and make sure that vendors show you a robust set of tests for bias using your data before you sign on the dotted line.

Following these principles will help your organization or agency build a solid technical foundation for running as a data-driven organization and work more easily within the ecosystem of service providers, funders, and data stewards that can benefit from transforming data to outcomes for communities. However, IT infrastructure in itself will not drive outcomes. There needs to be a simultaneous shift in how data are used to inform contracts and procurement in social services.

MOVING FROM ADMINISTRATIVE DATA TO "WORKING DATA" WITH OUTCOMES CONTRACTING

Pay for Success contracting, as well as other types of outcomes contracts, build on the principles of IT infrastructure procurement. At its core, Pay for Success is about incorporating an outcomes-oriented process into how the government spends its money, though its focus is services versus IT. While there is a spectrum of ways in which Pay for Success contracts may be structured or funded, the basic principle is using data to build an information feedback loop to inform government spending. By incorporating the collection, review, and interpretation of data as a byproduct of social services contracts, Pay for Success projects allow government to focus on the results of services versus the services themselves. However, this reality means that an outcomes-oriented IT infrastructure is a critical part of making Pay for Success contracts possible. The quality of government databases determines if and how you can procure for outcomes.

Government administrative data are essential for Pay for Success contracting because they "underwrite" all processes for the efficient operation, ongoing evaluation, and learning and improvement within Pay for Success programs. Some of these processes include:

- Identifying the programmatic areas and target populations with the highest need and largest potential benefit;
- Development of intervention hypotheses, initial pricing, and contract terms;
- Basic performance reporting and ex-post evaluation; and
- Use of data as an ongoing performance feedback loop with providers and government to learn and improve.

The last process—use of data for ongoing performance—is a distinction of Pay for Success programs, which are giving administrative data the chance to become "working data" by truly developing a feedback loop between service providers and the contracting government entity. This means that instead of submitting one annual report to SDWP about how many youth were served, providers in the youth employment contract may be able to review data about their effectiveness on a monthly basis. This gives them the opportunity to learn from their data and refine their work to maximize the chance that the young people being served become employed in meaningful career paths. By using live working data, both the provider and SDWP see meaningful results for their investment, and most important, more young people are gainfully employed.

Because data are so essential to Pay for Success, the way government agencies and service providers collect, store, analyze, and report that data can determine the success or failure of a Pay for Success initiative. Without the right kinds of systems and processes in place, Pay for Success contracting will remain difficult or impossible in many jurisdictions. Many have realized this and are working to solve the many and varied challenges. Yet this important problem-solving is happening completely separate from the administrative data community, which has also begun to coordinate efforts on improving local and national integrated data systems for better research and performance reporting. With both IT and outcomes-contracting movements proposing to "take government into the twenty-first century," why aren't they working together?

WHAT IT TAKES TO DRIVE PUBLIC-SECTOR OUTCOMES

To understand how IT and outcomes contracting can work together, it is necessary to consider what drives public-sector outcomes today. Breaking down the incentives across multi-agency systems, it quickly becomes clear that technology and contracting are not enough to drive outcomes. You also need policy that incentivizes funding outcomes and programs that are able to deliver results for America's most vulnerable populations. And you can't forget that people run these systems. The capacity of both government and nonprofits to implement performance contracting is in many cases the largest limiting factor to measurably improving lives. It is the combination of technology, contracting, policy, and capacity that can drive systems change.

Yet jurisdictions are continuing to take an agency-level approach to what is a cross-cutting government process and system—perhaps, in part, because it is easier to re-procure one large IT contract than to consider all social services contracts and change procurement policies across agencies. The result of this thinking is that public IT capital is under increased scrutiny as it spends billions on databases to support efficiency and compliance. But little energy is spent on deploying that data to get better results from contractors. Technology is being upheld as increasing government effectiveness simply because it is changing the face of it. But technology itself is not the answer. At the end of the day, the technology SDWP uses to identify and track the success of its youth is a tool; it does not directly result in employment or self-sufficiency outcomes in itself.

That is why driving public-sector outcomes will require systems innovation across policy, technology, contracting and implementation capacity, with each of these levers relying on providers and government to drive change management processes to ongoing results for communities.

CHALLENGES TO COMBINING TWENTY-FIRST-CENTURY TECHNOLOGY AND TWENTY-FIRST-CENTURY OUTCOMES

There are two major challenges facing both IT infrastructure and outcomes contracting reform. Each highlights the difficulty of the public-sector systems to properly incentivize their people and processes to be able to fund and build evidence for programs that measurably improve lives.

Current information technology and outcomes contracts are too bespoke. At this point, Third Sector, BrightHive, and those in the outcomes contracting field for IT or services are working on bespoke projects. Each of these has made important progress for individual agencies, yet falls short of jurisdiction-wide change. Projects are helping to build the case for systems change but are limited in their reach because of structural challenges to the procurement process, federal budgeting requirements, data-sharing agreements, and culture. Our work relies on those public servants willing to prioritize innovation and creativity and spend political capital to measurably improve lives. These everyday heroes are providing promising examples to inform policy, but they are expending immense energy, resources, and political capital on each project.

The very bureaucracy that was put in place to protect people is, in some cases, failing them. For example, those who qualify for food stamps have to muddle through paperwork to receive services. Data are used for compliance, not to learn if the program delivered the intended results. It then comes as little surprise that data created as a byproduct of compliance requirements are insufficient to underwrite outcomes contracts. Whatever your politics, it is clear America is unable to efficiently meet the needs of its most vulnerable, making it difficult to reduce demand for remedial services.

Yet while some write off ineffectiveness as an intrinsic quality of government, this is not the case. Government is still the largest funder of social services in this country, delivering trillions of dollars in health care, employment, and basic services to millions of Americans. The good news is that people join the public sector with a commitment to serve communities, and bureaucracy was never intended to prevent results. There is structural inertia that makes a culture of innovation both elusive and incredibly scalable if we are able to drive that inertia toward outcomes for the largest organization in service of humanity.

So what would it take to create a culture of innovation in government? We need to transform the processes across policy, technology, contracting, and implementation capacity if we are going to unlock innovation and drive better results for our communities. We also need to recognize that technology is not the answer—nor is a contract. It's about the ongoing conversation that both create amongst people within these institutions about the outcomes a government wants to achieve. The conversations can lead to a demand for continuous improvement to ensure every American gets equal opportunity.

PRINCIPLES FOR OUTCOMES CONTRACTING

Treat social-sector-outcomes contracting the same as information technology capital infrastructure. Organizations have come to view the cost of updating IT infrastructure as a capital outlay that pays for itself in the productivity gains of employees and the quality and efficiency of services. This model of a capital improvement project can be applied to updating the technical, legal, and human infrastructure necessary to procure services based on outcomes. A relatively small upfront investment can ensure outcomes across social-sector contracting. Take the time to not only procure an exceptional case management system and integrated data warehouses, but also to hire or train operational staff and management on new processes and metrics that will help drive the agency's outcome goals. It's an investment that will pay off in spades.

Ensure information technology infrastructure enables third-party access and front-end software innovation for tools for both government and service providers. Businesses have real-time data on products sold. Why doesn't SDWB have real-time data on whether their youth have jobs and whether they get raises after their training programs? Providers need access to these data just as much as government. Government doesn't have to build these provider tools. It can enable their creation by supporting modern data services on top of administrative data. This often means tackling privacy and data-sharing agreements in ways that protect people but also enables government to get the best results for its investment. However, emerging national standards for individual data-sharing consent put the power directly in citizens' hands to control their own data. They also allow the organizations supporting them to have access to the information they need to do their jobs better.

Develop new federal technical assistance models to support governments to embed data for decision-making. It will take significant resources to change the culture of government. Federal funding to technical assistance providers who can support change management within jurisdictions will be essential to create a culture of performance management within the public sector.

Use enabling legislation, incentives, and mandatory spending on outcomes as a way to ensure that government funding incentivizes a focus on ongoing results over time versus "silver bullet" programs or earmarks for specific interventions.

Revise federal regulations to ensure compliance is about outcomes. What if, instead of compliance and burden being yoked together, compliance became synonymous with outcomes and learning? The federal government should engage in true procurement reform by reviewing OMB federal circulars and legislative guidance on spending streams. State and local governments are often afraid they may be punished for moving away from funding programs to funding outcomes. America's jurisdictions need a strong, proactive message from federal budget and procurement offices that outcomes are encouraged—and required.

If we can use the power of federal bureaucracy to set compliance principles for innovation and provide incentives for outcomes, we can then let local governments define the spectrum of what they want to achieve for communities. This structure will unleash the power of local governments by empowering those that know their communities best to define success with them—not for them—and use data to spur public-sector innovation, ensuring improvement and results over time.

CONCLUSION

We have the opportunity to ignite a public-sector innovation revolution in our lifetime if we can deploy data for improved outcomes. Make no mistake, innovation of this sort isn't easy. The existing technological and contractual inertia in state and local government is difficult to overcome, and San Diego continues to face an uphill battle with the state to implement innovations. Even with the ongoing advocacy of institutions like Third Sector and BrightHive, paradigm shifts require persistence and constant pressure. But combining IT infrastructure and outcomes contracting empowers public servants to make decisions that measurably improve lives and ensures that government is truly working for its people. As communities collectively invest in combining administrative and operational data, they bring power back to constituencies and usher in transparency and accountability. But success is far from guaranteed, particularly if we do not complement technological innovations with systemic changes to procurement and compliance; that is, if we do not use our data to change how we deliver services to the people who need them most. Yet if we are thoughtful about this revolution, every contract in IT and social services may become an opportunity to move the needle on social problems and to make data underwrite outcomes for America's communities.

CAROLINE WHISTLER *is the chief executive officer and co-founder of Third Sector Capital Partners, Inc., where she leads the firm's work with state and local jurisdictions to drive government funding to outcomes-oriented programs that measurably improve lives. Under her leadership, Third Sector has launched six of the nation's Pay for Success projects and developed partnerships with New Profit, Ballmer Group, The Kresge Foundation, and Stanford Center on Poverty and Inequality. In 2016, her expertise in outcomes contracting and passion for public sector innovation was recognized by the* Chronicle of Philanthropy *("40 Under 40") and by Living Cities ("25 Disruptive Leaders"). Prior to Third Sector, Whistler researched nonprofit sustainability in Brazil as a Fulbright Fellow and structured growth capital campaigns that raised over $320 million for nonprofits at the Nonprofit Finance Fund.*

MATT GEE *is a data scientist and entrepreneur. He is the co-founder and chief executive officer of BrightHive Inc., which provides an open source data integration platform powering smarter government and more effective social service delivery. He is also a senior research scientist at the University of Chicago's Center for Data Science and Public Policy, where he leads a major research initiative harnessing the power of artificial intelligence to change the way American workers prepare for and find jobs. He is the co-founder of the Eric and Wendy Schmidt Data Science for Social Good Fellowship, and is a founding board member of several social enterprises using data and analytics to solve pressing social challenges, ranging from health service delivery in war-torn regions of the globe to how utilities and governments invest in reducing energy use. He is an open source software evangelist and an active advocate for improving access to STEM opportunities for disadvantaged youth.*

USING PAY FOR SUCCESS TO SOLVE THE "WRONG POCKETS" PROBLEM

Andy McMahon and Stephanie Mercier
CSH

The new county director of human services shook her head in frustration as she read a newspaper article highlighting the plight of Bob, a 56-year-old homeless man living on the streets for over two decades. According to the story, Bob was frequently intoxicated, which made it difficult to house him. He also faced serious mental health challenges and too often found himself in shelters, jails, or other crisis care. The director wanted to help Bob and others like him but wondered how best to tackle it during tough budget times.

She asked her staff to find a cost-effective solution for housing Bob and other chronically homeless individuals in the county. They presented her with a plan to create supportive housing, a proven, evidence-based intervention that delivers housing stability for individuals with complex needs. Bob would not need to give up alcohol before moving into an apartment and, once housed, could receive services that would reduce his time in homeless shelters and jails. Such results would mean better lives for people like Bob and less outreach and monitoring costs, saving crucial human services dollars. Embracing the plan and promise of future savings, the director scrubbed her budget for every penny and secured other resources to create 50 units of supportive housing and launch an independent evaluation to verify the value to her department.

Two years later, the evaluation demonstrated that Bob and the other chronically homeless served by the initiative remained in stable housing and reduced their time spent in shelters and jails. But the director noticed that the vast majority of cost offsets accrued to the sheriff's office, not to her budget. The savings resulting from less time in jails were so great they could have covered her department's cost for the supportive housing.

Although she was happy the intervention was succeeding, she faced the uncomfortable dilemma of how to justify the new costs now affecting her budget without the obvious offsets to human services programs.

The dilemma in this illustration is known as the "wrong pockets" problem, and it could happen in any county or community in the country. It occurs when the entity investing the resources in an intervention is not the sole—or even primary—beneficiary of the program's success.

In the scenario earlier, the department of human services paid for supportive housing because it was its strategic (and public) priority to house chronically homeless individuals, but the sheriff's office benefited most from the cost savings/offsets. In this case, the question about which budget should pay for the intervention is between two departments at a county level.

This challenge can be compounded if savings accrue to budgets on the city, county, state, and federal levels.

Health care service reduction is a good example of this complexity. Thorough analysis and evaluation would be needed to determine whether Bob's stabilized health led to savings that were realized at the local hospital level, in the state Medicaid budget, or both.

There may also be a situation in which savings generated across multiple systems—state Medicaid, federal Medicaid, county jails, state prisons, local health care—demonstrate a cost-effective program in aggregate but not enough savings to individual departments or government levels to warrant investment by any one of them alone.

Pay for Success is a model that drives resources toward proven, successful programs and offers opportunities to address the "wrong pockets" problem by providing a mechanism through which the comprehensive needs and costs of a particular target population are assessed, and budget allocations agreed to prior to implementing an intervention. It breaks down siloed thinking by taking a holistic view of an intervention's impact across all relevant systems. Furthermore, because payment is made only if success is observed, the primary end payer is guaranteed to pay only for pre-agreed outcomes of value.

For these reasons, Pay for Success is an attractive way to bring supportive housing to scale. If the director of human services had used Pay for Success, she would have realized that supportive housing required significant upfront resources and identified the various departments benefitting from its implementation. She may have agreed to pay for some of the supportive housing on the basis of length of stay, or she may have decided to ask the county administrator and budget office to fund the program on the basis of avoided jail days. Either way, she would have been clear about which agencies must participate and to what extent, as well as what the benefits would be and where they should, and could, be realized.

Our supportive housing Pay for Success transaction in Denver takes this holistic view by basing its success payments on anticipated reductions in jail days, police encounters, court costs, detox, hospital emergency department and other medical visits, as well as housing stability. There may also be savings that accrue to managed care organizations (MCOs) or state Medicaid based on a shift from emergency room usage to preventive care among members of the target population. Although these MCO and state savings add another wrinkle to the "wrong pockets" problem, as they are not being directly captured through the Pay for Success initiative, Denver is using this opportunity to push toward a more sustainable funding model for services in supportive housing and exploring potential roles for MCOs and the state in realizing that goal.

As Denver identified, the value of some outcomes goes beyond cost savings. In our illustration, the director of human services did not try to place a monetary value on successfully achieving a strategic priority for her department. She also did not consider the difficulty of transforming the life of a person who has struggled through homelessness, addiction, or similar challenges in her assumption of benefits. These intangible benefits should also form a component of the Pay for Success analysis.

Pay for Success is filled with opportunities, but continuous work to ensure the combined talents, efforts, and targets of the multiple entities involved is an absolute must if success is to be recognized. It has been described as an "admissions ticket" that serves as a lever to bring diverse stakeholders to the table and reorient systems around investing in and scaling what works. A Pay for Success initiative will not be successful if the participants remain focused on their own siloed missions and fail to look beyond their individual interests and budgets.

Nonetheless, the process of making partnership work can be challenging. Difficulties may arise in sharing data and information to identify status quo costs of the target population and evaluate potential savings. Data sharing protocols and memoranda of understanding need to be agreed upon, which can be a lengthy process. If the partners have identified a cohort for the target population, they may wish to try matching named data from across systems, which again requires maneuvering through bureaucratic approval and data sharing logistics.

Furthermore, the process of developing a Pay for Success model may highlight structural barriers when scaling interventions, such as supportive housing. For example, there are supportive housing programs in the pipeline that will likely reduce Medicaid expenses for a given population. Although these cost savings can be realized at the state level, the federal government also stands to benefit—but there is so far no mechanism to realize or use these federal savings in a Pay for Success project. The lack of shared federal and state Medicaid budgets means savings cannot be used directly to pay for the housing required to make the project sustainable.

In the short term, Pay for Success overcomes these challenges by empowering public agencies and investors to be comprehensive, inclusive, and transparent about what objectives are attainable, which entities are able to fund the housing required to make the intervention sustainable, and where benefits could be realized. While the partnership-building required to do this takes time, a successful approach results in a comprehensive understanding of the scope and scale of the opportunity.

As we move forward with Pay for Success, we must consider the creation of an approach in which savings or benefits accruing to one department can be applied to another. This could take the form of a scoring system in which realized benefits are valued even from different departments or levels of government.

At CSH, our role as technical advisor or intermediary in many Pay for Success transactions can help streamline collaborations and access to resources, as well as the process of receiving and distributing success payments—potentially serving as a mechanism to allow these to be pooled from multiple departments or entities.

If we collectively focus on the right priorities, Pay for Success can be a powerful tool to ensure that we fully understand the scope and scale of the challenges faced by vulnerable populations in our communities. It can also be a catalyst for the implementation of effective and efficient solutions that generate positive and far-reaching outcomes.

———

ANDY MCMAHON *is vice president of CSH's policy and external affairs team. McMahon has an MPA from Northeastern University and more than 20 years of experience working on issues related to homelessness, housing, health care, and reforming public policies to better serve our most vulnerable populations. McMahon leads work to impact funding and policy for housing, health, and homeless programs, spur innovation in the supportive housing industry, and expand its reach to additional sectors and populations nationally. Previously, as associate director for CSH's innovations team, McMahon led CSH's Returning Home, a national initiative focused on engaging corrections and criminal justice systems to create supportive housing and end the cycle of homelessness and incarceration. Prior to joining CSH, McMahon worked in Washington, DC representing state housing and community development agencies on issues related to affordable housing and homeless programs and policy.*

STEPHANIE MERCIER *has more than ten years of experience working with communities to strategically address the needs of their most vulnerable citizens particularly as it relates to homelessness and housing. As an associate director with CSH's strategy and impact team, Mercier focuses her efforts on developing the use of Pay for Success as a tool to scale supportive housing and drive system change. Prior to joining her current team, Mercier was on CSH's consulting and training team, providing training, facilitation and technical assistance to organizations working to address issues of housing and homelessness in their communities. Before coming to CSH, Mercier was a housing coordinator directly connecting shelter clients with housing in the community. Mercier has an MSW and an MBA from the University of Michigan.*

CLARITY AND FEEDBACK
How Information Can Drive Outcomes

Jacob Harold
GuideStar

One day in third grade my teacher walked us down the hall of Brunson Elementary School to the library. The librarian gave us a tour and explained how the books were organized: the Dewey Decimal System. She described the conveniently-numbered categories (Religion: 200! Science: 500!). I was fascinated. But I remember pausing for a moment as she walked through the subcategories for Literature, from 810 (American Literature in English) to 880 (Classical and Modern Greek) all the way to the lonely category 890: "Other." Non-European literature—the majority of the human story—was relegated to "Other."

I didn't have the language to describe my confusion. But that day in the library started me on a path to a simple realization: How we organize information matters for how we understand the world. And it matters for how we act in it. This is especially true in the work of social good.

INTENTION AND LEARNING

We ride toward the future on the tracks of our intentions. When we state a goal, we set a pattern in our minds and thus our actions. The first characteristic of effective social change is, therefore, *intention*. That intention should be aimed toward lasting results for a better world: We must judge our success not by completed actions, but by completed change. Or, in nonprofit-speak, organizations should seek to create lasting "outcomes" and not settle for just maximizing "outputs."

The second characteristic of effective social change is a stance of constant *learning*. For social change organizations to be effective, they need to learn from the world around them. It is the only way to adapt to a changing context, to adjust after a mistake, and, in simple terms, to get better.

Intention provides information. Learning requires information. So how should we organize this information? How might we ensure that the community of social change can access the right information at the right time? We need mechanisms to gather, structure, and distribute information. And to honor the diversity and complexity of social change, we need to do better than Melvil Dewey.

FOUR TYPES OF INFORMATION ABOUT SOCIAL CHANGE

There are four primary categories of information about social change. The first category is information about the social issue itself. If one cares about obesity in Birmingham, Alabama, for instance, it makes sense to ask: What is the obesity rate in Birmingham? The second category is information about interventions. What are the best ways to reduce obesity? Should one focus on nutrition programs in schools or advocate for walkable neighborhoods? The third category is information about organizations. What groups are working to address obesity in Birmingham? What are their goals and strategies? What do these organizations' beneficiaries think of their work? The fourth category is information about resources. What foundations are funding work on obesity in Birmingham? How have volunteers devoted time and energy to drive healthy choices in a community?

Each of these four categories is critical to effective social change. They have for too long been held in isolated silos. As the field learns to cross-reference across these different categories of information, we will unlock new levels of intelligence and effectiveness.

The organization where I work, GuideStar, is the leading data platform for the third category: information about nonprofit organizations. This essay will focus primarily on how we might best structure information about organizations, for it is through organizations that people act to create the change we wish to see.[1]

INFORMATION ABOUT ORGANIZATIONS

One of the many human biases revealed by behavioral science is "availability bias:" We pay attention to the information that is immediately

---

1 For most of the twentieth century, organizations devoted to a social mission tended to be nonprofits. But as the universe of the social sector expands, we cannot look only to tax status to understand social good. Social businesses, government entities, and unincorporated networks of people are often the vehicles for social good. Accordingly, I'll use the more general descriptors "organizations" or "social organizations."

available, even if it is incomplete or irrelevant. Availability bias has consistently undermined our understanding of organizations. This has been especially acute in the nonprofit sector, where nonprofits' publicly available annual filings with the IRS have provided the appearance of a comprehensive data set. Although immensely valuable, these filings—through the Form 990—are primarily composed of financial and operational data. The form has very little data about goals, programmatic strategies, or results. And although the financial data in the 990 provide a rich picture of certain aspects of a nonprofit organization's economics (e.g., the structure of the balance sheet), the form is limited in describing others aspects (e.g., the underlying drivers of revenue or costs).

We cannot allow availability bias to determine how we understand organizations, nor should we leave it to the IRS to determine how we think about organizational performance. Instead, we need a proactive framework. If the work of social change is complex, it stands to reason that we would need a multidimensional approach to understanding organizations. To start, let us consider a basic dimension, one that applies to all organizations: Some data come from *inside* organizations, and some come from *outside* them.

INSIDE-OUT: THE POWER OF CLARITY

The most important source of data about an organization is the organization itself. Indeed, for many kinds of information, the organization is the only possible source of information. Only the leadership of an organization can decide on the organization's mission or goals. For other categories—e.g., a list of board members—it may not be the only source of information, but it is the most efficient.

Self-reported data can enable rich insight into an organization's finances and operations. At best, it can give a sense of an organization's reach and its depth of impact. And there is an often-missed advantage to self-reported information. The way an organization talks about its work can itself be an indicator of its potential effectiveness. That insight may be found through a simple lens: clarity. An organization that can clearly state its goals and strategies will find it far easier to arrange its activities and is far more likely to achieve those goals. Clarity of action flows from clarity of goal-setting. Optimally, those goals are framed in the form of specific outcomes so they refer to lasting results and not just fleeting activities.

Moreover, an organization that can articulate its mechanisms of measurement, evaluation, and learning is far more likely to learn and change course as necessary. "Clarity" need not mean "certainty." Indeed, an organization that clearly articulates its uncertainties is an honest organization. And honesty is a foundation for learning: If we don't admit that we don't perfectly understand something, it is harder to adapt our understanding over time.

Optimally, a nonprofit's description of its work should be both qualitative (words) and quantitative (numbers). Words that describe goals and strategies should be matched with numbers that measure progress. Consider a job training program. It might track the number of volunteer trainers (an "input"), the number of trainings held (an "activity"), the number of people who complete the training (an "output"), and the number of people who got jobs (an "outcome"). These metrics form a causal chain that flows through to social good.

As a rule, it gets increasingly difficult to measure as one moves down this causal chain. But a serious organization has no choice but to go as far as possible. When we fail to interrogate the actual numbers that explain our organization's results in the world we, quite simply, betray our missions.

There are scoundrels in the nonprofit sector, those who lie to the world about their work. A bigger challenge, though, are the organizations that lie to themselves. By not paying attention to their own data they fail to see (or admit) the ways they are not succeeding. And that is one of many reasons why external perspective is also crucial.

OUTSIDE-IN: THE POWER OF PERSPECTIVE

The leaders of social change organizations toil for a better world. They are absorbed in the frameworks and language of their fields and their organizations. Familiarity breeds blindness. Those outside an organization can often see things those on the inside cannot.

That external perspective can be part of a formal institutional contract. An audit firm might provide an annual external perspective on an organization's financial controls and financial position. A third-party evaluator might offer expertise and neutrality when analyzing the impact—or lack thereof—of an organization's work.

Perspective does not require a formal arrangement with an outside firm. One can gain great insight through casual conversations with volunteers or a suggestion box at a homeless shelter. Direct engagement with constituents can also be highly structured: For example, a months-long community engagement process to decide how to rebuild a waterfront.

Effective organizations recognize that stakeholder engagement brings two distinct types of benefits: deeper loyalty and better insight. It is no small task to extract opinions from multiple stakeholder groups. Volunteers, donors, and partners might all require different processes. But it is only through seeking such external perspectives that organizations can respond to the world around them.

Different stakeholder groups offer different types of insight for different organizations. An organization that relies heavily on volunteers (e.g., the Greater Chicago Food Depository) should pay special attention to their opinions. An organization that directly serves an end beneficiary (e.g., the Kendall County Women's Shelter) will know the experiences of those beneficiaries are central to achieving the organization's mission. The best insights about an advocacy group (e.g., Natural Resources Defense Council) may come from experts, such as journalists, policymakers, and foundation program officers. Constituency voice is always important, though it will take various forms across the diverse social change community. And as with "inside-out" information, "outside-in" data can be both qualitative (e.g., stories of success or failure) and quantitative (e.g., satisfaction scores).

The business world spends billions of dollars each year learning from its constituents, whether through J.D. Power surveys or the Net Promoter Score. Social change organizations, from GlobalGiving to the Fund for Shared Insight, are now exploring sophisticated ways to bring the voice of stakeholders into nonprofit strategy. There is no perfect solution. But for now, the advice to organization leaders is simple: Just ask. Ask your stakeholders what they think. And listen to what they say.

Figure 1. Information About Social Change: Organizations

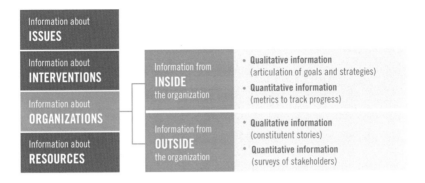

A DATA SYSTEM FOR SOCIAL CHANGE

As a field, we dream of multidimensional, contextualized data about social change. The emerging infrastructure of social change data offers a promise of a more efficient and effective field. In particular, we have a chance to orient the field's information systems around lasting outcomes, not mere activities.

Advances in technology provide an opportunity not just to collect that data, but also to distribute it and make it useful at scale. To get there, we will have to strengthen our data standards (unique IDs, taxonomies, and protocols), raise more capital, find new partners, and build new bridges with business and government.

If we do it right we can present the complexity of social change in a way that makes sense to human beings. This is a multi-decade challenge. But we are well on our way to a social sector defined by intention and enriched by learning.

JACOB HAROLD *is president and chief executive officer of GuideStar, the world's largest source of information about nonprofits. Prior to GuideStar he worked on climate change and philanthropic strategy at the Hewlett Foundation, the Bridgespan Group, the Packard Foundation, Rainforest Action Network, Greenpeace, and Green Corps. Harold earned an AB from Duke University and an MBA from Stanford University.*

NONOBVIOUS METRICS

Michael Weinstein
ImpactMatters

The Robin Hood Foundation makes grants of about $150 million a year fighting poverty in New York City. At first glance, its decisions might appear odd. Ponder three grant seekers (with made-up names):

1 Cool-Tax files for tax refunds on behalf of low-paid workers, recovering an average of $3,000 per worker. Impressive outcome. But Robin Hood does not fund Cool-Tax.

2 Cool-Loan lends small amounts of money to entrepreneurs to set up daycare services in their basements. Every borrower thrives. Impressive outcome. But Robin Hood does not fund Cool-Loan.

3 Cool-House spends $600,000 a year to provide shelter for 60 formerly homeless individuals. Not one returns to the streets. Impressive outcome. But Robin Hood does not fund Cool-House.

See a pattern? You might infer that Robin Hood makes dumb decisions. I prefer a different inference: Robin Hood's way of measuring success—its metrics system, dubbed Relentless Monetization—generates nonobvious decisions. Nonobvious but, I hope to convince you, correct. These decisions are examples of what happens when funders focus on correctly measured outcomes.

Let me explain.

Cool-Tax: Assume the taxpayers who flock to Cool-Tax would, in its absence, flock to H&R Block. Then Cool-Tax accomplishes nothing important other than to save filers a modest fee. The H&R Block option is known as a *counterfactual*—an assumption, which cannot be directly observed, about what would happen in the absence of an intervention that did indeed take place.

Cool-Loan: Assume the daycare businesses that Cool-Loan makes possible take customers from equally poor daycare providers down the block. If so, Cool-Loan accomplishes nothing important. It changes the name of those who are poor but not their number. The unintended harm that a grant does—in this case, to self-employed neighbors—is known as *displacement*.

Cool-House: Assume Cool-House spends $600,000 each year to provide services to the same 60 families. That's prohibitively expensive, compared with spending $600,000 each year providing services to *different* individuals (as would ordinarily occur if the intervention were training unemployed workers or teaching math to eighth graders). Relentless Monetization's discipline of trading off benefits against cost taps the workhorse of modern economics: benefit-cost analysis.

Here's an important point: Nonprofits habitually pay short shrift to counterfactuals, displacement, rate of return, and, as we'll see later, a correction called the "Robin Hood factor." These oversights produce not just error, but bias. They make nonprofits look more powerful than they truly are. No wonder these oversights persist.

When deciding whether to fund a nonprofit, Robin Hood applies a complicated algorithm. Let's start with the basics:

> **Step #1:** Robin Hood identifies outcomes that connect to its mission of fighting poverty.

> **Step #2:** They then assign a dollar value to each outcome (they "monetize" outcomes).

> **Step #3:** They then add up the separate benefits to calculate a total benefit of the intervention: the numerator of a benefit-cost ratio.

For example, imagine a grant to a middle school serving poor children.

First, what's the poverty-fighting outcome? Robin Hood funds the middle school to raise the probability that its students will graduate high school four years hence. Robin Hood does so because it believes earning a high-school diploma is the most important step that any of us take out of poverty.

Let me explain with an equation.

The numerator of the benefit-cost ratio:

45 x [[P.D.V. ($6,500/year for 20 years)] + [1.8 QALYs x $50,000/ QALY]] x [0.6 Robin Hood factor]

45: Robin Hood estimates that the school graduates 45 more students than would have graduated from neighboring schools. Simple enough statement. But behind the figure (45) lurks a lot of research and numerical estimation. It takes account of counterfactual success (how many students would have graduated from neighboring schools). It takes account of displacement (whether Robin Hood's grant unintentionally harms other low-income students in the host or neighboring schools). And so on.

P.D.V. *(present discounted value):* This is a reminder to take account of the fact that dollars enter and exit in different years.

$6,500: From research literature, we take this measure of the expected difference in future income between two otherwise identical workers, one of whom earned a diploma and one of whom did not.

1.8 QALYs *(quality-adjusted life years):* Though the literature does not speak with one voice, we take from it the plausible estimate that folks who graduate high school live, on average, two years longer and in better health than do identical students who don't graduate high school (separate from the impact of higher income on health). We measure the impact in QALYs, which account for morbidity and mortality.

$50,000:
Problem: If we agree that helping low-income residents live longer and healthier ought to be an important part of alleviating poverty, how do we combine the impact of our grants on income (measured in dollars) and on health status (measured in QALYs)?

Answer: We need to assign a dollar value to improving the health of the individuals we serve. Robin Hood has assigned a value of $50,000 to a QALY (helping an individual live one additional year in good health). They arrived at the $50,000 figure after sifting through the medical-economics literature, reviewing the practices of U.S. and U.K. government agencies, and sometimes making (arguable) judgment calls about inconsistent evidence.

0.6 Robin Hood factor: If Robin Hood is not the sole funder, it cannot claim credit for all of the school's success. Here, we estimate that without Robin Hood's help, 60 percent of the rise in graduation rates would disappear.

If you do the arithmetic, the numerator comes to $5.2 million. The cost to Robin Hood—the grant size—is $800,000. The benefit-cost ratio comes to 7:1. What does 7:1 mean? For every $1 Robin Hood spends on this grant to the middle school, the collective wellbeing of low-income New Yorkers rises by $7 (over their lifetimes). Wellbeing takes account of changes in future income and changes in a monetized value of future health status.

Robin Hood can compare the benefit-cost estimate for this middle-school grant to that of any other grant—whether it be, for example, teaching carpentry to chronically underemployed women, providing legal services for abused women, or screening adults for hepatitis C virus and treating those who test positive. The calculations often grow more complicated than the equation presented earlier. But the basic principle remains the same: Steer grant dollars to where they do the most additional good.

Do metrics matter? You bet. This example shows how. Metrics drive us to serve the most disadvantaged—those we can help the most. Metrics drive us away from most standalone after-school programs, steering us instead toward high-performing schools that seek money to run extended hours.

And on and on.

Of course, placing dollar values on services involves arguable judgment. What's the value of providing lawyers to help parents fight for custody of their children? Of course, monetizing value runs the risk of false precision. But the simple fact is that any funder that allocates a budget across options implicitly assigns a relative value to each option it chooses to fund and to each option it could afford but chooses not to fund. The major advantage of Relentless Monetization is that it makes judgments explicit and, therefore, debatable. Robin Hood posts on its website the 170 or so equations that it uses to assess the impact of grants, alongside the source of all cited numbers. They do so both to share what they've learned and to solicit suggestions for improving their metrics. Two key points:

1 Relentless Monetization focuses on outcomes—outcomes corrected for counterfactual successes and displacement—rather than inputs. Robin Hood doesn't measure how many students you teach. They measure how many *more* students you graduate.

2 Robin Hood's metrics assess the value of Robin Hood's grant, not the value of its grantees. The enrollees at Stuyvesant High School in New York are the highest-scoring students on citywide tests. We believe they would all graduate even if you locked them in a dark room for four years before letting them pop out to take exams. The fact that Robin Hood sees no impact from a possible grant to Stuyvesant reflects high regard for these students, not low regard for the school.

The upshot? Robin Hood's metrics system admittedly doesn't get everything right. But by tying grant decisions to *correctly measured* outcomes, Relentless Monetization steers grants where they pack the most wallop. At the very least, Robin Hood has shown that evidence-driven outcomes can move out of the classroom into the streets of New York. All in, Robin Hood estimates that its typical grant generates a ten-fold return: $150 million of annual grantmaking triggers a boost in the collective living standards of low-income New Yorkers by $1.5 billion or so.

Finally, the Robin Hood mantra: Never, ever make a grant on the basis of arithmetic alone. Benefit-cost ratios serve as one, but only one, key piece of information, much as SAT scores serve as one, but only one, key piece of information to college admissions offices. Numbers matter. But other types of information also matter.

Focusing on smartly measured outcomes does not come easily to funders. Adding to their discomfort, smart decisions can steer dollars in counterintuitive directions, away from popular organizations with enviable reputations. But one powerful thought need reign supreme: For funders to spend precious philanthropic dollars on the wrong interventions is unconscionable.

———

MICHAEL M. WEINSTEIN *holds a PhD in economics from the Massachusetts Institute of Technology and serves as executive director of ImpactMatters, which conducts impact audits to certify whether the claims made by nonprofits about their impact are backed up by a professional assessment of data. He previously served as chief program officer for The*

Robin Hood Foundation (2002 to March, 2017); founding director of the Greenberg Center for Geoeconomic Studies at the Council on Foreign Relations while holding the Paul A. Volcker chair in international economics at the council; member of the editorial board of The New York Times *and as* The Times' *economics columnist. He is founding chairman of Single Stop U.S.A., a national nonprofit that helps low-income Americans solve financial problems; founding board member of Just Capital, which ranks American corporations according to the public's perception of justness; and founding board member of ReServe, which matches recent retirees with nonprofits in deed of part-time talent. Columbia University Press published his co-authored book,* The Robin Hood Rules for Smart Giving *(2013).*

HOW OUTCOMES-BASED FUNDING MODELS CAN IMPROVE THE EFFECTIVENESS OF STATE AND LOCAL GOVERNMENTS

Jeremy Keele and Sara Peters
Sorenson Impact Center

State and local governments have deployed outcomes-based funding models for decades. In the late 1990s, for example, New York City dramatically changed the way it bought workforce development services from nonprofit providers working around the city.[1] Rather than pay for the cost of services up front and hope for the best, the city tied 100 percent of funding to measured performance—providers got paid only if they achieved clearly defined milestones (e.g., job placement, retention after set periods of time). The innovative focus on results yielded a number of benefits:

- Providers were incentivized to achieve outcomes that aligned with the city's policy objectives.

- Because the city contracted with multiple providers, it could compare results across different intervention models and identify best practices. Not surprisingly, higher-performing providers picked up market share at the expense of lower-performing models.

- The new market-based approach allowed the city to flexibly price (and re-price) outcomes it cared about while avoiding a more prescriptive, top-down approach to program design that can stymy innovation.

---

1 Swati Desai, Lisa Garabedian, and Karl Snyder, "Performance-Based Contracts in New York City: Lessons Learned from Welfare-to-Work," The Nelson A. Rockefeller Institute of Government (June 2012), available at http://www.rockinst.org/pdf/workforce_welfare_and_social_services/2012-06-Performance-Based_Contracts.pdf.

- Because milestones mattered, the city was forced to develop robust impact measurement systems to assess each program's effectiveness.

- Performance data could help the city make course corrections to the system as a whole. (When early program data showed poor job retention results, the city doubled down by changing payment formulas to incentivize longer-term retention outcomes.)[2]

- Individual providers could also feed performance data back into their interventions in a virtuous cycle of continuous improvement.

OVERVIEW

Historically, government agencies prioritized the general outputs that public funding achieved (e.g., individuals served, training opportunities provided) but were generally unsure of long-term results (e.g., job retention rates after five years). In an effort to better understand whether public programs and services deliver their intended results, state and local governments are now developing and monitoring a range of meaningful and rigorous short-, mid-, and long-term outcomes. The emergence of public data systems that can validate impact and innovative financing models that can support providers' working capital needs are helping to further accelerate uptake around the country.

More broadly, the development of today's outcomes-based funding landscape can be explained by a confluence of diverse factors, all of which have laid a strong foundation for the use of outcomes-based funding in state and local government. We live in a time of unprecedented digital access, and state and local governments are producing and collecting significant amounts of individual, community, and population-level data. Consequently, state and local policymakers have a growing amount of low-cost but highly valuable administrative data at their fingertips.

This era of big data has facilitated the use of more refined evaluations and a more scientific understanding of a range of social problems. Over the past several decades, academia has begun to partner more frequently with state and local governments to evaluate the effectiveness of public programs and services. As this information is published and disseminated, various public and private clearinghouses have started to aggregate and

2 Ibid.

identify promising and evidence-based programs and services across a host of issue areas. As a result, it is becoming more customary for state and local governments to consult these resources when choosing to implement or scale a program or social service.

Given the increasingly widespread application of rigorous evaluation methodologies to track and report outcomes, a heightened level of confidence can now be associated with the attainment of a range of social outcomes than previously experienced in government. The application of more robust quantitative and qualitative tools and techniques has been central to this development. The advent of certain digital technologies, including sophisticated statistical and management information systems, has facilitated the advancement of outcomes-based decision-making. Previously considered discretionary, various analytical capabilities are now regarded as critical components to government departments and agencies nationwide.

In fact, whole government offices and senior staff appointments are now dedicated to developing and enabling an outcomes mindset and facilitating a better understanding of what does and does not "work" in state and local governments. For example, the New York City Mayor's Office of Data Analytics was established in 2013, the state of North Carolina's Government Data Analytics Center was established in 2014, and the first director of data and innovation was appointed in Salt Lake County, UT, in 2015.

By attempting to more definitively quantify the impact associated with public programs and services, state and local governments also have been able to more precisely quantify the net financial benefits associated with particular interventions. The integration of financial analysis techniques with mainstream policy analysis tools has proven to be a major catalyst in the growth of outcomes-based funding in state and local government. It is also worth noting that immediately following the recession and over the past several years, many state and local governments have faced revenue shortfalls—which, in some cases, have been dramatic—and heightened fiscal constraints. Amid hard financial decisions, financial outcomes have become a key driver of public decision-making.

At the same time, the public sector has been tasked with meeting increasingly complex and escalating demands on public services. Faced with such issues as multigenerational poverty, unique population dynamics and sustainable development concerns, outdated public infrastructure, jail overcrowding, and public health and environmental risks, the use of public funding can be rife with difficulties. With increasing demands on a limited pool of public resources, it is no wonder that state and local governments have reoriented their budgeting practices around robust, objective outcomes.

In Salt Lake County, for example, policymakers recently grappled with a set of policy considerations relating to overcrowding at the county jail.[3] Rather than commit new funding to build more jail beds, the county decided to focus on the demand side and dedicate existing revenues to funding reductions in incarceration and recidivism rates. The decision was driven partly by thoughtful cost-benefit analyses that demonstrated the economic benefits of treatment and diversion over incarceration. In this particular case, a suite of evidence-based programs will be funded through a social impact financing mechanism. If incarceration rates drop by an agreed-upon threshold percentage over a five-year period, the county will repay the funders who provided the upfront bridge financing. If the programs are not successful, the county won't pay.

STRENGTHS

Linking state and local spending with outcomes has allowed government to get smarter about how and why it spends public money. In fact, outcomes have the potential to transform our relationship with state and local government; not only do they provide a vehicle for concerned citizens to better understand how public dollars are being used, but they also signal how state and local policy priorities actually translate into state and local spending.

Part of the beauty of outcomes-based funding is the freedom it provides local and state governments to assess the effectiveness of their services and programs; experiment, refine, and improve the execution of those services

---

3 Fox 13 Salt Lake City, media interviews with Salt Lake County elected officials (May 14, 2015), available at http://fox13now.com/2015/05/14/overcrowding-at-salt-lake-county-jail-means-fewer-bookings-come-summer-mayor-proposes-solution/.

and programs; and then redirect funding as deemed appropriate. State and local governments must then have the willingness and capacity to adapt and iterate in order to disrupt the status quo of more traditional government measurement and funding practices. That said, if state and local governments possess such a "learning mindset," outcomes-based funding can be an extraordinary tool for continuous quality improvement.

Because state and local governments are now better able to measure and assess the social and financial consequences associated with their program and service offerings, the sector is developing a menu of evidence-based interventions across specific areas of community need. A more granular understanding of the financial realities of working in particular policy areas (e.g., homelessness or recidivism interventions) and the net financial costs and benefits associated with specific intervention models within those policy areas (e.g., permanent supportive housing or transitional housing programs) helps governments choose an evidence-based intervention that makes sense—both for the people they intend to serve and the jurisdiction's own pocketbook.

More generally, outcomes provide common, objective benchmarks against which state and local governments can prioritize and guide their decision-making over time and, ultimately, hold their own spending decisions to account. In this sense, outcomes-based funding can serve as an established and respected process to help cut across the politicization of state and local government spending. Yet, the benefits of outcomes-based budgeting extend far beyond state and local government. The reliability that outcomes provide as a reporting tool is immensely valuable to the nonprofit, private, philanthropic, and academic sectors as well.

Outcomes provide a common language with which state and local governments and the nonprofit, private, philanthropic, and academic sectors can communicate their shared and competing visions and expectations of public programs and services. In this capacity, outcomes can spur innovative, multisector partnerships. They can also align program and service implementation with the varying expertise and decision-making preferences and styles of individuals from a multitude of backgrounds.

The increased understanding with regard to which public programs and services "work" and which do not has served to highlight the long-term effectiveness and cost savings associated with more preventative—versus predominantly reactive—social programs and services. However, although more preventative programming (for example, prioritizing the education of at-risk youth over more traditional juvenile justice programming) makes financial—not to mention ethical—sense over the long term, state and local governments often cannot afford the upfront costs required to administer this category of service delivery.

This allows philanthropic and private funders that are traditionally more removed from the public sector to bridge the financing gap. The growing and relatively newfound evidence base surrounding public programs and services is an attractive asset for these impact-oriented funders and enables them to provide financing based on expected future results. Further, the heightened confidence associated with the application of high-quality analytical methods is important for funders looking to quantify the risk that accompanies their investments. Notably, the involvement of somewhat unconventional funders in the public sector may fuel the appetite of state and local government decision-makers to continue to engage in outcomes-based funding.

Outcomes-based funding also has emboldened stakeholders that are traditionally removed from the public sector to take part in cutting-edge government funding collaboratives, such as social financing and impact investing models. These multisector partnerships and financing collaboratives provide important advantages to state and local government. On their own, the nonprofit, private, philanthropic, and academic sectors possess unique comparative strengths and attributes. Together, these stakeholders provide a mix of skill sets, knowledge, and experiences, all of which can complement state and local government program and service delivery and provide a collective vision for public growth and innovation.

Admittedly, much of the value of outcomes-based funding for state and local governments hinges on tracking, assessing, reporting, and, ultimately, funding the "right" outcomes. The involvement of the nonprofit, private, philanthropic, and academic sectors may prove critical for state and local governments as they work to develop and fund outcomes that provide both the appropriate level of rigor and nuance for jurisdictions' varying needs. For example, consider that in some instances job retention may be a worthy outcome; however, in other instances (e.g., if an individual was empowered to leave his or her employer for reasons of sexual harassment) job retention would not be a suitable outcome for a state or local government to fund.

Outcomes-based funding must accommodate the idiosyncrasies that characterize different communities of individuals residing within different state and local governments. No outcome or funding model will fit the needs of all jurisdictions. Rather, the intuition and expertise of state and local government decision-makers will be essential to properly using the funding mechanism and sustaining its effectiveness over time.

WEAKNESSES

Of course, defining, measuring, and funding the "right" outcome is difficult. If the proper questions are not being asked, the sophistication of data tracking and analytical tools and capabilities within a state or local government does not matter. In fact, without the proper benchmarks of success, more data may simply confuse the results. State and local governments must be extremely deliberate about: 1) how they define the success of their program and service offerings; 2) what data and information sources they intend to use; 3) how they decide to collect and evaluate this data and information; and 4) when they intend to refine their program and services to make improvements for communities in need.

Outcomes-based funding in the public sector is wholly different from the oft-used performance metrics of the private sector. Understanding such concepts as fixed and marginal costs for a 2,000-person county jail can be incredibly challenging. Moreover, determining whether a for-profit company is delivering on its sales objectives (e.g., meeting its monthly sales goals through predetermined consumer channels) is quite dissimilar from determining whether an intervention for individuals experiencing homelessness is actually reducing homelessness. In the case of the latter, for example, should a homeless intervention measure the number of people sleeping on the street on a given night, precariously housed individuals sleeping in cars and doubling up in apartments, and individuals sleeping in emergency and temporary housing, as well as include self-reported information? Ideally, the outcome measurement would include all of the above, but doing so would present obvious complications.

Given the complexity of choosing, measuring, and funding the proper outcomes, governments may turn to proxy outcomes to represent other more intangible but highly important outcomes (e.g., choosing specific health indicators to more generally represent the health and wellbeing of a community of individuals). However, while proxy outcomes may give the illusion of success in certain instances, they may not actually indicate an effective service or program. For this reason, state and local governments must be especially attentive to the evidence base surrounding a given intervention and understand that there is still significant uncertainty around the long-term impacts associated with many commonly accepted interventions.

Aside from choosing and measuring the appropriate outcomes for a given jurisdiction, it is also difficult to understand which government departments and agencies are primarily responsible for obtaining these outcomes. The issue areas that these public services and programs target (e.g., recidivism, homelessness, domestic abuse, education) are interdisciplinary in nature and thus require the attention of multiple government departments and agencies. In certain jurisdictions, however, these stakeholders may have never come together to serve a particular community of individuals in need.

The successful implementation of outcomes-based funding will require strong, interdepartmental leadership and a continued commitment to obtaining rigorous, meaningful outcomes. Accordingly, involved state and local governments must have individuals in place dedicated to incorporating program and service learnings into organizational decision-making and the adaptability to not institutionalize programs and services into the government budget. Rather, a government must have a proclivity toward continued measurement and growth across the full life cycle of the program or service and the willingness to end or alter a program or service based on the outcomes achieved.

BARRIERS AND THREATS THAT POTENTIALLY KEEP IDEAS FROM BECOMING POPULAR

Chiefly, as mentioned earlier, there is still major uncertainty about the effectiveness of common public programs and services. By and large, state and local governments spend money on public services and programs without measuring the level of impact gained or lost from that investment.

According to former U.S. Budget Director Peter Orszag, less than one percent of federal discretionary spending is supported by even the most basic evidence.[4] Against that backdrop, any expansion of high-quality programs and services that is data-informed, carefully tracked, and designed around specific outcomes is a significant leap forward.

However, a limited familiarity with more exhaustive forms of research and evaluation may preclude certain public decision-makers from engaging in outcomes-based funding models. There are complex, technical questions about how to set appropriate baseline outcomes for specific programs and services (i.e., effectively trying to understand what would have happened to people in the absence of those programs and services). Even where good baseline evidence exists, it can be difficult to link standardized assessment tools with downstream outcomes that can be measured and paid for.

State and local governments are not afforded the luxury of waiting for the perfect metric or data set to appear before beginning this work. Although academic and research experts can guide state and local governments in the scope of research and evaluation needed, major questions are left to the discretion of the state and local governments. Such questions include the following: given a limited pool of public resources, is there a preference to fund a more rigorous evaluation methodology (i.e., randomized controlled trial or quasi-experimental method) for select program(s) and service(s) or, instead, lower cost evaluation approaches, which may be less rigorous in nature but serve a greater number of program(s) and service(s)?

A key component that may preclude state and local governments from engaging in outcomes-based funding is the compilation and integration of relevant and timely data. Although governments may have access to a large quantity of administrative data, these data may not necessarily capture the full set of impacts needed to assess a particular program's or service's effectiveness. Given the interdisciplinary nature of many public issues, data from various sources—many of which may be incongruous—will need to be collected and consolidated. This process

---

4   John Bridgeland, U.S. House Ways and Means Committee Testimony (March 17, 2015), available at
    https://waysandmeans.house.gov/UploadedFiles/John_Bridgeland_Testimony_031715_HR2.pdf.

may involve creating new data management systems and tools to more systematically collect, organize, store, and analyze the relevant data.

Some governments will be more disadvantaged than others in assessing the outcomes of their programs and services. Not all state and local governments will have the same access to analytical tools and technologies, local research expertise, and, notably, a large enough population of individuals served by a program or service to generate sufficient statistical power. As a result, some governments will be less able than others to incorporate reliable success measures into their decision-making and budgeting practices.

CONCLUSION: PROMISE FOR WIDESPREAD USE AND ADOPTION OF STRATEGY

Fundamentally, outcomes are meant to tell us which programs work and which do not. Our children, families, and communities in need deserve to receive the programs and services that can serve them best. At the same time, this field is very much in its infancy; transforming the public sector into something more results-focused and measured is going to take many iterations. Keeping an open mind to substantive critiques of outcomes-based funding models will help ensure that the field is continuously improving and that state and local governments stand to gain the most from the funding models.

When practicable, government contracts and grants should encourage or require high-quality, evidence-based program and service delivery and incorporate outcomes accordingly. Of course, state and local governments cannot possibly evaluate every decision made and action taken (at least, not yet). In the meantime, a handful of well-defined and transparent performance indicators and outcomes will be far more important to state and local governments and the community of related stakeholders than an assortment of loosely defined, subjective metrics.

A potential strategy for state and local governments looking to begin the outcomes-based funding process would be to initially consider outcomes as starting points for growth and development for their public program and service offerings. In this sense, outcomes can provide a clearer picture of a jurisdiction's needs and help decision- and policymakers choose the most appropriate response. Furthermore, state and local governments may also choose to partner with external technical assistance providers to strengthen their technical capabilities and build their internal capacity to engage in outcomes-based funding models.

As state and local governments become more comfortable with the outcomes-based funding mechanism, the outcomes they choose will become more nuanced and the funding strategies more sophisticated. The proliferation of advanced data collection and analysis technologies will allow state and local governments to gain increased access to locale-specific data; this advancement in the field will be particularly important for adapting outcomes to the needs of various heterogeneous communities across the country. In addition, as service providers gain access to real-time performance data, service and program delivery will be more easily adapted to outcomes, and vice versa.

The systematic application of outcomes-based decision-making to a significant portion of government funding will be critical to the widespread adoption of outcomes-based funding. For this model to be successful, state and local governments cannot view outcomes-based funding as a side project. Instead, the principles of outcomes-based decision-making and funding should permeate the culture of state and local government operations. Creating a culture grounded in outcomes may be a powerful paradigm shift and will likely involve significant resources and time, dedicated staff and leadership, and buy-in from all levels of government.

———

JEREMY KEELE *is president and chief executive officer of the Sorenson Impact Center at the University of Utah's David Eccles School of Business and an adjunct member of the faculty of the Business School. Keele's work at the center is dedicated to developing innovative and data-driven approaches to difficult social problems. Prior to joining the University of Utah, Keele was senior advisor to Salt Lake County Mayor Ben McAdams from 2013 to 2015. During his time at Salt Lake County, Keele advised the mayor on his key policy initiatives, including financing, transportation, homelessness, criminal justice, health, culture and the arts and economic development. Prior to joining Salt Lake County, he practiced corporate transactional law in New York, London, and Los Angeles with the law firms of Cleary Gottlieb and Latham & Watkins, from 2006 to 2013. Keele received his JD from New York University,* an MPP from Harvard's Kennedy School of Government, and bachelor degrees in biology and French from Brigham Young University.

SARA PETERS *is director of social innovation at Sorenson Impact Center, providing social impact bond and pay-for-performance feasibility analysis, transaction structuring, and project management support. Prior to joining the center, Peters worked at several nonprofits in New York and Boston, as well as a Columbia University education policy and litigation think tank. Peters has a BA from Princeton University in politics and American studies and an MPP from the University of Cambridge.*

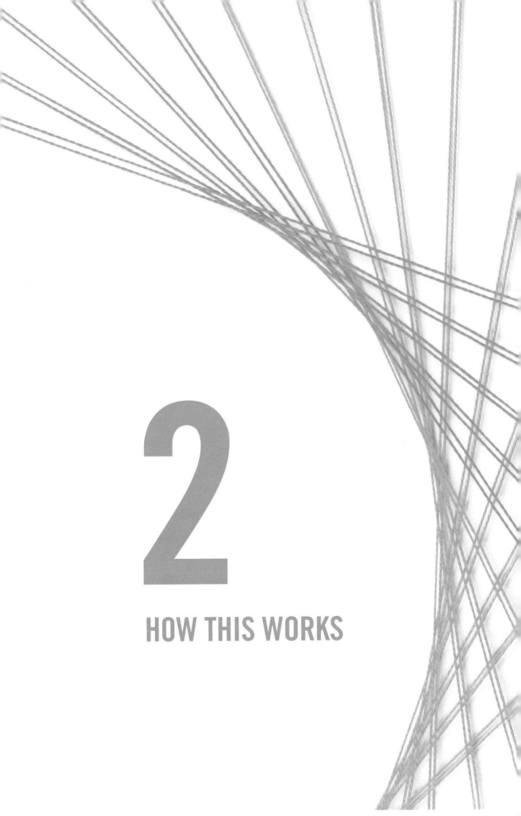

2

HOW THIS WORKS

How This Works
PROTOTYPES

FINANCING OUTCOMES THROUGH SOCIAL IMPACT BONDS

Tracy Palandjian
Social Finance Inc.

I n 1977, Dr. David Olds began testing a home-visiting program that paired nurses with first-time, low-income mothers. The Nurse-Family Partnership (NFP), a community health program that extends from pregnancy through the first two years of a child's life, has since become one of the most effective social interventions.

The results speak for themselves: across three randomized controlled trials, NFP improved birth outcomes, reduced childhood injuries, decreased special education needs, and even lowered rates of criminal activity decades later for participants. However, this program is just serving a small fraction of the 800,000 babies born to eligible low-income, first-time mothers each year in the United States.

So why hasn't NFP become the standard of care?

One reason is because the public and social sectors are largely not currently designed to reward what works or to allocate funding based on outcomes. Rather, funding is typically structured around services delivered.

Social impact bonds can be part of the solution. Social impact bonds sit at the center of three powerful twenty-first century movements: an ever increasing reliance on data and evidence in service of policymaking, the harnessing of capital markets in service of society, and growing momentum around tri-sector models. This partnership model aligns uncommon partners—policymakers, investors, and nonprofit service providers—around a common purpose, further blurring the ever more porous boundaries across the public, private, and social sectors.

In this essay, I discuss how social impact bonds—and the partnerships they foster—manage for performance and create value by tackling the root causes of persistent social challenges to measurably improve the lives of those in need.

DEFINING SOCIAL IMPACT BONDS

Social impact bonds are part of a broader suite of Pay for Success contracting mechanisms, which direct government resources to *outcomes achieved* rather than *services delivered*. Pay for Success approaches, including social impact bonds, performance-based contracts, and outcomes rate cards, all center on the same question: How can the public sector allocate resources more efficiently while improving outcomes for the most vulnerable?

In a social impact bond, intermediaries bring together impact investors, high-impact service providers, and government payers to implement preventative social services that, if successful, will lead to improved social outcomes and reduced government costs, generating both fiscal and intangible value for society.

THE VALUE OF SOCIAL IMPACT BONDS

Social impact bonds rely on an elegant, mutually beneficial framework:

- High-performing nonprofits get access to long-term, flexible funding, which allows them to grow—and links performance to further funding.
- Impact investors are able to reflect their values in their investment portfolios by receiving financial returns only when projects measurably improve people's lives.
- Governments gain a new level of accountability for taxpayer funds by only paying for results.

The end result is a new dynamic yielding multiple winners across sectors and a set of incentives that redirect society's resources toward measurable results for our most vulnerable communities.

WHY HAVE SOCIAL IMPACT BONDS ATTRACTED SUSTAINED ATTENTION?

The Value of Risk Transfer

Social impact bonds transfer performance risk from government to funders. Through social impact bonds, government is able to experiment with promising approaches for preventive programs or meaningfully scale a proven approach, but is obligated to pay *only if* the program works.

Focus on Outcomes vs Outputs

Government spends hundreds of billions of dollars each year to provide health care for sick people, support vulnerable children, help build our workforce, and provide other necessary human services. However, for the most part, government measures outputs, such as the number of people served, volunteer engagement, or money distributed. Outputs do not provide answers to the big question: whether we're moving the needle on our most intractable challenges.

Outcomes are what matter: ex-offenders getting employed and reintegrated into society, students graduating and connecting to the labor force, women delivering healthy babies. Outcomes are what we are after but evaluating, tracking and reporting on outcomes requires not only a significant investment in resources but also a shift in mindset. Social impact bonds provide one way to focus public sector attention and resources on the achievement of outcomes.

Orientation Around Prevention

Social impact bonds allow governments to invest early and upstream, focusing on prevention rather than remediation via the social safety net. Vaccines are cheaper than treating disease; job training and housing cost less than incarceration. And these are only the quantifiable monetary benefits, they do not capture the intangible value of a life better lived.

The Role of Active Performance Management

Through active performance management—a key feature of social impact bonds—project oversight, analyzing programmatic and administrative data, course corrections, financial management, and investor relations—Social Finance and project partners keep a social impact bond on track over the life of the project. Active performance management aligns the interests of governments and service providers in new, productive ways, resulting in closer working relationships and a coordinated focus on project goals.

With a focus on prevention and outcomes, alongside ongoing performance management, social impact bonds help drive systems change in government. Indeed, social impact bonds represent a unique form of impact investment, with financial returns generated by increased efficiency and effectiveness of taxpayer funds.

One powerful example is the Nurse-Family Partnership Pay for Success Project in South Carolina. Launched in April 2016, the project focuses on improving maternal and child health outcomes for 3,200 low-income families state wide in South Carolina over six years. The initiative mobilizes $30 million to expand Nurse-Family Partnership's services, with philanthropic funders committing $17 million to the project and $13 million of federal Medicaid funding via a 1915(b) Medicaid Waiver. All potential success payments repaid by South Carolina will be reinvested in future Nurse-Family Partnership programming.

THE STATE OF THE FIELD

The values of collaboration, responsiveness, and a focus on data position social impact bonds with other parallel global movements, and have captured the interest of policymakers, social sector leaders, and the investor community worldwide.

Since Social Finance UK launched the world's first social impact bond in Peterborough in 2010 aimed at reducing prisoner recidivism, more than 70 projects have launched in 18 countries, with 15 projects here in the United States. Supporters of social impact bonds cross political party lines with at least two dozen states—balanced between red and blue—pursuing social impact bond approaches. A bipartisan congressional coalition has formed around the model to provide federal support for social impact bonds in state and local governments. The federal government has also demonstrated its commitment through support for projects in education, health, housing, employment and reentry support, and veterans' affairs.

CHALLENGES TO THE FIELD

As with any innovation, there are challenges to be addressed and over-come. Tri-sector partnerships over a multi-year timespan require shifts in roles and mindsets on all sides. Structuring social impact bonds can be complex, and to date they have served a limited number of people in need.

The measurement and evaluation process can also pose challenges, but is essential for triggering repayment and guiding future policymaking. In these early years, we have come to understand that we must balance the complexity required to precisely measure impact with the transparency and simplicity required for government payment and broad policymaking.

Critics have pointed to the high costs associated with structuring social impact bonds, but we would argue that these costs are the price of good government at work. Essential components of social impact bond develop-ment, such as analyzing available data sources, identifying evidence-based practices, supporting service providers to implement with high quality, and measuring results, are integral to ensuring long-term success as governments work to serve those in need.

Finally, we must not judge the field too early. As the field grows—and as we work to standardize the model—we must be cautious to do so without losing nuance or crowding out needed innovation.

THE EVOLUTION OF SOCIAL IMPACT BONDS

In these early years, we have seen enormous growth and evolution in the model—including a greater diversity of social impact bond structures. New geographies are applying the concept to new issues and adapting the model to work with different sets of partners. Dynamic stakeholder ecosystems and new payment structures are emerging.

We see iteration and innovation happening across three core dimensions of social impact bond design: financial structuring, payer characteristics, and measurement and evaluation. Projects are being developed both as loans and as equity, drawing from a blend of investor types, with an increasing number of outcomes measurements (versus a single threshold), and with regular capital calls instead of lump-sum payments. Projects can have either single or multiple payers, and increasingly, new types of payers—such as health insurers and private institutions—are exploring these roles.

We are also working to create a more nuanced approach toward measurement and evaluation based on project context and stakeholder objectives. Randomized controlled trials, characteristic of many early social impact bonds, are often challenging to implement and can limit the number of people served. Given these constraints, they may play a more limited role in the future, utilized either in tandem with validated outcomes or to inform project learning rather than project payment structures. Such a shift would create additional flexibility, allowing interventions to adapt more rapidly to interim measurements and ongoing outcomes data.

There is no one-size-fits-all social impact bond model; developing the appropriate structure for specific goals and contexts is critical to producing positive and enduring long-term outcomes.

THE FUTURE OF SOCIAL IMPACT BONDS

Six years in, we have built a proof of concept. But these are still the early days of the social impact bond field, as we build and iterate on our collective experiences in service of our most vulnerable communities.

We are mindful that social impact bonds are not a panacea; bringing the best of what we've learned in social science and adapting it to the realities of public sector investments is not a linear process. But we are optimistic that, as we incorporate learnings from the initial social impact bonds, we will continue to advance the field to the next level.

As Robert F. Kennedy remarked, our Gross Domestic Product doesn't always measure what matters: "It measures neither our wit nor our courage, neither our wisdom nor our learning, neither our compassion nor our devotion to our country, it measures everything in short, except that which makes life worthwhile."[1]

We have been valuing what we can measure; with social impact bonds, we can begin to build a market towards financing outcomes and measure what we value most: what makes life worthwhile.

1   Robert F. Kennedy, "Remarks at the University of Kansas," John F. Kennedy Presidential Library and Museum (March 18, 1968), available at https://www.jfklibrary.org/Research/Research-Aids/Ready-Reference/RFK-Speeches/Remarks-of-Robert-F-Kennedy-at-the-University-of-Kansas-March-18-1968.aspx.

TRACY PALANDJIAN *is chief executive officer and co-founder of Social Finance Inc., a nonprofit organization dedicated to the development of Pay for Success, an innovative public-private partnership that mobilizes capital to drive social progress. Prior to co-founding Social Finance US in 2011, she worked at the Parthenon Group, Wellington Management Co., and McKinsey & Company. Palandjian is co-author of "Investing for Impact: Case Studies Across Asset Classes," and serves as vice-chair of the U.S. Impact Investing Alliance. She is a member of the Board of Overseers at Harvard University, and serves on the boards of Facing History and Ourselves and the Surdna Foundation. She is also a director of Affiliated Managers Group (NYSE: AMG). A native of Hong Kong, Palandjian is fluent in Cantonese and Mandarin. She holds a BA from Harvard College and an MBA from Harvard Business School, where she was a Baker Scholar.*

SOCIAL IMPACT GUARANTEES COULD ENABLE PAY FOR SUCCESS CONTRACTING TO SCALE MORE RAPIDLY

George Overholser
Third Sector Capital Partners, Inc.

Recently, a senior government official leaned over the table, looked me in the eye, and asked, "Is this going to get any easier?" "Yes, Pay for Success will get easier," I responded. "Much easier, I'm willing to bet. But only if we continue to innovate."

One innovation we are particularly excited about is something we are calling the social impact guarantee. If a government-backed social program fails to achieve social impact, the government gets its money back. And for service providers that don't want to take on the risk of providing their own money-back guarantee, private funders can offer social impact guarantee financing. That way, if the social service provider is called upon to pay back the government, social impact guarantee funders will step in to write the check. In contrast with the social impact bond (described in Tracy Palandjian's chapter in this volume), where private funders write checks at the beginning and the government (potentially) writes checks at the end, the social impact guarantee has the government writing checks at the beginning and private funders (potentially) writing checks at the end. You might say that a social impact guarantee is a social impact bond in reverse.

Both of these approaches reach a similar place. The government pays only if social impact is achieved. And both use private financing to offload performance risk from vulnerable service providers. But in many ways, the social impact guarantee approach can be simpler and philosophically more intuitive than the social impact bond.

To understand why, consider that one of the reasons that social impact bonds can be so difficult to implement is that the government is not accustomed to contracting for social services in a multi-year or contingent way. Even if government officials would like to take on multi-year Pay for Success obligations, laws and regulations may be a barrier. There are workarounds—waiver processes, legislative overrides, creation of special new spending streams with special use rules, elaborate sinking funds, and the like. But the workarounds are technical, expensive, uncertain, and time-consuming. Indeed, this has been a significant impediment to the growth of Pay for Success contracting.

A second technical problem with Pay for Success/social impact bonds is called "double capitalization." Originally, the idea was to reduce stress on government cash flows by providing private upfront social impact bond financing. But in practice, governments have needed to place capital into escrow accounts right from the start, so that social impact bond lenders feel confident that the government has enough cash lined up to make good on its Pay for Success payment obligations. This double capitalization has been necessary to give funders confidence, but it is an inefficient way to scale Pay for Success contracting more broadly.

HOW DOES THE SOCIAL IMPACT GUARANTEE HELP?

With the social impact guarantee, the model is flipped: Instead of the government, it is private funders who make a contingent promise to pay in the future. This allows the government to purchase social services in a way that more closely resembles its usual pay-as-the-work-is-done timing. Then, if social impact targets are missed, private funders write a check back to the government. For example, a group of private social impact guarantee funders might obligate themselves today to write a check three years from now, but only if a program fails to reduce the incarceration rate. The good news is that multi-year contingent promises are something private funders do all the time. No waivers needed, no new government spending streams with special rules. It's a lot simpler.

Technically, the government would implement social impact guarantees by inserting a penalty provision into its social services contract that makes clear to the organization awarded government funding to provide social services that if those services do not work, the government will have to be repaid some or all of its funds. Then the contract would specify impact metrics that determine what constitutes success and what would trigger the penalties. Luckily, penalty provisions are already common practice, and specifying impact metrics is no different from what is already done under the Pay for Success/social impact bond model.

The other good news is that the social impact guarantee does not require the government to place capital redundantly into sinking funds and the like. Instead, the government's money is used productively from the start. The problem with traditional penalty provisions is that they can disrupt or even bankrupt services providers who have to come up with money to pay back the government after they have already spent their funding on service delivery. That's where, in the social impact guarantee approach, private investors step in. They offer something akin to an insurance policy or a letter of credit, which means they (not the service provider) will ultimately be on the hook to cover the penalty. The insurance policy or letter of credit is a contingent promise to write a check in the future rather than provide an immediate outlay. In other words, there are no escrow accounts with money that simply sits there. Bottom line: The social impact guarantee would have less "double capitalization" than the social impact bond, and that makes it inherently less expensive.

Philosophically, I have felt that the social impact bond places too much emphasis on borrowing and not enough on insurance. Indeed, the central role of a social impact bond (and certainly of a social impact guarantee) is insurance. It insures against the risk of the government's allocating precious taxpayer money to programs that do not work. And it insures vulnerable nonprofit service providers from the financial peril of potentially never being paid.

Currently, social impact bonds are positioned as a lending product, prompting people immediately to ask whether the government really needs to borrow more money, especially when the investment returns typically demanded by investors for investing in social impact bonds are so much higher than, say, municipal bonds. With the social impact guarantee, everything begins to make more sense. This is not an interest payment; it is an insurance premium. And it is easy to explain how paying a five percent premium for something that might otherwise cost 100 percent is a good deal—especially in a world where so many social programs, when rigorously evaluated, are revealed to have been ineffective.

SOCIAL IMPACT BONDS AS A STEPPING STONE TO THE SOCIAL IMPACT GUARANTEE MODEL

Of course, as with any innovation, the social impact guarantee brings unique challenges. For example, the private funders that currently back social impact bond projects are typically set up to provide loans, not letters of credit or insurance policies, as social impact guarantees require. And the insurance companies that might ultimately be best suited to offer social impact guarantee policies are largely not engaged with the Pay for Success community.

To address this challenge, I propose that social impact bond loans be used as a stepping stone. Remember, with the social impact guarantee, a service provider has to be financially able to pay back the government at some future date, should that be necessary. While it would be most natural to take out an insurance policy for that purpose, the provider could instead borrow money and immediately place it into a reserve on its balance sheet, which would then be used to pay back the lenders once impact is proven. Alternatively, if necessary, the reserve could be used to honor the government's penalty provision.

Pencil this out and you will see that under this stepping stone approach, the lenders would experience something very much like a typical social impact bond. The money is drawn down gradually as the social services are provided, and the lenders get paid back only if the program works. Indeed, the one main difference—a simple reserve on the provider's balance sheet—would be celebrated by the social impact bond lenders as a safer form of "counterparty risk" than the complex government appropriations promises and sinking funds commonly used in the social impact bond model.

Some readers will note that this stepping stone loan approach does not solve the double capitalization problem. However, it would retain the benefits of simplifying the government side of the contracting process. Moreover, it would set the stage for a smooth transition toward using letters of credit (which are a promise to write a check in the future if needed), rather than outright loans. Ultimately, it will be ideal to tap into the immense balance sheets of major insurance companies. I expect this will eventually happen. But in the meantime, a letter of credit approach would be a powerful step in the right direction.

There will be other challenges as well. For example, in most jurisdictions, any money returned to the government might need to be directed to a general fund, rather than to the department that originally contracted for social services. Also, the payment of social impact guarantee premiums and other aspects of setting up the Pay for Success project may fall outside the permissible use of some of the spending streams that would be tapped. These are problems that already challenge the social impact bond market. They are also limited and solvable. Although the social impact guarantee approach does not avoid them, it addresses other concerns that make it considerably less onerous than the additional challenges we have dealt with while implementing social impact bonds.

At Third Sector Capital Partners, Inc., we believe that the social impact guarantee holds more than enough potential to merit testing, as it promises to simplify the contracting process (by employing already-existing techniques), lower project costs for governments (by reducing double capitalization and the amount of time it takes to construct projects), and tap into the immense world of mainstream insurance. Ultimately, we believe it could enable Pay for Success contracting to scale more rapidly, thus empowering more governments to pursue outcomes-based contracting that measurably improves the lives of our most vulnerable citizens.

We will most certainly continue to embrace social impact bonds, as they remain the de facto vehicle for financing Pay for Success projects in the United States. That said, we plan to pursue and implement the world's first social-impact-guarantee-financed project and grow the social impact guarantee market from there.

GEORGE OVERHOLSER *is board chair and co-founder of Third Sector Capital Partners, Inc., a leading nonprofit advisory services firm in the field of Pay for Success/social impact bonds. Prior to his 15 years as a social entrepreneur, he was a founding member of Capital One's management team and the co-founder of North Hill Ventures. He holds an undergraduate degree in physics from Harvard College and an MBA from Stanford's Graduate School of Business, and he currently serves as an executive in residence at Northeastern University's D'Amour-McKim School of Business.*

CAN PRIZES SOLVE PROBLEMS FACING VULNERABLE POPULATIONS?

Renya Reed Wasson
Children's Prize Foundation

Salman defied the odds. Prior to his birth, his 40-year-old mother had endured seven newborn deaths and five stillbirths in 14 deliveries. While pregnant with Salman, she suffered from both acute anemia and high blood pressure, and yet she was determined to follow tradition and deliver at home. Fortunately for Salman, the nonprofit Vital Pakistan had recently started providing an evidence-based maternal, newborn, and child intervention package in his village, Rethri Goth, on the outskirts of Karachi, Pakistan. Vital Pakistan services include training community workers to identify at-risk pregnancies and to encourage families to use skilled birth services. Thanks to Vital Pakistan and Aga Khan University Hospital, Salman is thriving today.

Salman is far from the only beneficiary. The neonatal mortality rate in Rethri Goth dropped 44 percent between 2013, the year before Vital Pakistan began offering services, and 2015. In absolute terms, neonatal mortality fell from 57 deaths per 1,000 live births in 2013 to 32 deaths per 1,000 live births in 2015. Pakistan's national neonatal mortality rate dropped only five percent in that period (from 47.4 to 45.5 deaths per 1,000 live births). Rough calculations based on Vital Pakistan's online progress report indicate that during the first two years of its operations, 51 infants survived the first month of life who otherwise would have perished.[1] The under-five

---

1 Assumptions: (1) The 2,710 births between May 19, 2014, and April 30, 2016, were split into two intervals (with the second interval experiencing slightly fewer births because it contains three fewer weeks); (2) The imputed neonatal mortality rates in the absence of the program were calculated by adjusting the starting neonatal mortality rate in Rethri Goth in 2013 to fall annually by the same percentage observed for the national neonatal mortality rate; (3) The imputed 2014 neonatal mortality rate was used to estimate the number of neonatal deaths without the program for the period between May 19, 2014, and May 18, 2015, and the imputed 2015 neonatal mortality rate was used to estimate the number of neonatal deaths without the program for the period between May 19, 2015 and April 30, 2016. Neonatal mortality data for Vital Pakistan can be obtained at http://www.vitalpakistantrust. org/progress-report.php and national data for Pakistan can be obtained at http://www.indexmundi.com/ facts/pakistan/mortality-rate.

mortality rate also fell in Rethri Goth due to the provision of services such as nutritional supplementation and immunizations. Salman's story is highlighted on Vital Pakistan's website and includes this heartbreaking quote from his mother: "I wish these services had come sooner."

Dr. Anita Zaid, the founder of Vital Pakistan, obtained her initial funding for the program in Rethri Goth by winning the inaugural $1,000,000 Children's Prize in 2013. She initially applied as an individual not affiliated with any nonprofit and, without a fiscal sponsor,[2] would have been ineligible for most grants. Foundations typically prefer to fund established nonprofit organizations capable of sustaining themselves.[3] Bank loans would also be exceedingly difficult to obtain in Rethri Goth, especially without collateral or a business plan. The Children's Prize filled the funding gap. Like many prizes, the Children's Prize accepts applications from individuals, nonprofits, and for-profits.

The Children's Prize Foundation tests the boundaries of philanthropy in two ways: how money is dispersed, and how projects are managed. Ted Caplow, an engineer and entrepreneur, created the Children's Prize after the birth of his triplets. Caplow was inspired by his belief that "all children are equally deserving of life and better health" and his desire to address the problem that "children and mothers die daily from preventable causes."[4] Caplow considered donating to existing, large foundations but was unconvinced that his donations would have much of an impact on reducing under-five mortality. He was also intrigued by the resurgence in science prizes, such as the Ansari XPRIZE for suborbital flight, which were yielding major breakthroughs. Caplow decided to design his own open global competition. Each year, the Children's Prize assembles a team of experts to pick the winners and then engages with the winners to support the projects. Funds are paid out in stages as quantifiable

---

2 According to Grantspace: "Fiscal sponsorship is a formal arrangement in which a 501(c)(3) public charity sponsors a project that may lack exempt status. This alternative to starting your own nonprofit allows you to seek grants and solicit tax-deductible donations under your sponsor's exempt status." For more information, see http://grantspace.org/tools/knowledge-base/Individual-Grantseekers/Fiscal-Sponsorship/fiscal-sponsorship.

3 Joanne Fritz, "6 Realities of Foundation Grants for Nonprofits: Grants Have Their Place, but Are Not a Cure-All," *The Balance* (August 21, 2015), available at http://www.thebalance.com/foundation-grants-for-nonprofits-2501773.

4 Children's Prize Foundation, "Our Story," available at http://www.childrensprize.org/our-story/.

milestones are reached. Given Caplow's technical background, it is not surprising that the Children's Prize wholeheartedly embraces the growing emphasis in the philanthropic sector on evidence-based programs. It requires "rigorous process accountability" and "insists on impact and data-driven rigor."[5]

TRENDS IN PRIZES

The Children's Prize is among the growing wave of organizations offering prizes. Unfortunately, the last systematic review of prizes offering awards greater than $100,000 was conducted almost ten years ago by McKinsey & Company.[6] McKinsey reported that in 2007, 80 percent of the extant 219 large prizes focused on technical challenges (aviation and space, science and engineering, and climate and environment). Prizes for the arts and "other" (which includes social concerns, such as health, poverty reduction, and education) accounted for ten percent each. Following precedent in the prize literature, the terms "prize," "contest," "challenge," and "competitions" are used interchangeably. The McKinsey report noted that over 60 of the large prizes were created after 2000 and estimated that the total prize sector was worth "as much as $1 to $2 billion."[7]

The proportion of prizes that address social challenges may be growing as well. Following on the success of the Ansari XPRIZE in 2004, the XPRIZE Foundation has launched four prizes for social challenges (women's safety, water abundance, adult literacy, and global learning), as well as 11 more prizes for specific technical goals (such as lunar robotic exploration). In 2015, the foundation launched XPRIZE India to solve development challenges in energy, food, learning, shelter, water, waste, and social justice. Many organizations, such as the Knight Foundation and Ashoka Changemakers, also now offer multiple prizes to address broad social concerns. Online prize platforms, such as Innocentive, allow both for-profit and nonprofit organizations to post challenges for

---

5 Ibid.

6 McKinsey & Company, "And the Winner Is: Capturing the Promise of Philanthropic Prizes" (July 2009), available at http://www.mckinsey.com/industries/social-sector/our-insights/and-the-winner-is-philanthropists-and-governments-make-prizes-count; The annual *Awards, Honors & Prizes*, published by Gale, does provide an extensive, but not exhaustive, list of all types of awards, not just prizes. For the past ten years, various editions have reported between 20,000 and 24,000 awards of all types.

7 McKinsey, "And the Winner Is" (July 2009).

a variety of problems. Most of Innocentive's current 73 prize offerings focus on scientific achievement, such as the $100,000 challenge for "Culture of Select Poultry Viruses in Immortalized Cell Substrates," but others focus on social challenges, such as the $50,000 "LIFTed Prize 2017—Innovation in Postsecondary Learning."

President Obama encouraged government agencies to increase their use of prizes in 2010, and many have followed through.[8] As of March 3, 2017, the Challenge.gov website listed 750 active competitions. Although most of the prizes listed on Challenge.gov focus on scientific goals, such as the $295,000 Nail to Nail (N2N) Fingerprint Challenge, others, such as the $1.2 million Aspire Challenge, address a social need. Up to 16 Aspire Challenge winners will be awarded $75,000 each by the U.S. Small Business Administration to implement their proposals "to spur the development and provision of innovative entrepreneurial development and access to capital resources for formerly incarcerated individuals or those who are non-violent ex-offenders."[9]

To understand how prizes can address the needs of vulnerable populations, it is important to recognize that there are three main types of prizes.[10] The prize types differ in the order in which applicants receive funds, complete their work, and enter the prize competition:

* Resource Prizes: Winners are given an award before they complete their proposal (Children's Prize, Aspire Challenge, Innocentive's Postsecondary Learning).

* Incentive Prizes: Winners are given an award after they complete the goal (Ansari XPRIZE, Nail to Nail, Innocentive's Poultry Virus Challenge).

* Recognition Prizes: Winners are given an award for work completed before competition (Nobel Peace Prize, Pulitzer Prize, Ibrahim African Leadership Prize).

---

8 Kathleen O'Neil, "Prizes and Competitions Spur Innovation in Government Agencies," American Association for the Advancement of Science (January 13, 2017), available at http://www.aaas.org/news/stpf/competitions-and-prizes-help-government-agencies-spur-innovation.

9 Aspire Challenge, "About the Challenge," available at http://www.challenge.gov/challenge/aspire-challenge/.

10 Renya Reed Wasson, "The Future of Prize Philanthropy," *Stanford Social Innovation Review* (Summer 2016), available at https://ssir.org/articles/entry/the_future_of_prize_philanthropy; McKinsey, "And the Winner Is" (July 2009).

Resource prizes are essentially technologically enhanced grants. Compared with grants, resource prizes typically are open to a wider audience, place a greater emphasis on measurement and outcomes, and are more likely to adopt a web-based prize platform to interface with applicants and to build an online community that promotes collaboration between current and past applicants.[11] Resource prizes can address broad social challenges, such as improving child and maternal health.

Incentive prizes, also known as inducement prizes, require the completion of a precisely stated specific goal to win an award. For example, the specific goal for the $10 million Ansari XPRIZE was "to build a reliable, reusable, privately financed, manned spaceship capable of carrying three people to 100 kilometers above the Earth's surface twice within two weeks."[12] Starting with the British government's Longitude Prize in 1714 for the first marine chronometer, incentive prizes have been used for centuries to spur technological breakthroughs.[13]

Recognition prizes, the last major type of prize, are awarded for work completed before the start of the competition. All three types of prizes can raise an issue's public profile and inspire future leaders.

Tiered-evidence provides another lens for viewing prize types. Borrowing from Feldman and Haskins' tiered-evidence grantmaking protocol, projects can be divided into three groups, depending on how much evidence is available, and each group can be mapped to an optimal prize/funding mechanism.[14] On the lowest step of the evidence ladder, development projects employ "high-potential and relatively untested practices." If these are relatively low-cost projects, or are conducted in industries with high earning potential, they could be designed as self-funded incentive prizes. If funding is an insurmountable barrier, development projects would need to be designed as resource prizes. At the next step of the evidence ladder, validation projects employ, "promising practices with existing moderate

---

11 Wasson, "The Future of Prize Philanthropy" (Summer 2016).

12 Ansari XPrize, "About the Prize," available at http://ansari.xprize.org/.

13 Robert Lee Hotz, "Need a Breakthrough? Offer Prize Money!" *The Wall Street Journal* (December 13, 2016), available at https://www.wsj.com/articles/need-a-breakthrough-offer-prize-money-1481043131.

14 Andrew Feldman and Ron Haskins, "Tiered-Evidence Grantmaking," Evidence-Based Policymaking Collaborative (September 9, 2016), available at http://www.evidencecollaborative.org/toolkits/tiered-evidence-grantmaking.

evidence," perhaps testing a proven practice in a novel environment or in a new bundle of services. These could be designed as incentive prizes, but if there is a strong profit potential, a prize sponsor would not be needed to facilitate the project. If a validation project needs to be offered as a prize to be completed, then it probably should be designed as a resource prize to cover implementation costs. Lastly, on the highest step of the evidence ladder, scale-up projects employ "replication of practices with existing strong evidence." Scale-up projects likely involve the adoption of a new long-term program and are best suited to contracts, rather than one-off prizes.

Thanks to the Ansari XPRIZE and other big prizes, much of the current hype surrounding prizes focuses on incentive prizes. Incentive prizes are great for achieving specific technological goals when applicants can either easily cover the cost of their activities themselves or find sponsors. However, they don't work as well for broad goals that insert subjectivity into the judging process, decrease the certainty of winning, and therefore increase risk for financial backers. Incentive prizes also do not work well when applicants do not have access to funds—a problem likely to plague projects that are unlikely to yield profits. As a result, many prizes aimed at broad social goals, such as the Knight Foundation's City Challenge (to make cities "more vibrant places to live and work")[15] or the Ashoka Changemakers' Co-Creating a Healthier World ("to spark the next generation of sustainable health solutions through collaboration with the business sector")[16] are resource prizes.

The XPRIZE Foundation has attempted to tweak its incentive prize model to make it applicable to broad social goals in areas where applicants are unlikely to be able to self-fund. In these situations, the XPRIZE Foundation focuses on technology-driven solutions that address a single aspect of a social challenge, and they offer a hybrid, multistage prize in which some rounds are paid for by XPRIZE. For example, applicants for the Adult Literacy Prize self-fund the development of a mobile literacy application in the first round. Judges select 15 semifinalists, whose software is field-tested for one year, with costs covered by the Barbara Bush

15 Knight Cities Challenge, "About the Challenge," available at http://knightcities.org/.

16 Ashoka Changemakers, "About Co-Creating a Healthier World," available at http://www.changemakers.com/makingmorehealth.

Foundation in the second round. The team that posts the largest 12-month literacy gain is declared the Grand Prize Winner and receives $3 million.[17]

PROS AND CONS OF EMPLOYING PRIZES

Resource and incentive prizes have enormous potential for addressing the problems that vulnerable populations face. As vividly illustrated by the Bill & Melinda Gates Foundation's Reinvent the Toilet Challenge,[18] a prize can shine a spotlight on problems that have plagued humanity forever, but are not necessarily very sexy. The toilet challenge was designed as a resource prize: From 2011 to 2013, winners were provided with funds to complete their proposals. By marketing their request for proposals as a "challenge" rather than a traditional grant, the Bill & Melinda Gates Foundation could piggyback on the excitement surrounding incentive prizes and tap into an innovator identity. Like most prizes, the Reinvent the Toilet Challenge awarded funds to a variety of applicant types, including universities, for-profits (Unilever), and nonprofits (RTI International). The Reinvent the Toilet Challenge also exhibited an emphasis on measureable outcomes typical of prizes. A prominent goal of the challenge was to create a toilet that cost less than $.05 per user per day despite being off the grid without access to water, sewer, or electrical lines.

While both resource and incentive prizes can add panache, publicity, openness, and technical emphasis to solving problems, incentive prizes offer several additional benefits. In an MIT Open Courseware publication,[19] Peter Diamandis, the entrepreneur who founded the XPRIZE, lists four benefits unique to incentive prizes:

1 Efficiency: Foundations pay the winner only once the goal is achieved.

---

17 The mobile literacy applicants must show promise that they can substantially improve the proficiency of adult readers at or below the third-grade reading level within 12 months. The top five mid-year performers are selected as finalists and receive $100,000 each. Other awards are granted based on performance in native language categories and for cities that encourage the greatest participation. See http://adultliteracy.xprize.org/about/overview for more information.

18 Bill & Melinda Gates Foundation, "Fact Sheet: Water, Sanitation & Hygiene: Reinventing the Toilet Challenge," available at https://docs.gatesfoundation.org/Documents/Fact_Sheet_Reinvent_the_Toilet_Challenge.pdf.

19 Peter H. Diamandis, "Using Incentive Prizes to Drive Creativity, Innovation and Breakthroughs," Massachusetts Institute of Technology (2009), available at https://ocw.mit.edu/courses/engineering-systems-division/esd-172j-x-prize-workshop-grand-challenges-in-energy-fall-2009/readings/MITESD_172JF09_Diamandis.pdf.

2 Leverage: A well-structured prize can spur investment up to 40 times the size of the award.

3 Industry Creation: When multiple applicants work in parallel, numerous approaches can be explored, unleashing new possibilities. The for-profit private space industry was born from the Ansari XPRIZE.

4 Paradigm Change: A well-structured prize "can change what people believe is possible."

However, if an organization is trying to solve a problem for which applicants cannot self-fund, then it cannot offer an incentive prize and must offer a resource prize instead. Fortunately, organizations can design resource prizes to partially capture Diamandis' four benefits: 1) organizations can pay winners at various milestones, so that the total award is paid only once the goal is achieved; 2) organizations can promote their finalists as well as their winners and help them leverage their finalist/winner status for more funds from other sources; 3) organizations can include a first round in which they support multiple semifinalists so that numerous approaches can be explored; and lastly, 4) if an organization sets an ambitious-enough goal, then a resource grant also can change what people believe is possible. Good prize design is critical, and many possibilities for innovations still exist.

Despite a long list of desirable features, prizes are not without their critics. Kevin Starr, the managing director of the Mulago Foundation, complained that incentive prizes are a waste of time for nonprofit applicants who cannot afford to self-fund their work, especially if there is only one winner, and that prizes put too much emphasis on innovation instead of implementation.[20] Other critics complain that offering prizes can distract a nonprofit from its mission and does not help solve big problems.[21] Rick Cohen, a national correspondent for *Nonprofit Quarterly* prior to his death in 2015, warned of the danger of using crowdsourcing to judge

---

20 Kevin Starr, "Dump the Prizes," *Stanford Social Innovation Review* (August 22, 2013), available at https://ssir.org/articles/entry/dump_the_prizes.

21 Maria Mottola, Gail Nayowith, and Jon Pratt, "Nobody Needs a 'Shark Tank' in Philanthropy," *The Chronicle of Philanthropy* (March 2, 2015); James English, *The Economy of Prestige: Prizes, Awards, and the Circulation of Cultural Value*, (Cambridge: Harvard University Press, 2009).

prizes.[22] Robert Lee Hotz, a science writer for *The Wall Street Journal*, has questioned whether prizes are just a marketing gimmick and has argued that incentive prizes allow organizations to take advantage of free labor.[23] Two other concerns that have received too little attention in the literature are:

1 Offering a prize is now easy and can be handled by a small organization, thanks to prize platform providers such as Skild and Big Ideas, but offering a prize is still not cheap. Running a successful prize requires considerable time and planning, communicating with applicants and judges, and working with both winners and losers.

2 Structuring an incentive prize and/or hybrid prize is very difficult to get right, even with months of planning and a deep field of experts. Several big incentive prizes have failed to produce a winner, including Robert Bigelow's $50 million America Space Prize, which expired in 2010.[24] The winning team of the Netflix Prize was awarded $1 million in 2009, but the company quietly announced three years later that it would not use the winning algorithm—Netflix had not sufficiently defined the parameters of its prize's goal.[25]

These criticisms can all be mitigated with good prize design, but, as evidenced by the Netflix Prize, good design is not easy or cheap.

CONCLUSIONS

Prizes are trendy for a reason: They hold great promise for solving both technical challenges and problems facing vulnerable populations. Incentive prizes have a long, successful history and have become much more valuable and easier to run in the information age. Resource prizes

---

22 Rick Cohen, "Contest Philanthropy at the Council on Foundations: A Troubling Dynamic," *Nonprofit Quarterly* (March 23, 2015), available at https://nonprofitquarterly.org/2015/03/23/contest-philanthropy-at-the-annual-meeting-of-the-council-on-foundations/.

23 Robert Lee Hotz, "The Science Prize: Innovation or Stealth Advertising?" *The Wall Street Journal* (May 8, 2009), available at http://www.wsj.com/articles/SB124173078482897809.

24 Kenneth Chang, "In New Space Race, Enter the Entrepreneurs," *The New York Times* (June 7, 2010), available at www.nytimes.com/2010/06/08/science/space/08space.html.

25 Casey Johnston, "Netflix Never Used Its $1 Million Algorithm Due to Engineering Costs," *Wired* (April 16, 2012), available at www.wired.com/2012/04/netflix-prize-costs/.

can be thought of as "grants 2.0," harnessing the power of communication technology and borrowing elements from incentive prizes.

To realize the full potential of prizes, prize sponsors need a forum for sharing best practices in this rapidly evolving sector. Organizations need to be able to learn from each other which types of prizes and/or hybrid prizes work best for different types of problems. Establishing prize conferences, prize journals, and prize trade organizations would help maximize the positive impact of prizes.

Going forward, prize sponsors need to continue innovating the delivery of funds. Although crowdsourcing may not be ideal for judging, perhaps it could be used to raise funds for applicants. Prize sponsors could function as a vetting service to help philanthropists select which projects to support on platforms like Go Fund Me. Perhaps eventually, most prizes could be structured as incentive prizes so that sponsors could realize all of Diamandis' four benefits. Prizes offer organizations the opportunity to buy the biggest impact bang for their buck.

RENYA REED WASSON *is a performance management consultant for nonprofit and municipal organizations in the Philadelphia area. She recently served as the global philanthropy impact specialist at the Children's Prize Foundation. Wasson is a PhD economist who has held faculty positions at Villanova University and Bryn Mawr College. She is currently pursuing an executive master of public administration at the Fels Institute of Government at the University of Pennsylvania.*

BUILDING A MARKET FOR HEALTH
Achieving Community Outcomes Through a Total Health Business Model

Tyler Norris
Well Being Trust

Jme McLean
Mesu Strategies

Jewel, eight, clasps her mother's hand as they enter the hospital elevator. As the doors slide shut, she manages one last peek at the brightly colored murals of the fifth-floor pediatric unit. Her mother, Elena, 30, squeezes Jewel's hand, anxiously fretting that she must do more to manage Jewel's weight and increasing risk of diabetes. Jewel's doctor has warned that if she doesn't eat better and move more, she must soon start on metformin or risk the fate that Elena herself could not avoid — type II diabetes and early cardiovascular disease.[1]

As the elevator drops to street level, Elena's mind races for a solution. A single parent, working more than 50 hours per week as a hairstylist, her income barely covers the rent and utilities of their one-bedroom apartment in a neighborhood long characterized by disinvestment. There is no full-service grocery store in their neighborhood, and though the corner store recently introduced a limited selection of fresh produce, the higher costs and longer preparation times make regular, healthy meals more of a distant goal than a daily reality. Meanwhile, her attempts to get Jewel out to play involve two bus transfers to the closest park and recreation center, which she can reasonably manage only about once per week. But Elena prioritizes this critical activity time, as it is unsafe for Jewel to play near the tough streets of their transitional neighborhood, and walking or riding a bike to school or other activities on busy roads without sidewalks is both dangerous and impractical.

When the doors slide open on the ground floor, Elena and Jewel step back into their daily lives, presented with a challenge confronting tens of millions in America today: how to achieve health in an environment that seems to conspire against it. Despite her mother's best intentions and efforts, at this rate, Jewel is likely to experience a future characterized by increased

---

1 This vignette of Elena and Jewel (not their real names) is adapted from composite archetypes of patients' lives and care experiences.

stress, declining physical health, reduced quality of life, and significant medical care procedures — at a financial cost that will only further exacerbate her stress. Indeed, unless policymakers, investors, civic leaders, and advocates working across sectors can reform and invest in the systems that produce health in the first place, our nation will likely see such personal challenges continue to drive the decline of population health, and accelerate the demand for costly health care services. While increasing spending on care services can be wildly profitable to private-sector entities in the business of sick care, these same profits are making health care more unaffordable for most Americans every day.

To contain costs and change the odds for Jewel and other families with adverse community experiences across the nation, we must reorient our health and social systems upstream, toward the outcome of total health, rather than focusing ever more resources on downstream clinical care interventions. By employing health-outcomes-focused policies, practices, and investments, many of the disease conditions our nation is battling could be avoided, along with their attendant costs. In a capitalist democracy, this calls for building a marketplace that values improvement in health outcomes, as an alternative to the existing marketplace that primarily rewards the volume of health care services provided. A marketplace for health outcomes would supply community members with the social, economic, and environmental conditions that produce longer, stronger, and healthier lives. Over time, such a market could reduce preventable demand for costly care services, making access to care more affordable for all Americans.

As an increasing number of health systems begin to explore value-based "at risk" payment arrangements and more fully embrace their stated missions to be accountable for the health of their communities, they are recognizing the benefits of a marketplace that values health. Indeed, some of these health systems are transforming their business models to move from volume (of care services) to value (of outcomes produced). They are increasingly investing in, and working in close partnership with, schools, low-income housing providers, local healthy food cooperatives, community development corporations and other "health-producing" community organizations—both to realize better health outcomes and to reduce unnecessary use of expensive care services that drive up avoidable costs.

A NATION AT RISK

Access to health care services is an essential human necessity, and continuing to ration access to health care by wealth or selected demographic group is untenable. Ensuring that everyone has access to a "medical home"—a regular and ongoing place that cares for his or her health and wellbeing—is both a moral imperative in a just society and a wise investment. While only ten to 20 percent of health outcomes are attributable to access to health care services, access to care contributes to increased wellbeing and functional health status, as well as to managing long-term costs. Expanding access for all Americans, especially to primary care and preventative services that integrate mental and physical health, promises to both improve health outcomes and contain preventable demand driven by costly illnesses in the first place.

America's treatment-oriented health care system comes at significant expense to the taxpayers, employers, and insurers who pay for it. These costs are only increasing. In 2015, national health expenditures accounted for nearly $3.2 trillion, or 18 percent of the gross domestic product (GDP).[2] These expenditures exceed 20 cents of every dollar when including the indirect costs associated with diminished worker productivity, tax revenue losses, and the significant emotional and psychological toll that illness takes on individuals and their families. Health care spending as a percentage of GDP is now twice the rate of what it was in 1980 (8.9 percent) and three and a half times that in 1960 (5 percent).[3] The rising supply-driven costs of pharmaceuticals, medical technology, and biotech devices further drive the growth of health delivery expenditures.

High and rising health care costs in a market that values treatment crowds out investments with higher potential to promote health and wellbeing. Nearly three-quarters of total U.S. health care expenditures are attributable to chronic disease, including those suffering with complex mental and behavioral health conditions. Much of this can be prevented by more effectively addressing an inextricably connected blend of economic, environmental, social, and cultural factors that influence health.

---

2   Centers for Medicare & Medicaid Services, "National Health Expenditure Data" (2016), available at http://www.cms.gov/research-statistics-data-and-systems/statistics-trends-and-reports/nationalhealthexpenddata/nationalhealthaccountshistorical.html.

3   Ibid.

A growing body of research shows that health outcomes are more directly shaped by economic, social, and environmental determinants within communities than by care services.[4] As such, initiatives that focus on resilient and equitable community development—safe affordable housing, active and accessible transportation options, healthy and affordable food, economic opportunity, and quality education, particularly in historically disinvested communities where health outcomes tend to be worse and threats of climate change are greatest—are critical, upstream drivers of health. Deeper investments in these non-health-care drivers of health outcomes are needed to improve health outcomes and slow the growth of health care costs.

Making these kinds of upstream investments and policy changes to improve population health outcomes will require a significant shift in both how we think about health and who plays a role in creating it. It calls for looking beyond the doctors, nurses, and care providers who address existing ailments and engaging the leaders in business, education, finance, and civic life, who can help prevent them in the first place. There are many complementary benefits in this equation, as the primary factors that shape health outcomes are the same ones that drive economic opportunity: equitable access to education, housing, transportation, and healthy foods, reducing stress and improving public safety, etc.[5] But for this leadership shift to happen, the health care sector must increasingly work closely with leaders in the finance and civic sectors to make these investments.

---

4   Sandro Galea et al., "Estimated Deaths Attributable to Social Factors," *American Journal of Public Health* 101 (8) (2011): 1456–1465, available at https://www.ncbi.nlm.nih.gov/pmc/articles/PMC3134519/. Finds that the number of deaths attributable to social factors in the United States (low education, racial segregation, low social support, individual poverty, income inequality, area-level poverty) is comparable to the number attributed to pathophysiological and behavioral causes.

Ali H. Mokdad et al., "Actual Causes of Death in the United States, 2000," *Journal of the American Medical Association* 291 (10) (2004): 1238–1245, available at https://www.ncbi.nlm.nih.gov/pubmed/15010446. Estimates that approximately 45 percent of deaths in the United States in 2000 were attributable to preventable ailments caused by tobacco use, poor diet, and physical inactivity, alcohol consumption, microbial agents, toxic agents, motor vehicle crashes, incidents involving firearms, sexual behaviors, and illicit use of drugs. Other unquantifiable causes of death included socioeconomic status and lack of access to medical care.

J. Michael McGinnis and William H. Foege, "Actual Causes of Death in the United States," *Journal of the American Medical Association* 270 (18) (1993): 2207–2212, available at https://galileo.seas.harvard.edu/images/material/2800/1140/McGinnis_ActualCausesofDeathintheUnitedStates.pdf.

5   Michael Marmot and Richard Wilkinson eds., *Social Determinants of Health: The Solid Facts*, 2nd ed. (Denmark: World Health Organization, 2003).

In the current health care marketplace, private and public insurers "supply" health care coverage to "buyers"—the people and businesses that purchase it. In the case of Medicare, Medicaid, and for the military, the supplier is the U.S. government. By offering products that spread risk, coverage makes health care more affordable and accessible to consumers and ensures that care providers (physicians and health systems) are paid fairly for the critical services they deliver.

In this volume-centric system, resources are primarily applied to health care interventions (e.g., treatment for chronic disease conditions, such as diabetes, hypertension, heart disease, and mental health disorders). This model, rewarding treatment rather than wellness, does little to incentivize improved health outcomes or cost containment. Even physicians' admonishments to their patients to change behaviors related to diet, exercise, and stress management often translate to little more than well-wishes, as there is little reward or accountability for assuring long-term health outcomes.

Also, in this volume-centric system, investments in the upstream determinants of health outcomes are not rewarded and, as such, are inadequately produced and delivered at a level sufficient to result in significantly better health outcomes. Furthermore, in a nation that tends to privatize gains while socializing costs and underestimating risk, funding for these health determinants is undervalued as a benefit to society, and as a result is woefully inadequate to address existing needs. Federal spending on Medicare alone exceeds both mandatory and discretionary federal spending on food assistance, transportation, housing, education, and unemployment programs combined.[6] Yet these nonmedical drivers of improved health outcomes and lower care costs over time are the top challenges identified in Community Health Needs Assessments. This result points to both a market failure and a market opportunity.

---

6 National Priorities Project, "Federal Spending: Where Does the Money Go," available at https://www.nationalpriorities.org/budget-basics/federal-budget-101/spending/; Juliette Cubanski and Tricia Neuman, "The Facts on Medicare Spending and Financing," Kaiser Family Foundation (July 2016), available at http://kff.org/medicare/issue-brief/the-facts-on-medicare-spending-and-financing/; Center on Budget and Policy Priorities, "Policy Basics: Non-Defense Discretionary Programs" (February 2016), available at http://www.cbpp.org/sites/default/files/atoms/files/PolicyBasics-NDD.pdf.

The health care sector is well positioned to unlock new sources of capital by helping to shift the health economy from its primary current focus on providing health care services to a concurrent focus on generating improvement in population health outcomes. In a new marketplace for health that seeks a return on increasing health and wellbeing, the actual "producers" of healthy people and environments (educators, land use planners, transportation agencies, affordable housing developers, food producers, and community development finance institutions) would supply health-promoting conditions to "buyers" of total health—the health care-sector actors (insurers, providers, integrated delivery systems, etc.) that are seeking to improve health outcomes and lower preventable spending for care delivery.[7]

In this new marketplace, the health care sector leverages and redirects existing and future assets to invest in community development factors that affect health outcomes. By investing in what gets and keeps people healthy, the sector is poised to increase health outcomes and, with time, reduce spending on unnecessary treatment and care. In this new health marketplace, health care systems "at risk for health" will increasingly value what community development institutions produce as purveyors of health. Under ideal market conditions, increased demand will boost supply and generate competition that creates equitable opportunity and access to the American Dream in the form of quality education, living-wage incomes, housing, food, transport, human connection, and the potential to build household wealth.

Opening this new marketplace for health will provide opportunities for a variety of actors to contribute to improving overall population health outcomes. Market mechanisms will create avenues for philanthropy, financial institutions, and others to work in coordination with community developers to augment the quality and volume of their "products." These mechanisms will also create roles for toolmakers and intermediaries across fields—from predictive data analytics to a continuum of nonmedical community health workers—to help translate the health demands and needs of "buyers." This marketplace can also spark innovation among

---

7 The typology of this market into "buyers of health," "sellers," and "connectors" was developed by Ian Galloway, Federal Reserve Bank of San Francisco, for the SOCAP Health conference in 2013. For more details on that conference, see the agenda and other content at http://www.frbsf.org/community-development/events/2013/september/socap-social-capital-markets-health/.

Figure 1. Health and Health Care / Supply and Demand

	BUYERS	COMMODITY	SUPPLIERS	RATIONALE
PRESENT **"VOLUME" TREATMENT AND SERVICES-ORIENTED**	Taxpayers (federal and state government for Medicare, Medicaid, military, and employees); businesses (for employees); individuals	Best quality care experience at best cost	Health care sector	The health care sector is incentivized to provide care to the sick and injured and to treat illness and injury.
DESIRED **"VALUE" OUTCOMES-ORIENTED**	Health care sector	Best quality care experience at best cost while improving population health Healthier people and places	Education, social services, transportation, affordable housing, healthy food access, urban planning	Health systems are incentivized to improve health and have interest in purchasing the outcomes that healthier communities exhibit.

smaller and local entrepreneurs to meet the increased demand for health by employing business models that create healthy community environments and behaviors.

PROFILE OF AN EARLY ADOPTER: KAISER PERMANENTE

Kaiser Permanente (KP), the nation's largest nonprofit integrated health system ($61 billion in revenue in 2015), provides both care and coverage. That is, KP offers its 10.6 million members across eight states and the District of Columbia both competitive insurance plans and care from more than 20,000 physicians. This structure incentivizes the organization not only to treat and care for existing and developing medical conditions, but also to help keep members from getting sick in the first place. KP seeks to make care and coverage more affordable by improving health and reducing preventable utilization, thereby increasing quality and managing costs.

As a mission-driven organization, the business challenge KP faces is that it is "at risk" for 100 percent of the health of its members, but as a provider of care services, it directly produces only ten to 20 percent of what creates health in the first place. In other words, KP as an insurer is accountable for covering the costs of Jewel's medical treatments, but by itself as a care provider, at first glance, it can do little more than effectively treat her worsening conditions, and support her in practicing healthier behaviors. Ultimately, the organization is at risk for that which is primarily outside of its direct control. This is similarly the case for any health care provider that enters into an at-risk or value-based risk-sharing arrangement. So to promote health, prevent disease, and manage conditions, care organizations need community partners.

As such, investments in resilient, equitable community development that create health have tangible value for KP, other insurers, and care providers increasingly engaging in at-risk arrangements. By promoting access to affordable housing, active transportation options, better schools, healthier and more affordable food, and safer communities—i.e., the social determinants of health—these health systems are increasingly able to address the 80-percent-plus nonclinical determinants of health; they are also better able to deliver on their mission to provide high-quality, affordable care and to improve the health of the communities they serve.

Recognizing this opportunity, KP has worked to creatively seek out and invest in *healthy community* strategies for the total health of its members. In effect, it has become a "buyer" of health in the marketplace for health.

- In Oakland, CA, leadership at KP is working closely with the mayor, city and county councils, school district, other health systems, foundations, and civic leadership via the Oakland Thrives Leadership Council to make a generation-long commitment to health, education outcomes, and equitable prosperity.

- In 2006, KP helped to found the Convergence Partnership, a collaboration of foundations and health systems aiming to accelerate a vision of healthy people and places by leading and supporting fundamental shifts in policy and practice across sectors. In more than a decade of strategic partnerships with government and nonprofit organizations, network- and capacity-building among foundations across the country, policy advocacy, and shared grantmaking, the partnership has influenced significant federal, state, and local policy changes related to healthy food financing, transportation equity, and resilient, equitable development.

KP has also recognized its role as a community anchor institution in and across its eight states and the District of Columbia.

- In 2015, $1.7 billion of a total of $20 billion of KP's purchasing nationally was made to women and minority suppliers. KP's national supplier diversity team is now working to localize that spending, creating local jobs and circulating wealth-creating resources in its footprint.

- KP's environmental goals aim to reduce the impact of its operations on population health. In recent years, this includes meeting over 50 percent of total energy needs with renewable sources, facilitated by an $800 million investment in solar and wind generation, creating green jobs and setting the pace for the health sector.

- KP has set up more than 60 farmers' markets in its communities—often at care facilities, for ease of access for employees and the community—as part of its efforts to deliver total health, leveraging all organizational assets and resources.

- Other total health levers at KP include workforce pipeline development into vulnerable communities, impact investing, and designing facilities and surroundings as drivers of vibrant places (e.g., placemaking)[8] that spark economic development and human connection.

GETTING THERE

Delivering significantly improved population health outcomes at significantly decreased costs will require a deliberate, long-term agenda that scales up the "dose" of health promotion and healthy communities. This must be core to the work of all nonprofit health systems with missions that call them to improve community health, not just those currently able to capture the economic benefit. Results from years of efforts in community benefit have led KP researchers to understand that the reach of an initiative (how many lives it touches), together with the intensity (strength of intervention) and duration (length of intervention), directly influence

---

8   Project for Public Spaces, Inc., "Improving Health Outcomes Through Placemaking" (2016), available at https://www.pps.org/wp-content/uploads/2016/12/Healthy-Places-PPS.pdf.

Figure 2. Total Health Impact: Leveraging Multiple Assets at KP

the initiative's impact.[9] In the marketplace for health, higher "dose" can be achieved through greater supply of, and demand for, the economic, social, and environmental determinants of health. Increased investment in resilient, equitable community development, greater and more diverse collaborative leadership, and a focus on low-income people, rural communities, and communities of color can substantially reduce disease rates.

One promising avenue to boost supply of health value production is through health systems (as well as universities, governments, and large

9   Pamela Schwartz, Suzanne Rauzon, and Allen Cheadle, "Dose Matters: An Approach to Strengthening Community Health Strategies to Achieve Greater Impact" National Academy of Medicine (August 2015), available at https://nam.edu/wp-content/uploads/2015/08/Perspective_DoseMatters.pdf; Pamela Schwartz, "Lessons Learned from Kaiser Permanente's Community Health Initiative (CHI) Evaluation," Kaiser Permanente (2014), available at https://share.kaiserpermanente.org/article/building-the-field/.

employers rooted in place) acting as anchor institutions in their communities. "Anchor institutions"—often the universities and hospitals in a city or region—wield significant power as engines of local economic growth and revitalization, and they have massive opportunity to deliver on community wellbeing and prosperity objectives.[10] Anchor institutions are usually the largest employers in their locales, with sizable human resource needs that can help to build out local workforce pipelines and training and career development opportunities for disadvantaged populations and workers across fields and skill levels. The fixed and expansive size of their footprints typically includes building and development demands that can lead to creative placemaking and fuel local construction trades. Their purchasing power in combination with the demands of their operations, when procurement is localized, can drive powerful wealth-multiplier effects across regions. Investing their pension funds and capital reserves for direct impact on the economic, environmental, and social determinants of health (from housing as a platform for health to healthy food and clean-energy enterprises that concurrently create local green jobs and wealth creation) can bring much-needed resources to places and sectors that have experienced disinvestment and that disproportionally contribute to chronic disease, mental health, and reduced economic opportunity.[11] For many leading health systems such as KP, community benefit work that initially led to healthy eating and active living initiatives, has expanded to an emphasis on policies, systems, and environmental changes, as well as prevention. As health sector leaders immerse themselves more deeply in this upstream work, dozens of health systems are coming to recognize that increasing dose also requires harnessing the full power of hospitals and health systems as community anchor institutions.[12]

---

10 Tyler Norris and Ted Howard, "Can Hospitals Heal America's Communities?" Democracy Collaborative (December 2015), available at http://democracycollaborative.org/content/can-hospitals-heal-americas-communities-0.

11 Enterprise Community Partners, "Health & Housing" (2017), available at http://www.enterprisecommunity.org/solutions-and-innovation/health-and-housing; East Bay Asian Local Development Corporation, "Healthy Neighborhoods" (2015), available at http://ebaldc.org/healthy-neighborhoods; Emerald Cities Collaborative, "Oakland Programs and Initiatives" (2017), available at http://emeraldcities.org/cities/oakland; Great Communities Collaborative, "Impact" (2017), available at http://www.greatcommunities.org/our-work/impact.

12 Nancy Martin, "Advancing the Anchor Mission of Healthcare," The Democracy Collaborative (March 8, 2017), available at http://democracycollaborative.org/content/advancing-anchor-mission-healthcare-report.

Another primary avenue for improving outcomes is through collaboration for clinical-community integration, especially around meeting the nonmedical (economic and social) needs of patients, from food security to affordable housing. This will require collaboration between health care providers and other anchor institutions (including banks, community development finance institutions, transportation, and housing) at a scale never attempted before. It will mean investing deliberately in the upstream public, nonprofit, and philanthropic capacities that advance healthy environments. It will mean building robust feedback loops for learning across fields and sectors about the social and economic environments that influence health.

One of the too-often-overlooked benefits of the Affordable Care Act is the important payment mechanisms and incentives for health care providers to move from volume (of care services) to value (for delivering health outcomes) via risk-sharing arrangements and global payments for defined populations. As such, hospitals and health systems and physicians are beginning to move toward an incentive model to deliver the best-quality care experience, at the best cost, while improving population health (the aptly named "triple aim").[13] In any reform scenario for the Affordable Care Act, it is vital that value-based incentives for providers to produce better outcomes at less cost are not only preserved, but expanded.

THE PROMISE OF AN OUTCOMES-BASED APPROACH TO HEALTH: THREE CALLS TO ACTION

A market that values health incentivizes an outcomes-based approach to improve Americans' health while reducing preventable use of health care services. By increasing health outcomes and making care more affordable, this approach also leads to increased family and community prosperity and security. Advancing this approach through cross-sector collaboration can serve as a boundary-crossing salve to the toxic partisanship that often thwarts meaningful progress on the contributors to population health and equitable economic opportunity. We offer three calls to action:

1 **Civic leadership and accountability.** Creating a marketplace for health that measurably improves outcomes will require significant

---

13 Institute for Healthcare Improvement, "The IHI Triple Aim" (2017), available at http://www.ihi.org/ Engage/Initiatives/TripleAim/Pages/default.aspx.

conversations and actions on complex social issues, engaging leaders across sectors and diverse communities to move from doing good things to being accountable for results. This means setting a table that engages both traditional leaders—the politicians, executives, and civic leaders whose institutions can significantly impact community outcomes—and nontraditional community leaders who shape the social, cultural, and economic landscapes of our communities. This must include residents with innate expertise and lived experience in the viability of potential improvements to community conditions; educators and service providers intimately acquainted with local needs and assets, taking trauma-informed approaches; and the advocacy and philanthropic organizations that are fueling social change. Professionals deeply engaged in shaping the form and function of communities—transportation and land use planners, affordable housing developers, real estate investors, community development finance institutions, banks, and so on—must also have a voice. Civic discourse must be strong enough and long enough to match challenging, longer-term forces at play in communities, such as gentrification, displacement, and persistent, concentrated poverty in urban and rural areas. To create a sustainable infrastructure of health and opportunity, this work must transcend election cycles, grantmaker initiative periods, organizational timeframes, and generational divides to meaningfully address the health conditions that manifest across lifetimes and persist across generations.

For health systems, this means stepping up to the civic table with other leaders across sectors to identify roles and opportunities for driving equitable community development strategies that produce health. For nonprofit, mission-driven health systems, this work is essential to delivering on their stated commitment to measurably improve health in the communities they serve.

2 **Health in all investments, policies, and practices.** Advancing total health outcomes will require fearlessly and relentlessly improving our organizational practices and policies and making necessary investments at a sufficient scale. We must ask whether and how every operational decision affecting the economy, society, and the environment can contribute to positive health outcomes.

For health systems, this means embracing the triple aim of a high-quality care experience, cost reduction, and creating healthier people and communities; making the assessment of and referral to basic human needs a standard of care; and embracing health care's role as an anchor institution with significant economic leverage.

3 **Innovating, tracking outcomes, learning.** Continually improving results will require better (more timely, transparent, granular, accessible) real-time data and predictive analytics to understand and act on the complex interplay between the economic, social, and environmental issues facing our communities. This requires a disciplined focus to generate, assess, and learn from actionable information and to share results in a way that builds understanding, accountability, and action. It means disaggregating data by race and other socioeconomic factors to understand disparities in impacts and investments, and how such disparities might (or might not) align. This information should always inform strategies and partnerships.

For health systems, this means leveraging existing resources (such as Community Health Needs Assessments), building new partnerships (with community development organizations and other anchor institutions to share existing data and generate shared data), and innovating on data collection, analysis, and reporting in creative and intentional ways (through improved efforts around learning, measurement, and assessment).

By partnering with the health sector, community development leaders and those who finance their activities hold the greatest promise for improving population health, reducing preventable costs, and paving the way to a healthy, more equitably prosperous nation. Given that economic and social factors are the primary drivers of health outcomes, a community development approach to health can be coupled with deeper investments in disease prevention and clinical-community integration to reduce preventable use of services and, in turn, reduce demand-driven care costs. This is a call to leadership to accelerate the transition from volume to value, and from a market that primarily values health care services to a market that primarily values and rewards health outcomes. A market that values health is America's key to unleashing the innovation and investment that can create more afford-able health care—and better health for all.

Jewel, now 30, releases her daughter Leticia's hand as they approach the sidewalk from the crosswalk, where cars and bikes anticipate the walk signal. Giggling, eight-year-old Leticia dashes past the storefront of the hair salon that Jewel owns and manages to the community play lot on the far corner, where she marvels at the brightly colored new mural on the building wall. From the fresh produce market across the street, her grandmother Elena, 52, shouts and waves hello. The incredible changes she has seen in this neighborhood over the past 22 years have made all the difference for her granddaughter. Leticia might never know of the many difficult but critical investments and policy changes that community leaders made two decades before; she may also never know of the daily challenges that childhood obesity and chronic disease can bring over a lifetime.

———

TYLER NORRIS *is chief executive of the Well Being Trust and previously served as vice president of total health at Kaiser Permanente.*

JME MCLEAN *is principal at Mesu Strategies and previously served as associate director for PolicyLink and the Convergence Partnership.*

ADVANCE MARKET COMMITMENTS
Rewarding Innovation Without Picking Winners

Ruth Levine
William and Flora Hewlett Foundation

Babies cry when they get a jab, but parents feel good knowing that immunization prevents a lifetime of disability or even death. In the United States, Canada, and Europe, vaccine manufacturers have developed remarkably safe and effective products, pushing scientific boundaries to reduce or even eliminate the risk of such infectious diseases as polio, measles, pertussis, tetanus, pneumonia, and now human papilloma virus.

In deciding to dedicate precious research and development (R&D) resources to vaccines, those firms haven't been responding simply to a public health imperative; they also have been seeking rewards in the market. Private insurers and government health programs have been willing to pay a price for newly developed products that compensate companies for capital-intensive R&D, regulatory approval, and manufacturing capacity. As a result, vaccines are universally available to children in wealthy countries, and new ones are in the pipeline.

These same market incentives are not at work in low- and middle-income countries, where the majority of the world's children live. Traditionally, vaccines have not been affordable to governments in the developing world until long after the patents have expired and generic manufacturers have stepped in to sell a high volume of low-cost products. Moreover, private pharmaceutical firms view developing vaccines for diseases that are unique to poor regions, such as malaria and dengue, as an unattractive way to invest their scientific brainpower and capital.

The author is grateful to professors Michael Kremer and Prashant Yadav, as well as the editors of this volume, for comments on an earlier draft, though they bear no responsibility for any of the content herein.

Recently, the business case for global vaccines has grown stronger, particularly with the creation in 2000 of the Global Alliance for Vaccines and Immunization (GAVI), a public-private partnership funded by the Bill & Melinda Gates Foundation, the United States, the United Kingdom, Norway, and other donors. GAVI has financed the introduction of relatively high-priced products into low-income countries. At the same time, it has sought to negotiate long-term prices that are more affordable to national governments.

However, GAVI's purchases of existing products haven't been enough to induce large pharmaceutical companies to undertake costly R&D or brick-and-mortar investments in manufacturing plants for new products, particularly vaccines that would be well suited to poor countries. So, to try to solve that problem, several philanthropic and public-sector funders started exploring ways to pay for R&D, particularly through public-private partnerships with specific pharmaceutical manufacturers.

The traditional approach would have been to fund innovators who were most likely to succeed in developing a new vaccine, essentially attempting to "pick winners" among possible innovators and pay for their research. But a technical working group convened by the Center for Global Development, a Washington, DC think tank, proposed a novel application of an idea first suggested by noted Harvard economist Michael Kremer:[1] What if GAVI instead could make a binding promise to buy a not-yet-developed vaccine at a price that would make a firm's investment pay off, if and only if the vaccine met preset standards? Rather than paying for research by pre-identified innovators, they would instead pay anyone who achieved the outcome of producing a vaccine that met the needs of public health officials and people in poor countries. Might this promise incentivize innovation by manufacturers in search of a profit while permitting funders to hold onto their money until the product they wanted was brought to market?

This insight about the potential to orient funding around desired outcomes rather than the activity required to get there led to the creation of the first advance market commitment (AMC). The AMC was created

---

1 Michael Kremer and Rachel Glennerster, *Strong Medicine: Creating Incentives for Pharmaceutical Research on Neglected Diseases*, (Princeton, NJ: Princeton University Press, 2004).

to spur the final stages of development and investments in scale manufacture of a pneumococcal vaccine that would protect against strains of the disease common in the developing world: a disease that kills more than half a million children each year.[2] The governments of the United Kingdom, Norway, Canada, Russia, and Italy, along with the Gates Foundation, pooled a total of $1.5 billion to back a deal: any company able to make a pneumococcal conjugate vaccine that met predetermined safety and efficacy standards would be guaranteed a relatively high price for the early doses.

The AMC sought to mimic key aspects of a market—innovators take a risk when they envision a possible payoff down the line; consumers buy a product that suits their needs if and when it is developed. As in any attractive market, the total potential revenue from the deal would be set at a level sufficient to cover the development and manufacturing costs of the product with a modest markup. That potential revenue would then permit firms to make the R&D investments. Funders would not pick the winning firm(s) in advance by funding the R&D itself or offering a purchase guarantee. They would pay only for the product and would buy it from any firm(s) producing it. If no product is developed, they would not pay a penny.

The AMC had one special feature that made it particularly useful for incentivizing innovations that would benefit low-income countries. Any supplier reaping the rewards of the AMC would have to accept a relatively low price for the product after the "payment pot" was exhausted and would have to commit to continuing to supply the product. This would help to ensure that the benefits of the AMC funding would be sustained even after the original money was gone.

The result? By 2010, pneumococcal conjugate vaccine from the first eligible manufacturer was available to countries receiving GAVI support. Subsequently, one other company's product was also deemed eligible. As of 2016, the AMC-funded vaccine was protecting children in 54 countries around the world, and about one-quarter of the original AMC payment

---

2 Advance Market Commitment Working Group, "Making Markets for Vaccines: Ideas to Action," Center for Global Development (2005).

pot still remained as an incentive for additional manufacturers to get in on the deal.

As the vaccine case illustrated, an AMC is a way to make a future market opportunity visible to businesses that are choosing among alternative ways to use capital today, while permitting funders to pay only for results. For most not-yet-developed products, an AMC is neither necessary nor feasible because the normal workings of the marketplace suffice to stimulate innovation. But for some—particularly products where the social value exceeds the perceived willingness to pay—an AMC may be the most efficient way to create an incentive for costly R&D and manufacturing. And for funders, it may be far better than making upfront investments in R&D. Funders don't have to pick winners among companies that think they are on the path toward a viable product, and they don't have to bear the R&D risk.

In its most generic form, an AMC is an open offer committing the purchaser to pay a relatively high unit price for the first units of a product that meets the preset eligibility requirements. To simulate a natural competitive market, the sales may go to any company with an eligible product. In turn, participating companies commit to supply the product at a lower unit price (also called a "tail price") in future years after the original payment pot is exhausted.

An AMC has four core elements, each of which constitutes a design challenge.

1 **Guaranteed funding.** The AMC commits to future purchases— potentially many years hence. In the case of the pneumococcal conjugate vaccine, most of the R&D had already been done, thanks to a lucrative market for a similar product in industrialized countries. Still, the guarantee has had to be in place for several years to allow for late-stage development, regulatory approval, and the build-up of production capacity. Most products would require a similar, or longer, timeframe. Although private funders, such as foundations and some national governments, are able to make legally binding commitments, many governments (including the United States) cannot do so without special legislative action.

2 **A target product profile.** The exact, observable specifications of the product must be described *ex ante* (based on essential requirements rather than actual results). In the case of a health product, for example,

specifications may include everything from the safety and efficacy levels to the required storage conditions, means of administering the drug or vaccine, and single- or multi-dose packaging. This can be challenging for products that are many years away. Setting the bar too low may allow suboptimal products to get to market, while setting the bar too high may discourage innovation.

3 **A means of assessing eligibility.** A regulatory agency, commission, or other entity that is seen by both purchaser and supplier as legitimate, unbiased, and technically competent is essential. In the case of health products, the U.S. Food and Drug Administration or a comparable national regulatory authority can serve this purpose. For other types of products, investors in the AMC would have to create a specialized process to adjudicate whether the product meets the specifications.

4 **Established set prices at the start and end of the AMC purchasing period.** An AMC design specifies the high starting price and a ceiling for the lower tail price. This AMC element represents the biggest departure from a normal market—and potentially the most problematic, because it requires educated guesswork about production costs. To avoid a situation that would be financially nonviable for the firm(s), the tail price must at least be greater than the likely production cost once manufacturing capacity is scaled up. Although this is challenging, it also represents an opportunity to signal to firms that they need to consider the eventual production cost during R&D; there's no point in developing a product that will be unaffordable to potential purchasers. When done well, this price signal further defines the outcome that the funder values—not only the production of a viable vaccine but its on-going availability at affordable prices.

In addition to these core elements, it is useful to have a credible demand forecast for the product. Although "demand risk" is a normal part of life in the private sector, the strength of the AMC incentive is greatest when accompanied by a credible estimate of year-on-year demand so that firms can better estimate the potential ease or difficulty of recouping their investment. In the case of the pneumococcal AMC, a credible demand forecast was augmented by a volume guarantee—a commitment by GAVI to purchase a certain minimum number of units in the early years.

Beyond the application of an AMC to develop a pneumococcal vaccine, other vaccines may also be appropriate targets. Think, for instance, of an AMC to incentivize development of a vaccine to prevent Zika or Ebola, or of any vaccine that could be viable without refrigeration. A similar case might be made for some types of drugs, such as antibiotics, and health-related devices, such as improved female condoms. In fact, structuring some of the reimbursement for pharmaceutical products under Medicaid and Medicare into AMCs could help shift public spending on drugs away from "me too" products, which are just costly versions of existing generic medicines, toward products that yield far greater health benefits.

Moving out of the health sector, agricultural applications of the AMC have been explored. New, environmentally friendly fertilizers and pesticides, for example, or better seeds for crops that are staples in poor countries could be good targets for a future AMC. An AMC could potentially be a useful means of attracting innovators to work on improved safety gear for firefighters and other first responders. If police departments across multiple states pooled funds, they might be able to incentivize the development and manufacture of "personalized guns" that could be used only by a particular police officer. An AMC might be the right way to incentivize the creation of technologies for clean transportation or solutions to other parts of the clean-energy puzzle and, eventually, even innovations that address complex social challenges, such as homelessness. In all of these cases, the public sector would need to be likely to buy the products if they existed—and an AMC could help to make that future market visible to innovators and investors today.

AMCs are a clever addition to our toolbox of innovation incentives.[3] The experiences with the pneumococcal AMC, now well along in implementation, offer confidence that such a tool can be created to solve a specific problem—and can work. The trick now is to match the concept of an AMC with a particular innovation challenge and to find funders who are ready, willing, and able to send a strong signal that today's R&D effort will be duly rewarded tomorrow.

---

3 Center for Accelerating Innovation and Impact, "Health Markets for Global Health: A Market Shaping Primer," U.S. Agency for International Development (2014).

RUTH LEVINE *is the program director of global development and population at the William and Flora Hewlett Foundation, and previously was the deputy assistant administrator for policy, planning and learning at the U.S. Agency for International Development. She has a PhD in economic demography from Johns Hopkins University, and led the Center for Global Development's work on global health policy from 2002 to 2010.*

SCALING PROGRAMS THAT WORK BY PAYING FOR SUCCESS

Tamar Bauer and Roxane White
Nurse-Family Partnership

If parenthood is the toughest job you will ever love, then Pay for Success may be the most grueling growth strategy we will someday celebrate. We often get asked about Pay for Success and how to put together "a deal." And we find that the best guidance we can provide is under the category of "lessons learned" or "things I wished I'd known." As two experienced professionals with expertise in the nonprofit and governmental sectors, we often remind each other that these deals are among the most complicated and interesting (on good days) work that we have done.

Our goal with this essay is to honestly reflect on some of what we have learned with the hope that the paths become easier. And we start with a caveat: Because Pay for Success is labor-, and resource-intensive, we recommend that it be the "last and also the latest tool in the toolbox." At this early stage in the development of this field, we urge policymakers not to use Pay for Success to replace existing funding streams but instead to supplement them. Otherwise, while deal construction is underway and when some deals fall apart, families will be left with fewer services and agencies will struggle with unpredictable futures.

At the same time, we are excited about ways to simplify Pay for Success and also use new innovations in outcomes-oriented funding to expand services and reach more people. We see in Pay for Success the potential to scale programs in a way that aligns funding with the outcomes orientation we have built over decades at Nurse-Family Partnership (NFP), a national program serving first-time, low-income mothers with home visits by certified nurses. The promise of unlocking new sources of aligned capital to expand services for the families and communities that need them is worth fighting for.

SHIFTING TO AN OUTCOMES MINDSET

Due to decades of ongoing work by Dr. David Olds and colleagues, there is a powerful body of evidence demonstrating the impact of the NFP model and a national quality assurance system that supports communities in replicating NFP with fidelity. But because, like all social service providers, we operate in a funding system that pays for activities, not results, we have grown by shoe-horning activities-based funding (e.g., government contracts that allow NFP to hire more nurses or to bill for more services provided to mothers) into our outcomes-oriented organization that carefully tracks the difference these services make in the lives of mothers and children. Pay for Success is attractive to us because it aligns funding with the focus on outcomes, which has always been core to NFP.

Our research partners were invaluable in the first step required to engage in Pay for Success work, delving into identifying three to five viable outcome metrics for Pay for Success from NFP's larger body of demonstrated outcomes. We worked on model impacts, health economics, and replication data. We focused on those outcomes that achieve the most meaningful impacts for mothers and babies, produce the most significant savings for state governments, and can be efficiently measured in the Pay for Success measurement period.

The second step is the most complex: using existing and often imperfect data on baseline levels of impact to project the size of the effect in that community for the selected outcome metrics. Given the many "what ifs," it is challenging to negotiate reasonable effect sizes that ultimately drive success payments. Some examples include the difficulty of reliably predicting future trends in community demographics and population health that can and will change the impact that any individual model, like NFP, can have. This work requires intensive analysis during deal construction but does not require a shift in how we deliver our services. In contrast, there is an intensified focus on enrollment as a result of Pay for Success.

One observation about our South Carolina deal may be useful. In South Carolina, a randomized controlled trial evaluation will be used to assess whether NFP can achieve the outcome metrics while also reducing costs through model modernization strategies, such as telemedicine and tailoring visit schedules to align more closely with the risk levels of each mother. This is requiring a deep dive to determine more precisely which program elements are most critical to outcomes achievement.

REFLECTIONS ON LESSONS WE LEARNED

Emphasizing that we are very much in the early stages of Pay for Success, and learning each day, we can safely share these thoughts.

First, to make future projects more efficient to develop and launch, we are refining a national Pay for Success framework for NFP. This includes outcome metric options, but also a plan for which issues to tackle first in the deal construction process so we know if there is enough alignment in priorities to invest more time. Another element to this is the need for a contingency fund as part of the budget, since modeled programmatic costs will have some variation in practice.

Second, governments have surprisingly different appetites to pay for tangible vs. intangible outcomes, which is key to determining whether the math will work for the deal. For example, fewer child injuries requiring hospitalization reduces health care costs, a tangible savings to government. In contrast, improvements in quality of life from lower infant mortality rates produce intangible savings to society, measured in the value of a child's life. It is also important which level of government benefits from outcomes. Federal participation in paying for outcomes would be very helpful for NFP, given that 62 percent of our government savings accrue to Medicaid.[1]

Third, there are key partners that have to be included. For providers, this work would be very difficult, especially at this early stage, to complete without an intermediary like Social Finance and the Harvard Kennedy School Government Performance Lab Innovation Fellows, but it is critical for providers to be at the table to reflect the needs of families served. Influential funders can play a vital role in encouraging state and community leaders to move a Pay for Success project forward in a responsible way and in creating a sense of urgency. Pay for Success deals seem to periodically run into a risk of crumbling under the weight of their complexity, and funders can be helpful in mobilizing toward the end goal.

---

1 Ted R. Miller, "Projected Outcomes of Nurse-Family Partnership Home Visitation During 1996–2013, USA," *Prevention Science* 16 (6) (2015): 765–777. Return cited here is based on investment calculator updated by Dr. Miller on March 7, 2017.

Fourth, prepare for a roller-coaster ride. We have worked with three separate states on Pay for Success deals for the past two years and have launched one project (in South Carolina) so far. We often resort to labeling our Pay for Success projects as in the "zombie stage." It can be hard to decipher when the projects are dead and when they will resurface. For example, in South Carolina, there were numerous points when the complexity of data sharing and evaluation or significant staffing changes resulted in long, painful delays. A major health crisis led to delays in another state. Pay for Success is unlikely to be the top priority for any government, but with persistence and lots of weekend and holiday work, the projects have come back to the priority work list and proceeded with great speed—only to completely stall a few weeks later.

Finally, enabling legislation for outcome payments is useful, but it also may be helpful for success payment funds to be captured in a place where they cannot be swept away in the future. This is why we needed Children's Trust of South Carolina, where funds could not be re-appropriated by a new administration.

LOOKING FORWARD

Even for an organization celebrated for its data-driven culture and outcomes focus, NFP has had to put our performance management "on steroids" to meet the requirements of the South Carolina Pay for Success project. Pay for Success typically requires providers to develop and adhere to monthly enrollment schedules that are tied to project budgets. To stay on schedule and within budget, we now track enrollment daily rather than retroactively reviewing it each month or so. This requires dedicated staff and is part of what is transformative about Pay for Success. This will lead to more efficient use of public dollars by making sure that every available dollar is used to serve as many families as possible. But might it also perversely drive enrollment away from those with the greatest needs?

During the deal construction phase, it is important to recognize when to persevere and when to exercise the discipline to say no. It is important to recognize when Pay for Success is not the right tool to reach the people you are serving. For example, size matters. Small projects may lead to unacceptably high costs per person served overall due to fixed Pay for Success transactional costs, as we found in one potential deal so far. Or small projects may present challenges with statistical power, where we have too small of an intervention or a control group to be able to prove causality.

Pay for Success is very complex work that requires staying power. The headaches are worth it if we can simplify the process and allow successful programs to keep serving families. Sustainability could be a powerful provider incentive. If a provider delivers on the promise of Pay for Success and meets outcome metrics, government should make success payments and also commit to sustaining services going forward. That would be truly transformative.

If Pay for Success works at a larger scale, then NFP can realize a vision that we've shared with supporters for years: reaching every mom who needs us, sparking multi-generational change, and creating pathways out of poverty. Pay for Success holds the same promise for other participating nonprofits striving to reach their goals. In that way, despite challenges and drawbacks, Pay for Success holds the exciting promise of unleashing major, new sources of funding that can become models for a new wave of highly effective public-private partnerships.

———

TAMAR BAUER *is chief policy and government affairs officer of Nurse-Family Partnership (NFP). Bauer leads a national team that develops and executes Pay for Success, health care integration, and other strategies to catalyze government support for NFP's evidence-based home visiting model for first-time, low-income women and children. Bauer holds a BA in history and music from Wesleyan University and a JD from Rutgers University School of Law.*

ROXANE WHITE *was appointed president and chief executive officer of Nurse-Family Partnership (NFP) in November 2014. Prior to that time, she was chief of staff for mayor of Denver and then governor of Colorado, John Hickenlooper. She was head of the Denver Department of Human Services and Medicaid before her appointment as chief of staff. White was a 2015 Aspen Ascend Fellow and serves as a member of the Urban Institute U.S. Poverty/Mobility Partnership Group. Under her leadership, NFP launched the first Pay for Success project in South Carolina, which will allow an additional 3,200 babies and moms to enroll and benefit from this high-impact intervention.*

THE STRONG FAMILIES FUND
Outcomes-Driven Resident Service Coordination

Kimberlee Cornett
The Kresge Foundation

The need for quality affordable housing is large and growing: 54 percent of families pay more than half of their monthly income on rent. Having a stable, safe place to live that doesn't cost an entire paycheck is crucial to low-income Americans participating fully in the economy. Beyond that fact, research also shows strong physiological connections between poverty and toxic stress and health outcomes for children and families. In one distressed ZIP Code in St. Louis, 52.5 percent of families live in poverty. A child born and raised here is expected to live only 69 years—ten years below the national average, per a PolicyLink report.[1] And children born into poverty usually stay there; data show children born into the bottom quintile in terms of family income have only an eight percent chance of moving to the top quintile.[2]

Research also shows that outcomes can improve when a social service coordinator is available to families living in affordable housing. This coordinator helps connect residents to services onsite and in the community, including transportation, banking and financial coaching, food, quality early childhood programs, children and youth educational and enrichment programs, health care, job skills and workforce training—you name it. These coordinators also increase the social cohesion of affordable rental property communities, creating opportunities for people to engage in community activities, rely on and learn from their neighbors, and experience less isolation along the way.

---

1 Kalima Rose and Teddy Ký-Nam Miller, "Healthy Communities of Opportunity: An Equity Blueprint to Address America's Housing Challenges," Policy Link (2016), available at http://www.policylink.org/sites/default/files/HCO_Web_Only.pdf.

2 Raj Chetty et al., "Where is the Land of Opportunity? The Geography of Intergenerational Mobility in the United States" (June 2014), available at http://www.rajchetty.com/chettyfiles/mobility_geo.pdf.

So we know families thrive with access to better supports that connect them to a range of services that can help them obtain successful employment, education, and health outcomes. But service coordinators are generally paid for through cash flows generated by the property, grants secured by the developer, or agreements with third-party service providers. Long-term, stable funding for service coordination is elusive. That's why The Kresge Foundation's social investment practice team began to hunt for a solution through a pay-for-performance investment.

The road to this innovative investment opened only after Kresge's human services team, in response to growing demand from the field to enhance the quality and resources available to tenants in affordable housing, first made a grant to the Stewards of Affordable Housing for the Future to develop new metrics related to outcomes for low-income housing residents. It was the first attempt to create a standard "menu" of metrics for multiple developers to use to assess the link between their housing developments and the outcomes of the people living in them. It included performance measures from income and assets, health, housing stability, community engagement, and education. It would become a crucial underpinning of our pay-for-performance work, giving us the firm data and consistent reporting criteria—across developers and developments—to assess outcomes and make a larger argument about the cost-effectiveness of service coordination.

With that matrix in hand and the desire to put it to use, we centered on our guiding question: How could a fund be structured to incentivize developers and investors to invest not only in building housing units but also to implement high-quality, outcomes-driven service coordination?

The result was the Strong Families Fund, a Kresge–led, multi-partner effort to fund up to ten years of resident service coordination in Low Income Housing Tax Credit (LIHTC)–financed family housing through a pay-for-performance, incentivized loan structure. In a LIHTC deal, a developer applies for, and is awarded by a housing finance agency, a certain number of tax credits for an affordable housing project. The developer then takes those credits to a bank or other investor to sell a partnership interest in the project, to get the upfront capital needed to build the development. The banks (now partners) use the tax credits to offset future federal taxes (and in some cases, meet their obligations under the Community Reinvestment Act), saving themselves on next year's tax bill, while the developer now has the cash on hand to construct or rehabilitate the property. The developer agrees to keep the property affordable for 15 years. Using pay-for-performance mechanics, the Strong Families Fund was built to provide LIHTC developers a ten-year funding source for resident service coordination when there is evidence that resident outcomes are tracked and are improving.

The Strong Families Fund, which closed in 2015, proposed to include $50 million in tax equity from Goldman Sachs and Key Bank, along with grants, guarantees, and loans from Kresge and the Robert Wood Johnson Foundation. Kresge invested in four organizations participating in the fund: a $2 million guarantee to the National Affordable Housing Trust and a $1.5 million guarantee to Cinnaire, Inc., both syndicators of LIHTC equity; a $3 million program-related loan to Community Development Trust, a community development financial institution (CDFI) and the provider of permanent financing; and Kresge's human services program made a $1.25 million grant over three years to the Corporation for Supportive Housing, also a CDFI, which would provide technical assistance and support the fund's operations. To support "performance payments" to developers, the Robert Wood Johnson Foundation will make up to $5 million in grants available.

To generate a funding source that would enable developers to consistently provide high-quality service coordination, the effort called on using the following levers:

- The release of three months of the operating deficit reserve (and replacement with the Kresge guarantee) to pay for service coordination in years one and two;

- Up to $90,000 annually in performance payments to developers in years three through ten; and

- An additional equity payment from the LIHTC investor to the developer in year ten if outcomes are achieved.

Projects that received investment agreed to establish baseline measures at the start, implement a data-driven service coordination program in

Figure 1. Strong Families Fund

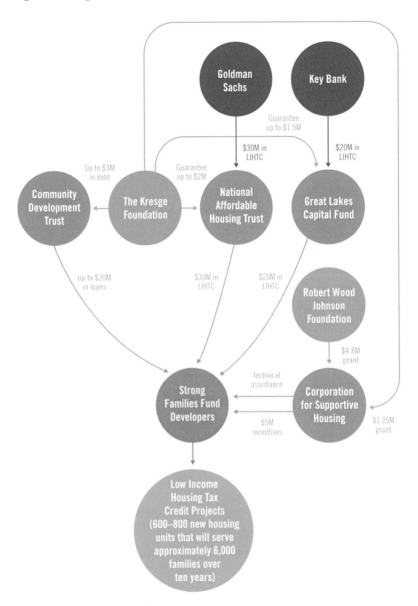

collaboration with the Corporation for Supportive Housing, and report on the results annually. Developers are required to report the resident data and, if outcomes improve, will earn a performance payment up to

$90,000 annually for ten years—funded through grants from Kresge and the Robert Wood Johnson Foundation.

Reaching agreement with so many parties required enormous perseverance and commitment on the part of many. Everyone was optimistic about the opportunity to influence the field and improve outcomes for families. Going in, we thought the Strong Families Fund would finance up to eight projects, generating 600 to 700 new units of service-enriched housing. We believed then, as we do now, that through an outcomes-oriented development, we could strengthen the connection between better service coordination and improved resident and property outcomes. We also hoped to create a business case to attract housing finance agencies, private investors, or other public agencies to step up to provide the incentive payments—after seeing the data demonstrating the cost-effectiveness of such an approach.

Less than two years in, we have some lessons learned and an emerging question to wrestle with: Were we a little too early, a bit ahead of the market, to test this model?

The developers involved were all financially and operationally strong, they were all mission-driven, and most had participated in the creation of the outcomes menu. This group was advanced in its understanding of how to operationalize service coordination. The first challenge was reaching consensus about what measures were meaningful and could be tracked accurately and consistently at a series of properties owned and managed by different developers.

It made sense to work with the strongest affordable-housing developers. But unexpected challenges soon emerged. Because of their relative strength, these developers can command very high equity pricing for their LIHTC deals—in some cases, higher than what was offered through the Strong Families Fund. And, although it offered additional financial benefits via the performance payments, developers often saw it in their best business interests to get the highest equity pricing possible at closing and not take a chance on the performance payments down the road. It's basically like this: If I offered you $100 for running a mile now or $130 in three years, but only if you improved your time in the mile each year, which deal would you pick? Although these developers are undoubtedly committed to the principles of service coordination, we realized there is a lot of truth in the adage "cash is king."

These challenges led to a slower-than-anticipated deployment of the Strong Families Fund's capital. By the end of 2016, only three transactions had closed. All parties involved discussed whether there was still enough to be learned from the experiment. Ultimately, we believed three more properties were in the pipeline and would close in 2017.

And then we had an election.

With the new administration, uncertainty hit the markets as all waited to see what the election results would mean for so many related areas of work. Early on, there was one area with a high degree of clarity: Throughout the 2016 presidential campaign, conversation centered on tax reform and, specifically, cutting the corporate tax rate. Minimizing a company's federal tax liability is the primary reason that banks and corporations invest in the LIHTC market. Banks are also motived by receiving Community Reinvestment Act credit for their investments in LIHTC projects. With the prospect of lower taxes and reduced value of the credits to corporations, the market for tax credits slowed considerably, even before the new president took office. In some cases, transactions can still be financially viable—even with lower equity prices—but others will need to find capital resources to fill the funding gaps. Although the Strong Families Fund partners are optimistic that the remaining three deals will close, the outcome for the winter of 2017 is less certain.

So back to our question: Were we too early for this model? And what lessons can we offer to others? There is plenty to be learned about what to do and what not to do when trying to introduce a new pay-for-performance element into an established market, such as LIHTC equity. We clearly had assembled the right panel of partners who were all aligned around the goals and ambitions of the Strong Families Fund. However, we had not assessed the business drivers of those partners fully, and that proved to be an unexpected and high hurdle. We also learned that new products and fund structures take much longer to be accepted in the marketplace; development projects tend to take at least two years to get online. And, we learned that you never know for sure what significant political-context changes are coming or how they might impact the market.

Is the Strong Families Fund worth the investment and the effort? In terms of outcomes, the initiative, at a minimum, will collect and understand resident and property data outcomes for residents in 370 units across three affordable housing developments, with the potential for data from an additional nearly 520 units as more transactions close. We don't regret investing our capital toward this effort and are waiting to see if that investment can produce the impact we truly wanted to make.

There are also positive lessons we see now. The Strong Families Fund has given momentum to establishing a uniform set of metrics in the affordable-housing sector, to the value of connecting residents to services, and to the importance of finding a predictable funding source for service coordination. Development and testing a protocol for data collection remains a fruitful and positive idea in an increasingly outcomes-driven market.

If we want the housing sector to strive not only to produce units but also to improve residents' lives, we need policies, public agencies, and nonprofit and for-profit developers to focus as intensively on outcomes as they do on the costs of "sticks and bricks." Over the next ten years, the Strong Families Fund will be able to tell a data-driven story of exactly how far six developments and their residents have gone toward achieving that goal.

KIMBERLEE CORNETT *is director of the social investment practice at The Kresge Foundation where she oversees the foundation's $350 million impact investing commitment. She guides the foundation's efforts to use a range of capital tools—debt, deposits, equity, and guarantees—to affect complex social problems. Before joining the foundation in 2010, Cornett was vice president at Enterprise Community Investment where she led the investment management division. Earlier in her career, Cornett was a White House Fellow in the Clinton administration and served at the executive level of the U.S. Small Business Administration. She is a graduate of Hood College.*

THE POWER OF INCENTIVE PRIZE COMPETITIONS

Jennifer Bravo, Christopher Frangione,
and Stephanie Wander
XPRIZE Foundation

At the Wendy Schmidt Ocean Health XPRIZE awards ceremony, murmurs rippled through the crowd. The $2 million prize competition to develop better pH sensors for the measurement of ocean acidification (the increasing chemical imbalance in our oceans due to excessive carbon in our atmosphere) resulted in some surprising outcomes. The competition had two tracks — one for better accuracy (best performance) and one for affordability (cost and ease of use). In an unlikely victory, team Sunburst Sensors, a small business and relatively new market entrant based in the landlocked state of Montana, had won both first-place prizes, garnering $1.5 million. Their approach was novel: using an autonomous spectro-photometric process in ocean conditions. Their technology demonstrated unprecedented accuracy in both coastal and deep-sea environments up to 3,000 meters. Sunburst Sensors is currently looking to expand its small company and bring high-tech jobs to Missoula. In the accuracy competition, Sunburst Sensors had beaten industry leader and incumbent Team DuraFET, who won the second-place prize. Gracious in defeat, Team DuraFET announced that they would donate their second-place purse of $250,000 to the University of Washington to enable them to add pH sensors on profiling floats around the world, further expanding oceanographic and ocean acidification monitoring. Met with resounding applause, both teams illustrated the power of prizes to inspire teams to compete — not just for the purse — but to achieve innovative breakthroughs for the betterment of humanity.

We are living in extraordinary times, when technology is allowing ordinary individuals to accomplish what was once the province of only the wealthy and powerful. Small teams of innovators are creating breakthroughs that touch the lives of billions, tackling challenges and solving problems once thought to be solely the domain of governments. Incentive prize competitions can challenge these innovators to solve some of our most difficult, grand challenges.

Incentive prize competitions are different from *post facto* awards for accomplishments, such as the Nobel Prize and Pulitzer Prize. Instead of serving as an acknowledgement, the purse (cash or, in some cases, resources or opportunities) works as an incentive to motivate innovators to address a particular problem, usually one where the best solution or approach is unknown. It can also be used to draw public attention to an important issue facing humanity. Although the purse/prize itself is important (prizes can range from opportunities alone to millions of dollars), it is important to note that it is often not about the money for competitors and that a well-defined and executed prize competition can have extraordinary results.

Historically, governments used prizes to solve large, intractable problems. In 1714, the British government used a prize to challenge innovators to measure longitude, a barrier facing the maritime industry. Deviating from the more traditional approach of celestial navigation, clockmaker John Harrison cracked the problem by creating an extremely accurate maritime clock, radically improving the safety and efficiency of global trade.

Most people are familiar with Charles Lindbergh's extraordinary transatlantic flight in 1927, but what few people know is that he did so in pursuit of the Orteig Prize, a $25,000 purse to the first person to complete a nonstop, solo voyage between New York and Paris (or Paris and New York). Lindbergh's winning flight captured the attention of the press, public, and investors, accelerating the development of the aviation industry as we know it today.

For a time, prizes fell out of favor as research and development primarily became the purview of governments. But in 1996, Peter Diamandis launched the Ansari XPRIZE for private spaceflight, resulting in a prize renaissance where prize competitions are frequently used by both the public and private sectors.

PRIZES ARE POWERFUL

Prize competitions are powerful tools that anyone, including corporations, nonprofits, and governments, can use to address specific challenges. They promote innovation, offer financial benefits, and increase public awareness.

Prizes promote innovation by: 1) encouraging new ideas; 2) proving the hardest test cases; 3) building community; and 4) democratizing innovation. Prizes define problems rather than solutions, allowing a diverse crowd of innovators to develop a wide variety of possible solutions. In effect, they allow investors to bet on a portfolio of ideas versus investing in only a few organizations with a narrow set of solutions. Prizes can be designed to address the most difficult aspects of a problem, such as the most critical use cases or the hardest-to-reach constituents. Frequently, the resulting solution has a much wider application. Not being near the ocean, Sunburst Sensors might have been overlooked, but by participating in the Wendy Schmidt Ocean Health XPRIZE, they were able to validate a different technological approach and see it pitted side-by-side with the current best-in-class solution. Also, they proved their solution at depth and far from the coast, one of the world's most challenging environments for pH sensors, thus proving that it will function in less difficult conditions.

Prizes build community. They are as much about collaboration as they are about competition. Prize competitions galvanize resources, encourage conversations, and engage supporters in pursuit of a common goal. Where permissible, teams sometimes combine to improve their chances of winning, but they have also been known to make selfless gestures in support of other teams because they believe in the importance of solving the problem or appreciate another team's efforts. In addition to donating their prize purse to the University of Washington, Team DuraFET supported and collaborated with other teams, including donating to one team's crowdfunding campaign to raise the funds needed to attend competition trials and collaborating post-prize with another team whose goal is to enable surfers to capture ocean health data via their surfboards. These acts occur so frequently during XPRIZE competitions that they are referred to as "coopetition."

Prizes also offer unique financial benefits by: 1) paying only for successful outcomes; 2) potentially resulting in exponential gains; and 3) providing financial leverage. The largest expenditure for a prize occurs only after a solution that meets the criteria is achieved. In this way, it makes highly efficient use of limited resources. Prizes can result in extraordinary and exponential advancements by requiring teams to address well-scoped problems with non-prescriptive solution requirements which, if solved, might enable several additional problems to be solved down the line. Prizes incentivize many teams to work on a solution. This increases the amount of aggregate investment in research and development to solve a problem and reduces the risk that a successful solution will not be developed. Teams competing for the Ansari XPRIZE for private space flight spent a combined $100 million in pursuit of a $10 million purse. The challenge was audacious but achievable, well-scoped, and non-prescriptive: The winning team must build a reliable, reusable, privately financed, manned spaceship capable of carrying three people to 100 kilometers above Earth's surface twice within two weeks. This one challenge dramatically accelerated the private space flight industry.

Prizes also build awareness by influencing, exciting, and educating the public. Prizes issue a clear call to action and tell a simple, yet powerful, story about a challenge that needs to be addressed. In the Wendy Schmidt Ocean Health XPRIZE, the competing teams and XPRIZE spent hundreds of hours engaging with the press and social media, garnering significant media attention as well as direct engagement through education and aquarium outreach programs.

Prize competitions democratize innovation, meaning that they ask innovators from anywhere, with any background or experience, to tackle a challenge and create diverse solutions. Most important, good prizes endeavor to create as objective and fair a playing field as possible, enabling great ideas from unlikely sources to shine. It does not matter how old participants are, where they went to school, or how long they have been working in the field—if they can solve the challenge, they win. This is even more relevant today, as teams have the ability to take advantage of exponential technologies (e.g., artificial intelligence, virtual reality, big data) to develop solutions in pursuit of prizes. Prizes democratize innovation because they encourage the creation of diverse, cross-disciplinary teams, and incentivize and validate new or unlikely thinkers. Good prizes allow anyone to compete, encourage teams to identify and incorporate people with diverse skills sets into their teams, and often provide incentives (e.g., solution testing, deployment, training) to support teams as they attempt to reach the goal set by the competition. These resources help prepare teams for a successful run in competitive markets after the prize is completed.

For example, in 2010, a team of high school students from West Philadelphia High School Academy of Automotive and Mechanical

Engineering competed in the $10 million Progressive Automotive XPRIZE. Despite coming from an economically disadvantaged and very low-performing school, this student team competed against teams of well-funded, seasoned engineers. The Hybrid X team made a strong showing in their attempt to build a car capable of achieving 100 miles per gallon equivalent. Although Hybrid X did not win the prize, they won the hearts and minds of all who heard their story. As part of their incredible journey, in 2011 they sat with Michelle Obama at the State of the Union, were featured in newspapers, and were lauded by Philadelphia's mayor. Members of the team were later accepted to The New School and Penn State. Their story showcases the power of a prize competition to incentivize innovators from anywhere to tackle our toughest challenges and change their own lives in the process.

PRIZES ARE VERSATILE AND EFFECTIVE BUT ARE NOT SUITABLE FOR ALL PROBLEMS

Prizes are strong yet flexible tools for creating change. Prizes are especially effective for engineering challenges and validating technology. The Ansari XPRIZE required scientists and engineers to tackle the challenge by applying and integrating known technology and approaches to the space race is new ways. It also had a clear and simple method for proving that the challenge criteria had been met. An important value offered by a prize competition can be the testing of solutions, especially prototypes, to identify which one is truly superior at solving the problem.

Prizes work best when targeting a specific problem and can be highly effective when addressing a critical piece of a larger, more systemic problem. By defining specific elements to target, a prize competition can help chip away at larger, less tractable problems. Prizes work well by addressing necessary elements on the path toward addressing the problem in its entirety. For example, the Wendy Schmidt Ocean Health XPRIZE may unlock exponential advances in addressing ocean acidification and climate change by enabling oceans to be healthier and more accurately measured, understood, and managed by the world's scientists.

It is important to note, however, that a prize competition may not be the right tool for tackling a problem in the following circumstances: 1) when a large systemic problem needs to be solved in its entirety; 2) when policy or regulatory barriers exist; 3) when a thriving market or many players exist with significant funding; or 4) when basic research is needed. A prize may not be able to address all aspects of a systemic problem that may have many barriers to solutions. For example, a prize attempting to cure a disease or "end" homelessness may be too complex or inoperable or may require such large incentives as to be unrealistic.

TIPS FOR DESIGNING EFFECTIVE PRIZES

Prizes should be considered one of many innovation tools that can help us solve difficult problems. Even though prizes are powerful, they are not a panacea. Prizes must be well-designed, well-targeted, and well-operated to be successful. Good prize designers: 1) understand what a prize can and cannot do; 2) ensure that a prize has sufficient resources; 3) design to the market; 4) incentivize the right thing; and 5) consider the timing. Prizes succeed when they target areas where they are most effective, are scoped to balance expectations, and are part of a supported ecosystem that includes staff to operate the competition, judges to validate the competition, and resources that directly support teams, such as by providing access to experts and funding.

Good prize design identifies barriers to innovation in a market and overcomes or bypasses those barriers. When designed properly, prizes can catalyze stagnant markets and stimulate innovation. "You get what you incentivize" is the prize designer's mantra. Be careful not to include too many criteria or inadvertently incentivize an unintended outcome. The best prize designs are simple, elegant, and clear. Good prizes have a sufficiently long timeline to allow for innovation, yet are short enough so as to not lose the attention of the audience or allow market forces to move faster than the competition itself. Tougher problems usually take longer to solve, so consider the time horizon carefully. Look out for accelerating and advancing markets, as advancement is sometimes unpredictable.

By following these principles, XPRIZE has become increasingly effective at designing prizes. It has expanded to new topic areas and implements prizes in new ways. For example, XPRIZE has expanded from prize competitions for the development of novel technology and hardware solutions (e.g., Ansari XPRIZE and Wendy Schmidt Ocean Health XPRIZE) to population- and application-based competitions, where teams compete to show that they can help a group of people acquire new skills or apply exponential technologies to grand challenges in novel ways (e.g., Global Learning XPRIZE; Barbara Bush Foundation Adult Literacy XPRIZE presented by Dollar General Literacy Foundation; and IBM Watson A.I. XPRIZE, a Cognitive Computing Challenge).

PRIZES FOR SOCIAL OUTCOMES

Although prizes may not be the best solution to address social problems in totality, they can be very effective at accelerating progress and advancement. A well-designed prize targeted at the right part of a systemic problem can tip over a pivotal domino in a problem chain and result in exponential benefits. Through the Barbara Bush Foundation Adult Literacy XPRIZE presented by Dollar General Literacy Foundation, XPRIZE challenged teams of educators, mobile developers, and innovators to develop mobile learning solutions that would improve the basic English literacy skills of adults in the United States. The competition catalyzed a network of partners, including Comcast, the Philadelphia Mayor's Office of Adult Education, the Los Angeles Unified School District, and the Dallas County Community College District, and resulted in a 20-fold increase in the number of mobile learning apps available to adults at these lowest literacy levels, both by accelerating the pace at which incumbents transitioned to mobile platforms and by bringing new entrants into the field. By improving the literacy skills of adult learners and providing low-cost, easily accessible learning solutions, the prize will increase the percentage of adult learners able to access educational services, improve participants' access to information, improve their navigation of health and financial challenges, and increase their children's chances of succeeding in school.

Prizes create an incredible platform to compare and test solutions, especially where the best approaches may not be known. Imagine a competition to help change outcomes for a population of people experiencing homelessness, where teams compete to see which program provides the best improvement in people's access to care and housing. Imagine teams of technologists and educators competing to reduce achievement gaps in schools or improve entry-level employees' access to the skills they need to succeed in the workplace.

THE PROMISE OF PRIZES

Prizes hold significant promise for widespread use. They can enable us to solve global challenges by identifying the right problems to tackle, by motivating solvers to come to us, and by bridging the gap in incentives to bring solutions to market. Prize competitions are proven tools that enable us to crowdsource solutions to some of the world's grand challenges. They tell powerful stories and change how people view global problems and their solutions.

XPRIZE believes that the prize model is one tool to harness technological advances and the crowd to help achieve a world of abundance—food, water, education, health, and wellbeing—for all of our planet's inhabitants. XPRIZE believes that there are no problems that cannot be solved. There are plenty of untapped minds out there just waiting to solve them.

———

JENNIFER BRAVO is a senior director at the XPRIZE Foundation. Bravo leads a core pillar of the foundation's work (Visioneers), which leverages XPRIZE's global community of innovators, thought leaders, and entrepreneurs to design competitions that tackle the world's grand challenges. Prior to leading Visioneers, she was an integral member of the foundation's prize development team. Before joining XPRIZE in 2013, Bravo worked closely with government agencies, nonprofit organizations, and academic institutions for over a decade to develop and implement policy in the public interest. She earned her BA from California State University, Sacramento in anthropology, and her MPP from the University of Southern California.

CHRISTOPHER FRANGIONE is the executive director of prizes at the XPRIZE Foundation, overseeing the department that designs and operates XPRIZE's incentivized innovation competitions. Frangione also runs XPRIZE's government relations initiative. He speaks often on exponential technologies, the incentivized prize model, and harnessing the crowd, and has testified in front of both the U.S. House and Senate. Frangione holds a BA in environmental policy from Colby College and master's degrees in business administration and environmental management from Duke University.

STEPHANIE WANDER is a senior manager of prize development at the XPRIZE Foundation, where she recently led the design of the IBM Watson AI XPRIZE: A Cognitive Computing Challenge, as well as the design of competitions for workplace skills, urban aviation, and tissue engineering. She is also a contributing designer on the Wendy Schmidt Ocean Health XPRIZE and the Global Learning XPRIZE competitions. Wander is a graduate of the UCLA Anderson School of Management and Northwestern University. She serves on the advisory board of the Brink Institute.

CAN THE HOUSING TAX CREDIT BE A MODEL FOR CONNECTING CAPITAL TO MORE HUMAN-CENTERED OUTCOMES?

Terri Ludwig
Enterprise Community Partners, Inc.

In Cleveland's Buckeye neighborhood stands Saint Luke's Manor, a former hospital that closed in 1999 and remained vacant for more than a decade. Over time, Saint Luke's became a target for vandalism, an eyesore for residents, and a symbol of neighborhood neglect and decay. Its surrounding streets became lined with empty lots and boarded homes.

Fast-forward to today. Saint Luke's is an anchor for the community: home to 137 quality, affordable senior apartments, office space for nonprofits, and an 80,000-square-foot learning campus that hosts a top-performing charter school and after-school programs through the local Boys and Girls Club. Saint Luke's is located on the transit line and is surrounded by new homes being built and sold on adjoining streets, reflecting the broader neighborhood's revitalization. One current tenant of Saint Luke's says, "I have no fear now that I live at Saint Luke's to leave my windows open. I am proud to be living in such a beautiful place."

What explains this transformation? How did a complex, multi-faceted effort requiring millions of dollars in financing—far more than the local government or foundation dollars available to meet it—come together so effectively? The answer: the federal tax code.

In addition to the determination and effectiveness of local partners, the transformation was made possible by investment tax credits that encourage the flow of private capital into low-income communities and demonstrate outcomes-based financing in action—in particular, the Low Income Housing Tax Credit (the Housing Credit).

HOUSING TAX CREDITS ARE A LONGSTANDING PAY FOR SUCCESS PROGRAM

For three decades, the community development sector has used the Housing Credit to provide housing for people who would otherwise struggle to find an affordable place to call home. The Housing Credit is an undeniable success story in public-private partnerships, financing virtually all of the country's affordable housing construction since the late 1980s—over three million affordable homes and counting.[1]

We should be proud of this. These are quality homes that give people stability and an essential platform to opportunity—quality education, jobs, health care, transportation, and other critical community services. Less understood is that the Housing Credit is a true pay-for-outcomes financing program: The federal government pays for those high-quality homes only if and when the homes have been built and leased to the target population.

The success of the Housing Credit invites us to consider how we might build on the model. Could we use this proven approach to physical capital development (real estate) to develop *human* capital (health, education, etc.)? What if we were to include metrics that revealed how the residents in homes financed by the Housing Credit are doing, such as their health or their access to quality schools and jobs? What if we had an evaluative component that goes beyond the "bricks and sticks" and creates financial incentives to reward developers who can demonstrate that their residents are positively, *measurably* transforming their lives? And what if we provided resources and incentives to reward those outcomes? What if, instead of—or in addition to—tying capital to the provision of quality, affordable homes, we tied it to outcomes like "ready to learn at kindergarten," or "graduation from high school," or the "successful long-term employment for a former prisoner?"

Three decades after the origination of the Housing Credit, the time is right to look ahead to the next three decades. In addition to expanding the Housing Credit program to enable the provision of more badly needed affordable homes, we should consider how we might build on the model to produce all types of transformative outcomes for residents—not just

---

1   National Council of State Housing Agencies, "2016 Message on the Housing Credit" (February 26, 2016), available at https://www.ncsha.org/resource/2016-message-housing-credit.

by providing access to housing, but by ensuring that their homes serve as true platforms to good health, quality education, employment, and whatever else they need to prosper.

How the Low Income Housing Tax Credit Works

For a project to be eligible for the Housing Credit, a certain percentage of units must be rent-restricted and occupied by households earning below a certain income level. Private investors, not the government, provide money to cover development costs and are on the hook for most financial risks. In exchange, the investor is given a federal tax credit, redeemable only when construction is completed and the low-income residents move into the new homes. The final payments come when the investor receives IRS Form 8609, a certification of a successfully operating affordable housing project that is leased to low-income renters.

Importantly, the rent must stay affordable for a minimum of 30 years (although in most cases the affordability restrictions are longer), and there is also ongoing monitoring of the property to ensure that it stays affordable. During the initial 15-year window, the government can recapture tax credits in the event of noncompliance. This pay-for-performance mechanism has an elegant way of infusing market discipline while ensuring that the federal government pays only when the desired outcome is achieved.[2]

Building on the success of the Housing Credit, the New Markets Tax Credit was created in 2000 to encourage private investment for "near bankable" deals in low-income communities where capital doesn't naturally tend to flow.[3] The program allows individual and corporate investors to reduce their federal income tax burden in exchange for a qualified equity investment in a community development entity, which uses that money to fund businesses and real estate projects, such as charter schools, health care clinics, and other key community assets.

---

2 For an overview of the Housing Credit, see David J. Erickson, *Housing Policy Revolution: Networks and Neighborhoods* (Washington, DC: Urban Institute Press, 2009).

3 For a good overview on the origins of the New Markets Tax Credit program, see Benson F. Roberts, "The Political History of and Prospects for Reauthorizing New Markets," *Community Development Investment Review* 1 (1) (2005): 21–32, available at http://www.frbsf.org/community-development/files/cdirvol1issue1.pdf.

When used together, these two tax credit programs can have a transformative impact on low-income communities. Saint Luke's Manor, for example, received over $19 million in Housing Credit equity, helping to finance the affordable homes for seniors mentioned earlier. The other facilities, including the charter school and after-school program center, were made possible by $5 million in New Markets Tax Credits.[4] All told, it took multiple creatively assembled sources of financing—a "capital stack" of tax credit equity, multi-sector partnerships, and local support—to pull off the successful six-year revitalization effort in this historically disinvested community. Without the tax credits, none of it would have been possible.[5]

Building on a Successful Model

A Housing Credit investment generates a clear, positive social outcome: an affordable home. The social benefits of an affordable home cannot be overstated; they include physical, emotional, and financial stability for residents—a true springboard for opportunity.

But it invites us to ask: What if we built on this model, using financial incentives linked directly to outcomes for the residents (the people as well as the place)—their improvements in health, financial growth, educational advancements, or employability? What might that look like?

Consider the basic characteristics of the Housing Credit program. For one, you have a clear and measurable *outcome* you are looking to achieve (an affordable home over a sustained period of time). You also have a *market incentive* that attracts investment toward that outcome, as well as a *monitoring and measurement requirement* to ensure that the outcome has, in fact, been achieved. There is also a *policy structure* that catalyzes public-private partnerships on a large scale and a mechanism to *recapture* the investment if the outcome is not achieved. These are the core components.

Using these essential ingredients of the Housing Credit program to engineer a model designed around a different type of outcome, we arrive at a potential path, one that builds on Housing Credit investments with additional tax credits tied to a layered-on outcome—what we might call "extra credit(s)." Below is a glimpse of how such a program could look.

---

4   The Saint Luke's Manor project was also made possible by Historic Tax Credit equity.

5   Enterprise Community Partners, Inc. worked in close partnership with Pennrose Properties and Cleveland Neighborhood Progress on Saint Luke's Manor.

Adding Human Capital Outcomes to Investment Tax Credits

The Housing Credit program works remarkably well to produce housing and it should be maintained (in fact, the program should receive dramatically more federal funding to address the severe shortage of affordable units). But imagine if we also took the Housing Credit one step further—by adding on tax credits that are tied to more human-centered outcomes. It is one thing to build a financial model around the occupancy or conditions of a unit. It is quite another to build a model around a parent's rising wages or a student's educational advancement. But it can be done.

For this to work, a critical support activity would be offered on a Housing Credit property (e.g., onsite daycare, after-school transportation, job training, or a partnership with a health clinic for youth or senior wellness visits), which would require an upfront investment that covers startup and ongoing operating costs. That activity would be supported by an award of additional tax credits, which could come in a lump-sum using equity from an investor who buys the tax credits.

One of the virtues of the Housing Credit program is that through the allocation process, states are able to address the needs unique to their local communities, such as housing in rural areas or supportive housing designed to serve especially vulnerable populations, such as frail elderly or formerly homeless. In the same way, extra credit funding could be matched with existing social programs, building on the successful work already being done and tailored to local needs. The program could even require a match to improve the leverage of the extra credit program, and municipalities that are currently providing funding for existing programs could use the extra credit program to make their local dollars go even further.

Imagine, for example, a "Bright Eyes Education Tax Credit" (per Len Syme's dedication in this book), where credits are issued as a child moves through the education system successfully. You could imagine a tax credit certification at the following stages: 1) the completion of successful post-partum home visiting sessions; 2) arriving at kindergarten ready to learn; 3) reading at grade level in third grade; 4) math proficiency in eighth grade; and, finally, 5) high school graduation.[6]

---

6 For more information, a similar concept was explored by Ian Galloway in "Charter School Tax Credit: Investing in Human Capital," Federal Reserve Bank of San Francisco (December 1, 2010), available at http://www.frbsf.org/community-development/publications/working-papers/2010/december/investment-tax-credits-charter-schools/.

Or consider a "Jobs for All Tax Credit," where credits are issued when certain workforce milestones are reached for an adult struggling to find or hold employment, such as: 1) an effective onsite jobs training program is held; 2) a job is secured by the individual; and 3) he or she is still employed after two years. Or something along those lines.

Such programs would apply to people living in Housing Credit properties, hence the "extra credit" aspect. So, imagine if an 80-unit property receiving Housing Credits also received $2,000 per year per unit to spend on programs that directly served the residents, and one-third of the cost for the first five years would come from the extra credits, with the remainder from local sources. In this example, the extra credit proceeds would total $267,000, which could only be used for a resident-focused program or set of programs that were defined in advance of allocation — such as the Bright Eyes Education Tax Credit or the Jobs for All Tax Credit.[7] Over the course of the five-year pilot, outcomes generated by those programs would be carefully measured and evaluated against certain milestones like those above, and the government would allocate credits if and when the milestones are achieved.

The same core mechanisms in the Housing Credit program would be featured in the extra credit program. You would have clearly defined *outcomes*, such as those suggested in the examples earlier. Your *market incentives* would be similar to those of the Housing Credit — the prospect of a dollar-for-dollar reduction on investors' tax liability, as well as the potential for financial returns. Also, like the Housing Credit program, you would have a *monitoring and measurement requirement*, carried out perhaps by the relevant city or state agency, depending on the nature of the program (monitoring of Housing Credit properties, for example, is typically done by state housing agencies). And, of course, the extra tax credit program would need the enabling *policy structure*, including changes in the tax code.

As with any new program, we could start small, test it, adjust it, and then expand it. We could experiment with a program like this in several states so that we have comparative approaches for implementation. From there,

---

7 How the $267,000 figure was derived: an 80-unit project in which $2,000 per unit is allocated over five years (80 x 2,000 x 5 = 800,000); one-third of that cost is covered by equity from the "extra credits" (800,000/3 = $267,000).

if successful, the program could expand and become a permanent feature in the federal tax code.

Building on Low Income Housing Tax Credits and Investing in What Works

With such a model, all stakeholders stand to win: Investors have a financial incentive to provide additional funding; the federal government's dollars are being put to good use since it is paying for what works; local governments, who provide funding for local supportive services (which is usually insufficient to meet the needs), are able to further leverage what they are already doing; and, of course, residents themselves benefit from services that are stronger and held to greater accountability.

The investment tax ecosystem for physical capital development is scaled and sophisticated and involves the necessary expertise from a range of industries: law firms, Wall Street, real estate investment, design and construction, and human services providers. We have shown that when the federal government uses subsidy dollars to create an outcomes orientation — or quasi market — it can create enormous efficiencies and incredible transformations, such as Saint Luke's Manor in Cleveland.

More human-centered transformations, such as education outcomes for children or sustained employment for adults, require more complex interventions over longer periods of time than making homes affordable. But that is no reason to doubt that we can create the sophisticated and scaled ecosystem to execute on these types of outcomes, too. The time has come to use the Housing Credit's core mechanisms—that have worked for over 30 years—to create a new market and policy infrastructure that helps us turn the tide on inadequate educational achievement, insufficient job opportunities, health disparities, and other inequities that prevent people from reaching their potential.

TERRI LUDWIG *is president and chief executive officer of Enterprise Community Partners, Inc., a national nonprofit that creates affordable homes and strengthens communities across the United States. Enterprise has pioneered innovative neighborhood solutions, transformative policy, and community development financial products for over 30 years, having invested over $28 billion in that time. Ludwig has over three decades of experience in investment banking and nonprofit leadership. She previously served as president of the Merrill Lynch Community Development Company, president and chief executive officer of ACCION New York, and in several executive leadership roles at Credit Suisse and Merrill Lynch.*

INVESTING IN INNOVATION AND OUTCOMES
The Story of DC Water's Environmental Impact Bond

Beth Bafford
Calvert Foundation

Mark Kim
DC Water

Eric Letsinger
Quantified Ventures

Combined sewer overflows (CSOs), the unfortunate byproduct of old sewage systems and increased weather severity, are a major source of pollution, a cause of poor water quality, and a health threat. CSOs have become an increasingly urgent environmental challenge as a result of climate change, which has intensified both the severity and frequency of the rainfall events that overwhelm aged stormwater infrastructure.[1] In Washington, DC, the water utility, DC Water, operates under a landmark legal settlement that requires a substantial intervention to reduce this damage.

There are two main ways to address challenges with CSOs: gray infrastructure (tunnels) and green infrastructure (mimicked natural habitats). Gray infrastructure is a known, trusted, and tested solution. Green infrastructure has great potential and many positive externalities but is largely unproven at scale.

After years of negotiations, DC Water reached an agreement in 2015 with the U.S. Environmental Protection Agency, U.S. Department of Justice, and District of Columbia that modified their legal settlement to allow DC Water's Clean Rivers Project to deploy large-scale green infrastructure installations to reduce CSOs to the Potomac River and Rock Creek. So

---

1 When a rainfall event exceeds the capacity of a combined sewer system, a CSO event occurs in which untreated stormwater and raw sewage are discharged into local waterways to prevent the system from backing up. In an average year, approximately 2 billion gallons of CSOs pollute the Anacostia and Potomac Rivers and the Rock Creek in the District of Columbia.

when faced with a choice, DC Water's chief financial officer, like all entrusted stewards of public funds, was haunted by the simple question, "What if green infrastructure does not achieve the outcomes we need?"

Fast-forward 18 months to September 2016, when DC Water issued the nation's first environmental impact bond (EIB) to finance its maiden green infrastructure project. This $25 million deal was sold in a private placement to Calvert Foundation and Goldman Sachs' Urban Investment Group, with Quantified Ventures serving as DC Water's Pay for Success transaction coordinator.[2] This was not only DC Water's first foray into green infrastructure, but also the first large-scale green infrastructure project in the District. Because the effectiveness of green infrastructure depends on local climatic conditions, DC Water faced a challenge in measuring the risk of performance outcomes. The resulting EIB represents a groundbreaking approach to partially transfer the risk of performance outcomes from the issuer to the investor, allowing DC Water to move forward confidently with its green infrastructure experiment.

The EIB is unique in many respects. With the assistance of Quantified Ventures, DC Water structured the EIB with an outcomes-based financing mechanism that leveraged private impact capital to support public "interventions" to produce measurable social and environmental outcomes for the community. Payment on the bond will depend on the intervention's demonstrated success, as measured by a rigorous evaluation that will be independently validated. To date, such contracts, also known as social impact bonds, have been used to address critical social issues, such as prisoner recidivism and homelessness. Unlike previous social impact bonds in the United States, DC Water's EIB is the first Pay for Success deal structured as a traditional bond instrument, and the first to fund environmental interventions like green infrastructure. At $25 million of investor capital, it also represents the largest Pay for Success transaction in the United States.

The defining characteristic of DC Water's EIB is that the total rate of return to the investors will depend on the green infrastructure's performance in managing stormwater runoff. Standard municipal bond

2   Other parties to the transaction included Public Financial Management, Inc. (financial advisor), Harvard Kennedy School Government Performance Lab (technical advisor), Squire Patton Boggs LLP (bond counsel), and Orrick, Herrington & Sutcliffe LLP (investors' counsel).

investors invest solely on the creditworthiness of the issuer. In contrast, DC Water's EIB investors are "betting" on the outcome of the funded project—in this case, the green infrastructure's ability to reduce the volume of stormwater runoff, thus decreasing the incidence of CSOs. DC Water accomplished this by embedding a two-way contingent payment feature into the bond itself, the first time a tax-exempt municipal security explicitly tied financial payments to measurable outcomes. If the green infrastructure outperforms mutually agreed-upon performance targets, DC Water will make an additional "outcome payment" to its investors. If the green infrastructure underperforms, the investors will make a "risk share payment" to DC Water, partially offsetting the expense of testing this solution. If the green infrastructure meets performance expectations, the EIB will pay the investors the stated interest rate on the bond.

With this structure, all parties' interests are well-aligned. The investors, seeking ways to leverage private capital to promote innovation for greater social and environmental impact, are able to share risk with DC Water and help induce the agency to apply a green infrastructure approach with positive externalities that the investors value. DC Water, interested in testing green infrastructure but with a mandate to make the best financial decisions on behalf of its rate payers, is able to shift downside risk to a third party so that they are comfortable taking this promising but unproven approach.

Incentivizing this innovative approach could reap outsized benefits for DC Water, its citizens, and other communities. If the green infrastructure outperforms, DC Water will prove, with a scientific and verified evaluation, that green infrastructure is as effective as gray infrastructure, allowing it to manage a growing problem at likely a lower cost. This will trigger at least six additional green infrastructure projects across the Potomac and Rock Creek sewer sheds. In addition, DC Water's experiment will give U.S. communities a new tool to manage similar waste- and stormwater system challenges. In addition to reducing stormwater runoff, this tool improves local air quality, generates more resilient local habitats, and creates quality, local green jobs,[3] all without the cost and disruption that large-scale gray infrastructure projects cause.

---

3 U.S. Environmental Protection Agency, "Benefits of Green Infrastructure," available at https://www.epa.gov/green-infrastructure/benefits-green-infrastructure.

This cross-sector, multi-stakeholder approach to financing innovation was not without its challenges. Creating a common language among mission-driven investors, a water utility, green infrastructure engineers, bond counsel, and many more parties required a collaborative and open approach to problem-solving along the way. The cultural and knowledge gaps that were unveiled early and often were overcome by listening, learning, and trusting that all actors were committed to shared objectives.

Investors have expressed a strong interest in the EIB model, highlighting its transparency, simplicity, rigor, and scalability. We believe these are the primary drivers that can lower transaction costs and enable faster deployment of impact capital for vexing social and environmental challenges, and we are excited to share our lessons to facilitate more of these deals.

Beyond its application to infrastructure projects, we can envision this outcomes-based financing mechanism being leveraged so that public officials, alongside private investors, are comfortable pushing the envelope in pursuit of more effective solutions. The core insight—that identifying the outcomes a project requires and then organizing financing that shares the risk and cost of generating these outcomes—can support public officials as they embrace innovation when the status quo is proven but the alternative can potentially deliver better long-term results. We have seen this approach applied in other areas, ranging from criminal-justice reform to health care to education, and we hope that this EIB will serve as a template that local authorities can replicate as they evaluate green infrastructure and other innovative social and environmental interventions.

BETH BAFFORD is director of investments at Calvert Foundation, a nonprofit financial intermediary, where she works on domestic and international transactions across impact sectors with a focus on health and place-based community development. Prior to joining Calvert Foundation, Bafford was a consultant at McKinsey & Company. She has also worked at the White House Office of Management and Budget, on the 2008 Obama for America campaign, and at UBS Financial Services. Bafford received her BA and MBA at Duke University.

MARK T. KIM *serves as chief financial officer for the District of Columbia Water and Sewer Authority (DC Water). He is responsible for the financial management of the utility and its $1 billion operating and capital budgets. Kim holds a BA from Northwestern University, JD from Cornell Law School and a PhD in public policy from Harvard University.*

ERIC LETSINGER *is chief executive officer of Quantified Ventures, whose mission is to simplify access to impact capital in order to scale what works. He has an MBA from the Yale School of Management and a BA in urban studies from Northwestern University. A tri-sector, cross-industry executive with more than 25 years of public-private partnership expertise, he is currently structuring multiple Pay for Success transactions across the health, environment and education fields. In 2016, he served as the Pay for Success transaction structurer on the nation's first Environmental Impact Bond with DC Water.*

HOW TO FINANCE OUTCOMES/RESULTS THROUGH GOVERNMENT PRIZE COMPETITIONS

Jenn Gustetic
NASA

Many of us know the frustration of sitting down for dinner and having the phone ring with an illegal, pre-recorded message marketing a scam.[1] The U.S. Federal Trade Commission (FTC) receives between 125,000 and 200,000 complaints each month regarding these harassing calls. As of May 2016, the FTC had brought more than a hundred lawsuits against over 600 companies and individuals responsible for billions of illegal robocalls and other Do Not Call violations.[2] The FTC also has tried another innovative approach: It has supported a series of prize competitions to develop technology-based solutions to reduce the number of illegal robocalls.

In 2013, the first FTC Robocall Challenge offered a $50,000 prize purse for the creation of innovative solutions to block illegal commercial robocalls. The FTC, the "seeker," received nearly 800 eligible submissions from individual solvers and teams. All of the developers and engineers who created the winning solutions were new to this problem—a powerful example of how prize competitions can attract out-of-discipline experts to unlock innovative solutions to vexing problems. One of the winning solutions, "Nomorobo," developed by Aaron Foss, is a free technology service that routes incoming robocalls to a second telephone line that can identify and hang up on these calls. Nomorobo has blocked more than 80

---

1 Office of Science and Technology Policy, "Implementation of Federal Prize Authority: Fiscal Year 2013 Progress Report" (2014), available at https://obamawhitehouse.archives.gov/sites/default/files/microsites/ostp/competes_prizesreport_fy13_final.pdf.

2 Federal Trade Commission Consumer Information, "Robocalls," available at https://www.consumer.ftc.gov/features/feature-0025-robocalls.

million robocalls to date.[3] Compared with lawsuits and enforcement, this prize competition was a remarkably cost-effective approach to reducing the amount of illegal robocalls and driving meaningful change for citizens.

Engaging the public through incentive prizes offers a revolutionary way to bring in new groups of people to address important societal problems. Moving beyond traditional contracts and grants, incentive prizes harness the public's ingenuity to solve tough challenges, drive outcomes, and address societal needs, while paying only for solutions. These prize competitions are one approach that federal agencies can take to encourage innovation and better outcomes—whether technical, economic, or social. They allow the seeker to: 1) define the outcomes it wants to see and fund the best solutions to deliver those outcomes; and 2) establish an important goal without having to pre-select the approach or the team it anticipates as most likely to succeed. Prize competitions often stimulate private-sector investment that is many times greater than the cash value of the prize.

Incentive prizes have an established track record of spurring innovation in the public, private, and philanthropic sectors, including the 1714 Longitude Prize, which stimulated the development of the world's first practical method to determine a ship's longitude, and the Orteig Prize, which motivated Charles Lindbergh to fly nonstop from New York to Paris. The Obama administration took important steps early on to accelerate public-sector adoption of these innovative tools.[4] In his "Strategy for American Innovation," President Obama called on all agencies to increase their use of prizes to address some of our nation's most pressing challenges.[5] Subsequently, the White House Office of Management and Budget (OMB) issued a formal policy framework to guide agencies in using prizes to mobilize American ingenuity and advance their respective core missions.[6] Soon thereafter, in December 2010, Congress passed the America COMPETES Reauthorization Act, providing all federal agencies

---

3 For information on robocalls see https://www.nomorobo.com.

4 Office of Science and Technology Policy, "Implementation of Federal Prize Authority" (2014).

5 Executive Office of President Barack Obama, "Strategy for American Innovation: Executive Summary," available at https://obamawhitehouse.archives.gov/innovation/strategy/executive-summary.

6 Executive Office of The President, Office of Management and Budget, "Guidance on the Use of Challenges and Prizes to Promote Open Government" (March 2010), available at https://obamawhite-house.archives.gov/sites/default/files/omb/assets/memoranda_2010/m10-11.pdf.

broad authority to conduct prizes. As a result of these key policy actions, the use of public-sector prizes has been increasing steadily, with progressively more ambitious outcomes being sought. Since the U.S. General Services Administration (GSA) started the Challenge.gov program to provide a one-stop-shop for all federal prizes in 2010, more than 80 federal agencies have engaged 200,000 Americans through over 700 challenges with more than $220 million in prizes. Harvard recognized the Challenge.gov program with the Innovations in American Government Award in 2013.

Prizes can be designed in an almost infinite number of ways, for a variety of different outcomes. The Deloitte University Press studied more than 400 challenges that have been conducted since 2009 and identified six outcomes the U.S. Government is seeking through prizes, falling along two dimensions:[7]

- Developing ideas, technologies, products, or services to:
  - Attract new ideas
  - Build prototypes and launch pilots
  - Stimulate markets
- Engaging people, organizations, and communities to:
  - Raise awareness
  - Mobilize action
  - Inspire transformation

An example of a public-sector prize that seeks to both stimulate markets and mobilize action is the U.S. Department of Energy's Sunshot Catalyst Prize. Catalyst is an open innovation program that aims to encourage the rapid creation and development of products and solutions that address near-term challenges in the U.S. solar and energy efficiency marketplaces. This $2 million prize has backed 36 early-stage teams developing prototypes and supported five teams with more extensive funding through two rounds of incubation. All five incubation teams are still in business and growing as they bring their energy services and products to market. The

---

7 Kwasi Mitchell et al., "The Craft of Incentive Prize Design," Deloitte University Press (June 18, 2014), available at http://dupress.com/articles/the-craft-of-incentive-prize-design/.

five companies collectively raised $1 million in 2015 from private investors and created 20 to 25 new jobs.

A very different example sought to attract new ideas and inspire transformation in how public spaces were designed and built in the wake of Hurricane Sandy. The U.S. Department of Housing and Urban Development (HUD), in collaboration with the Hurricane Sandy Task Force, launched Rebuild by Design, a multistage regional design competition to promote resilience for the Sandy-affected region.[8] The competition aimed to attract world-class talent, promote innovation, and develop projects that would actually be built. The $2 million prize purse was funded entirely by HUD's philanthropic partners, led by The Rockefeller Foundation. Approximately 148 teams from more than 15 countries submitted proposals; ten teams were selected as finalists. These finalists each received $200,000 in awards and provided their unique insights to community leaders and stakeholders through public meetings, facilitated field visits, and one-on-one discussions. According to an evaluation released by the Urban Institute, finalist design teams contributed work effort between three and six times the amount of the cash prize awards they received in the competition.[9] Of these ten finalists, HUD incentivized the implementation of seven of the winning designs by committing $930 million through the Community Development Block Grant Disaster Recovery (CDBG–DR) program to leverage other public and private funds.

According to HUD's reporting on this prize, "The use of a prize competition was selected to help provide solutions to problems that are larger or more complex than individual jurisdictions have the capacity to solve independently."[10] This challenge was innovative in a number of ways but had a substantial impact because it combined the tools available to the federal government to stimulate and support innovation. Rebuild by Design leveraged a prize competition approach—a public-private partnership to bring new ideas into a pipeline for more traditional, discretionary,

---

8   The author joined the board of trustees of the Van Alen Institute, one of the implementing partners of the Rebuild by Design Challenge, in January 2017, after the challenge was completed.

9   Carlos Martin et al., "Evaluation: Rebuild by Design Phase I," Urban Institute (October 13, 2014), available at http://www.urban.org/research/publication/evaluation-rebuild-design-phase-i.

10 Office of Science and Technology Policy, "Implementation of Federal Prize Authority: Fiscal Year 2014 Progress Report" (May 2015), available at https://obamawhitehouse.archives.gov/sites/default/files/microsites/ostp/NSTC/fy14_competes_prizes_-_may_2015.pdf.

federal grant funding. According to the Urban Institute, this combination of support vehicles was critical to the competition's success. "Leadership among the core partners and the magnitude of the $1 billion in CDBG-DR funding for awards motivated all of the key stakeholders in spite of an expedited timeframe and daunting requirements."[11]

The flexibility of this tool can drive diversity in federal prize designs and outcomes. However, it can also paralyze some federal decision-makers, since there isn't yet a clear understanding of how to identify which portions of a portfolio would benefit most from this approach. Additionally, even though the federal government has conducted more than 700 prize competitions, most program managers are not aware that this approach is available to them. Building decision-maker awareness of this new tool is crucial to expanding adoption. But since these tools do not have uniform step-by-step guidance, significant learning must happen each time a new program or office attempts to use this approach. GSA's Challenge.gov program and NASA's Center of Excellence for Collaborative Innovation[12] are working to address the knowledge-management and scaling issues through federal-wide communities of practice, training, mentoring programs, the development of a toolkit,[13] and government-wide shared services for prize design and implementation.

These forums and documentation efforts to capture lessons learned are critical as the art of designing prizes is further developed. Several parts of prize design and implementation are notoriously difficult, including:

* Defining your problem in a way that thoroughly considers and challenges the assumptions made in prior problem-solving approaches. Prizes seek to discover new solutions and pay only for the best performance against measurable outcomes. These outcomes should be tied to a clear understanding of the desired future state that could be achieved through a prize. Designing a prize requires the prize designer to think about *what* should be accomplished through a prize, articulating the starting line (point A) and the finish line (point B), and not *how* to best get from point A to point B. Focusing on the what instead of the

---

11 Martin, "Evaluation: Rebuild by Design Phase I" (2014).

12 For more information on the NASA Center for Excellence see https://www.nasa.gov/offices/COECI/.

13 For more information on the Challenges and Prizes Toolkit see http://www.challenge.gov/toolkit.

how can be unnatural and difficult for people accustomed to solving problems (how), rather than defining them (what). It also forces people to question prior assumptions about what's possible.

- Balancing the need to create an open-solution space when defining the problem that encourages entirely new thinking while ensuring that promising solutions can be reintegrated into your program. This requires a delicate compromise in the way requirements are written — not so specific that they constrain innovation, but not so broad that there is no way to reintegrate resulting solutions.

- Setting the prize purse and suite of incentives to attract the right types of solvers to your problem. There are at least four core rewards that drive participants to compete for prizes: "goal, glory, guts, and gold," according to Ken Davidian, formerly of NASA's Centennial Challenges Program.[14] These incentives should be customized to incentivize your target solver communities.[15]

- Creating communications and engagement strategies that get solvers' attention beyond the "usual suspects." Often breakthroughs in one domain come from practices that are commonplace in other domains, but not yet applied to the domain in question. Engaging diverse viewpoints, both from other domains and sectors of the population that might have a more difficult time accessing traditional channels, expands the seekers access to innovative approaches to solving their problem.

- Setting expectations up front between the seeker and solver, and more clearly and definitively articulating the time and resources necessary to participate in the full process.

Despite these challenges, government incentive prizes, when used the right way on the right problems, can be transformative (and cost-effective) in driving outcomes. These approaches should be considered alongside more traditional approaches, such as contracting and grantmaking, to encourage innovation and increase participation to solve national problems. As awareness of this approach increases across sectors and as more experienced prize designers are available to support implementation,

---

14 McKinsey & Company, "'And the Winner is'…:Philanthropists and Governments Make Prizes Count" (July 2009), available at http://mckinseyonsociety.com/capturing-the-promise-of-philanthropic-prizes/.

15 The White House Office of Social Innovation and Civic Participation, "Prizes and Challenges," available at https://obamawhitehouse.archives.gov/administration/eop/sicp/initiatives/prizes-challenges.

managers will begin to identify opportunities to build this type of outcome-driven approach into their own program planning. There is immense promise for ambitious and high-impact prizes in such important societal areas as clean energy, education, and public health. Prize initiatives in these national priority areas will have a higher likelihood for sustained support, impact, and reach if they are conducted through cross-sector collaborations, as some of the most ambitious prizes conducted recently have been.

Finally, the increased use of prizes within the government is also encouraging broad discussions of outcome-driven procurement approaches.[16] This is not surprising, as designing prizes forces seekers to focus on outcomes in order to establish a transparent judging process. Prize designers are adept at focusing on outcomes, and their experience should be part of broader discussions within government about buying outcomes and paying for success. The lessons learned from more than 700 pay-for-performance prizes are critical data points to drive a more outcome-focused government.

———

JENN GUSTETIC *is the Small Business Innovative Research (SBIR) program executive for NASA headquarters in Washington, DC. Previously she served as the assistant director for open innovation at the White House and the prizes and challenges program executive for NASA. She holds a master's degree in technology policy from the Massachusetts Institute of Technology and a bachelor's degree in aerospace engineering from the University of Florida.*

16 Partnership for Public Service, "Innovation is a Contract Sport: Ways that Agencies Can Achieve Innovative Outcomes Through Acquisitions" (February 6, 2016), available at http://ourpublicservice.org/publications/viewcontentdetails.php?id=918.

OUTCOMES RATE CARDS
A Path to Paying for Success at Scale

Lara Metcalf
Social Finance Inc.

Andrew Levitt
Bridges Fund Management

Consider Jason and Emily, two young people living in the north of England. Jason, from just outside Liverpool, struggled to find employment, even after completing his Level 1 plumbing training.[1] Emily, from Manchester, was in danger of dropping out of school without graduating; she lacked self-confidence and a sense of responsibility.[2] Both were at risk of becoming "NEET" (not in employment, education, or training),[3] but they faced their own unique challenges.

Fortunately, Jason and Emily were each connected with programs that met their individual needs. For Jason, this was a program called Career Connect, a nonprofit organization that provides career-focused support for disadvantaged 14- to 19-year-olds.[4] For Emily, it was Teens and Toddlers, a nonprofit organization that runs an 18-week mentoring program pairing teenagers from disadvantaged communities with toddlers in nurseries.[5]

Though they didn't know it at the time, Jason and Emily were able to change their lives for the better as a result of the world's first outcomes rate card, developed by the United Kingdom's Department for Work and Pensions.

An outcomes rate card is a list of outcomes government wants to achieve in order to advance its policy priorities, and the monetary value (i.e.,

---

1 Career Connect, "Jason Moved from Unemployment to Level 2" (2016), available at https://www.careerconnect.org.uk/Jason-moved-from-unemployment-to-Level-2-c1.html.

2 Richard Garner, "Teenagers' Exam Results Boosted Through Scheme Pairing Them to Work with Small Children," *Independent* (August 20, 2015), available at http://www.independent.co.uk/news/education/education-news/teenagers-exam-results-boosted-through-scheme-pairing-them-to-work-with-small-children-10463801.html.

3 U.K. Parliament, "NEET: Young People Not in Education, Employment or Training," Research Briefing (2016), available at http://researchbriefings.parliament.uk/ResearchBriefing/Summary/SN06705#fullreport.

4 For more information on Career Connect see https://www.careerconnect.org.uk.

5 For more information on Teens and Toddlers see https://www.teensandtoddlers.org.

price or rate) it is willing to pay for each outcome. A government entity uses the rate card as the basis for a procurement process. The selected service providers receive payment only when the stated outcomes are achieved and participants' lives are positively affected.

A NEW APPROACH TO A PERSISTENT PROBLEM

In the United Kingdom, as in many parts of the world, young people have faced barriers to employment and limited access to high-quality educational training programs in the wake of the Great Recession. In the first months of 2016, 865,000 young people in the U.K.—roughly 12 percent of all 16- to 24-year-olds—were considered at risk of becoming NEET. Each young person who fits this description will cost the U.K. economy an estimated £56,000 over the course of his or her lifetime, through lost taxes and increased dependence on public services.[6] The total cost to the taxpayer is much greater when you take into account the broader social costs, including health care, homelessness, and contact with the criminal justice system.

The Department for Work and Pensions is the U.K.'s biggest public service department, responsible for welfare and child maintenance policies. It administers the state pension and a range of other benefits. In June 2011, the department launched a two-phase pilot Innovation Fund to "test new social investment and delivery models to support disadvantaged young people" by paying for outcomes that were "directly related to increasing future employment prospects."[7]

The department selected ten nonprofit organizations to deliver programs as part of the Innovation Fund that would go on to serve approximately 17,000 young people over the next three years.[8] This approach brought together government, service providers, and impact investors to tackle the challenges facing disengaged youth. The development of the rate card

---

6 Bob Coles et al., "Estimating the Life-Time Cost of NEET: 16–18 Year Olds in Education, Employment or Training: Research Undertaken for the Audit Commission," University of York (2010).

7 Cabinet Office: Centre for Social Impact Bonds, "Department for Work and Pensions Innovation Fund," available at https://data.gov.uk/sib_knowledge_box/department-work-and-pensions-innovation-fund.

8 Emily Gustafsson-Wright, Sophie Gardiner, and Vidya Putcha, "The Potential and Limitations of Impact Bonds: Lessons from the First Five Years of Experience Worldwide," Brookings Institution (July 2015), available at https://www.brookings.edu/wp-content/uploads/2016/07/Impact-Bondsweb.pdf.

facilitated a rapid scaling of Pay for Success, enabling government to test the efficacy of diverse approaches to solving this social issue.[9]

DEVELOPING AN OUTCOMES RATE CARD

An outcomes rate card requires government officials to go a step further than setting policy priorities and goals. They must define how much they think those goals are worth in financial terms and determine how much they will pay for progress toward those goals. Typically, the rate card will set a payment for a number of outcomes and populations.

Governments, often working with an intermediary like Social Finance, analyze existing administrative data and define a price for each outcome, such as the value of successful entry into employment. Usually, they will incentivize certain early milestones (e.g., completion of certain levels of skills training or qualifications) that have a proven correlation with the ultimate desired outcome (e.g., entry into first employment).

Prices on an outcomes rate card may be informed by policy priorities, in addition to potential monetary savings. For example, government can use higher outcome rates to incentivize providers to focus on achieving outcomes for the hardest-to-serve populations. Service providers pick which outcomes they want to focus on, and in which geographies, rather than having to change their services to fit a single, government-mandated outcome.

As initial results clarify which early milestones best contribute to ultimate success, and what payments attract service providers' interest, government can tweak the rates. Figure 1 shows how the Department for Work and Pensions used this iterative approach in the second round of the Innovation Fund. Based on the first-round results, including feedback from providers and other stakeholders, the rate card in the second round increased payment rates for some outcomes and completely eliminated others.[10] The importance of having an engaged service provider commu-

---

9   A note on terminology: We will use "Pay for Success" as an umbrella term to describe government human services or health system contracts commissioned on an outcomes-focused basis. By "social impact bonds" (the more common term in the United Kingdom), we mean the subset of Pay for Success projects (Pay for Success financings), where a social or impact investor provides the upfront working capital to social sector organizations delivering the program.

10 Rita Griffiths, Andy Thomas, and Alison Pemberton, "Qualitative Evaluation of the DWP Innovation Fund: Final Report," Department for Work and Pensions (July 2016), available at https://www.gov.uk/government/uploads/system/uploads/attachment_data/file/535032/rr922-qualitative-evaluation-of-the-dwp-innovation-fund-final-report.pdf.

nity that feels its full costs can be covered by achieving a portfolio of outcomes it has signed up to achieve cannot be overemphasized.

PROCUREMENT WITH AN OUTCOMES RATE CARD

Once a government has created an outcomes rate card, it begins the procurement process to select the organizations it believes can best achieve the outcomes. Impact investors and intermediaries often work with service providers to review their delivery plans, hone their bids, and provide the upfront working capital for successful bidders. Typically, investors need to fund only one-third of the total service delivery budget, because once the early-milestone outcome payments are achieved, these can be recycled to finance the later stages of the program.

The focus on outcomes represents a fundamental shift from government's traditional fee-for-service approach. However, there are some long-standing precedents, which helped inform the development of rate cards and important improvements. Early precursors for the concept stem from New York City welfare-to-work contracts, which were launched through the Human Resources Administration in the 1990s.[11] The contracts used a 100 percent performance-based model with a series of milestone payments. Today, $55 million of New York City's newest round of Human Resources Administration welfare-to-work contracts (totaling $180 million) is allocated toward performance-based payments linked to the successful achievement of employment milestones.

In the New York City Human Resources Administration contracts, prede-termined milestones drive service provider performance; outcomes rate cards combine aspects of this approach with the risk-sharing and private financing model of Pay for Success. Thus, rate cards represent a positive evolution from the performance-based contracts that preceded them, with tweaks that help address some of the challenges service providers have

---

11 Swati Desai, Lisa Garabedian, and Karl Snyder, "Performance-Based Contracts in New York City Lessons: Learned from Welfare-to-Work," Rockefeller Institute (June 2012), available at http://www.rockinst.org/pdf/workforce_welfare_and_social_services/2012-06-Performance-Based_Contracts.pdf.

12 HM Government, "Innovation Fund: Key Facts" (2017), available at https://www.gov.uk/government/uploads/system/uploads/attachment_data/file/212328/hmg_g8_factsheet.pdf; Cabinet Office: Centre for Social Impact Funds: "Department for Work and Pensions Innovation Fund," available at https://data.gov.uk/sib_knowledge_box/department-work-and-pensions-innovation-fund.

Figure 1. Selected Outcome Prices from Department for Work and Pensions Innovation Fund Rate Cards[12]

NATURE OF OUTCOME	INNOVATION FUND ROUND ONE	INNOVATION FUND ROUND TWO
	(Maximum price of outcome)	
Per participant age 14-24 classified as NEET		
Improved attitude to school/education	-	£ 700
Improved attendance at school	£ 1,300	£ 1,400
Improved behavior at school	£ 800	£ 1,300
QCF Accredited entry level qualifications (below GCSE)	-	£ 900
First QCF Level 1 Qualification	£ 700	£ 1,100
First QCF Level 2 Qualification	£ 2,200	£ 3,300
First QCF Level 3 Qualification	£ 3,300	£ 5,100
Entry into Education at NQF Level 4	£ 2,000	-
Successful Completion of an ESOL Course	£ 1,200	-
Entry into First Employment	£ 2,600	£ 3,500
Entry into Sustained Employment	£ 1,000	£ 2,000

experienced in the past. When providers partner with impact investors to cover working capital needs, they shift all or part of the financial risk to investors. Additionally, investors provide technical assistance for providers with their rate card bids and program delivery, helping them focus on outcomes that align with their service model and enabling them to create a sustainable project budget.

OUTCOMES RATE CARDS AND PAY FOR SUCCESS PROJECT DESIGN

All Pay for Success projects involve detailed work to identify a target population, select outcomes, and set a value for those outcomes. But when Pay for Success projects are developed in response to an outcomes rate card, that work is front-loaded—government sets the prices, terms, and timeline before the procurement process.

Crucially, moving the process of setting outcome metrics and payment levels ahead of procurement has a powerful, positive effect on the timing of project design and service launch (Figure 2). Although the work involved in setting and pricing outcomes is similar for both the single-intervention Pay for Success model common in the United States today, and the outcomes rate card Pay for Success model used in the U.K., the former leads to one project, while the latter can yield multiple projects. Service providers, with investor support, bid specifically on their ability to deliver selected outcomes on the rate card, targeting the outcomes they are best suited to achieve. After service providers are selected, contracts are often required to be finalized within four weeks. As a result, the average timeline for an outcomes rate card project is over 50 percent shorter than the current average Pay for Success timeline in the United States.[13]

Although a strength of the model is its ability to standardize the Pay for Success development process, the process of rate card development must take into account the needs of the local provider community. Governments must carefully identify outcomes and prices such that they both incentivize providers to meet beneficiaries' needs and fairly compensate providers for the cost of services.

ALIGNING OUTCOMES RATE CARD DESIGN WITH DESIRED RESULTS

Focusing on improving long-term life outcomes — but paying for early engagement, too. A well-designed rate card should have both early and late indicators and metrics, which result in payments dispersed throughout the life of the project.

Relying on strong data systems to set rates, monitor performance, and make payments. Management of outcomes rate cards requires government administrative data systems to be integrated, to analyze data and value outcomes, and to track and pay for outcomes. Data sets are also necessary to stratify rates, depending on the target population: Providers should be paid more when they achieve outcomes with harder-to-serve segments of the population, and less when they achieve outcomes with easier-to-serve segments, to avoid "cherry picking" or "cream skimming."

---

13 Social Finance, "Outcomes Rate Cards: Frequently Asked Questions," available at http://socialfinance. org/content/uploads/OutcomesRateCard_FAQ.pdf.

Figure 2. Current Pay for Success Negotiated Development Process vs. Outcomes Rate Card Pay for Success Development Process

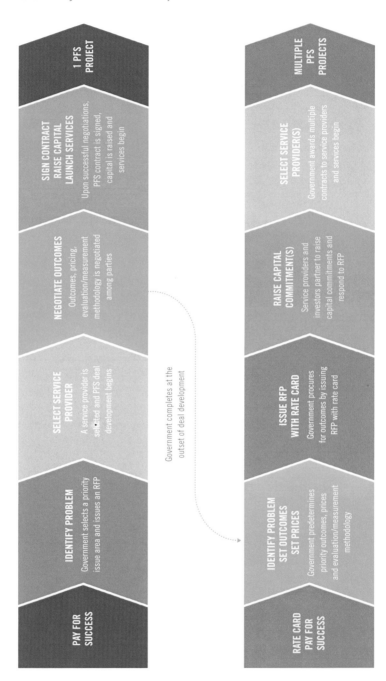

PAY FOR SUCCESS

IDENTIFY PROBLEM
Government selects a priority issue area and issues an RFP

SELECT SERVICE PROVIDER
A service provider is selected and PFS deal development begins

NEGOTIATE OUTCOMES
Outcomes, pricing, evaluation/measurement methodology is negotiated among parties

SIGN CONTRACT RAISE CAPITAL LAUNCH SERVICES
Upon successful negotiations, PFS contract is signed, capital is raised and services begin

1 PFS PROJECT

Government completes at the outset of deal development

RATE CARD PAY FOR SUCCESS

IDENTIFY PROBLEM SET OUTCOMES SET PRICES
Government predetermines priority outcomes, prices and evaluation/measurement methodology

ISSUE RFP WITH RATE CARD
Government procures for outcomes by issuing RFP with rate card

RAISE CAPITAL COMMITMENT(S)
Service providers and investors partner to raise capital commitments and respond to RFP

SELECT SERVICE PROVIDER(S)
Government awards multiple contracts to service providers and services begin

MULTIPLE PFS PROJECTS

Outcomes rate cards will be most useful in jurisdictions with reasonably strong data systems.

Using adaptive learning and feedback loops to drive better outcomes. By incentivizing providers to focus on published outcomes, rate cards create constant feedback loops. Ongoing active performance management, typically provided by a specialized third party, helps the service provider observe, diagnose, and adapt. Government can monitor effectiveness and performance.

THE PROMISE OF OUTCOMES RATE CARDS

Because of their success with at-risk youth like Jason and Emily, Career Connect and Teens and Toddlers last year became the first two social-impact-bond service providers in the world to be recommissioned to deliver a second program. The two service providers will now reach an additional 5,781 at-risk youth. Bridges Fund Management, which provided the working capital and hands-on capacity building to the two providers in the first round, was fully repaid and has signed on to provide further funding in this second round. These factors signal the early success of this iterative, outcomes-based tool for all parties involved.

In a time of rising need and shrinking resources, we need to embrace innovation and give government multiple tools with which to tackle social challenges. Outcomes rate cards provide one promising solution to drive improved social outcomes for people in need worldwide.

––––––

LARA METCALF *is managing director of Social Finance Inc., a nonprofit that mobilizes capital to drive social progress, where she is responsible for overseeing strategy and operations and developing and executing innovative financings that drive better life outcomes for at-risk people and communities. At Social Finance, Metcalf has overseen the development of six Pay for Success projects, four of which have launched service delivery funded by $68 million in new capital. Metcalf has deep experience in the public and private sectors, including 18 years on Wall Street at world-class financial institutions, as well as four years as chief financial officer and chief financial and administrative officer at Harvard University's John F. Kennedy School of Government. Metcalf is a graduate of Boston College and earned her MBA from the Kellogg School of Management at Northwestern University.*

ANDREW LEVITT *is a partner at Bridges Fund Management, a specialist sustainable and impact investor. Levitt manages the Bridges Social Impact Bond Fund, the world's first and only dedicated social impact bond fund. He has invested in and overseen the delivery of 15 social-impact-bond-backed programs —three of which have now completed, delivering significant social impact and positive returns to investors. Levitt was previously chief executive officer of MicroCred Banque, the largest microfinance bank in Madagascar, and before that spent eight years working in cooperatives and mutuals in the U.K. banking and insurance industry. He is an On Purpose mentor, and lectures about social impact bonds at London Business School, Saïd Business School, INSEAD, and HEC.*

THE IMPACT SECURITY
Reimagining the Nonprofit Capital Market

Lindsay Beck and Catarina Schwab
NPX

Anna Pinedo
Morrison & Foerster LLP

I n recent years, institutional investors, fund managers, and retail investors have expressed increased interest in aligning their investment objectives with furthering social impact. The development of social impact bonds has been an important first step toward meeting this objective. Social impact bonds incorporate pay-for-performance features that bring together donors, governmental entities, and investors to fund a nonprofit organization's achievement of specified impact objectives. Donations and investments are tied to the advancement of the nonprofit organization's initiatives, which promotes accountability and transparency.

The potential of pay-for-performance investments has not been fully realized through existing examples of social impact bonds because they are so complex. Today's social impact bonds are not actually "bonds," but rather bespoke contractual arrangements entered into among institutional investors, philanthropic foundations, governmental entities, and nonprofit organizations.[1] Some of these arrangements have taken the form of loans or credit facilities, while others have been structured as investments in special purpose investment vehicles. The type of players and variety of legal structures for these arrangements has contributed to limiting the universe of potential nonprofit organizations and investors.

THE IMPACT SECURITY SOLUTION

Now, what if the attractive pay-for-performance elements of existing social impact bonds were incorporated into a simpler, more familiar

---

1 The exception being DC Water's Environmental Impact Bond, which is profiled in this book (Bafford/Kim/Letsinger) and has less of an explicit focus on social outcomes.

What Matters: Investing in Results to Build Strong, Vibrant Communities

structure that could be readily offered publicly to socially-minded investors, including individuals? The Impact Security approach accomplishes just this.

The Impact Security is a debt security issued by a nonprofit organization, foundation, government or supranational entity featuring variable returns that are contingent on the achievement of predetermined impact metrics. The Impact Security has the following five characteristics:

1 The issuance proceeds, excluding transaction fees, are deployed exclusively to advance an entity's charitable mission;

2 The terms of the instrument specify a predetermined set of impact outcome(s);

3 The terms of the instrument include the public reporting of an objective, predetermined process for third-party measurement and/or evaluation of impact outcome(s);

4 A predetermined outcome payer(s) undertakes responsibility either to guarantee the issuer's obligation to repay investors, or to make payments of the contingent returns to the investors on the issuer's behalf; and

5 A variable financial return based upon predetermined impact outcome(s).

Purchasers of an Impact Security are not making a donation, but rather seeking a financial return while furthering, through their investment in the security, certain social objectives.

TERMS OF AN IMPACT SECURITY

The Impact Security is a debt instrument, or bond. Most investors are familiar with bonds. Large, well-established companies, as well as municipalities and governments, regularly issue bonds. In this case, an Impact Security will be issued by a nonprofit, foundation, government or supranational entity. Like any other bond, the Impact Security represents a promise by the issuer to make certain payments to the holder of the security. The terms of the security may be structured to provide for interest payments and/or principal payments that are tied to, or contingent upon, the issuer's achievement of predetermined impact outcomes.

A donor, or a payer, either will guarantee the nonprofit issuer's payment obligations to the Impact Security holder or will make the contingent payments due to the holder on the issuer's behalf to the extent that the impact outcomes are met. An Impact Security holder's return is variable based on impact. The nonprofit issuer will deploy the proceeds of issuance of the Impact Security, excluding transaction fees, to advance the entity's charitable mission.

Like traditional bonds, the Impact Security will be issued pursuant to an indenture or an issuing and paying agency agreement and may be marketed by financial intermediaries, acting as "underwriters," to the public. Given that the instrument is a debt security issued pursuant to agreements familiar to investors, a high level of standardization can be attained. The Impact Security will bear a security identifier (i.e., a CUSIP number), can be held in an investor's brokerage account, and can be readily transferred or sold among interested investors.

ASSESSING IMPACT

The hardest part of structuring an Impact Security is not the legal structure itself, but all of the other considerations, namely, impact assessment.

Impact evaluation is often the anticipated red herring; however, it is less daunting than one may imagine given the great advancements made in the impact field over the past decades, including GIIRS, IRIS, GuideStar, and Impact Genome.

The Impact Security can be applied to any intervention with measurable impact. Impact metrics are predetermined by the donor and/or nonprofit organization, laid out clearly with a sliding scale of outcomes each tied to specific payment triggers and audited by an independent third party.

Similar to other standardized financial products deployed by different issuers and even by issuers in different industries, there will be some variances among the terms of an Impact Security issued by different nonprofits. By way of example, the terms of a municipal bond issued in connection with a toll road differ from the terms of a municipal bond issued in connection with the construction of a new stadium, which may incorporate different terms and payment features; however, both are still municipal bonds. Similarly, an Impact Security issued for a healthcare project will have different terms and features than one issued to advance an education initiative, but both will have the same basic, familiar structure and documentation.

The donor in an Impact Security can be a private donor (individual, family office, private foundation, corporate foundation, etc.), government, or supranational entity—anyone seeking to make a performance-based donation. Expanding beyond government to include private philanthropy and supranational entities dramatically increases the amount of capital and types of interventions that can benefit from the pay-for-performance model, which is currently limited to those that save the government money.

For example, The Last Mile, a 501(c)(3) nonprofit organization, intends to issue an Impact Security with the support of donors that have pledged amounts that will provide for payment to investors if The Last Mile achieves predetermined impact metrics. The upfront capital will be used by The Last Mile to launch the first-ever web development shop inside a U.S. prison. Highly vetted inmates at San Quentin that graduate from a one-year coding training program are eligible to work inside the "dev shop" where contract work is brought in from the Bay Area's biggest tech firms. The impact metric on the deal is hours worked, which will be audited annually by an independent third party and trigger donation payments from the fund.

ADVANTAGES OF THE IMPACT SECURITY

This novel approach has the potential to transform social impact investing because it promotes:

- **Standardization**—Studies have shown that there are growing numbers of investors committed to making investments that further their social objectives. These investors favor products that are familiar in format, do not require customization, can be readily held in brokerage accounts, and are transferable.

- **Efficiency**—A standardized approach permits many more nonprofit organizations to access the capital markets and replicate an established structure, with appropriate modifications made to the impact metrics, in order to raise funds. This will reduce transaction costs for nonprofit organizations, donors, and payers and also will improve speed of execution.

- **Expanded investor access**—If the debt security is issued by a nonprofit organization, foundation, or governmental or supranational entity, the offering of the security would be exempt from SEC registration. This exemption allows the security to be offered publicly to all investors, accredited and non-accredited, which expands the pool of eligible investors.

- **Transparency**—Using a debt security facilitates public disclosure and reporting, which leads to enhanced transparency and more efficient pricing.

- **Market integrity**—The rigors associated with reporting impact metrics will promote market integrity. Donors and payers will be able to have reliable data, rather than relying on anecdotal evidence, regarding the effectiveness of their sponsored programs and initiatives. Eventually, investment dollars and donations will follow results.

CHALLENGES TO BROAD ADOPTION

Despite these obvious benefits, the Impact Security faces some hurdles to broad adoption. Quite surprisingly, donors (or outcome payers) are the biggest limiting variable to scale despite the novel risk-sharing mechanism built into the performance-driven structure. A donor's best option prior to the Impact Security was to donate and then hope for impact. By contrast, the Impact Security offers a built-in investor match, audited impact evaluation, and the obligation to donate if and only if impact is achieved. Changing donor mindsets and behavior so that capital is explicitly linked to impact is critical to adoption.

Another barrier is getting impact investors to consider alternatives to social impact bonds. Although only 15 social impact bond transactions have been completed to date in the United States, market participants tend to be creatures of habit who find comfort in the familiar, even when presented with a more efficient alternative.

The rigors associated with impact reporting might also discourage some nonprofit organizations and foundations from embracing the Impact Security. One of the key benefits associated with the Impact Security is that it introduces market discipline by aligning dollars with impact achieved. Stakeholders, including foundations and governmental entities, may not agree on the metrics to be reported or the regularity of reporting; they also may be reluctant to share results broadly.

Lastly, fear of the unknown may inhibit nonprofit organizations from offering Impact Securities. Personnel within nonprofit organizations may require the assistance of advisers with the requisite financial and legal expertise to help them evaluate this important alternative.

In our view, success entails mass adoption of a standardized financial product that explicitly links capital with impact, thereby maximizing donor capital, catalyzing investor capital, unlocking impact data, and, ultimately, transforming the way the world finances impact.

———

LINDSAY BECK and **CATARINA SCHWAB** *are co-founders and co-chief executive officers of NPX, where they are working with innovative donors, impact investors, and nonprofit organizations to transform the way that impact is financed in the nonprofit sector.*

ANNA PINEDO *is a partner at Morrison & Foerster LLP in the capital markets group, where she specializes in securities and derivatives, including structured notes and other hybrid and structured products.*

EQUITY WITH A TWIST
Getting to Outcomes With Flexible Capital

Nancy O. Andrews
Low Income Investment Fund

Janis Bowdler
JPMorgan Chase & Co.

Pay for Success approaches have focused almost exclusively on scaling evidence-based interventions within single sectors. They are hard to structure, carry a high level of risk, and have been slow to get off the ground. LIIF and JPMorgan Chase believe that there is a need for a different kind of outcomes-based capital tool—one that is more flexible and user-friendly, and which intentionally supports innovative and cross-sector approaches to tackling poverty. Structuring and executing new approaches, demonstrating impact, and gaining investor acceptance is difficult and time-consuming work.

Equity with a Twist (EQT) is our attempt to solve that problem and one other. At the highest level, EQT is intended to demonstrate that integrated, outcomes-driven approaches can alleviate poverty. Second, EQT is meant to be much more user-friendly than current outcomes-based capital tools like social impact bonds or Pay for Success structures. EQT has a stream-lined, customer friendly structure that relies upon existing knowledge about what works, with a lighter touch for data collection than other forms of outcomes-based financing.

EQT is an outgrowth of the explosion of social sector evidence over the past decade. It demonstrates that the age-old debate about people- vs. place-based strategies is over—and both sides won. We now understand that it takes more than housing, more than community building, more than health or education alone to change life trajectories. We must braid together various lines of social investment to make a difference. We need a more united vision of what works, coordinated by a community quarterback or integrator organization, with funding that rewards positive outcomes: healthy children and families, excellent schools, safe communities, more viable life trajectories. EQT builds on this understanding and rewards integrated, outcomes-driven work.

EQT works on a simple but revolutionary premise: We know what works to address poverty, but we are funding it chaotically, with a vision that is blinkered by traditional program silos. EQT rests on the idea that there are three important levers in creating successful anti-poverty outcomes and that these should be coordinated by a community quarterback focused on getting results:

1 Mixed-income housing, to provide families with affordable homes in healthy, diverse communities;

2 Early learning and child development programs, to ensure young kids are ready to learn when they enter first grade; and

3 Excellent education, providing a pipeline to well-paid careers.

EQT requires that these three elements are included in all place-based programs receiving its support. Furthermore, EQT supports community quarterbacks overseeing the integration of these elements, measuring the success of the program and making adjustments to the community model as required to achieve success. EQT is the only existing community development financing source that is not project-specific, but that funds the quarterback at the organizational level. EQT provides enterprise-level capital, not project-specific capital, with a ten-year success horizon.

Until now, place-based anti-poverty support has largely been project-specific, built on the premise that one program or another—a housing development, a child care service center, a great school—would be enough to move the dial on poverty. EQT argues that doing these things individually is like singing the notes of a song in random fashion. The result will not be music, but cacophony. To produce results (music, in this analogy) we need to organize and coordinate the inputs, so they produce the outcomes we want. EQT sets forth a framework for this, requires that outcomes are measured and provides unsecured, patient ten-year capital to the quarterback willing to pull it all together.

HOW EQUITY WITH A TWIST WORKS

LIIF and JPMorgan Chase launched EQT in early 2016 as an initial $6 million pilot to provide flexible and low-cost enterprise-level investments to support organizations quarterbacking integrated and outcomes-driven solutions to poverty. These organizations agree to track common process and performance measurement throughout the term of the investment.

EQT is "equity-like"—no collateral is required and the terms of repayment can vary enormously. For example, an EQT investment could be structured with even repayments over the life of the investment. Or it can be structured with no repayments at all until the final year. Unlike a typical loan, which is focused on supporting a given project, EQT supports an organization in any way that makes sense for the organization, as long as it is committed to providing an integrated program that incorporates mixed-income housing, early learning programs and high quality education, with outcomes measurement.

In an effort to simplify the data collection component of this work, EQT investees agree to track progress on five common measures over the term of the investment:

1. Resident health
2. Neighborhood safety
3. Child development
4. Education
5. Real estate market strength

Reporting social outcomes against benchmarks in five common areas:

1. Child progress on a standard measurement tool
2. Third grade reading and math scores
3. Health and wellbeing (can be measured by resident perception)
4. Community safety (can be measured by resident perception)
5. Improvement in market value of neighborhood

EQT is designed to support innovation within the common framework noted above. There is a preponderance of evidence in each area—mixed-income neighborhoods, early learning, and quality education—that suggests that an integrated model, led by a data-driven community quarterback, can deliver even greater benefits to families and neighborhoods.

Figure 1. Risk/Return Continuum

| Financial return to investor based on financial success of project (less risk) | Traditional Senior Debt | Equity with a Twist (EQT) | Pay for Success | Financial return to investor based on social impact achieved (more risk) |

EQT is outcomes-driven and also customer-friendly for organizations working on the ground, especially with regard to data collection and reporting. The recipient of EQT does not require perfect evidence to demonstrate success (using a randomized controlled trial, for example).

EQT falls somewhere in the middle of the spectrum of social impact investing. As shown in Figure 1, because it is unsecured and because there is no pre-determined repayment schedule, EQT is much riskier than traditional debt. However, it is less risky than the Pay for Success approach that bases return entirely on achieving the desired social impact.

EQT also does not require that public sector savings be used for repayment to investors. Rather, it relies on the strength of the organization for repayment, tantamount to a corporate guarantee. And, perhaps most importantly, EQT works across program silos, requiring integrative, outcomes-driven work. Pay for Success examples, like social impact bonds, tend to derive return on investment through the savings of a single program silo, such as housing for the homeless, reduced incarceration, or early learning programs. Moreover, EQT's ten-year horizon and its unsecured structure make it unusually patient and flexible, since it depends on the organization itself, not a specific project, to achieve social impact. EQT sets a favorable financial yield hurdle (two percent in early experimental investments), relying upon "social return" as the main benefit to investors, in addition to a modest financial return.

There are few financial instruments—perhaps none—that call out the quarterback role and support it directly. Given the lack of support for silo-busting work and quarterback organizations, EQT seeks to fill an otherwise large gap in the social investment spectrum.

CASE STUDIES

The first two EQT investments, $2 million each, were made in BRIDGE Housing and the Bayou District Foundation (BDF). BRIDGE will use EQT to support its work transforming dilapidated public housing sites in San Francisco (Potrero Terrace & Annex) and Los Angeles (Jordan Downs) into mixed-income communities with a range of new programs and services. In particular, BRIDGE plans to use EQT funds to continue their evolution from a housing developer to an organization with a comprehensive, holistic approach to community building. EQT's flexible capital structure will allow BRIDGE to accelerate its innovation by adding staff to implement key programs, and launching its new Trauma Informed Community Building vision and strengthening the planning and investment required to build a data platform. Importantly, EQT also requires ongoing evaluation and measurement of the five core outcomes noted earlier.

EQT allowed BRIDGE to be far more efficient in the use of staff resources. It precludes the need for BRIDGE to fundraise in the short term, and enables them to delay repayment to investors until they earn developer fees and project reimbursements at a later date.

The Bayou District Foundation (BDF) will use its EQT investment to replicate the Purpose Built Communities model in New Orleans. BDF is continuing the development of Columbia Parc, a master-planned community in New Orleans on a former public housing site, with mixed-income housing, a health clinic, high-quality early childhood education, and a planned K-8 charter school. BDF plans to use EQT funds to bridge fundraising in one of these real estate development projects, but it is free to change course as it sees fit because EQT investees are not obligated to any particular use of funds. EQT has thus enabled BFD to accelerate its timeline in implementing its comprehensive strategy, in addition to increasing the organization's capacity around impact assessment.

At the time of this book's publishing, LIIF and JPMorgan Chase had made an EQT commitment to an organization in Cincinnati as well.

EQT AS AN OUTCOMES-FOCUSED TOOL

EQT has both advantages and limitations as a financial product and as an outcomes-based funding approach in particular. First, as previously noted, there are no other dedicated sources of funding to support community quarterbacks. Enterprise-level capital that is low-cost and long-term, which allows uneven repayment and deferred revenue for investors, is exceedingly rare in community development finance. This scarcity makes EQT especially valuable for organizations pursuing complex poverty alleviation strategies that must be sustained over many years. Further, the tool incentivizes innovation on the ground by: 1) supporting integrated strategies, and 2) requiring social outcomes tracking—an easy to understand, but hard to accomplish goal when faced with the urgencies and day-to-day realities of being a practitioner organization. EQT's approach to evaluation and tracking social impact is user-friendly for investees.

By the same token, EQT might be more accurately characterized as an outcomes-*driven* funding tool than outcomes-*based*. Unlike with most Pay for Success approaches to date that have focused on scaling evidence-based practices within single sectors, repayment to EQT investors is not contingent upon generating social benefits of a pre-defined magnitude. Instead, the initiative is tailored to reflect LIIF and JPMorgan Chase's goal to support innovation within a broader framework which shows promise in generating significant benefits for families and neighborhoods. Importantly, investees are free to shift approaches over time—and the areas to which they allocate EQT funds—based on results that they collect along the way. This flexibility is critical for supporting real-time innovation on the ground, ultimately allowing organizations to figure out what works in their neighborhoods.

Equally important, EQT encourages more organizations to: 1) work across silos, 2) measure outcomes, and 3) adjust their strategies to achieve stronger and better outcomes. If we can demystify this way of working, if we can make it easier for others to adopt, we will have achieved our purpose.

Looking forward, EQT may help practitioners evolve and become more comfortable with integrated strategies. It may also set the stage for outcomes tracking as a condition for favorable financing. Despite limitations in its evaluation design, EQT may generate important lessons for practice and contribute to a growing body of suggestive evidence that could eventually be verified through more rigorous experiments.

NANCY O. ANDREWS *is president and chief executive officer of the Low Income Investment Fund (LIIF), a community development financial institution that has invested $2 billion in community projects. She serves on numerous community development and environmental boards and committees. Her 30 years in community development include positions as deputy director of the Ford Foundation's office of program-related investments, chief financial officer of the International Water Management Institute, and consulting for the U.S. Department of Housing and Urban Development and the U.S. Department of Treasury during the Clinton administration. Andrews received an MS in urban planning with a concentration in real estate finance from Columbia University.*

JANIS BOWDLER *is a managing director within global philanthropy at JPMorgan Chase & Co., responsible for setting and driving the firm's philanthropic and corporate responsibility strategy in financial capability, community development, and small business. Prior to joining JPMorgan Chase in 2013, Bowdler served as the director of economic policy at the National Council of La Raza (NCLR), the largest national Latino civil rights and advocacy organization in the United States, and as project manager at Famicos Foundation, a community development corporation working in Ohio. Bowdler received her MS in urban policy from Cleveland State University and her BA in political science and history from Malone College.*

INVESTING IN HEALTH FROM THE GROUND UP
Building a Market for Healthy Neighborhoods

Maggie Super Church
CLF Ventures

I f you had the chance to invest in new technology that was proven to reduce the burden of chronic disease and cut health care costs for thousands of people, would you do it? What if that same technology also reduced greenhouse gas emissions, improved mental health, and cut crime rates? The investment I'm talking about is deceptively simple—and we already know how to make it. It's not an app or a mobile device. It's a well-functioning neighborhood.

The market for improving health in the United States is vast and growing. Venture funding for digital health surpassed $4 billion in 2014, nearly equivalent to the prior three years of funding from 2011 to 2013 combined.[1] In 2014, the top six categories of venture funding for digital health were Analytics and Big Data ($393 million), Healthcare Consumer Engagement ($323 million), Digital Medical Devices ($312 million), Telemedicine ($285 million), Personalized Medicine ($268 million) and Population Health Management ($225 million).[2] In the context of this growing and dynamic market, there is clearly enormous opportunity to drive investment toward interventions that improve population health.

Neighborhoods conditions, including the quality and cost of housing and transportation, access to jobs, education and services, and the availability of healthy food and safe places to walk and play are primary drivers of

---

1   Malay Gandi and Teresa Wang, "Digital Health Funding: 2014 Year in Review," available at https://rockhealth.com/reports/digital-health-funding/.

2   Ibid.

how long and how well we live.[3] Together, they create an environment that shapes the choices we make every day, from how we get around and where we work to how much physical activity and sleep we get and how well we know our neighbors. Hostile environments can exacerbate poor mental and physical health through a cascade of stressors including exposure to violence, housing instability, and financial insecurity. These stressors, and the environmental conditions that underpin them, are more prevalent in low-income communities and communities of color, contributing to profound inequities in health outcomes. For example, a 2009 study from the Agency for Health Care Research and Quality found that hospital admissions rates for diabetes-related complications were 77 percent higher for people living in the poorest neighborhoods in the United States.[4] A 2014 study by the U.S. Centers for Disease Control and Prevention found that more than 50 percent of Hispanic men and women and non-Hispanic black women are predicted to develop diabetes during their lifetime, compared to 40 percent of the general population.[5] Diabetes and its complications accounted for $245 billion in direct and indirect medical costs in 2012.[6]

Despite overwhelming evidence linking neighborhood environments to health and health care costs, there is a dearth of investment in healthy communities. "On a Mission: Investing for US Health Impact in 2014," a survey conducted by the California Health Foundation, provides an overview of mission investing in health (defined as investing that aims to generate both social and financial returns). The survey identified 16 organizations that made health impact investments in 2014 totaling more than $120 million altogether. Of these investments, only 21 percent, or approximately $25 million, focused on the environmental and social

3 Amy Edmonds et al., "How Do Neighborhood Conditions Shape Health? An Excerpt from Making the Case for Linking Community Development and Health," Center for Social Disparities in Health, Build Healthy Places Network, and Robert Wood Johnson Foundation, available at http://www.buildhealthy-places.org/content/uploads/2015/09/How-Do-Neighborhood-Conditions-Shape-Health.pdf.

4 Lauren Wier et al., Statistical Brief #73: "Hospital Stays Among People Living in the Poorest Communities, 2006," Agency for Healthcare Research and Quality (May 2009), available at www.hcup-us.ahrq.gov/reports/statbriefs/sb73.pdf.

5 Edward Gregg et al., "Trends in Lifetime Risk and Years of Life Lost Due to Diabetes in the USA, 1985–2011: A Modelling Study," *The Lancet Diabetes & Endocrinology* (2014), available at http://www.sciencedirect.com/science/article/pii/S2213858714701615.

6 American Diabetes Association, "Economic Costs of Diabetes in the U.S. in 2012," *Diabetes Care* 36(4): 1033–1046 Apr 2013, available at http://care.diabetesjournals.org/content/36/4/1033.

determinants of health.[7] This is less than one percent of the venture capital invested in digital health companies in the same year. Although existing federal programs, including the Low Income Housing Tax Credit and New Markets Tax Credit, are critical resources, they are not enough.

Why is it so difficult to finance the development of healthy neighborhoods when the benefits to people, communities, and the economy are so profound? The answer, at least in part, lies in the fact that these benefits are not generally measured or accounted for in any systematic way. Healthy Neighborhoods Equity Fund (HNEF) is a pioneering, $30 million real estate investment fund in Massachusetts that grew out of the recognition that mixed-income, mixed-use, transit-oriented development (TOD) projects in historically disinvested neighborhoods are both challenging to complete and transformative for communities. HNEF is sponsored by two regional organizations, the Massachusetts Housing Investment Corporation, a 26-year-old community development financial institution (CDFI) with $1.2 billion in assets under management, and the Conservation Law Foundation, New England's oldest and largest environmental advocacy organization. HNEF provides "patient" equity for catalytic TOD projects in neighborhoods where the cost to build exceeds today's market value. The fund can invest in residential, office, retail, light industrial, or mixed-use projects, and typically supports five to 25 percent of the total project cost. HNEF has a longer time horizon and lower target return than typical private equity funds, which allow the fund to invest in projects and neighborhoods that would otherwise be unable to access this type of financing. A significant layer of "first loss" capital[8] absorbs some of the risk if projects do not perform as expected and offsets the lower rate of return for private investors. Equally important, projects seeking an investment from HNEF go through a rigorous review process using a scorecard that integrates more than 50 qualitative and quantitative measures that assess the project's likely community, environmental, and health impacts. HNEF also provides ongoing monitoring to document the effect of these projects over the ten-year life of the investment.

---

7 California Health Care Foundation, "On a Mission: Investing for US Health Impact, 2014" (June 2015), available at http://www.chcf.org/~/media/MEDIA%20LIBRARY%20Files/PDF/PDF%20M/PDF%20 MissionInvesting2014.pdf.

8 In an investment fund, first loss capital is used to cover losses that may occur before they are passed on to other investors.

The structure of HNEF, which aligns financial returns with community, environmental, and health benefits, is made possible by a fundamental shift in the real estate market nationwide. In their recently released paper, "Foot Traffic Ahead 2016," Christopher Leinberger and Michael Rodriguez found that, "For perhaps the first time in 60 years, walkable urban places in all 30 of the largest metros are gaining market share over their drivable suburban competition—and showing substantially higher rental premiums."[9] As a result, communities with the core characteristics of place that support walkable urban development, including a mix of uses, higher densities, access to transit, and connected street networks, have strong potential for long-term growth in value. These same characteristics are also important for increasing economic opportunity, health, and wellbeing for residents. HNEF is taking advantage of this overlap to drive greater investment in struggling neighborhoods that are in the early stages of development and are also facing significant health and environmental challenges. Recognizing the potential risk of displacement as real estate values rise, HNEF is supporting the development of mixed-income communities that include both affordable and market-rate housing.

The current HNEF project pipeline is concentrated in Boston, with some projects in downtown areas and around commuter rail stops in surrounding cities and towns. The first HNEF investment of $894,500 in the Chelsea Flats project was finalized in December 2014, and an additional $16.8 million of HNEF investment in five other projects has since been approved. These six projects have leveraged an additional $121.5 million of private and public investment in low- and moderate-income neighborhoods. In total, they will create 528 new housing units, of which 26 percent are affordable to households earning 80 percent of Area Median Income (AMI) or less. Starting rents for market-rate apartments range from 78 to 129 percent of 2016 AMI, affordable to working families. These six projects will also create over 106,000 square feet of commercial space, including neighborhood retail and office space, and generate nearly 1,100 new construction jobs and over 140 new permanent jobs. Across all phases of development, including those that HNEF has invested in, these projects will create 975,000 square feet of

9   Christopher Leinberger and Michael Rodriquez, "Foot Traffic Ahead: Ranking Walkable Urbanism in America's Largest Metros," George Washington University School of Business (2016), available at https://www.smartgrowthamerica.org/foot-traffic-ahead-2016.

new mixed-use development near transit that is home to nearly 1,800 new residents and employees. These projects will also support three new or improved parks and trails, a new grocery store, and several healthy food outlets. Equally important, these projects will contribute to safer and more walkable neighborhoods with new jobs and amenities that benefit current as well as future residents.

The Melnea Hotel and Residences in Boston's Dudley Square neighborhood is a prime example of the type of transformative development HNEF was set up to support. Located on a long-vacant piece of publicly-owned land at the intersection of two major streets that form a gateway to the commercial center, the site will soon be home to a new mixed-income, mixed-use development with 50 residential units, a Marriott flagship hotel, and ground-floor retail space. The project is located just 0.3 miles from Dudley Station, a major transit hub that includes regional bus service, and 0.7 miles from the Ruggles subway station. The project is one of several recent public and private developments in and around Dudley Square, a historically African-American neighborhood that is beginning to rebound after years of community-driven reinvestment activity.

Starting rents at Melnea Residences will be affordable to households earning 110 to 129 percent of AMI, with seven units set aside for households earning less than 70 percent of AMI. These units serve an important segment of Boston's housing market. The city's rental housing population grew by 23 percent from 2006 to 2013 while the number of rental units grew by only 15 percent, contributing to low vacancy rates and rising rents across the city.[10] Despite the prominence of the site and the overall strength of the Boston housing market, the Melnea Residences project would not be possible without HNEF financing owing to the perceived risk of achieving market rents and the longer time horizon required to pay back investors.

Melnea Hotel and Residences will create approximately 50 new jobs in hotel operations, residential management, and retail. Starting wages at the hotel will be $18 per hour, and the hotel operator is contributing $400,000 to the city of Boston for a job-training fund. Project sponsors

---

10 Zeninjor Enwemeka, "In Boston, Renters (And Rents) Are on the Rise but Available Units Are Not, Report Finds," WBUR News (May 28, 2015), available at http://www.wbur.org/news/2015/05/28/boston-rent-report.

have committed to local hiring targets, including 51 percent of construction worker hours performed by minority workers, with a preference for Roxbury residents (the larger neighborhood around Dudley Square), and 70 percent of hotel jobs to be filled by community residents and/or lower-income people. They have also committed to the participation of minority-business enterprises (MBE), including 40 percent of the construction contract value being performed by MBEs. In addition to construction and permanent jobs created on the site, 33 percent of the region's jobs are available within a 45-minute transit commute, opening up additional opportunities for residents of the project.

Beyond the creation of new housing and jobs, Melnea Hotel and Residences will contribute to measurable improvements in safety and walkability in the surrounding area and take advantage of a number of health-promoting features nearby. The project is expected to produce a 77.3 percent increase in the State of Place index, a block-by-block audit tool that measures the qualities empirically shown to be associated with walking.[11] This will not only promote physical activity but also improve community safety by creating more "eyes on the street." In addition, the project will provide secure indoor bike parking and enhance the existing South Bay Harbor bicycle trail that runs along the edge of the site. Finally, the project is flanked by a large complex of recreational fields and a newly constructed full-service grocery store, Tropical Foods, both of which support the health of residents in the area.

This type of development is important to Dudley Square for several reasons. The poverty rate for the half-mile area around the project is 34.5 percent, more than three times the state poverty rate, and unemployment is 13 percent, or 2.8 times the state rate.[12] In 2012, life expectancy in Dudley Square was a shocking 58.9 years, compared with 91.9 years for the Back Bay neighborhood just two miles north, and 80.5 years for the

---

11 The State of Place Index is comprised of ten urban design features–the State of Place Profile–empirically known to impact people's decisions to walk. The State of Place algorithm aggregates 290 data points into an index from 0–100 that indicates how walkable–convenient, safe, comfortable, and pleasurable–a block, group of blocks, or neighborhood is.

12 Metropolitan Area Planning Council Analysis for HNEF (internal document).

state as a whole.[13] Between 2010 and 2013, nearly one in three people (32.1 percent) in ZIP Code 02119 reported their general health status was fair or poor, twice the rate for Boston as a whole (15.7 percent).[14] Chronic disease is disproportionately high; the three-year, age-adjusted rate for diabetes in-patient hospitalizations was 1,466 per 100,000 residents, nearly 11 times the rate for Massachusetts as a whole, and the three-year age-adjusted rate for mental health emergency department visits was 40,235 per 100,000 residents, 18.3 times the state rate.[15]

Improvement on any of these measures would have a significant impact on residents, the neighborhood, and the health care system. Although no single project can bring about these kinds of large-scale improvements, a coordinated approach to public and private investment, guided by authentic community engagement and thoughtful planning, offers the best prospects for sustained change. The availability of patient equity through investment funds like HNEF can play a pivotal role in reversing decades of disinvestment in struggling communities across the country.

For these kinds of investments to take root in more places, we need the ability to measure and describe the social good the investment is creating. That is why we created a scorecard for HNEF (the HealthScore) that integrates data from a variety of sources and allows us to measure and monitor the impact of HNEF investments. To assess the need and opportunity for healthy neighborhood development and the likely impact of a proposed project, the HealthScore integrates primary data on walkability and quality of the built environment with secondary data on neighborhood conditions, demographics, and health outcomes. In addition, the HealthScore includes a qualitative assessment of the local planning and

---

13 Emily Zimmerman et al., "Social Capital and Health Outcomes in Boston: Technical Report," Virginia Commonwealth University Center of Human Needs (September 2012), available at http://www.society-health.vcu.edu/media/society-health/pdf/PMReport_Boston.pdf; Kristen Lewis and Sarah Burd-Sharps, "American Human Development Report: The Measure of America 2013–2014," Social Science Research Council, available at http://www.measureofamerica.org/wp-content/uploads/2013/06/MOA-III.pdf.

14 Boston Public Health Commission, Boston Behavioral Risk Factor Surveillance Study, 2010 and 2012 combined. For more information, see http://www.bphc.org/healthdata/Pages/Boston-Behavioral-Risk-Factor-Surveillance-System.aspx.

15 Center for Health Information Analysis (CHIA), Uniform Hospital Discharge Database System (UHDDS), Inpatient Hospitalization and Emergency Department Data, Calendar Years 2010–2012. For more information, see https://www.apcdcouncil.org/sites/apcdcouncil.org/files/media/state/ma-apcd-overview-2014.pdf.

development context, community engagement process, and partners. Finally, the HealthScore contains a detailed assessment of building uses, design, site plans, and programming. This scoring process relies on partnerships and agreements with our state public health department, regional planning agency, and several private contractors as well as conversations with project sponsors and other stakeholders in the neighborhood. The HealthScore also provides baseline data on a number of measures that can be monitored to determine whether conditions are changing over time. Although many of these conditions are not likely to change solely as a result of HNEF investment, we can use the baseline and monitoring data to gauge progress on key measures. As this type of neighborhood-level data becomes more widely available and accessible, the opportunity to use it for investment screening and monitoring will only grow.

What would it look like to make strategic, data-driven investments in healthy communities at scale? What could we achieve? The equity gap for mixed-use, mixed-income TOD projects is a challenge in markets across the country, and hundreds of community-based organizations and developers are seeking to build projects that address health and environmental challenges. Although the target rate of return and relative proportion of public, philanthropic, and private capital may vary, the concept of a blended capital stack can be replicated nearly anywhere. Individual and institutional investors, including banks, hospitals, and health systems, can bring new resources to the table, bolstered by first-loss capital from the public and philanthropic sectors. On the fund management side, CDFIs are widespread across the United States and can serve as effective intermediaries, combining local market knowledge with the ability to aggregate and deploy capital. Universities and nonprofits with expertise in data collection can support impact measurement. Similarly, county and state public health departments can bring deep expertise in gathering, tracking, and reporting health outcomes. Fusing these collective resources and capacities through a structure similar to HNEF has enormous potential to drive change at a scale that would not otherwise be possible.

MAGGIE SUPER CHURCH *is the health strategy and metrics consultant for CLF Ventures, the nonprofit strategy consulting arm of the Conservation Law Foundation. She is a 1994 Truman Scholar and holds a BA in architecture from Yale University, a master's degree in city planning from the Massachusetts Institute of Technology and a master's degree in urban design from the Edinburgh College of Art in Scotland. She lives in Lawrence, Massachusetts with her husband and two children.*

How This Works
BETTER RESULTS FOR VULNERABLE COMMUNITIES

MORE SERVICES, LESS WASTEFUL SPENDING
Pay for Success as an Innovative Strategy to Combat the Opioid Crisis

Katherine Klem
Institute for Child Success

Communities across the country are coping with a crisis of opioid use disorders that ravage lives by the day. The Centers for Disease Control and Prevention (CDC) reports that opioids claimed the lives of more Americans in 2015—over 33,000—than in any other year on record.[1] The annual number of opioid overdose deaths, the CDC also notes, has almost quadrupled since 1999.[2]

And yet, many of the best-intentioned policymakers are struggling to effectively address this mushrooming problem. One reason is that state and local government budgets are already severely strained. Communities may recognize that, as the federal government has shown, about one of every ten Americans who needs treatment for substance use is actually getting it.[3] And they may even know about evidence-based interventions, as well as promising new programs, that have been proven to work in other communities. But government leaders are not sure how to fund these interventions that could successfully ameliorate, if not eradicate, this crisis. And even if they did find the dollars, if government operated as normal, it would simply fund expanded activities by service providers rather than ensuring that their funding ultimately improves people's lives.

---

1 Centers for Disease Control and Prevention, "Opioid Overdose," available at https://www.cdc.gov/drugoverdose/.

2 Centers for Disease Control and Prevention, "Wide-Ranging Online Data for Epidemiologic Research (WONDER)," National Center for Health Statistics (2016), available at http://wonder.cdc.gov.

3 Substance Abuse and Mental Health Services Administration (SAMHSA), "Results from the 2015 National Survey on Drug Use and Health: Detailed Tables," Table 5.58B (September 2016), available at http://www.samhsa.gov/data/sites/default/files/NSDUH-DetTabs-2015/NSDUH-DetTabs-2015/NSDUH-DetTabs-2015.pdf.

So what's a community to do?

In the midst of these challenges, one potential solution, one tool in the proverbial toolbox, has emerged: Pay for Success.

If you're like most Americans, you've never heard of Pay for Success. But this wonky model, which is quietly gaining traction, may be one of our best hopes for tackling the undeniable toll of opioid use disorders—and other seemingly intractable issues of our time.

Pay for Success is a strategy to produce better outcomes, like fewer opioid overdoses, by paying only once an intervention (e.g., services, technology, medication) works. Instead of paying upfront without regard to results, government provides payment only once an intervention produces certain positive outcomes, as determined by an independent evaluator. For example, payment could flow after a program of medication-assisted treatment, in conjunction with behavioral counseling, reduces the rate of substance use relapse by eight percent over six years across a state, hitting the preset goal.

Meanwhile, the organization providing the intervention may well need dollars to cover its upfront costs. Impact investors—wealthy individuals, banks, or charitable foundations—are recruited to provide this capital (called Pay for Success financing).[4] And if the evaluator deems that the project hit its outcomes goals, then government pays back investors and provides a modest return. If the intervention does not achieve its intended impact, investors are not repaid.

The potential benefits in a case like tackling the opioid crisis are clear:

- The organization offering services to individuals who are experiencing substance use disorders and those at risk is freed from the narrow confines in which it may normally operate, given its traditional funding sources. They are no longer mandated by many grant rules—for example, to provide very specific services regardless of what its clients truly need in real time. The organization is also liberated from the

---

4 Pay for Success financing is sometimes known as a social impact bond, though the arrangement usually is not technically a bond.

tyranny of daily fundraising when it has an inflow of upfront capital to cover its costs, allowing staff to focus on mission over money.

- Government is able to preserve its limited taxpayer dollars for interventions that work. And helping a person overcome his or her substance use disorder may ultimately be far less expensive to taxpayers than paying for the costs that substance use can incur through increased crime, homelessness, and foster care demands. Although it is true that government will likely need to set aside the funds now for outcomes payments that it may or may not make down the road, it is still able to hang onto those dollars until lives are improved. And if the intervention produces cashable savings or avoids costs that it would have otherwise incurred, government could make its outcomes payments with dollars it didn't have available before.

- Investors not only stand to make a return, but they can do so in a way that aligns with shared values. As pointed out by David Wilkinson, a Pay for Success expert with whom I used to work at the White House, some investors put their dollars into private prisons and profit when more people are sent to jail, for example. Through Pay for Success, he'd note, impact investors can profit when ex-offenders do not return as a result of programs that reduce recidivism by tackling substance use disorders.

- The person ultimately served—say, someone with a substance use disorder who needs treatment—is receiving services he or she may not have otherwise been able to access. And with service providers whose reputation is on the line and investors who get paid only if outcomes improve, all under the watchful eyes of an independent evaluator, there is a good chance that the ecosystem will do everything it can to ensure the person's life is genuinely, measurably improved.

Thus, it's no surprise that national leaders on both sides of the aisle, from former President Obama to House Speaker Paul Ryan, have endorsed this model: more services for those in need, more efficient spending. There's a lot to like there.

Opioid use disorders are, in theory, a great fit for Pay for Success approaches. And innovators have taken notice. Connecticut has launched a Pay for Success project that is expanding services available to parents to enable them to keep their families together and their children out of foster care. Addressing substance use disorders is a major component of this work. A group of investors is providing $11.2 million to finance Family-Based Recovery, an intervention that includes home visits to families to help parents develop stronger skills, receive substance use treatment, and take toxicology screens. The evaluators at the University of Connecticut will measure the results, and the state will repay the investors if parental substance use, among other negative outcomes, decreases due to the intervention, saving the state substantial costs by helping to avoid foster care placements.

Beyond this pilot, Pay for Success approaches can take different shapes and forms in different communities. It could be used to expand evidence-based practices or pilot innovative ones. It can base only part of a funding stream, instead of all of it, on achieving outcomes. A Pay for Success project could involve multiple entities paying for the outcomes, and government need not be one of them. Hospitals, foundations, and others may be interested in paying for reduced substance use. Pay for Success could even be used to advance environmental outcomes instead of outcomes related to human lives. The possibilities go on.

Of course, Pay for Success has some limitations. One is that Pay for Success does not provide a quick solution to the opioid crisis and other pressing problems. Developing a carefully constructed project that guards against unintended consequences and wins the approval of all parties involved takes time. But like so many other urgent issues, the opioid crisis requires an all-hands-on-deck approach, and we need short-, medium-, and long-term approaches. Pay for Success is not designed to fix every-thing that needs fixing. It is meant to be one helpful piece of the puzzle, bringing together the sectors in a common mission to improve people's lives in the midst of some real constraints, often raising some sorely needed capital.

But even when funding for the opioid crisis is easier to find, Pay for Success will still be a relevant tool. The fact that Pay for Success can surface millions of dollars for services is a convenient, helpful feature of the model. Its core value is in guaranteeing that lives will be improved before govern-ments (or other "payers") pay for something. We need governments, service providers—the whole social sector—to embrace what works, improve or discard what doesn't, and test what is unknown. All involved need to be prudent stewards in times of tight budgets, but even more important, they need to be moral stewards in any budgetary environment.

Scripture tells us, "...where your treasure is, there will your heart will be also."[5] For our hearts to be linked in solidarity with those among us who most need support, including those wrestling with an opioid use disorder, we must usher in a different way to spend our collective treasure. And that's exactly what Pay for Success offers.

―――――

KATHERINE KLEM *is director, policy innovation and impact at the Institute for Child Success, where she advances the Pay for Success model and contributes to the organization's other policy priorities to improve the lives of our youngest children. She is a former senior policy advisor at the White House Office of Social Innovation and Office of National Drug Control Policy. Klem earned an MPP from the Harvard Kennedy School of Government and a BA with high distinction from the University of Virginia.*

---

5   The King James Bible, (Matthew 6:21).

IMPROVING EARLY LEARNING OUTCOMES THROUGH AN OUTCOMES-BASED FUNDING MODEL

Janis Dubno
Sorenson Impact Center

A small group of fifth graders performing at the top of their class sat around a table and discussed their life ambitions with a teacher. When asked who expected to go to college, each student raised his or her hand. The fifth graders shared what they would like to be when they grow up — an English teacher, a lawyer, an athlete. What is unusual about this conversation is that each child seated at the table is growing up in a high-poverty neighborhood with few family resources, and each tested significantly below his or her peers in language skills and cognitive development at preschool entry. The trajectory of children starting life so far behind is not very promising.[1] Indeed, 36 percent of children who spend half their childhood in poverty do not graduate from high school, compared with six percent of children who have never been poor.[2]

What changed the odds for these children was access to a free, high-quality preschool program. High-quality preschool can change the odds for low-income children by improving kindergarten readiness. But school readiness and longer-term outcomes for low-income children who attend preschool vary across programs.[3] The magnitude of the impact of early education programs on a child's learning and development and

---

1 Betty Hart and Todd Risely, "The Early Catastrophe: The 30 Million Word Gap by Age 3," *American Educator* (Spring 2003), available at https://www.aft.org/sites/default/files/periodicals/TheEarlyCatastrophe.pdf.

2 Donald Hernandez, "Double Jeopardy: How Third Grade Reading Skills and Poverty Influence High School Graduation," Annie E. Casey Foundation (2012), available at http://www.aecf.org/m/resourcedoc/AECF-DoubleJeopardy-2012-Full.pdf.

3 Hirokazu Yoshikawa et al., "Investing in Our Future: The Evidence Base on Preschool Education," Foundation for Child Development (October 2013), available at https://www.fcd-us.org/assets/2013/10/Evidence20Base20on20Preschool20Education20FINAL.pdf.

the persistence of early gains vary by type of program.[4] High-quality preschool programs produce the best and most lasting gains for low-income children, including improved academic achievement, less need for remedial services, increased high school graduation, reduced juvenile and adult crime, lower unemployment, and increased earnings.[5] However, even programs that have similar characteristics (such as credentialed teachers, evidence-based curricula, staff-child ratios) vary in the degree of impact and return on investment. Moreover, there is a need to promote innovation and leverage recent advances in the science of brain development to further improve outcomes for children.[6]

AN OUTCOMES-BASED FUNDING MODEL FOR EARLY EDUCATION

Typically, government funds upfront the activities of an intervention and that intervention may or may not achieve its desired outcomes for the participants. An outcomes-based funding model, rather than funding activities upfront, pays an agreed upon amount for the outcomes that the intervention seeks to achieve after they have been realized. An outcomes-based funding model for early education would direct investment to early education programs that best improve outcomes for children and, consequently, provide the greatest return (both monetary and non-monetary) on public investment. It could also foster innovation by focusing on and rewarding improved results, rather than prescribing specific program activities. By shifting the risk of program performance, government would be free to promote and reward experimentation and innovation. Early education providers would not be constrained to implement old program model characteristics but could innovate and expect compensation if they succeed.

In an outcomes-based funding model, government must identify valid, measurable outcomes that are indicative of future student and life success and meaningful for the community and government. Outcomes can be tied to direct fiscal savings or future cost avoidance, or government can

---

4 W. Steven Barnett, "Preschool and Its Lasting Effects: Research and Policy Implications," National Institute for Early Education at Rutgers University (September 2008).

5 James J. Heckman, "Early Childhood Education: Quality and Access Pay Off," The Heckman Equation, available at https://www.heckmanequation.org.

6 Center on the Developing Child at Harvard University, "From Best Practices to Breakthrough Impacts: A Science-Based Approach to Building a More Promising Future for Young Children and Families" (2016), available at http://www.developingchild.harvard.edu.

pay for an outcome it values even if not directly linked to monetary or cashable savings. Yet, focusing only on a narrow set of short-term outcomes that may be easier to measure and quantify may lead to under-valuing the true benefit of effective early education. Similarly, excluding certain outcomes because they are more difficult to precisely measure or are too far in the future could undervalue early education and result in underinvestment. What government pays for specific outcomes should accurately reflect the full value of effective early education programs, especially for economically disadvantaged children.

One of the advantages of this approach, as mentioned, is a more efficient allocation of public resources and greater investment in what works best to improve early learning outcomes. Other advantages include a systemic change in government to invest in what works in real time, as well as a systemic change that fosters innovation. Funding outcomes, rather than activities, will also facilitate systemic change in government and the early education sector more broadly. In the government sector, a focus on funding improved outcomes in one issue area can have a "spillover" effect of focusing on the outcomes of public investment throughout government. Considering the full range of benefits, including those in health, justice, welfare, and workforce development, government can shift from its silo-centric approach to one that is more comprehensive and child-centered. In the early childhood sector, this will facilitate a greater focus on what is best for improving child outcomes. In turn, it will foster the greater use of data to inform instruction and practices that improve early learning outcomes, rather than activities that do not produce real and lasting impact.

One case study of how an outcomes-based funding model can foster systemic change occurred in Salt Lake County and the state of Utah. In 2013, the United Way of Salt Lake and Voices for Utah Children part-nered with Salt Lake County, Goldman Sachs Urban Investment Group, and J.B. Pritzker to launch the country's first early childhood education Pay for Success project. The project's policy goal was to provide access to preschool in the Granite School District, Park City School District, and three community-based providers to children who were on the waiting list. Through its participation in the project, Salt Lake County has changed how it evaluates its budget and funding decisions, focusing more broadly on outcomes rather than the activities of programs. In

2014, the Utah State Legislature passed the Utah School Readiness Act, which appropriated funds to continue the High-Quality Preschool Pay for Success Project. Similarly, participation in the project subsequently led to a more explicit focus on outcomes and return on investment by the Utah Governor's Office of Management and Budget (GOMB). In January 2017, the Pew-MacArthur Results First initiative ranked Utah number two in evidence-based policymaking, citing GOMB's requirement that state agencies show the need for the service, the expected outcomes, and whether the program is evidenced-based and supported by research, data and evaluation.

As a result of the five-year High-Quality Preschool Pay for Success Project, 3,500 children who otherwise would not have had the opportunity to attend preschool will be given access. The High-Quality Preschool Pay for Success Project also made the case for investing in preschool for economically disadvantaged children; in 2016, the Utah Legislature appropriated $33 million (in addition to the Pay for Success funding) over three years to scale up preschool for economically disadvantaged children statewide through direct funding.

The outcome measure chosen in the Utah project was the reduction in the need for future special education. This measure was chosen because the research supported it, reliable data existed, and it was easy to measure and quantify. While the evaluation methodology has come under criticism (there is no control group), neither Salt Lake County nor the state of Utah are paying for any of the other short- and long-term benefits from this intervention. There are many additional benefits to both government and society that are likely to transpire, including increased kindergarten readiness, improved reading and math proficiency, future increases in high school graduation, and reduced interaction with juvenile and adult criminal justice. One reason these measures were not included in the project was the lack of data to either measure or quantify these benefits. In other words, because of a lack of data and credible methods to measure and quantify the broader impact of high quality preschool, the project focused on just one measure of success.

Data availability is critical to fully estimate the value of the range of outcomes associated with high-quality preschool. This is true at the program level, within the education system more broadly, and across government. Increased investments in data capacity and analysis, which are needed to implement an outcomes-based funding model, will improve overall information and services and shift government toward broadly promoting data-driven policies and investments and evidence-based policy.

Clearly, one limitation of this approach is the constraints regarding the availability of reliable data. What are kindergarten readiness and reading and math proficiency truly worth? What is the value of improved social and emotional benefit and high school graduation? How do you scientifically extrapolate with validity the longer-term impact based on shorter-term outcomes within a specific time horizon? These are not simple questions, and the answers can vary across jurisdictions and for different demographic characteristics of the children served. It is important to note, however, that approaches developed to answer these questions and help determine what government should pay for improvements in early learning outcomes need not be perfect. But these approaches should be based on reliable data and rigorous research; they should also be reasonable and practical. Over time, data capacity and analytical methods will improve through the implementation of this type of funding model precisely because of the need to answer these questions as accurately as possible.

Caution is needed to ensure that paying for outcomes does not create perverse incentives. This is particularly important if one of the outcome metrics is the reduced need for remedial services. Systems must be in place to ensure that the funding model does not influence program-level decisions about whether a child is eligible for these services. The risk of creating perverse incentives can be successfully mitigated by putting processes in place to ensure that the funding model does not impact eligibility determination.

Similarly, particularly in early education, the funding model should not incentivize "teaching to the test." This can be avoided by considering the full range of benefits across development domains as outcomes, including the "softer skills" of social-emotional growth, executive functioning skills, and impact on health. This can also be mitigated by making sure that the outcomes associated with the funding model are consistent with historical outcomes for the specific program being funded, achieved without the presence of an outcomes-based funding model. Further, including longer-term benefits—such as attendance, high school graduation, reductions in juvenile crime, and employment—as outcome measures can mitigate this risk. The evaluation methodology can also lessen the risk of perverse incentives. For instance, random assignment to a treatment and control group, whereby the independent evaluator is the only entity that knows which children are in each group, can mitigate perverse incentives. When this is not possible, a well-planned, quasi-experimental evaluation design can serve the same function.

Although an outcomes-based funding model presents an opportunity to build data capacity, the current lack of data availability presents a barrier to implementation. Lack of political leadership and will can be another barrier. Change can be difficult, and the increased transparency and accountability inherent in an outcomes-based funding approach for both government and providers can be daunting. Another obstacle is the added time and costs of implementing, at least initially, this type of funding model, including ongoing, rigorous program evaluation. Political opposition from some in the early childhood advocacy sector presents another barrier.

CONCLUSION

High-quality preschool programs can improve short- and long-term outcomes for economically disadvantaged children, but the degree of impact and return on public investment varies by program. An outcomes-based funding model for early education promises to direct public investment to effective early childhood programs that best improve child outcomes, incentivize data use for continuous program improvement, foster systemic change, and promote innovation. What government pays for each outcome and the range of outcomes it measures and values is critical to fully realizing the value of a successful early education program. Inadequate compensation has historically been a problem in the early education sector. Thus, by accurately measuring the true value of an effective early education program, government can allocate more resources to adequately compensate providers for the impact they achieve. This can be one approach to ensuring that compensation is commensurate with the value provided, attracting talented professionals to the field, and improving retention of good teachers. The first step, however, is to promote the measurement of and funding for meaningful outcomes. Only in this way will public-sector dollars be used as efficiently as possible to improve the academic and life success of our most vulnerable children.

───

JANIS DUBNO *is a director with the Sorenson Impact Center, David Eccles School of Business, University of Utah. She recently completed a fellowship at the U.S. Department of Education where she was responsible for developing and leading the department's Pay for Success initiative. She was formerly the director of early education policy at Voices for Utah Children, where she developed the Utah High-Quality Preschool Pay for Success Project. Dubno is a former investment banker with 15 years of experience in finance.*

PAY FOR SUCCESS CREATES IMPACT-DRIVEN PARTNERSHIPS THAT BENEFIT HOMELESS FAMILIES

David Merriman
Cuyahoga Job and Family Services

In 2000, I worked at the Cuyahoga Department of Children and Family Services, the public child-welfare agency charged with ensuring the safety and security of children in our county. It was a few months after a "staffing" that I was assigned a custody case of a family that I had known as an AmeriCorps volunteer managing a soup kitchen. Staffings are meetings with the parents, their family and advocates, and an objective reviewer from the agency to review the county's safety concerns before taking custody of the child(ren). This family's needs (trauma, housing instability, and mental health) were significant, and it was not clear that the children would be reunified with their parents. I am not sure if this family would have met a formal definition of homeless, but they clearly had what we now call housing insecurity. The family ultimately addressed their case plan goals, so the children and parents were reunified.

I was grateful that I did not have to file for permanent custody of the children and that the family worked out their issues. I left the agency within a year of their reunification, but I still had glimpses of them. I had been assigned cases from the area of the county where I lived, so I would see the family in the store or walking in my neighborhood. I also saw the news report of the accidental death of one of their children, and I saw the children as adults start to hang out at area drop-in centers for the homeless. I had a sense the family continued to struggle, but I don't know if they ever used any county services. I continue to wonder what more I could have done to help address their housing issues, trauma history, and very limited resources.

I'm grateful for the opportunity to be writing about systems coming together to change themselves and become more responsive to individuals and families. Six years ago, the George Gund Foundation arranged for me to attend the 2011 White House Convening on Pay for Success. The night before the convening, I attended a networking social organized by Nonprofit Finance Fund, where I joined a learning community that would be critical to Cuyahoga County's launching the first county-level, and first child welfare, Pay for Success project in the United States. We're a little over halfway into our Pay for Success project's intervention period. I'm excited about this work, and the process as well as early experiences have energized us.

Through Pay for Success we are providing intensive, evidence-based interventions to homeless families that have lost custody of their children and we will use randomized controlled trial findings to determine payment. We have developed a social-impact-driven public-private partnership, which is key to our project's successful launch. FrontLine Services and Enterprise Community Partners, Inc. (our respective lead service provider and project manager/fiscal manager) had worked together and with the county on other projects and national grant applications, and the county's growing permanent supportive housing portfolio showed that we could develop and manage meaningful public-private partnerships.

All of our Pay for Success partners brought resources to the project and agreed to share in the risks of the deal. These resources included local philanthropic funding for technical assistance and then investment in capital, early university research and access to a longitudinal, integrated data system, and openness of local government to change policy to accommodate innovation. Each of these contributed to the focus on the families we would better serve though the intervention, and each served as a bulwark to the stress of the shared risks of the deal.

I recognized the value of being impact-driven in the partnership context while attending a national forum on Pay for Success. I was there with a service provider staff member and it was near the end of the forum that we noticed there was little to no discussion about the lives of the people, children, and families that these great projects would serve. For the Cuyahoga partnership, our conversations revolved around the improvements we targeted for the homeless families. Yes, we spent hours talking about counterfactuals and the associated costs that lead to families' homelessness and county custody, but the deal construction did not drive our motivation. We found our purpose in service workers' direct observations that came while they talked to a family on a porch, in a shelter, or at a court hearing, and those experiences helped ground us to the impact.

There's great pride in being first in something, but in the project's toughest moments, the pursuit of that status is not what sustained and carried the partnership forward. We knew that by working together, we could develop a meaningful response to the child welfare and homeless systems' inability to align resources and outcomes and that we could launch that response at those systems' level. The impact-driven public-private partnership launched a Pay for Success project by focusing on the lives our clients are living and the work needed to help make the parents and children safe and stable.

We spent three years developing our project, and it will run for five. Few local government projects are sustained over eight years, although many of those with an extended term (e.g., permanent supportive housing and universal pre-K programs) have some of the best outcomes and potential for impact. Still, it is difficult to maintain a partnership over so many years, and one clear weakness is susceptibility to leadership transition. We would have struggled to complete the deal if any of the major partners had left during the development or contracting stages. Staff members have since left the project, and their replacements have brought new energy to the team; however, there was fragility in the partnership during the development. Staff interacted in new ways, and we had to learn together. Risk sharing at the organizational level was also challenging, and each partner had to get comfortable with some exposure. We all were working from a new program design paradigm that carried a heavy workload, partially because there was no example to follow.

It is also important to recognize how political cycles can drive policy agendas and the transition between administrations can blunt impact or end partnerships. I saw this occur as another group that was exploring the development of a Pay for Success project outside of Ohio experienced the election loss of its executive. All of the group's work was suspended, and staff began leaving the administration. In 2013, the county executive during the development of our deal decided to run for another office, so it became clear that the deal needed to be complete by the end of his term to ensure executive support. It turned out that the next county executive, Armond Budish, began assigning transition staff during the project's legislative work and became very familiar with it. As soon as he was elected, he received a brief and became a strong supporter. Executive Budish was such a strong supporter that when he was forced to address a significant budget deficit in his first year, he did not cut the project, even though it was developed by his predecessor and Budish's administration would be responsible for its outcomes and any potential payments. This would have been an easy time for the county to withdraw (a real concern of some investors), but Executive Budish and his chief of staff, Sharon Sobel Jordan, both recognized the potential of the impact-driven public-private partnership. They both became committed to the partnership and to the social impact it drove.

I still support our Pay for Success project, but I now work in the county's public assistance system. Like the child welfare and homeless systems, we have been charged to be more responsive to the workforce needs of our families. The county executive visited 100 businesses in his first 100 days in office, and he heard repeatedly that they needed help filling vacant jobs. At the same time, when people come to our public assistance office, most say they will work if offered a job. Our programs can help people get training, education, and employment. Unfortunately, very few clients receive these benefits because we focus more on the mechanics of the eligibility process than on career goals and wage growth. We also pay more attention to services with the highest compliance, rather than the highest success rates. Executive Budish heard this when he visited our busiest waiting room one day. A young man approached him, and Budish asked why he was there. The client said, "I want to get a job." At that point, a probation officer stepped from behind the client and said, "He's here to apply for food assistance." We gave him the food assistance, and he found a low-wage, limited-hour, seasonal job elsewhere. In time, he disappeared from our system.

We need impact-driven public-private partnerships across our public systems to make us more responsive to the needs of our residents and communities. It is only through partnerships that we can change policy and focus on impact over compliance, develop meaningful goals instead of achievable outputs, and commit the time and resources to work through decades of failed policies. Cuyahoga County exists to ensure that all residents have access to prosperity. It is through this work that we can ensure that all residents thrive, but neither public systems nor external advocates can do this on their own.

Through Pay for Success, we created an innovative program that offers a solution to family homelessness and child welfare by working with partners in a new and open manner, and we also have begun to transform our public assistance programs into a career and wage advancement system. Pay for Success is just one form of impact investment, and I believe that social impact bonds, mission investment, and other emerging impact-driven investment strategies have tremendous potential to accelerate the shift to an outcomes orientation to address social problems. The case for investment in this transformative work is clear. We can either continue with our existing resources and program models to ensure that safety net services meet families' basic needs, or we can build successful partnerships and systemic approaches that lead individuals and families from poverty to prosperity.

I have wondered what would have happened if the homeless family I served almost 20 years ago had access to the services our Pay for Success project provides. This drives me to think of the families receiving our TANF (cash assistance) and SNAP (food stamps) compliance-driven services—or worse, those sanctioned from these programs who now may have no support. We are currently opening up our public assistance system and developing new workforce partnerships, and I hope for a glimpse of that young man whom our executive met in my office. I will look for him in the career pathway programs we are developing, supported by area universities and credentialed training providers that are connected to our county's growing industries. I hope to see him someday walking the neighborhood with his family or into a store with his children, and I expect they will have the same resources as my children. These expectations are reasonable when providers come together and commit to achieving them.

DAVID MERRIMAN *is director of Cuyahoga Job and Family Services in Cleveland, OH. He is a social worker who has worked in child welfare, infant mortality prevention, and HIV/STD prevention and support systems. In his current role, Merriman serves as county administrator of the Medicaid, SNAP, and TANF programs.*

AN OUTCOMES-BASED APPROACH TO CONCENTRATED POVERTY

Carol Naughton
Purpose Built Communities

I n the 2012 edition of *Investing in What Works for America's Communities*, my colleagues Shirley Franklin and David Edwards wrote about the transformation of the East Lake Meadows public housing development in Atlanta and the partnerships and investments that made it successful.[1]

A local philanthropist, a tenant association leader, and the head of the local housing authority were willing to take big risks for an even bigger social return: Transforming a distressed neighborhood into a healthy one with a holistic approach that tackled housing, education, and community wellness simultaneously. This approach wasn't about doing more of the same, but about doing virtually everything differently than it had been done in the past.

In 2016, 21 years after the revitalization efforts began, Dr. Douglas Jutte, a pediatrician from California, visited East Lake to see the results of the transformation up close. After spending time in East Lake's Charles R. Drew Charter School, he inquired what accounted for the lack of obesity among the student body. A large majority of the students at Drew qualified for free and reduced lunch and were African American. In his experience as a pediatrician and public health practitioner, communities with similar demographics often experience higher than average rates of obesity. Was there a particular anti-obesity effort? My answer surprised him. I told him that all Drew students learn to play the violin in third grade. I wasn't being glib. When Drew Charter School opened in 2000, obesity was common among students. What changed? It was not one

---

1 David Edwards and Shirley Franklin, "It Takes a Neighborhood: Purpose Built Communities and Neighborhood Transformation," *Investing in What Works for America's Communities: Essays on People, Place & Purpose*, edited by Nancy O. Andrews and David J. Erickson (San Francisco: Federal Reserve Bank of San Francisco and Low Income Investment Fund, 2012).

thing—the entire neighborhood and its institutions had changed through a series of concurrent investments with excellent execution across sectors by best-in-class partners that fundamentally altered the environment in which children were growing up. High expectations, high opportunities, and high support throughout the community resulted in children who were slimmer and healthier than they were just a few short years ago.

Over a 20-year period, the East Lake initiative has successfully reduced the neighborhood's overall crime rate by more than 70 percent, with a reduction of 90 percent in violent crime. The gains in education were even more impressive. Over the same period, the percentage of fifth-graders meeting state standards in math went from a tragic five percent to an astonishing 99 percent. The employment rate went from a mere 13 percent to 100 percent among working-age adults who were not disabled or going to school. Average household income for families receiving rent assistance increased four-fold.[2] Low-income children in the neighborhood charter school perform at the same or higher levels than non-low-income children in the city and state.[3]

Purpose Built Communities, a nonprofit, pro bono consulting group, was created expressly to help local leaders replicate the success of the East Lake initiative. The approach used in East Lake to create a healthy neighborhood that includes broad, deep, and durable pathways out of poverty has been codified, and we now call it the Purpose Built Communities model. Central to this approach is the focus on a defined and relatively small geography—what people locally would recognize as a neighborhood. Although we have known intuitively that place matters, we now have research that proves the point. The ZIP Codes in which people are born are the single-biggest predictor of their life outcomes. If people are born in neighborhoods of concentrated poverty, the overwhelming odds are that they will live in poverty for the rest of their lives, and so will their children.[4]

2 East Lake Foundation, "East Lake Foundation Annual Report 2015" (2015), available at https://issuu.com/eastlakefoundation95/docs/elf_annualreport_2015.

3 Georgia Department of Education, "2013–14 CRCT Statewide Scores" (2015), available at https://www.gadoe.org/Curriculum-Instruction-and-Assessment/Assessment/Pages/CRCT-Statewide-Scores.aspx.

4 Raj Chetty and Nathaniel Hendren, "The Impacts of Neighborhoods on Intergenerational Mobility: Childhood Exposure Effects and County-Level Estimates," Harvard University and NBER (May 2015), availible at http://www.equality-of-opportunity.org/images/nbhds_paper.pdf.

The Purpose Built Communities model disrupts this cycle of poverty by transforming neighborhoods so that people can reach their full potential. Executed by local leaders with strategic and technical assistance from Purpose Built Communities, these initiatives bring new investments, best-in-class partners, and an insistence on excellence in the execution of all strategies to neighborhoods that have suffered chronically from disinvestment and hopelessness. Within a clearly-defined neighborhood, local leaders and their partners develop mixed-income housing, create a cradle-to-college education pipeline, and provide community wellness programs and facilities. These strategies are all guided by a community quarterback organization, a nonprofit whose sole mission is to focus on the overall health of the neighborhood, coordinating efforts among best-in-class partners from the private and public sectors and attracting the necessary resources to bring the highest level of quality to each of these activities and investments. It is the role of the community quarterback to hold partners accountable and maintain high standards in execution.

Too often in community development efforts in neighborhoods of concentrated poverty, marginally better outcomes are deemed satisfactory. In the Purpose Built Communities model, "good enough" is not good enough! By focusing on a specific neighborhood geography and demanding excellence from everyone involved, breakthrough outcomes become possible over the long term. In our experience, it takes at least ten years for breakthrough outcomes to materialize—the kinds of outcomes we see at East Lake—and it takes leadership in the form of a community quarterback committed to long-term success.

We recognize that all neighborhoods are intrinsically local, and therefore our model must be highly adaptive to meet the needs of local communities around the country. We believe that our model could be adapted for use in approximately 825 urban neighborhoods around the country. However, we don't believe it is a satisfactory strategy in neighborhoods where the larger region lacks economic vitality, nor do we have experience to know that it will work in rural areas. Our model is a neighborhood intervention strategy, not a regional economic development strategy.

We believe housing that serves families across a very broad range of incomes is critical to community vibrancy. Housing can serve not only as a platform for stability for low-income residents, but also as a catalyst for growing social networks, services, and infrastructure that ultimately benefits all residents. The introduction of high-quality, multi-family developments with rents at various levels of subsidy and market rates help create mixed-income neighborhoods that attract new services, jobs, and private investment. For the lowest-income residents, a mixed-income environment creates social connections, which benefit both children and adults and seldom exist in low-income housing developments. Many of these developments have work requirements as part of their leases, with exceptions for those who are in school, elderly, or disabled.

We've seen successful adaptations that are an improvement on what was possible in East Lake in the mid-1990s. For example, East Lake relied on a housing mix of 50 percent market-rate rental homes (no restrictions on either income or rent) and 50 percent deeply subsidized by the Atlanta Housing Authority. However, other initiatives we support are using a more refined mix that is based on one-third of the rental homes being available at true market rates, one-third for rent-restricted low- to moderate-income families, and one-third deeply subsidized through project-based assistance from a local housing authority. This mix creates a better financial model for the developer while creating a more economically diverse community. The lowest-income families, who might be worried that they can never make the jump from deeply subsidized to market rents, see the rent-restricted units as an achievable stepping stone as they work to gain financial stability and greater wealth. Other initiatives have demonstrated that having a significant component of rental homes available at true market rates is important for destigmatizing the neighborhood. Having a mere ten percent of the rental homes available at market rates will not attract additional investment to the community or result in the neighborhood's being perceived as a neighborhood of choice—something we believe is essential for creating the conditions that will attract additional investment into neighborhoods that are desperate for it.

Although the East Lake initiative focused on developing mixed-income rental housing, many of the Purpose Built Communities network members include a homeownership component as well. In Birmingham, in addition to new, beautiful townhomes available to low- and moderate-income families, the community quarterback is developing new, single-family homes that will be available at market rates. This strategy was employed simply because the state of Alabama made mixed-income rental housing almost impossible to finance. The community quarterback also raised funds for a single-family home-improvement program and renovated more than 65 homes for homeowners who would not have been able to afford those improvements, many of which were desperately needed. They repaired roofs, renovated kitchens, replaced heating and cooling systems, reattached porches to houses, and repaired dilapidated plumbing. This program largely benefited longtime homeowners who now have improved homes in an improving neighborhood.

Another innovation in mixed-income housing comes from the world of philanthropy. In several communities, local foundations are making significant investments in housing. Often, these investments are not designed to finance the affordable housing component, as one might expect, but are, in fact, used to help subsidize the market-rate housing, where financing is harder to secure. Frequently in the form of program-related investments, these investments in housing can be used to help reset the market. When they are repaid, often after 40 years, the funds can be used for other needs in the community.

On the education side, our network members (those community quarterbacks who have demonstrated both capacity and commitment to implementing this model) continue to push the envelope to create excellent, neighborhood-serving education pipelines in their neighborhoods. For example, the Charlotte Mecklenburg Housing Authority invested $5 million to support early learning at Renaissance West. This money wasn't put into the capital structure of the early learning facility, as might have been expected. Rather, the housing authority specifically contributed these funds to close the quality gap in providing excellent early learning for low-income children in the community. We know what it costs to deliver high-quality early learning that will prepare all children for success in kindergarten and beyond, and the public funds available are simply inadequate to meet the need. This creative, upstream investment will pay dividends long after children have moved beyond early learning and into the K-12 system. We've helped community quarterbacks negotiate memorandums of agreement with local school systems to bring charter-like flexibility to traditional public schools. Omaha Public Schools has worked with 75 North, the local community quarterback, and our sister program, Purpose Built Schools, to reconstitute a chronically underperforming elementary school. A year-long principal fellowship and ongoing support during the first year of the new principal's tenure has set the school on a new trajectory. One of the reasons we believe this approach will be effective is the complete buy-in and participation of Omaha Public Schools' leadership. Without that deep partnership and commitment, this approach would not likely be sustained beyond the tenure of the new principal. The deep commitment of Omaha Public Schools' central office staff and their board makes us optimistic that the approach is sustainable beyond the tenure of any one person. Of course, this is a marathon and not a sprint, so we really won't know for several more years how successful this approach will be.

We also have evidence from East Lake now that demonstrates that high-quality education sustains not only the human-capital transformation but the real-estate revitalization as well. In fact, as Drew Charter School has sustained its reputation for excellence and built out a new high school, more people are drawn to the neighborhood, and parents who live outside the neighborhood want to get their children into Drew. In fact, the school had a waiting list last year of about 2,500 children, most of whom lived outside of the East Lake neighborhood. Because children who live in the Villages of East Lake are given first priority to attend Drew Charter School, rents in the market-rate apartment homes in the Villages of East Lake are higher than they have ever been, despite the fact that the property is now almost 20 years old. Families pass up newer, shinier homes so they can live at the Villages of East Lake because they want their children to be part of the East Lake education pipeline. Although the market-rate rental homes attract higher-income families, low-income families continue to live in the Villages of East Lake and pay rent based on their income. As Drew Charter School becomes a more mixed-income school (Drew's target is for 65 percent of students to come from low-income families; approximately 60 percent do today), we are seeing significant growth of social networks—not just for students but for their parents as well. We know that social networks are an important tool that people use to get their next job or learn about a new opportunity. The combination of an excellent mixed-income school and high-quality, mixed-income housing creates a fertile environment for new relationships and opportunities.

Our network members and their partners continue to adapt the model on the health and wellness front as well. In East Lake, the YMCA was one of the first-in partners. Although they had been serving the neighborhood for years, their facility was closing because it had outlived its useful life. The YMCA jumped at the chance to become a founding implementation partner in East Lake, and in addition to serving as the tip of the spear in community building, it created a wonderful health and wellness center that continues to bring people together across race, income, religion, ethnicity, and gender. In Fort Worth, TX, the YMCA partnered with the city to build a new YMCA, including a city-financed outdoor pool that the YMCA will manage. In Spartanburg, SC, the Mary Black Foundation—a health-conversion foundation—has invested broadly in the initiative, including in the new early learning facility and in the community quarterback itself. The city of Spartanburg is building a first-rate health and recreation center in the community. Spartanburg Medical Center, with about a half-billion dollars of construction planned over the next decade, has developed a workforce development program to hire people from the Northside neighborhood in construction trades. Spartanburg Medical Center also has revised its background standards and training protocols to hire people who historically would not have qualified and is paying these trainees well during the training period. Working with the Goizueta Business School at Emory University, the East Lake Foundation piloted a new entrepreneurship program called Start:Me that is now being replicated in Spartanburg and other communities. The Bayou District Foundation, the community quarterback in New Orleans, has just opened a new, tournament-quality golf course in City Park. It will serve triple duty as a revenue generator for ongoing programs in the Bayou District, an economic engine supporting tourism in New Orleans, and the home of the First Tee of New Orleans, a youth development program that uses golf as a platform to deliver its curriculum.

As we have worked with local leaders to customize our model to meet the needs of their communities, we have experienced an expected tension between our desire to see the model executed with fidelity and the desire of local communities to customize, sometimes beyond where we feel comfortable about the ability to deliver exceptional results. For example, one school district unexpectedly pulled back on its commitment to operate a school on an extended-day model, which had been part of the plan from the start and is necessary to deliver the full school design that had been planned for the past three years. Although we will continue to support the school and the community, we are less certain about the ability to deliver dramatically-improved outcomes for students.

We have developed a performance scorecard to measure the impact of investments and provide insights to ensure ongoing improvements. All network members agree to measure certain metrics around student achievement, safety, productivity, neighborhood health and safety, and income and property values. Most network members have additional metrics that are meaningful to their work locally. Although it is much too early to know whether each network member will be successful, the preliminary data are very positive.

As of this writing, there are 16 Purpose Built Communities network members in 16 different cities across the United States. They include: Atlanta, GA; Birmingham, AL; Charlotte, NC; Columbus, OH; Fort Worth, TX; Houston, TX; Indianapolis, IN; Kansas City, MO; New Orleans, LA; Oakland, CA; Omaha, NE; Orlando, FL; Raleigh, NC; Rome, GA; Spartanburg, SC; and Tulsa, OK. Our goal is to add three or four more high-quality initiatives every year, and we have developed a pipeline of prospects to meet that goal.

As of January 2017, at least part of the educational pipelines of 13 of the 16 network members is operational; this includes 39 schools (including eight early learning centers), with a total of 17,338 students. Across the network, 2,194 apartment rental homes, serving 5,254 residents, are occupied by families across a broad range of incomes. There are another 612 apartment homes under construction, as well as three additional early learning centers and a new K-8 elementary school. All 16 network members are currently executing initiatives to support health and wellness for their residents.

Safety has improved dramatically in the Bayou District in New Orleans, along with incomes and employment rates for families receiving rental assistance. Young children have access to high-quality early learning at the Educare New Orleans, the first Educare Early Learning Center in the Deep South. A new K-8 KIPP school will open in the Bayou District in

July 2018. Other outcomes will take a few more years to bear fruit, but early progress is encouraging.

What do the outcomes in East Lake and the early data from other network member initiatives mean? First, the scale of the investments is necessary to help neighborhoods that have suffered from decades of disinvestment catch up with neighborhoods that have enjoyed more consistent investment. Tinkering around the edges of neighborhoods suffering from profound generational disinvestment won't create transformational outcomes. The Selig Center at the Terry School of Business at the University of Georgia looked at the economic impact of the East Lake revitalization in 2007 and determined that the initial $125 million invested in the initiative was recouped in just 18 months of operation.[5]

More important, the outcomes and return on investment from this approach beg another question: Who would be willing to pay for the outcomes that our model delivers? Who would be willing to pay for a solution to the costs associated with concentrated poverty? Clearly, local and state governments, the federal government, and public school systems should be willing to pay for the outcomes because the costs incurred in poverty alleviation, safety, and special education, for example, should all drop dramatically. Tax revenue, through increased property and income taxes, should increase. Investments at scale in our model will save all levels of government money and could ultimately reduce the tax burden.

Likewise, foundations, particularly health-conversion foundations, may also be interested in exploring how they could buy these outcomes.

Hospital systems, health insurance companies, and others in the business of improving health should be motivated to invest in neighborhood-level improvement. Despite the fact that our work was not designed as a health intervention, we have successfully moved the social determinants of health for entire communities, which should result in lower costs associated with delivering medical care. Academic outcomes, incomes, housing stability, and safety have improved, all of which predict better outcomes

---

5 Selig Center for Economic Growth, "Economic Revitalization of Atlanta's East Lake Community: A Chance to Succeed" Terry College of Business, University of Georgia (Fall 2008), available at https://www.terry.uga.edu/media/documents/selig/east_lake_study.pdf.

at the community health level. These outcomes have value to hospital systems, insurance companies, and others in this field. The challenge now is to measure the impact, quantify the value, and create mechanisms to appropriately allocate risk and reward.

Although the idea of selling a solution to concentrated poverty is alluring, the genius is in the details, all of which still need to be fleshed out. Before taking this idea to market, we will want to better understand any additional data that need to be collected and determine if a neighborhood intervention strategy can reach the scale necessary to make this kind of investment worthwhile for a buyer of better community outcomes. Our approach typically impacts about 15,000 people per neighborhood, and we have yet to determine whether that scale is sufficient.

At Purpose Built Communities, we are still learning what is possible and how quickly transformational outcomes can be achieved. With more high-caliber work, study, and evaluation, a place-based approach to eradicating poverty—by selling the outcomes to those who would benefit economically from the results—could emerge sooner than we think.

CAROL NAUGHTON *is president of Purpose Built Communities, a comprehensive community development organization. She is responsible for leading the teams that support revitalizations in 16 cities, as well as the teams currently vetting opportunities in 35 additional cities, including several in metro Atlanta. Previously, Naughton served as the executive director of the East Lake Foundation, the community quarterback organization that developed and continues to implement the model of community revitalization that Purpose Built Communities is charged with replicating around the country. Prior to joining the East Lake Foundation, she was general counsel and deputy executive director for legal and nonprofit affairs for the Atlanta Housing Authority. Before joining the housing authority, Naughton was an attorney with Sutherland, Asbill & Brennan's real estate group, where she primarily represented developers, lenders, and asset managers. She serves on the board of directors of the Low Income Investment Fund (LIIF), the board of advisors of the Build Healthy Places Network, the national steering committee of LOCUS, and is an alumnus of the 2016 class of Leadership Atlanta. She is a graduate of the Emory University School of Law and was executive editor of the* Emory Law Journal, *and graduated cum laude with a BA in political science from Colgate University.*

FROM EVIDENCE-BASED POLICIES TO POSITIVE OUTCOMES
How to Fund What Really Works in Child Welfare

Susan M. Snyder
Georgia State University

Matthew was 11, John was two, and Lisa was a newborn when they were removed from their mother's care because of her drug addiction and placed in the foster care system.[1] Instead of helping, the foster care system further traumatized the children. The children's first foster home was de-licensed after another child was severely physically abused in the home. The siblings were then separated, and John was beaten with a belt in his next foster placement. The newborn was placed in a home with a convicted rapist. Matthew began having behavior problems and engaging in gang activity. Although their mother loved her children, she needed help herself, and the addiction and parenting support programs available to her were ineffective.

Perhaps the most distressing part of this story is how common these circumstances are for child-welfare–involved children. As many as 80 percent of parents whose children are in foster care suffer from a substance abuse disorder.[2] And while removing children from their original homes can be essential in many circumstances, it also increases their risk of engaging in delinquent

---

1 Pseudonyms have been used to protect the identities of Lisa, John, and Matthew.

2 Arazais Oliveros and Joan Kaufman, "Addressing Substance Abuse Treatment Needs of Parents Involved with the Child Welfare System," *Child Welfare* 90 (1) (2011): 25–41, available at http://www.ncbi.nlm.nih.gov/pmc/articles/PMC4158612/; Nancy K. Young, Sharon M. Boles, and Cathleen Otero, "Parental Substance Use Disorders and Child Maltreatment: Overlap, Gaps, and Opportunities," *Child Maltreatment* 12 (2) (2007): 137–49, available at http://cmx.sagepub.com/content/12/2/137.

behaviors,[3] substance use,[4] and ultimately ending up in prison.[5] The long-term societal costs of removing children from their original homes, rather than seeking to treat parental addiction issues and preserve families where possible, are enormous — and sometimes continue for generations.

Regardless of whether children are removed from their homes, child maltreatment is a public health problem with substantial costs to society. A study by the Centers for Disease Control and Prevention found that the total cost of child maltreatment is $124 billion each year.[6] Despite these enormous costs, few evidence-based interventions address the needs of either maltreated children[7] or their parents.[8] The situation may be exacerbated because federal child welfare expenditures have decreased, even though the number of child maltreatment reports has increased across the country. As a result, child welfare services are increasingly reliant on

3 Susan M. Snyder and Darcey H. Merritt, "Do Childhood Experiences of Neglect Affect Delinquency Among Child Welfare Involved–Youth?" *Children and Youth Services Review* 46 (2014): 64–71, available at http://www.sciencedirect.com/science/article/pii/S0190740914002941; Joseph P. Ryan and Mark F. Testa, "Child Maltreatment and Juvenile Delinquency: Investigating the Role of Placement and Placement Instability," *Children and Youth Services Review* 27 (3) (2005): 227–49, available at http://www.sciencedirect.com/science/article/pii/S0190740904002026.

4 Susan M. Snyder and Rachel E. Smith, "Do Physical Abuse, Depression, and Parental Substance Use Influence Patterns of Substance Use Among Child Welfare Involved–Youth?" *Substance Use & Misuse* 50 (2) (2015): 226–35, available at http://www.ncbi.nlm.nih.gov/pubmed/25338287; Amy Heneghan et al., "Mental Health Problems in Teens Investigated by U.S. Child Welfare Agencies," *Journal of Adolescent Health* 52 (5) (2013): 634–40, available at http://www.ncbi.nlm.nih.gov/pubmed/23375826.

5 Sara McCarthy and Mark Gladstone, "State Survey of California Prisoners: What Percentage of the State's Polled Prison Inmates Were Once Foster Care Children?" *Policy Matters* (California Senate Office of Research: 2011), available at http://www.sor.govoffice3.com/vertical/Sites/%7B3BDD1595-792B-4D20-8D44-626EF05648C7%7D/uploads/Foster_Care_PDF_12-8-11.pdf; Susan M. Snyder and Rose Anne Medeiros, "Typologies of Substance Use and Illegal Behaviors: A Comparison of Emerging Adults with Histories of Foster Care and the General Population," *Children and Youth Services Review* 35 (5) (2013): 753–61, available at http://www.sciencedirect.com/science/article/pii/S0190740913000509.

6 Xiangming Fang et al., "The Economic Burden of Child Maltreatment in the United States," *Child Abuse & Neglect* 36 (2) (2012): 156–165, available at http://www.sciencedirect.com/science/article/pii/S0145213411003140.

7 Mary Dozier et al., "Developing Evidence-Based Interventions for Foster Children: An Example of a Randomized Clinical Trial with Infants and Toddlers," *Journal of Social Issues* 62 (4) (2006): 765–783, available at http://onlinelibrary.wiley.com/doi/10.1111/j.1540-4560.2006.00486.x/full; Nancy Rolock, Susan M. Snyder, and Cynthia Tate, "Formative Evaluation: A Case Study of the Illinois Birth-to-Three IV-E Waiver," *Journal of Evidence-Informed Social Work* 12 (5) (2015): 37–41.

8 Joan E. Zweben et al., "Enhancing Family Protective Factors in Residential Treatment for Substance Use Disorders," *Child Welfare* 94 (5) (2015): 145–166, available at http://www.ebcrp.org/wp-content/uploads/2016/02/150612_Enhancing-family-protective-factors-in-residential-treatment-for-substance-use-disorders.pdf; Richard Barth et al., "Parent-Training Programs in Child Welfare Services: Planning for a More Evidence-Based Approach to Serving Biological Parents," *Research on Social Work Practice* 15 (5) (2005): 353–371.

dwindling state and local funds.[9] Thus, social impact bonds may provide a way to address child welfare service needs that cannot be met in the current economic climate.

Children like Lisa, John, and Matthew might be far more likely to have better outcomes if our child welfare policies focused on what really works. Although we spend a great deal on social programs, seldom are the results of programs adequately assessed, which allows programs that don't work to endure far too long and draw resources from other, more effective interventions.[10] This chapter discusses social impact bonds, which strive to fund child welfare programs that achieve desired outcomes without wasting resources on programs that don't work.

OVERVIEW

A predecessor to social impact bonds, called performance-based contracts, emerged in the early 1990s as one way to fund what works in child welfare.[11] Rather than paying for a unit of a particular service (e.g., an overnight stay in a foster home), performance-based contracts can reward private agencies that achieve or exceed specific outcomes and/or penalize agencies that fail to achieve specific outcomes (e.g., children are reunified with parents, children are adopted, or parents are able to provide a safe and supportive home environment).[12] At least 27 states have experimented with performance-based contracts for one or more child welfare services.[13]

9   Kristina Rosinsky and Dana Connelly, "Child Welfare Financing SFY 2014: A Survey of Federal, State, and Local Expenditures," Annie E. Casey Foundation (October 2016), available at https://www.childtrends.org/wp-content/uploads/2016/10/2016-53ChildWelfareFinancingSFY2014.pdf.

10   Eric Trupin, Nicholas Weiss, and Suzanne U. Kerns, "Social Impact Bonds: Behavioral Health Opportunities," *JAMA Pediatrics* 168 (11) (2014): 985–86, available at http://archpedi.jamanetwork.com/article.aspx?articleid=1900479.

11   Crystal Collins-Camargo and Karl Ensign, "Driving Case Outcomes in Child Welfare: Are Performance-Based Contracts the Answer?" *Policy & Practice* 68 (3) (2010): 11, available at https://www.questia.com/magazine/1G1-229069168/driving-case-outcomes-in-child-welfare-are-performance-based.

12   Bowen McBeath and William Meezan, "Governance in Motion: Service Provision and Child Welfare Outcomes in a Performance-Based, Managed Care Contracting Environment," *Journal of Public Administration Research & Theory* 20 (suppl_1) (2010): i101–i23, available at https://jpart.oxfordjournals.org/content/20/suppl_1/i101.short; Emma Tomkinson, "Outcome-Based Contracting for Human Services," *Evidence Base* 1 (1) (2016): 1–20, available at https://journal.anzsog.edu.au/publications/20/EvidenceBase2016Issue1Version1.pdf; Charlotte McCullough, Nancy Pindus, and Elizabeth Lee, "Preparing Effective Contracts in Privatized Child Welfare Systems," HHS Office of the Assistant Secretary for Planning and Evaluation (2008), available at https://aspe.hhs.gov/basic-report/preparing-effective-contracts-privatized-child-welfare-systems; Lawrence L. Martin, "Performance-Based Contracting for Human Services: Does It Work?" *Administration in Social Work* 29 (1) (2005): 63–77.

13   Crystal Collins-Camargo and Karl Ensign, "Driving Case Outcomes in Child Welfare: Are Performance-Based Contracts the Answer?" *Policy & Practice* (3) (2010): 11, available at https://www.questia.com/magazine/1G1-229069168/driving-case-outcomes-in-child-welfare-are-performance-based.

Social impact bonds, part of a broader suite of outcomes-based contracting approaches, constitute a relatively new variation of performance-based contracts that focus on funding effective programs in child welfare. Social impact bonds are public-private partnerships that shift risk from the government to investors: An intermediary raises private capital, chooses service providers to provide an evidence-based intervention, and selects an independent assessor to determine performance outcomes and the evaluation approach.[14] Government is required to pay only if the intervention works as intended.[15]

Because of the size and complexity of the child welfare system, ensuring that social impact bonds can be effective in that context requires starting with a well-designed study, with the following components: a clearly defined population and problem, an intervention, a comparison, and the desired outcome.[16]

It is best practice for evaluations of social impact bonds to include a comparison or counterfactual, which is a way to see what would happen if the intervention were not given. One way to provide counterfactuals is to use randomized controlled trials.[17] In randomized controlled trials, participants are randomly assigned by an impartial method, such as a flip of a coin, to determine whether they receive the intervention the social impact bond provides. Although randomized controlled trials are considered the gold standard for scientific research, they are sometimes not used because some argue that it is unethical to withhold a treatment that could work. The irony is that failing to use randomized controlled trials may do more to withhold effective interventions, because that can allow treatments that may not work to be scaled up, wasting limited resources.

---

14 Ibid; Jeffrey B. Liebman, "Social Impact Bonds: A Promising New Financing Model to Accelerate Social Innovation and Improve Government Performance," Center for American Progress (2011), available at https://www.americanprogress.org/issues/general/report/2011/02/09/9050/social-impact-bonds/.

15 Laura Callanan, Jonathan Law, and Lenny Mendonca, "From Potential to Action: Bringing Social Impact Bonds to the US," McKinsey & Company (2012), available at http://www.payforsuccess.org/resources/potential-action-bringing-social-impact-bonds-us.

16 Nancy Rolock, Susan M. Snyder, and Cynthia Tate, "Formative Evaluation: A Case Study of the Illinois Birth-to-Three IV-E Waiver," *Journal of Evidence-Informed Social Work* (2015): 1–12, available at http://www.ncbi.nlm.nih.gov/pubmed/25826248; W. Scott Richardson et al., "The Well-Built Clinical Question: A Key to Evidence-Based Decisions," *ACP Journal Club* 123 (3) (1995): A12, available at https://acpjc.acponline.org/Content/123/3/issue/ACPJC-1995-123-3-A12.htm.

17 Liebman, "Social Impact Bonds" (2011).

EXAMPLES

States, counties, and child welfare agencies are beginning to embrace social impact bonds to reduce costs and improve outcomes. Connecticut, for example, obtained $12.5 million in private investments for a social impact bond using the Family-Based Recovery (FBR) intervention, which researchers from Yale University and the University of Connecticut found to be an effective treatment intervention for parental substance abuse.[18] FBR is an in-home, intensive, long-term clinical treatment intervention to keep families of children under the age of eight intact while providing the services needed (e.g., substance use treatment, parent-child relationship support, developmental guidance, and case management) to ensure that the home is a safe and supportive environment.[19] In Cuyahoga County, Ohio, a $4 million social impact bond is housing and providing supportive services to 135 homeless parents with children in foster care, to reduce the children's length of stay in foster care.[20] In Illinois, the Dually-Involved Youth Project was developed to target youth who are involved in both the juvenile justice and child welfare systems, since nearly two-thirds of those youth spend time in costly institutional care and half recidivate within two years.[21]

Although the literature regarding the strengths of child welfare social impact bonds is sparse, there are indications that social impact bonds may have the potential to strengthen the child welfare system. Axford and Morpeth suggest that the outcomes-based focus of social impact bonds may be a better fit for employing programs with a proven track record (i.e., evidence-based practice) than providing traditional public

18 Kyle Constable and Jacqueline Rabe Thomas, "New Program Announced for Substance Abuse Treatment," *The CT Mirror* (February 16, 2016), available at https://ctmirror.org/2016/02/16/new-funding-to-boost-substance-abuse-treatment/.

19 Yale School of Medicine, "Program for Families Affected by Substance Use (FBR)" (2017), available at https://medicine.yale.edu/childstudy/family/fbr.aspx; Karen E. Hanson et al., "Family-Based Recovery: An Innovative In-Home Substance Abuse Treatment Model for Families with Young Children," *Child Welfare* 94 (4) (2015): 161–83.

20 Patrick Lester, "Pay-for-Success in Child Welfare: A Case Study," Social Innovation Research Center (2015).

21 Illinois Department of Children and Family Services, "Illinois Dually-Involved Youth Pay for Success Initiative Ramp-Up Fact Sheet" (2015).

child welfare services without such contracts.[22] Liebman asserts that social impact bonds could provide a means of helping foster youth and youth involved in juvenile justice to successfully transition to adulthood.[23] Hawkins et al. contend that social impact bonds could effectively support the widespread use of preventive interventions.[24] With this in mind, evidence-based prevention and intervention programs could be initiated to address a wide range of issues pertaining to child welfare over the course of development. One example of a prevention program is SafeCare,[25] which is an in-home program for at-risk or maltreating parents that could be implemented in more communities throughout the world.[26] Examples of programs that address trauma include the Attachment and Behavioral Catch-Up for children from birth to 24 months, Parent-Child Interaction Therapy for youth from two to 12 years old, and the Safe Harbor program for youth six to 21 years old.[27]

Despite their potential, social impact bonds also have some weaknesses. Service providers may be deterred by the risk that the intervention could fail, or they (or their investors) may require large fees to assume the risk. Scaling up social impact bonds can be difficult because what works for one population may not work for another.[28] Social impact bonds may also cost more than programs that government delivers directly.[29] Another

22 Nick Axford and Louis Morpeth, "Evidence-Based Programs in Children's Services: A Critical Appraisal," *Children and Youth Services Review* 35 (2) (2013): 268–77, available at http://www.sciencedirect.com.ezproxy.gsu.edu/science/article/pii/S0190740912003994.

23 Jeffrey B. Liebman, "Building on Recent Advances in Evidence-Based Policymaking," Results for America and The Hamilton Project (2013), available at http://www.hamiltonproject.org/assets/legacy/files/downloads_and_links/THP_LiebmanF2_4-13_1.pdf.

24 J. David Hawkins et al., "Unleashing the Power of Prevention," Institute of Medicine of the National Academies (2015), available at http://aaswsw.org/wp-content/uploads/2013/10/Unleashing-the-Power-of-Prevention-formatted-4.29.15.pdf.

25 For more information see http://safecare.publichealth.gsu.edu/safecare/safecare-research/; Anna Edwards and John R. Lutzker, "Iterations of the SafeCare Model: An Evidence-Based Child Maltreatment Prevention Program," *Behavior Modification* 32 (5) (2008): 736–56, available at http://bmo.sagepub.com/content/32/5/736.short.

26 See additional examples for a range of preventative programs at https://www.childwelfare.gov/topics/preventing/programs/.

27 See additional examples at http://www.nctsn.org/resources/topics/treatments-that-work/promising-practices.

28 Liebman, "Social Impact Bonds" (2011).

29 Callanan, "From Potential to Action" (2012).

possibility is that service providers may avoid providing services in difficult cases that are less likely to succeed when compensation is tied to measurable success.

GIVEN THE EVIDENCE, WHY AREN'T SOCIAL IMPACT BONDS MORE WIDESPREAD?

A few barriers have prevented more widespread use of social impact bonds in funding the child welfare system, including their complexity. Service providers may already struggle to engage in performance-based contracting without the added layers of investors or intermediaries. Additionally, it can be harder to measure real change than other metrics that are easier to quantify but do not necessarily signal improvements in care. According to Stid, it is easier to quantify the resources that go into an intervention (inputs) and the products produced, such as the number of parenting training sessions (outputs), than the actual measurable changes the intervention produces (outcomes).[30] Martin's survey of 614 members of the National Institute of Governmental Purchasing found that only 39.9 percent of new contracts or contract extensions were awarded based on performance outcomes, as opposed to other measures like inputs and outputs.[31]

Another factor that may prevent social impact bonds from spreading in the child welfare field is that children in foster care have complex needs and are served by multiple agencies and programs across local, state, and federal government. This is particularly true of the high-needs users of child welfare services, such as children with severe emotional and behavioral problems. Additionally, individuals at each agency may have disparate and conflicting interests that may prevent needed collaboration and lead to competition for credit. Consequently, it may be difficult to track costs and service utilization, which is essential in order to pay off the intermediaries and investors. Finally, the failure of these programs could attract negative media attention.[32] The impact of such attention in child welfare may be particularly profound because the general public

30 Daniel Stid, "Pay for Success Is Not a Panacea," *Community Development Investment Review* (2013): 13–18, available at http://www.frbsf.org/community-development/files/pay-for-success-not-panacea.pdf.

31 Lawrence L. Martin, "Performance-Based Contracting for Services: A Survey of NIGP Members," (Orlando, FL: GSA Training Conference and Expo 2010), available at http://208.112.78.139/gsaSchedule2010/training/ppt/PerformanceBasedContractingForNIGP.ppt.

32 Stid, "Pay for Success Is Not a Panacea" (2013).

may be outraged if children are harmed by a program that was perceived as having a profit motive.

CONCLUSION

Although there are challenges, social impact bonds can play an important role in advancing child welfare. Science and ethics must play a central role in any such venture, and political will must be built among participating stakeholders to ensure optimal designs at every phase. Because the stakes are so high, social impact bonds should be considered as an option for child welfare only when the most rigorous evaluation approaches are used. In addition, child welfare social impact bonds require robust data systems to capture integrated data from each service provider children encounter, so that we can investigate fully what factors influence desired outcomes, both positively and negatively. Finally, it is imperative that all parties involved in social impact bonds are honest when interventions fail, because children like Lisa, John, and Matthew deserve interventions that work.

SUSAN M. SNYDER is an assistant professor in the department of social work at Georgia State University. Dr. Snyder has over a decade of practice experience in the field of child welfare, which informs her commitment to advancing research in the field. Dr. Snyder investigates the sequelae of problem behavior, including substance use and illegal behaviors, among maltreated and system-involved youth.

BRINGING TOGETHER COLLECTIVE IMPACT AND PAY FOR PERFORMANCE
A New Approach to Breaking the Cycle of Poverty

Kate Howard
City and County of San Francisco

Fred Blackwell
San Francisco Foundation

Picture an isolated, dilapidated public housing project built 60 years ago as temporary shelter and now home to the city's poorest residents, most of them people of color. There are no nearby grocery stores, no convenient buses, not even a neighborhood fire station, and most young adults are not working or in school. Now imagine this community transformed into a vibrant mixed-income development with beautiful homes, robust businesses, and thriving, productive residents.

HOPE SF, San Francisco's signature anti-poverty and equity initiative, is translating that vision into reality in four public housing communities. It is doing so without displacing current residents but instead by engaging them in charting the course to a prosperous future and embedding comprehensive services that support them along the way. HOPE SF aims to ensure those services actually deliver results for a significant number of low-income people by tying payments to resident outcomes.

It is among the nation's first large-scale housing transformation collaboratives that invests both in people and place to disrupt concentrated, generational poverty and spur economic mobility. It is also the first initiative that marries the multi-strategy, cross-sector approach of collective impact and a pay-for-performance model.

The collective impact partnership that manages HOPE SF brings together leaders from the community, city government, philanthropy, and business, including the co-authors of this chapter (Fred Blackwell serves as the steward on the philanthropy side and Kate Howard is responsible for allocating the city's dollars that advance the HOPE SF vision.) Our partnership has taken on the challenge of combining collective impact and results-driven contracting for an urgent reason: San Francisco needs a completely new approach to break the cycle of poverty and ensure that low-income people participate in and benefit from the city's stunning growth and prosperity. Conventional anti-poverty, workforce training, and community development strategies have failed. Residents rightly expect something better.

The city has the nation's fastest rates of job growth and economic expansion and one of the highest levels of income inequality.[1] The average income for the top five percent of households was $423,000 in 2013.[2] Meanwhile, HOPE SF communities in the city's southeast—home to 4,000 people, mostly of color—have a household median annual income of $14,000.[3] Cut off from opportunity, more than two-thirds of HOPE SF residents aged 16 to 24 are unemployed and either not in school or not on track to graduate. Many lack the training, work experience, and positive role models necessary to achieve financial security and sustainable livelihoods; they also are burdened by chronic trauma, and they distrust the systems that have let them down.

Against this backdrop, we in philanthropy and government recognized the need to shake up the way we do business in and with low-income communities. After decades of programs and services, it was painfully clear that disparate, narrowly focused interventions, created and implemented for residents, do not work. We need better tools and more powerful

---

1 Jennifer Warburg, "Top Analysts Predict Another Year of Growth for SF Economy," SPUR News (February, 15, 2015), available at www.spur.org/news/2015-02-20/top-analysts-predict-another-year-growth-sf-economy.

2 Alan Berube and Natalie Holmes, "Some Cities are Still More Unequal than Others – an Update," Brookings Institution (March 17, 2015), available at www.brookings.edu/research/reports2/2015/03/city-inequality-berube-holmes.

3 LA Group: Learning for Action, "Hope SF Baseline Evaluation Report" (June 2012), available at http://sfmohcd.org/sites/default/files/FileCenter/Documents/7645-3-HOPE%20SF%20Baseline%20Data%20Report_Final_7%203%2012.pdf.

approaches that focus on results. We also realized that philanthropy and government had to embark on this venture side by side, in deep partnership with residents, with all of us committed to common goals, a clearly articulated set of outcomes we intend to achieve, and evidence-based solutions.

Through flexible dollars, philanthropy has the ability to seed new strategies, advance learning through evaluation, bring promising practices from the field, and apply the influence that keeps the needs of vulnerable communities as a top San Francisco priority. For its part, city government can use one of its most powerful tools—contracts potentially worth millions of dollars—to support, scale, and sustain programs that make a difference in the lives and economic prospects of vulnerable populations. For those of us concerned about race, place, and trauma in San Francisco, collective impact and outcomes-driven contracting is a powerful combination to address the shameful, wasteful paradox of a resource-rich, yet outcomes-poor, city.

COLLABORATIVE ACTION TO CLOSE THE OPPORTUNITY GAP

Let's talk first about the collective impact piece of our effort, which has guided HOPE SF since 2010. The framework is an important acknowledgement by partners across sectors that none of us, alone, can fix economic inequality, racial inequity, and concentrated poverty. Rather, it takes intentional collaborative action driven by the community and focused relentlessly on results. It takes long-term commitments. And it requires multiple approaches aimed at improving the lives of individuals and families, strengthening neighborhoods, and changing the systems that shape, and too often impede, opportunity. HOPE SF has identified five overarching, interconnected trauma-informed strategies: equitable mixed-income development, health and wellness, education, community building, and economic mobility. This final one, mobility, is the target of our first venture in paying for results.

Collective impact provides a natural framework for the venture, committing HOPE SF partners to focus on meaningful outcomes and use shared data to track them, continually improve performance, and make the case for systems change. The determined focus on results inspires a spirit of innovation not typically seen in large bureaucracies or multi-agency initiatives. It also got us thinking about bringing a pay-for-performance model to the complicated environment of our multi-faceted, community-driven collaborative. We knew, of course, that previous models such as Pay for Success were based on single-issue initiatives. But life isn't so tidy. And in low-income communities, especially, the challenges pile up and compound one another. All need to be addressed, thoughtfully and simultaneously, if we want to get mobility and opportunity right.

We realized that results-driven contracting requires flexibility and creativity to ensure that our investments are evidence-based and that their outcomes are borne out by data. Moreover, we must do this while staying true to a core HOPE SF principle: engaging community voices in guiding the initiative's direction and in shaping programs. With technical assistance awarded by the Harvard Kennedy School Government Performance Lab, the HOPE SF team developed a results-driven payment pilot with one outcome in mind: improving economic mobility for young people aged 16 to 24 over the next five to seven years. We launched it in the spring of 2016.

PAYING FOR WHAT WORKS

We selected a group of providers, all of which have deep roots in the community, to form a collaborative, the Phoenix Project. It will pilot a model for comprehensive, integrated programming and multi-year intensive mentoring that uses data to track progress and improve outcomes. Collectively, the providers offer a full range of social, health, and workforce training services. But until they came together as the Phoenix Project, they ran separate, uncoordinated programs and did not have the capacity to use data to inform their decisions or measure client progress.

The two-year planning and ramp-up phase, supported by philanthropy and currently underway, focuses on developing the collaborative intervention and building the organizations' data capacity. At the same time, city agencies responsible for youth programming, human services, and workforce development have begun to align and restructure in order to support a new kind of contract with the Phoenix collaborative beginning in July 2018. That contract, which will be structured based on what is learned during the current ramp-up phase, will extend over multiple years and make payments based on outcomes, not activities or numbers of clients served.

A pay-for-performance contract will be a major departure for community-based service providers, who have historically received grant payments upfront and then reported on a set of activities upon completion of the grant period. To prepare them for the shift, our philanthropic partners have structured a planning grant to tie payments to specific benchmarks and deliverables in order to facilitate the discipline, coordination, and learning necessary to move the project in that direction. The grant is disbursed in four payments, contingent on the completion of key milestones. While these interim benchmarks are tied to the development and testing of program intervention as well as the new organizational and data infrastructure, the outcomes related to the 2018 contract will focus on social and economic wellbeing of the participants (increased income, educational completion, health and wellness, and reduction in convictions). We believe this interim grant structure will facilitate the discipline, coordination, and learning necessary for all partners to move in the direction of results-based payments.

We are enthusiastic about this joint approach because it allows us to both pilot new ideas and commit to long-term funding for those that work. The philanthropic partners are excited to support this initial phase because we have assurance that the city and county of San Francisco will pick up and increase funding after strategies are tested and scalable plans are developed. How many times have we funders supported programs, only to see them vanish when foundation support dried up? On the city side, we are excited about the opportunity to support services that have demonstrated they actually work for these young people in need.

Like many new marriages, this one faces challenges. Collective impact and results-driven contracting are complicated; joining them is a heavy lift. Service providers accustomed to going it alone must quickly learn to work in a tight, efficient collaboration marked by trust, shared goals and intended outcomes, and accountability to the people they serve. Government agencies and foundations, which have traditionally measured effectiveness by the number of clients on a roster, must realize that is not a mark of impact. What matters is how many people move to self-sufficiency and stay there. This is a huge change in thinking and practice.

But the opportunities are even bigger. Philanthropy and city government are fully invested in working together to move from a foundation-funded pilot to a city-funded program, to broader systems change in the way San Francisco advances equity and inclusion. Phoenix Project providers rank among the most dedicated, effective, respected organizations in the community. And the young people we work with in HOPE SF communities remind us of what's at stake. Elizabeth Luna, a 23-year-old mother of two, struggled mightily to find a job. After participating in a HOPE SF workforce training program and working closely with her job coach, she landed a full-time position. Now she's thriving. "This program motivated and inspired me," she said. "It has changed my life."

In HOPE SF communities, many more stories should end this way. By elevating our collective impact practice, engaging communities as full partners, strengthening the capacity of service providers, and tying dollars to outcomes, we can build a city that works for all.

――――

KATE HOWARD *is deputy chief of staff for San Francisco Mayor Edwin M. Lee. In this capacity, she advises the mayor on operations and policy issues, oversees the city's open data and innovation initiatives, and monitors and assesses the effectiveness of key policy initiatives on behalf of the mayor. Since 2007, she has worked in the San Francisco mayor's office under both Mayor Lee as the city's budget director and former Mayor Gavin Newsom. Prior to her work in the mayor's office, Howard worked at a nonprofit focused on community-based conflict resolution. She holds an MPP from the University of Maryland and a BA in politics with a minor in women's studies from Oberlin College in Ohio.*

FRED BLACKWELL *is chief executive officer of the San Francisco Foundation, where he leads one of the largest community foundations in the country working to ensure shared prosperity, innovation, and equity in the Bay Area. Blackwell, an Oakland native, is a nationally recognized community leader with a longstanding career in the Bay Area. He holds a MA in city planning from University of California, Berkeley and a BA in urban studies from Morehouse College.*

TOWARD THE NORTH STAR
Reorienting Workforce Development to Improve Long-Term Outcomes

Carrie McKellogg and Carla Javits
REDF

I t took the stress of the Great Recession and the resulting crisis of millions of unemployed workers of all skill levels who depend on the workforce system to give real momentum to outcomes-based funding for workforce development.

The recovering economy has failed to lift all boats. Workforce participation overall is at its lowest point in many years.[1] Although partly a result of demographic change, the drop has also been caused by those unemployed during the recession who stopped looking for work and by the millions of adults who face the most significant barriers to accessing it. To move the needle, it is critical to prioritize reducing long-term unemployment, transparently measuring results against that objective, and incentivizing performance improvements.

In workforce development, it is time to ask what we are accomplishing rather than continuing to merely report the number of hours or dollars spent on programs that do not lead to long-term employment. Federal support for essential workforce development programs has declined by 20 percent since 2010 alone. Investment requires results. As workforce leader Steven Dawson notes in a new series on job quality, "The workforce community's ultimate purpose should be to achieve sustained employment...at a minimum at least one year beyond initial job placement."[2] And Third Sector Capital Partners' Celeste Richie highlights that we have a special opportunity now to make this shift, "Over the next few years, the U.S. Department of Labor (DOL) will be baselining Workforce

---

1 U.S. Department of Labor, "Labor Force Statistics from the Current Population Survey," Bureau of Labor Statistics (January 3, 2017), available at https://data.bls.gov/timeseries/LNS11300000.

2 Steven L. Dawson, "Targeting Workforce Dollars: You Don't Get What You Don't Pay For," Pinkerton Foundation (October 2016), available at http://www.thepinkertonfoundation.org/wp-content/uploads/2016/10/Pinkerton-Papers-No3-Web-Final.pdf.

Innovation and Opportunity Act (WIOA) performance measures, making it a great time for providers and government to reset their expectations and goals for program performance."[3]

Although there are several factors at play, our insufficient attention to outcomes is one of the reasons that the labor force participation rate has dropped by almost five percentage points in the past ten years.[4] Perhaps even more important, employers report a persistent gap between their hiring needs and the preparation provided by the workforce development system,[5] and they generally do not look to that system for talent.

Until the Great Recession, and despite modest attempts to gear the system toward outcomes, publicly-funded workforce programs were incentivized to concentrate on short-term outcomes only. This, in turn, focused the workforce system almost exclusively on people who had recently been employed and needed short-term retraining, followed by job placement. Mechanisms to serve people who were long-term or chronically unemployed and faced greater discrimination—such as older workers, workers with histories of homelessness or incarceration, youth disengaged from work and school, and those with a range of disabilities—were neglected and virtually disappeared.

The reauthorization of WIOA in 2015 signaled the intent of Congress to drive toward long-term outcomes and innovative new mechanisms to achieve them—specifically through Pay for Success and performance data requirements, paired with an explicit mandate to serve those facing greater challenges. The establishment of outcomes-based performance standards is a positive first step, but to meet the mandate of increasing services to people who face greater barriers, workforce boards need to adjust performance objectives. For example, performance standards around retention of a job with the same employer are not appropriate

3 Celeste Richie, "WIOA Pay-for-Performance Is a Critical Tool for Equity and Opportunity," Third Sector Capital Partners, Inc. (November 17, 2016), available at http://www.thirdsectorcap.org/social-innovation-fund/wioa-pay-for-performance-is-a-critical-tool-for-equity-and-opportunity/.

4 U.S. Department of Labor, "Labor Force Statistics" (2017).

5 Pam Goins, "Top 5 Issues for 2015 Expanded: Workforce Development," The Council of State Governments (January 12, 2015), available at http://knowledgecenter.csg.org/kc/content/top-5-issues-2015-expanded-workforce-development.

in a transitional social enterprise context, where progress is defined by transitioning from the social enterprise to a competitive employer.

The changes bring WIOA into better alignment with social-sector leaders, philanthropy, and impact investors who are increasingly experimenting with outcomes-based funding. Social enterprise is an employment model that can bridge the gap between the hardest-to-employ and the needs of employers if it can continue to demonstrate results, access public funding, and benefit from tax and other incentives previously restricted to for-profit employers.

To get better results, we agree with Dawson's observation that we must be able to answer three essential questions: Who is being served? What is their sustainable employment rate of success at one year? And what does each success cost?

OVERVIEW

Reorienting the workforce system toward long-term outcomes of greater economic security and mobility for many more people is essential for our economy and our country to flourish. Richie suggests three remedies: refine performance measures to focus on those most at risk; shift the emphasis from quantity to quality; and adjust performance requirements to take into account the barriers job seekers face.

Social enterprise is an example of an intervention with a growing evidence base and a sustainable business model that—if widely embraced by philanthropy, government, and business—is poised to deliver results for many more of the people who face the greatest barriers to sustained employment.

The country's largest and most experienced tier of social enterprises initially began with legislatively mandated "anchor contracts" from the federal government. The Javits-Wagner-O'Day Act of the 1970s created the federal AbilityOne public procurement preference for socially-oriented businesses that employed people with severe disabilities.

The participating companies today employ about 140,000 people and in general have diversified beyond the federal government to private-sector customers. Some of these companies have also expanded their services to people with mental health and other disabilities, as well as people who face barriers, such as criminal justice system involvement, homelessness, and chronic unemployment.[6]

Although the network has been criticized—justifiably for paying roughly ten percent of workers below minimum wage—most of the companies pay at or significantly above minimum wage. Several offer outstanding examples of what social enterprise can be at scale, such as Orion Industries in Seattle, a manufacturing company that won the Boeing Global Supplier of the Year award.[7]

SOCIAL ENTERPRISE: AN INVESTMENT THAT WORKS

Meanwhile, during the past several decades, many more social enterprises were started by local entrepreneurs with no connection to government or the AbilityOne program. These are businesses with a social mission to provide transitional employment in a supportive setting to those who face a wide array of barriers to work.

This approach, which began at the turn of the twentieth century with St. Vincent de Paul and Goodwill affiliates providing long-term employment in general, rather than "transitional" jobs, has emerged across the United States in many different forms.

Social enterprise is an outcome-driven solution by nature because the model ceases to function without results and employer "connectivity." The enterprise must generate business results, or it fails. The employees must contribute to business performance even while working on developing their essential work skills (or soft skills), or the business fails. Because the model is employer-based from start to finish, it offers a promising way to close the persistent gap between workforce development and long-term competitive employment.

Social enterprise is a field under construction. The enterprises that make up the field have successfully brought people with barriers back into the workforce through a supported transitional job. The challenge now is

---

6   U.S. AbilityOne Commission, "AbilityOne Program—History" (2016), available at http://www.abilityone.gov/abilityone_program/history.html.

7   The Boeing Company, "Press Release: Boeing Honors 12 Suppliers for Outstanding Performance in 2015" (April 28, 2016), available at http://boeing.mediaroom.com/2016-04-28-Boeing-Honors-12-Suppliers-for-Outstanding-Performance-in-2015.

to transition these employees to competitive jobs and definitively prove the social enterprise model's ability to deliver long-term job retention, economic mobility, and greater financial security.

RAISING THE ANTE ON RESULTS

As a California-based venture philanthropy that has invested for almost two decades in the growth of social enterprises that are in the business of workforce preparation, REDF has always focused on measuring not just the beans—inputs and outputs—but outcomes. Our measures focus on job retention and economic self-sufficiency.

Social enterprises funded as part of REDF's portfolio regularly assess business and social outcomes against agreed-on annual and multiyear goals, and they use the information to continuously improve performance. REDF's approach to assessing social return on investment has been widely credited as the foundation for social-return-on-investment tools and assessment frameworks. Many of the 60-plus social enterprises REDF has supported in California embedded outcome tracking and related performance improvement systems into their daily operations, which have generated more than $220 million in revenue since REDF began investing.

In 2015, REDF undertook a third-party evaluation of its California portfolio. The data demonstrated that the incomes of those employed rose by 268 percent, the employment rate tripled, and the social enterprises covered most costs with business revenues, making them more sustainable than programs that are fully grant-funded.[8] Individuals who received a job in social enterprise were 19 percentage points more likely to be working a year later than a comparable group receiving traditional workforce services. The third-party data were the underpinning of a subsequent cost study demonstrating a 123 percent social return on investment.[9] This, in turn, has led the federal government's Social Innovation Fund and private supporters to commit $50 million to scale up the approach nationally.

Roca, a new entrant into the REDF portfolio, is an example of social enterprise at work. Founded by visionary chief executive Molly Baldwin, it serves young people in Massachusetts who are involved in the criminal

---

8 REDF, "Press Release: REDF Jobs Report" (February 5, 2015), available at http://redf.org/jobsreport/.

9 Ibid.

justice system and gangs—individuals targeted by very few programs. Roca runs supervised work crews under contract with municipal public works departments and private companies, providing maintenance, landscaping, painting, cleaning, and other services. Roca works with more than 300 young people each year, supporting their evolution through stages of change in behavior. Roca's theory of change is that it takes many months of losing and regaining social enterprise employment before young people complete 60 consecutive days of work—a key objective. Roca also applies relentless internal evaluation with a performance-based management system. Using Roca's intervention model, the staff served 659 high-risk, formerly incarcerated young men. The retention rate was extremely high at 84 percent, and they were retained 24 months or longer in the program. Nearly all had no new incarcerations, and 92 percent had retained employment for at least 90 days.[10]

A new report by JPMorgan Chase & Co. and ICIC offers another data point from a broader perspective. It urges city leaders to support the growth of small businesses with the resources dedicated to large companies, because small businesses are especially important to solving the problem of unemployment in distressed inner-city neighborhoods.[11]

IMPROVING OUTCOMES WITH EVIDENCE

Evidence-based approaches require practitioners, funders, and the public sector to become more comfortable acknowledging outcomes that do not meet expectations and valuing the learning opportunities presented therein.

As an example, data from the evaluation of social enterprises that REDF sponsored highlighted positive outcomes, like a dramatic increase in earned income from wages (268 percent) and a tripling of the retention rate one year later. However, the data also showed that despite the rise in wages, social enterprise employees faced a significant decline in government benefits and virtually no net increase in income. Government benefits are often cut sharply when incomes rise, creating a "benefits cliff" that is a significant disincentive to work. Coupled with a drop-off in

---

10 Roca, "Outcomes," available at http://rocainc.org/impact/outcomes/.

11 JPMorgan Chase & Co. and ICIC, "The Big Impact of Small Businesses on Urban Job Creation: Evidence from Five Cities" (October 2016), available at http://icic.org/wp-content/uploads/2016/10/JPMC_R1_BigImpact_FINAL_forpost.pdf?af674c.

employment over time and the low wages earned relative to increased cost of living, REDF observed that a social enterprise job is a first but insufficient step to medium-term financial security for people facing barriers.

In response, REDF and our social enterprise partners made programmatic adjustments; they also focused on the need to educate policymakers about alternatives to the benefits cliff, like gradual reductions in subsidies as incomes rise and stabilize.

REDF looked for the bright spots, basically who was beating the average. There were social enterprises that delivered better results. Notably, 70 percent or more of those employed by some social enterprises were still working a year later. These findings, in turn, challenged REDF and its partners to learn from those achieving better results and concentrate greater attention on increasing economic security and mobility. This led to a much tighter focus on the connectivity to employers, the transition into competitive employment, and the investment in residual supports that social enterprises continue to provide.

"Devil in the details" policy implementation issues also need to be addressed for social enterprise to scale up its impact across the United States. Although WIOA performance data put the onus on local and state workforce investment boards to match participant data with wage records to show how many participants got jobs and to assess average earnings, the same workforce investment boards need to track and care about how many participants keep jobs in the long run. To do so at a reasonable cost requires routine access to data that are currently hard to access. University of California, Berkeley's O-Lab has been exploring the privacy concerns that limit data access and is piloting a new initiative to move beyond the current impasse.[12] The Stanford Center on Poverty and Inequality and Third Sector Capital Partners (a Pay for Success intermediary) are providing technical assistance to local governments administering outcomes-oriented projects to link federal data (U.S. Census, IRS, etc.) with local data to evaluate program effectiveness.

---

12 University of California, Berkeley, "Press Release: Unlocking Government Administrative Data with New California Policy Lab" (November 29, 2016), available at http://news.berkeley.edu/story_jump/unlocking-government-administrative-data-with-new-california-policy-lab/.

However, it is still unclear which entity—at the federal, state, or local level—will focus on, track, and invest in long-term employment outcomes for people overcoming multiple barriers.

SOCIAL ENTERPRISES: AN EVIDENCE-BASED APPROACH SCALES UP

WIOA now allows a set-aside of up to ten percent for Pay for Success projects to incentivize state and local workforce boards to experiment with paying for outcomes like medium-term job retention. Several states, including California, have indicated interest in their initial WIOA plans submitted to the federal government, although Pay for Success in the workforce arena faces the challenge of identifying the public entity with "repayment" responsibility. This is a more complex question than, for example, in the area of recidivism to prison, where one system can be identified that benefits most from improved outcomes.

An Irvine Foundation report on Pay for Success in the workforce context flags these factors as most important: state government support and pre-existing momentum, proven interventions/service providers with rigorous performance data, intermediary involvement, and dual recidivism and employment goals.[13]

Social enterprises are well-suited to participate in Pay for Success transactions because their financial performance and employee outcomes are both embedded in their double-bottom-line accounting.

Beginning in fiscal year 2012, the DOL awarded funding to projects that engaged social enterprises to deliver outcomes in two large-scale Pay for Success projects: New York State (the Center for Employment Opportunities) and Massachusetts (Roca).

Work is underway to lay the foundation for Pay for Success projects with local workforce boards. Notably, five cities were recently selected to receive technical assistance to scale high-impact youth workforce

---

13 Nonprofit Finance Fund (NFF) and The Joyce Foundation, "Pay for Success in Workforce Development: What We've Learned and What's Next" (March 2014), available at http://www.payforsuccess.org/sites/default/files/resource-files/PFS%20in%20Workforce%20Development.pdf.

development strategies with long-term improvements in youth employment and earnings.[14]

Funding social enterprise through outcomes-based instruments like Pay for Success is also driving greater connectivity between workforce preparation and the labor market. More broadly, such funding is creating a new pathway for government and philanthropy to support greater scale for interventions that demonstrate publicly valued outcomes.

Generally, social enterprises offer an evidence-based approach to workforce development for those who face significant barriers to employment. The growth of this sector can and should be supported on a bipartisan basis by the business community, philanthropy, and government.

Businesses that are increasingly concerned about finding employees who are prepared for the basic demands of work can hire those prepared to work by social enterprise. They also can include social enterprises in their supply chain for products and services, fueling their growth and stability.

Philanthropy and government programs that are currently funding traditional workforce development for populations with barriers can access and expand similar programs at a fraction of the "subsidized" cost.

The aim of the social enterprise business model is to earn revenue from the sale of products and services, leveraging these funds to offset most of the cost of work preparation and employee supports. And because of their business orientation, social enterprises bake in outcomes measurement, performance improvement, and customer service—meeting employer demand for prepared workers and quality products and services.

The specific ingredients that would fuel growth include:

- Increased private and public procurement of goods and services offered by social enterprises;

- More direct hiring by competitive employers of those prepared by social enterprise to work;

---

14 Third Sector Capital Partners, Inc., "Press Release: Social Innovation Fund: Cohort 2" (April 13, 2016), available at http://www.thirdsectorcap.org/sifcohort2/.

- Funding of growth capital for social enterprise expansion and replication to new communities; and

- Continued support for employees as they transition out of social enterprise into the job market.

The field is ready to scale up. REDF's recent national competition revealed 209 social enterprises in 36 states—which we know, because of the limited outreach and timeframe, revealed only a fraction of the employment-focused social enterprises in the field nationwide. The 80 or so that REDF selected to assess for funding as part of our rigorous due-diligence process reported that collectively they could employ 160,000 people over the next five years. With the right growth capital and investment in technical assistance to these companies, the country could develop a base of social enterprises capable of employing several hundred thousand people each year. Business partnerships and support structures would result in most of them moving into competitive employment and staying in the workforce.

REDF's work on the pioneering "LA:RISE—Los Angeles Regional Initiative for Social Enterprise"[15] in partnership with the Los Angeles Mayor's office and workforce system, as well as the private business community, is an example of the type of partnership that scales up the impact to meet the need. In cities and communities across the United States—from Austin to Chicago, Denver to Boston—struggling with crises of homelessness, disconnected youth, and an influx of citizens returning from the criminal justice system, social enterprise is emerging as a concrete first step in re-establishing hope and possibility to thousands.

CARRIE MCKELLOGG *is REDF's chief program officer, overseeing REDF's grantmaking activities and impact data, as well as the organization's support of the social enterprise field nationwide through knowledge sharing, supporting the practitioner community, and policy and advocacy efforts. Prior to directing funding for social enterprises domestically at REDF and internationally at the Multilateral Investment Fund, she was an economist at the U.S. Treasury.*

---

15 For more information on LA:RISE—Los Angeles Regional Initiative for Social Enterprise please see http://ewddlacity.com/index.php/employment-services/la-rise.

CARLA JAVITS *is president and chief executive officer of REDF, a California-based, national nonprofit venture philanthropy and intermediary that is leading the pioneering effort to create jobs and employment opportunities for people facing the greatest barriers to work. Through her stewardship, REDF has expanded from the San Francisco Bay Area throughout the United States, helping to impact the lives of thousands of people in need of jobs by investing capital and expertise in social enterprises. These mission-driven businesses focus on hiring and assisting people who are willing and able to work but have a hard time securing employment. Inspired by REDF's founder, George R. Roberts of KKR, REDF focuses on achieving measurable results by building the partnerships and systems to provide a business solution to joblessness among those overcoming the most significant challenges.*

BETTER OUTCOMES FOR CHRONICALLY HOMELESS "FREQUENT USERS"

Louis Chicoine
Abode Services

Allen was living on the streets of San Jose for more than six years. He occasionally slept in shelter beds when they were available but more frequently stayed under freeway overpasses. He had an extensive history of incarceration, cycling in and out of jail in his home state of Colorado, typically after parole violations. He was eventually given a bus ticket to California, and he arrived in Santa Clara County with no resources, no social networks, and a criminal history that prevented him from finding work. Shortly after arriving, he was diagnosed with schizoaffective disorder. He also suffers from serious arthritis and chronic obstructive pulmonary disease, which were compounded by his extended homelessness. With a mostly untreated mental health disability and numerous acute medical conditions, he was hospitalized 15 times in two years but remained homeless during that time. He was placed in permanent supportive housing as part of Project Welcome Home (PWH) in September 2015. Since then, he has received regular medical and mental health care, taken scheduled medication, and attended weekly respite support groups. He has remained stably housed and re-established a relationship with his son (from whom he had been estranged for 18 years). His hospitalization rate has decreased sharply.

I n Santa Clara County, there are more than 2,200 chronically homeless people living on the streets at any point in time, of whom more than 90 percent are unsheltered.[1] Like Allen, many receive a fragmented and inconsistent array of services from the county's emergency system, and some cycle in and out of jail. Without a safe, permanent place to live, they remain disconnected from the comprehensive, coordinated care they need to address their physical and mental health issues. This is not just an inhumane situation; it is a costly one. According to a

---

1 Applied Survey Research, "Santa Clara County Homeless Point-In-Time Census & Survey" (2015), available at https://www.sccgov.org/sites/oah/coc/census/Documents/SantaClaraCounty_HomelessReport_2015_FINAL.pdf.

study commissioned by the county in 2015, the costs associated with a chronically homeless person cycling through their emergency systems can exceed $83,000 per year, without actually ending that person's homelessness. By contrast, well-designed permanent supportive housing costs much less (under $20,000, in some cases) and, more important, significantly reduces human suffering.[2]

At Abode Services, we are familiar with the immense benefits of permanent supportive housing for the people we serve. We provide housing to roughly 1,100 people on any given night through our various housing programs and have seen the incredible improvements that people can make in their lives when connected to a safe, stable place to live. When we learned that the county wanted to try the Pay for Success model within a permanent supportive housing program, we were immediately attracted to the opportunity. The idea was that rather than pay us directly to connect chronically homeless people to permanent supportive housing, the county would define the success that it expected from our work, a group of investors would pay us the real cost of meeting those success targets, and the county would pay back the investors only when we reached them. In some cases, the "success payments" to investors were calculated to include modest returns that would be realized only if the program was fully successful. Researchers at the University of California, San Francisco (UCSF) would evaluate the project's success.

Some of the benefits were very clear. The county would pay only for programs that worked. And investors could make a socially responsible investment in a complex social problem and generate a modest return. As the service provider, we saw the possibility of bringing our track record of successful permanent housing programs to greater scale while getting paid for the full cost of running the program, instead of relying on a bare-bones budget so common in nonprofit contracting.

Another appealing feature for Abode was that, unlike many other Pay for Success models, we did not need to prove that our intervention saved the county money directly in order to be deemed a success. The county was

---

2 Kaitlyn Snyder, "Study Data Show that Housing Chronically Homeless Peoples Saves Money, Lives," National Alliance to End Homelessness, available at http://www.endhomelessness.org/blog/entry/study-data-show-that-housing-chronically-homeless-people-saves-money-lives.

confident that permanent supportive housing would be more cost-effective than providing emergency services on an irregular basis. As such, for the purposes of triggering repayment to the investors, success would be defined as housing stability alone. The UCSF evaluation would also assess reductions in service utilization, but those were ancillary outcomes. That was a big selling point for us—we wanted to rely on success metrics that we had used before and according to which we had already demonstrated success.

One of the initiative's larger benefits was that it offered a concrete and visible representation of the county's growing commitment to performance measurement within its larger system of homeless service delivery. Faced with limited resources, the county increasingly focused on measuring performance at both the program level and system level and wanted to invest resources in the interventions that had the greatest impact.

The deal construction was like no other contract negotiation Abode Services had ever participated in. It took nine months to carefully determine the success metric, develop project budgets, attract and secure investors, and develop and enter into legal agreements. In the end, project investors were local and national foundations (Google.org, Sobrato Family Foundation, Health Trust, The James Irvine Foundation, California Endowment, Laura and John Arnold Foundation), national community development financial institutions (The Reinvestment Fund, Corporation for Supportive Housing), and Abode Services in the form of at-risk deferred program fees. It was also determined that Abode Services would not only manage the program but would play the Pay for Success manager role, which in previous deals was the responsibility of a third party. In this role, Abode Services handles all project finances and convenes a quarterly meeting of the investors to report on project metrics.[3]

After winning a competitive bid process and working through a nine-month deal construction period, PWH was launched. PWH combines permanent housing (in site-based and scattered-site apartments) with wrap-around supportive services—such as outreach and engagement, intensive case management, and specialty mental health services (offered according to the Assertive Community Treatment model)—for 112 chronically homeless

---

3 Nonprofit Finance Fund, "Project Welcome Home" (2017), available at http://www.payforsuccess.org/project/project-welcome-home.

Figure 1. Santa Clara Pay for Success Overview

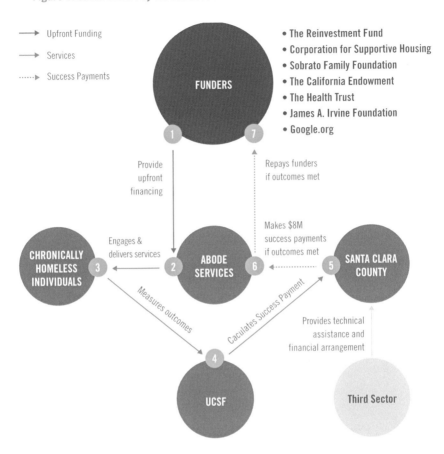

people at any point in time. At the time of writing, Abode was nearing month 16 of operations, with all 112 people placed in housing.

The PWH team has thus far met the housing stability targets built into the first five quarters of success projections and has generated the projected amount of success payments for investors. We know that long-term housing stability for chronically homeless people can take years in some cases, but we are cautiously optimistic that the program's success will continue. We are hopeful not just that the project investors will be repaid, but that housing stability and the reductions in service utilization will provide a solid evidence base for the county to continue to invest in permanent supportive housing. In that sense, the Pay for Success model has provided a great opportunity for Abode to do more of what we know works and, in partnership with the county, broadcast that success to generate additional support and investment. We are grateful for the opportunity.

That said, the model does have some drawbacks, which any interested service provider should consider before diving in. We have spelled out some of those challenges below, not to discourage prospective providers, but with the hopes of preparing them for the journey ahead.

Prepare for a sizable investment of staff time and resources. Government contracting is often unilateral. Local governments tell service providers what they expect and how much they will pay. However, there is no such simplicity or clarity in Pay for Success deal construction, and our team had to weigh in at every turn. This was empowering and likely resulted in a program design that truly served us. But it also meant that our agency leadership had to be available, capable of tracking several complex deal elements at the same time, and comfortable making very important decisions with little time to reflect. In addition, our deal involved multiple investors who came to the table at different times, each with unique expectations and due-diligence needs. Any organization considering a Pay for Success deal should ensure that there is a relatively high-level staff member who will devote 60 to 80 percent of his or her time to deal construction for several months.

Greater efficiencies are needed with respect to defining success. How a local government defines success and the degree to which a group of investors will agree with the rigor and/or reasonableness of that definition both depend on who is sitting at the deal construction table. As a provider of permanent supportive housing, we believed that the case for our success in the field was well established. We have been measuring and reporting our program outcomes according to U.S. Department of Housing and Urban Development standards for years. However, our investors wanted a finer-grained success metric, which meant that we had to rely on a measure that we had never used before. This was harrowing for us, as we did not want to agree to something that we were not sure we could achieve. To confirm that we could, we chose to pull individual client records manually and test the proposed measure, which was arduous and time-consuming.

Ultimately, Pay-for-Success-funded programs should have similar definitions of success; otherwise, economies of scale or efficiencies will not be attained as more deals are finalized.

The politics of negotiation can place service providers in an uncomfortable spot. When it comes to setting the success target, there is an inherent tension between the imperatives of the local government funder (who wants to pay only for true success) and those of the investors (who want to be sure that they get paid back). Each entity has its own risk calculation. The reputational risk assumed by the service provider is often ignored in this negotiation. If the target is too low, the provider looks unimpressive, but if the bar is too high, the provider can do an excellent job but still look like a failure. In our case, the county initially proposed a success rate that we did not believe was attainable, but one of the potential investors countered with a rate that would have been embarrassingly low. This uncomfortable position required us to respectfully stand up to our local government partner—and to a table of financial and philanthropic institutions—and assert a target that we thought was reasonable but challenging. Without strong agency leadership, excellent relationships with our funders, and confidence in our data, success negotiations may not have turned out as well.

There is not yet full fidelity to the model and spirit of Pay for Success. In theory, Pay for Success shifts the role of local government from bureaucratic contract management to performance measurement. Investors ostensibly enter the deal when their due-diligence demands are satisfied, then retreat to the background and wait for their success payments to start flowing in. Reality and theory are not totally aligned just yet. We learned from our deal that local government agencies—and some funders—still feel the need to closely manage the budget and other operational elements of the program, in the spirit of being responsible stewards of public funds. As understandable as this may be, our reporting requirements have doubled, with the standard reporting requirements (of which we were supposed to be free) now layered on top of the new, more intensive, reporting requirements associated with program success. And our investors remain closely involved, regularly attending monthly meetings, monitoring our housing placements, and at times asking for additional reports. In sum, a number of the philosophical elements of the

Pay for Success model have not translated into program operations. As such, any service provider contemplating involvement in Pay for Success should build into the program the bandwidth to satisfy these additional reporting requirements, at least until investors and government funders are more comfortable with the model.

The Pay for Success model is still very new. Only a handful of Pay for Success programs are operational, and only two have reached a point where program success or failure can meaningfully be measured.[4] Our program is in its initial stage, and the conclusions we draw five years from now will likely differ from those reflected here. In addition, as the field grows, we are likely to see many more lessons learned, improvements, and efficiencies. In the meantime, for providers who are thinking about diving into these relatively uncharted waters, it is our hope that these observations and recommendations help to inform your decision and ensure your success.

———

LOUIS CHICOINE *has successfully led Abode Services' development into one of the San Francisco Bay Area's most effective and far-reaching agencies providing social services. Starting with his promotion to executive director in 1995, Chicoine guided the agency through almost two decades of responsible growth, building the capacity required to respond to the urgent needs facing homeless and low-income families and individuals in the Bay Area. He holds a BA in philosophy and MS degrees in social work administration and pastoral ministry.*

---

4 Donald Cohen and Jennifer Zelnick, "What We Learned from the Failure of the Rikers Island Social Impact Bond," *Nonprofit Quarterly* (2015), available at https://nonprofitquarterly.org/2015/08/07/what-we-learned-from-the-failure-of-the-rikers-island-social-impact-bond/; Jeff Edmondson et al., "Pay-For-Success is Working in Utah," *Stanford Social Innovation Review* (2015), available at https://ssir.org/articles/entry/pay_for_success_is_working_in_utah.

How This Works
FIELD AND SECTOR IMPLICATIONS

BETTER OUTCOMES FOR THE NONPROFIT SECTOR

Muzzy Rosenblatt
BRC

How do you know? Sixteen years ago, as a new nonprofit executive director, I asked that question repeatedly about our impact, efficiency, quality, financial stability, reputation, and so on. We didn't know then how well we performed by any of these measures; today, we do.

While visiting programs in those early days, I'd ask staff how they knew if we, the organization, and they, the staff, were good at what we did. It wasn't a trick question. As the new guy, I was eager to find the secret to our success and the areas in which we needed to improve. The response was always a moving story of a client and the details of how this program and that staff helped him or her achieve sobriety, stabilize mental health, find a job, and eventually obtain housing. But when I asked how often that occurred, what contributed to the result, and what it would take to increase the rate of these incredible, positive outcomes, I might as well have been speaking a foreign language. Nobody knew; all they could tell me was the story of their client.

The overwhelmingly positive energy from staff passionate about their work and the people they serve might have been sufficient for some (particularly in a sector where the workforce often feels insufficiently supported and morale can be low). But as powerful as that impression was, what I found even more striking was the absence of any sense of the systemic impact of their work, of the outcomes they achieved, and of how, with all their passion, they could—we could—do more good, more often, for more people.

Further, like many nonprofits, we were facing huge financial challenges. I knew that if we could grow by replicating the work we did well, the economies of scale (combined with other efforts) could improve our financial condition, while simultaneously advancing our mission and enabling us to help more people. But to make the case for growth to our funders, I needed to demonstrate impact.

Our organization was founded nearly 50 years ago by recovering alcoholics living in New York City's Bowery flophouses. They were "the homeless" of their era, before the phrase was coined. Today, we stay true to their belief that no matter how far someone has fallen, he or she can climb back and achieve if given an opportunity and support. We provide holistically integrated services and housing to make that possible for anyone willing to try, no matter what came before. More simply, we offer a hand up instead of a handout and provide the opportunity for our clients to achieve their potential.

As I listened to the individual stories in those early days, I was humbled by the challenges our clients overcame. Yet we cannot run, sustain, and grow our organizations by relying solely on emotion. We need proof of our impact and evidence of the key variables that contribute to the results. So we created a system for measuring performance and management, assessing our work, and instilling a culture that values inquiry and encourages adaptive management.

This led us on a journey of inquiry and analysis, of acquiring knowledge and learning from it—a journey that continues today. There was fear when we began: Would the pursuit of data change our mission or cause us to focus our energy only on clients likely to succeed? Would people lose their jobs if their outcomes weren't good enough?

What I said then, and say today, is that we must strive to manage with data, not to it. Am I excited when a program achieves a good outcome? Absolutely. Am I concerned when it does not? Of course. But I am much more interested in why. Data are not an outcome but an accounting instrument. Like staff, facilities, and dollars, they are a tool and resource with which we manage. How we use these resources determines how we achieve outcomes. Sustaining and replicating success is unlikely if we don't understand how it happened. Similarly, if we understand why some results aren't what we expected, we have the ability to turn them around.

Here's an example. We assess the performance of our homeless shelters largely by their success at helping people find and retain housing. We measure how many people get housed (overall and as a percentage of those served), how quickly that happens, and whether those who leave us stay housed. A few years ago, we noticed that performance was declining. We were initially patient; it was important to know whether this was a trend. Because a key staff member was on family leave, it seemed reasonable to attribute the drop in performance to her absence. The trend continued when our staffer returned, so we dug deeper. Might the performance of our complementary workforce development program be impacting the shelter's outcomes? The data said no; in fact, our clients were entering the labor force at ever greater average wages and were sustaining employment at consistently high rates. Further analysis revealed the source of the decline: Our working clients had fewer housing options, a result of the well-documented elimination of nearly all rental subsidies for housing, compared with prior years.[1] As a result, it was taking them longer to save enough to move out on their own, they were moving to less secure situations (renting rooms without tenancy rights; sharing costs with roommates; renting apartments they could not afford), and therefore were more at risk of losing their housing and returning to the shelter. Thus, we realized that our shelter's performance was declining despite, not because of, our efforts.

We set out to find a new way to improve our ability to meet our clients' needs for affordable housing that would also decrease lengths of shelter stays and reduce the likelihood that they would return to the shelter. We realized that in order to more positively impact our clients' lives, and our performance, we would need to focus on producing low-income housing. So we developed a financing model to build housing they could afford, and now we are building that housing: 135 apartments in the Bronx with rents that will be affordable to our clients (studios for less than $500 per month for people earning less than $20,000 per year). It's half of an innovative financing model that also includes the development of a new homeless shelter. It leverages revenue from the shelter—what would otherwise be the profit we generate for a private developer when we lease our shelters—and repurposes these dollars to provide the operating subsidy needed to make the housing affordable. It's a model that can

1 Matt Chaban, "Tenants and Landlords Fret as Sequester Cuts Hit Section 8 Subsidies," *Crain's New York Business* (2013), available at http://www.crainsnewyork.com/article/20130609/ REAL_ESTATE/306099969/tenants-and-landlords-fret-as-sequester-cuts-hit-section-8-subsidies.

be replicated to develop housing and strengthen nonprofits' financial condition.

If we had not been outcome-oriented, we might never have realized the challenge and devised a solution. That said, it's important to be cautious when using data to evaluate performance. The decline in our ability to move clients to housing had occurred despite our best efforts and was attributable to external factors. Yet, if we had been funded by a typical performance-based contract, we would have lost income and likely not been able to invest in analysis and innovation. This is because current performance-based contracts have two major flaws: 1) they set performance targets and evaluate them on an absolute basis, without considering context, and 2) they provide reduced payment when targets aren't hit. There is a better, more productive way to configure outcomes-based contracts, one that would ultimately drive better results for the clients of homeless services organizations. What could that look like?

Nonprofits and those who fund them should care about and measure performance; more important, they should identify and account for what drives the data. Rather than setting a target of a specific number of units, funders could say: I'll pay you for putting as many people as possible into permanent housing and keeping them there. They pay for results on a per person basis, and can consider relative performance across organizations. This allows them to ask: For every 100 clients served, how many was organization A able to successfully transition to permanent housing? How about organizations B, C and D? That in turn creates a level playing field and doesn't penalize organizations for external factors outside of their control (e.g., skyrocketing real estate prices, government policy changes).

Secondly, we must stop the practice of paying reduced amounts as the penalty for not hitting performance targets. Many organizations have operated on shoestring budgets for decades; reducing their payments and asking them to do more with less money is a recipe for failure. Instead, funders should pay the full amount the first time an organization underperforms, and tell them they need to improve. Expectations should be clear and direct, and the nonprofit's leadership should be given a reasonable timeline to make improvements. If results don't improve in that reasonable timeline, all of their funding should go to other organizations that are better achieving results for clients. We have all become accustomed to getting paid for effort, not outcomes. And while the sector's effort is laudable, perhaps a little competition is healthy for us. And ultimately healthy for the clients we all serve.

This approach to nonprofit management is imperative at a time when skepticism is growing about the integrity of all institutions. Nonprofits cannot expect to be, or ask to be, exempt from this scrutiny because of their mission's worthiness. Therefore, it is not sufficient for us to take comfort in leading our own high-performing organizations; those of us who value this accountability have a responsibility both to assist our peers who seek to follow suit, and to call out those who do not. The further transformation of our sector toward one that values and speaks thoughtfully about outcomes, and not simply effort, will fundamentally improve the lives of those we serve, consistent with our missions. If we fail to do so, we should not be surprised by nor bemoan those who question the value of our sector or seek to disinvest from it.

I'm proud of what we do and how well we do it. I know we have room to improve, and I know where. And I still ask that same question: How do you know? Only now, we have a system to generate the answers.

———

MUZZY ROSENBLATT serves as the president and chief executive officer of BRC, a $75 million nonprofit with 825 staff, which provides comprehensive, integrated services and housing, enabling its clients to achieve their potential, overcoming the challenges of homelessness, addiction, physical and mental illness, and unemployment. Rosenblatt guides BRC's strategic growth to achieve greater impact for the people and the city it serves by recruiting and retaining exceptional talent, applying evidence-based management practices that drive innovation, ensuring rigorous financial management practices, and articulating thoughtful perspectives to shape public policy and philanthropy. Prior to BRC, Rosenblatt held positions in New York City government under Mayors Koch, Dinkins and Giuliani. He earned his MPA from New York University and BA from Wesleyan University. He frequently serves on the boards of nonprofit organizations and on government task forces.

CHARTING NEW TERRAIN IN SOCIAL HEALTH

Prabhjot Singh and Anna Stapleton

Arnhold Institute for Global Health

Somewhere in America, a boy is born. Because his parents don't make much money, Medicaid pays for his birth and for visits to a pediatrician. When he's diagnosed with asthma at age five, Medicaid pays for his inhaler, but not for the cleaning service that would remove the aggravating mold from the house where he lives. Every time the spores overwhelm his weak lungs, Medicaid pays for his trip to the emergency room. By the time he's 18, he has dropped out of school because of too many missed days. Inactivity due to the asthma leaves him overweight. When he develops diabetes at age 25, Medicaid pays for his insulin, too, but not for the dietary education that would help him control his blood sugar, or for the training that might help him find a job. By the time he hits 50, Medicaid has funded the amputation of three toes and treatment of extensive ulcers on his lower extremities. Then his kidneys begin to fail, and despite dialysis (also paid by Medicaid), his health steeply declines. By the time he dies at just 60 years old, Medicaid has invested more than half a million dollars in clinical care. For this patient, that investment kept him alive through acute illness but never truly stabilized or improved his health. Multiply that number by the thousands of Americans for whom this story plays out, and we see how the United States spends trillions of dollars every year on health care while millions of our citizens see their futures stripped away by poor health.

Investing in clinical care alone is bankrupting our country and leaving Americans with poorer health than our peer nations. Yet we continue to concentrate our efforts within the narrow space of clinical needs because that approach is simpler and more direct than the poorly defined, unbounded, and complex space of social needs. We can map human anatomy, and even the human genome. But we have not yet been able to map the multitude of interacting contextual factors that shape health over the human lifespan. To solve the dual disaster of unsustainable health spending and endemic poor health in America, the health care sector must be willing to step outside the controlled space of the clinic and into the uncharted territories of the social contexts that create, support, or destroy health. We must apply the resources and innovative spirit present in the health care sector to develop systems capable of sensing, analyzing, and addressing complex social contexts that generate poor health. To be sustainable, these care models will require value-oriented financial contracts that incentivize collaboration between the health care and social sectors.

In communities across the country, local entrepreneurs with one hand in each sector are already showing us how building these integrative care models can create and support health. In Dallas, Ruben Amarasingham and Anand Shah at Parkland Health and Hospital System have led a multidisciplinary team to create software capable of uniting data from clinical health records and community-based social service providers, called Pieces. This innovative combination of data sources enables proactive identification of individuals at risk of a health crisis. For example, a patient who shows up in the emergency room week after week in urgent need of thyroid medication might also be living at the Salvation Army homeless shelter across the street. If the shelter and the hospital are connected via Pieces, the emergency room physician can, with the click of a button, notify Salvation Army staff about the dollar-a-day medication that keeps the patient healthy. When the charity is able to provide the medication, his health stabilizes. He stops coming to the emergency room and can focus on finding more permanent housing. The key is to put all the "pieces" of the puzzle—clinical and social—together in one place to achieve a better health outcome.

Another example is City Health Works, an organization in New York City that matches patients with high health care utilization to health coaches. Health coaches are selected for their ability to listen empathetically. They are trained in motivational interviewing to help patients understand how their health conditions intersect with their personal goals, such as attending a grandchild's graduation or maintaining their independence. By building a trusting relationship with patients, the health coach serves as a bridge between the community and the clinic. An important part of the role is knowing when to "escalate"—or communicate significant changes or needs in a patient's life to the clinical care team, helping the patient reach the appropriate point of care. This essential exchange of information is enabled by mobile communications technologies that allow health coaches to record and share key data points such as changes in patient health status, or challenges and successes in compliance with care team instructions.

New financial partnerships must underpin collaborations between the health care and social sectors. For both Pieces and City Health Works, the final barrier to achieving impact at scale is achieving sustainable financing. Both organizations relied on short-term philanthropic funds to stand up operations and provide services to an initial set of clients. Having demonstrated positive impacts on health outcomes, both now seek to develop new financing models based on the value they provide to health and social sector clients. Capturing the value created by improved health outcomes—being able to assign it a dollar amount and demonstrate to whom it accrues—is perhaps the single largest barrier to transformative innovations bridging the gap between health and social needs.

A significant portion of that challenge derives from a mismatch in the organizational tendencies of the health and social sectors. Health systems represent massive accumulations of capital, which must now be infused into the social sector. But from the perspective of a health system leader, the social sector is something of a black box: a diffuse network of organizations hugely diverse in terms of size, mission, and capabilities. To create sustainable partnerships, both health systems and social sector organizations will need to be educated in the workings of the other sector and be given guidance to become reliable partners in value-driven arrangements. The forcing function of these new partnerships will likely serve to make each partner more efficient and effective, sharpening the focus on delivery of services that directly support health and wellbeing.

One strength of this approach is that it makes health equity not only attainable but essential. It focuses our efforts on the human, rather than on a false delineation between clinical and "other" factors. This approach also encodes the absolute importance of matching every individual with the resources best able to meet his or her needs, whether those needs arise from geography, socioeconomic circumstances, racial or cultural factors, or gender.

The orientation toward value can also drive the health care and social sectors toward greater efficiency, as we redeploy limited resources into interventions that truly support health. Ultimately, by coordinating health care and social sector services to meet patient needs, we can improve health while meeting the core business needs of a health care system increasingly held financially responsible for the health outcomes of the patients it serves.

Although pioneers in this area are already demonstrating its promise, we still have much to learn about how social and environmental factors interact over time to create health outcomes at the individual and community or population levels. Although the scientific literature currently reflects concrete links between a list of discrete factors and specific health outcomes—for example, mold in housing and uncontrolled asthma—we are not yet able to paint a functional picture of the full terrain of social health. Charting this terrain requires that we apply new advances in data analytics to help us understand how the interplay of a seemingly infinite number of factors over the lifetimes of not only individuals, but communities, create patterns of health and disease, opportunity and limitation. Exploration of this new frontier can be launched only from bright spots of work, like those in Dallas and New York.

Despite its underlying promise, the integration of health and social care toward a common goal of healthier lives faces great challenges from the status quo. Federal and state regulatory barriers function to sequester health care dollars in clinical care, preventing the funds allocated for America's safety-net insurance systems of Medicare and Medicaid from fully collaborating with the social systems their beneficiaries commonly need. The federal and state governments have opportunities to remove those barriers—to advance the health of our nation, they must. Even when those walls do fall, we will need motivated innovators across technical and social disciplines to invent and implement new people-centered information and analytics technologies capable of fully supporting the integrated system of health and social care we imagine. Ultimately, this transformation will require a massive cultural shift within both medicine and the social service sector, away from old thinking that segregated clinical and social needs and toward a new understanding of the human whole.

As our nation's health care sector works its way through the ongoing shift toward value-based care, we already see health systems across the country expressing hunger for opportunities to address a fuller range of their patients' needs through strategic partnership with social service providers. Fully realizing this new approach requires that innovators across sectors come together to generate new care models, technologies, and financial arrangements. Old barriers persist, and the path ahead remains uncertain. But in working to get this transformation right, we have the opportunity to revolutionize the efficiency and efficacy of our health care and social sectors—and, ultimately, the health of our nation.

————

PRABHJOT SINGH *is director of the Arnhold Institute for Global Health and chair of the department of health system design and global health at the Icahn School of Medicine at Mount Sinai, as well as special advisor for strategy and design at the Peterson Center for Healthcare. Prior to joining the Mount Sinai Health System, Dr. Singh was a professor of international and public affairs at Columbia University and director of systems design at the Earth Institute, where he was chair of the One Million Community Health Worker Campaign. He completed an MD at Cornell University and a PhD in neural and genetic systems at Rockefeller University, with a post-doctoral fellowship in sustainable development at Columbia University. His book about how to better anchor healthcare to communities,* Dying and Living in the Neighborhood: A Street-Level View of America's Healthcare Promise, *was published by Johns Hopkins University Press in 2016.*

ANNA STAPLETON *is program manager for policy at the Arnhold Institute for Global Health at the Icahn School of Medicine at Mount Sinai. She holds her BA in sociology from the University of Chicago, and recently led production of a report on sustainable community health programs in the United States in partnership with the Office of the UN Health Envoy.*

OUTCOMES-BASED FUNDING AND THE COMMUNITY FINANCE ECOSYSTEM

Annie Donovan
CDFI Fund

Outcomes-based funding can be a powerful tool for shaping fiscal policy. Community finance plays an important role in the quest to transform funding systems toward a focus on outcomes.

In the United States, outcomes-based funding is often coupled with outcomes-based financing. Let's clarify the difference between "funding" and "financing" because although it may seem subtle (and frankly, confusing), the distinction is important for understanding how the momentum toward outcomes-based funding is currently being achieved.

"Funding" refers to making payments with no expectation of being paid back. In today's world, success is typically measured by outputs, rather than outcomes. For example, a success measure for a childcare program may be the number of low-income children served (the output), rather than the developmental milestones those children achieve by the time they leave the childcare program (the outcome). In the case of outcomes-based funding, payments would be provided only once the outcomes have been demonstrated. If funders shift toward funding only after an outcome has been achieved, where will the resources come from to support the delivery of services in the meantime? That's where outcomes-based financing comes in. In outcomes-based financing, the money is loaned to the service provider for the period of service provision. The outcomes-based investor is then repaid by the government funder when the agreed-upon outcomes are delivered.

Whether referred to as outcomes-based financing, Pay for Success, social impact bonds, or any other name, this innovative form of financing has

---

The views expressed in this paper are those of the author and do not necessarily reflect the policies or views of the U.S. Department of the Treasury.

What Matters: Investing in Results to Build Strong, Vibrant Communities

helped catalyze the movement toward funding based on outcomes. Initially, an outcomes-based financing investor, who is confident in the eventual program outcomes, provides funds to the service provider until the outcomes are established. This allows the government to invest its resources in a program or an intervention only if it is successful, thereby transferring the implementation risk from the public sector to the investor. This transfer of risk helps to overcome political resistance governments may have to funding innovative approaches. Outcomes-based financing is the bridge to creating a world in which outcomes-based funding is the norm.

As a tool for improving the efficient and effective use of resources to solve intractable social and economic problems, outcomes-based funding is promising. However, it has its limitations; chiefly, reliance on evidence to drive funding means that it is not likely to be used to *create* social innovation, but rather to *scale* it. For that reason, it will always need an ecosystem to support its potential. Private- and public-sector partners who invest in innovation will remain essential to both outcomes-based funding and outcomes-based financing. Fortunately, community development financial institutions (CDFIs) can be such partners when it comes to advancing outcomes-based financing.

The case has been made elsewhere in this publication regarding the considerable benefits of outcomes-based funding. There are many evidence-based strategies that we already know create better outcomes and save taxpayer money, such as early childhood education, cognitive behavioral therapy for youth offenders, assisted living in lieu of skilled nursing, energy-efficient retrofits of public housing—to name just a few.

Despite a growing movement to support evidence-based policy- and decision-making, it has been slow to gain traction within government, in part because it requires government to shift longstanding ways of operating. For example, the period of availability of annual appropriations for many federal agencies may inhibit outcomes-based funding of projects with longer time horizons.

Though more must be done to support outcomes-based funding, we can't lose sight of the importance of funding for innovation. In fact, "innovation-based funding" has greatly enhanced the adoption of outcomes-based financing in the United States.

The CDFI Fund has played an essential role in innovation-based funding. At the CDFI Fund, we support both the growth of the community finance ecosystem and the innovation potential of individual CDFIs. CDFIs are mission-driven financial organizations that come in a diversity of forms. Currently, there are more than 1,000 CDFIs, certified by the CDFI Fund, operating nationwide. There are CDFIs in all 50 states, the District of Columbia, and most U.S. territories. From regulated banks and credit unions to unregulated for-profit and nonprofit loan funds, venture capital funds, and microfinance funds, CDFIs share a common mission of providing access to capital for people and communities on the economic margins. These are often the same communities targeted by outcomes-based strategies.

You will find CDFIs in markets that traditional financial institutions do not serve regularly, if at all. Some markets are geographically defined and characterized by high rates of poverty, unemployment, and other measures of economic distress. Other markets are thought of by traditional investors as inefficient to serve or higher in risk, such as the small-business market. Many markets served by CDFIs are driven by government funding and are therefore less attractive and more difficult to underwrite for conventional lenders, such as community health centers and charter schools. Where there are gaps in access to capital and high social returns to be had, you will find CDFIs.

CDFIs do not act alone. They are a collaborative force that brings together diverse private- and public-sector investors in ways that mitigate risk, reduce inefficiency, and make it possible for profit-maximizing investors to engage more fully in distressed or underserved markets. CDFIs do this by engineering transactions and taking risk positions that allow private sector investors to realize risk-adjusted rates of return.

Since 1994, the CDFI Fund has supported the growth and capacity of CDFIs through its various programs. Unlike most federal programs, the CDFI Fund provides funding at the enterprise level, rather than the project level. Like a venture capital investor, it evaluates the strength of business plans and management teams and provides flexible funding that must be leveraged with matching funds from other sources. By enhancing the net assets of CDFIs through this funding, the CDFI Fund allows them to take risks, innovate, and build financial strength—all in pursuit of their mission to solve tough economic and social problems. To date, the CDFI Fund has provided more than $2 billion directly to CDFIs.

Thus, it's no mystery that CDFIs were among those who were first on the scene as the concept of outcomes-based financing, then referred to as social impact bonds, made its way to our shores in the United States. In 2011, The Rockefeller Foundation, having made a pioneering program-related investment in the first social impact bonds in Peterborough, England, wanted to test this new innovation in America. Whom did it turn to? Nonprofit Finance Fund (NFF), a certified CDFI that has received considerable support from the CDFI Fund over the years.

The Rockefeller Foundation grant was used to explore the feasibility of this new approach to social finance and to investigate how it might be adapted for the U.S. market. At that stage, there was no evidence that it would succeed. In fact, for many reasons, such as unconventional primary and secondary sources of repayment, it looked like a long shot. However, NFF was in a position to play a catalytic role in testing the concept, jump-starting the practice, and advancing its development. In 2012, it received a grant from the CDFI Fund to make subordinated debt investments in three of the earliest Pay for Success transactions in the market, incentiv-izing other investors and further fueling the development and practice of the Pay for Success field.

Since then, other agencies have leveraged the power of CDFIs to support the Pay for Success model. In 2014, when the Corporation for National and Community Service's Social Innovation Fund provided grants through the inaugural competition of its Pay for Success program, nearly 40 percent of the $12 million available went to CDFIs—an indication of their readiness and capacity to take on development of this new financial instrument.

One of the first Pay for Success transactions to be completed in the United States was in Cuyahoga County, home to the city of Cleveland. The targeted problem was homeless families with children. Evidence shows that children with homeless caregivers spent considerably more time in out-of-home foster care than children with housing-secure caregivers. This extended time in the child welfare system has historically resulted in poor outcomes for the most vulnerable families and has led to higher costs for local government.

In Cleveland, many local partners came together to create a program to reduce the time children of homeless parents spend in foster care and to accelerate the process of reconnecting children with their parents or caregivers in stable, affordable housing. When no conventional financial institutions stepped forward to finance the Pay for Success transaction, not even the local bank, two CDFIs collaborated with several nonprofit and philanthropic partners to close the deal. The senior debt was taken on fully by the Reinvestment Fund, with NFF holding a subordinate position along with other subordinated debt investors.

The financial strength and innovative capacity of CDFIs has enhanced the development of outcomes-based funding in the United States. Movement toward outcomes-based funding at all levels of government will aid in the accomplishment of more wisely spent taxpayer dollars. However, outcomes-based funding can succeed only to the degree that there is a pipeline of innovative, evidence-based solutions—and if flexible partners are available to finance transactions that build this evidence. The way in which the CDFI Fund invests in CDFIs supports them to be good partners, to innovate, and to discover what works.

———

ANNIE DONOVAN *is director of the United States Department of the Treasury's Community Development Financial Institutions (CDFI) Fund. She has been chief executive officer of CoMetrics, Inc, senior policy advisor for the White House Office of Social Innovation, and chief operating officer of Capital Impact Partners.*

NARROWING FOCUS WAS THE KEY TO TRANSFORMING THE LIVES OF HIGH-RISK YOUTH IN MASSACHUSETTS

Molly Baldwin
Roca

At Roca, we know from experience that good intentions don't always produce good results.

In the early days of the 1990s and early 2000s, Roca was a loosely defined youth development organization that wanted to help everyone we could. Just over the Mystic River from Boston, Roca's big white building stood out as a beacon of hope in the otherwise economically and socially depressed community of Chelsea.

In this gateway city, a harbor for the region's poor and largely disenfranchised minorities, youths as young as eight and all the way up to 25 struggled to leave the streets and avoid gang life; to make it through school without becoming pregnant or addicted to drugs; to deal with complicated immigration statuses; to protect themselves from domestic or peer violence; to just make it to adulthood, relatively unscathed.

But no matter your problem, Roca (which means "rock" in Spanish) was there to help solve it—or at least we'd try. A de facto multiservice and multicultural community center at that time, we didn't just provide street outreach to high-risk young people, as we continue to today. We also ran dance classes, summer leadership programs, social ventures, afterschool tutoring, fitness classes, a music studio, and sports leagues.

At times, the one focus we had—youth—felt too narrow, even selfish. So we also ran a weekly food pantry for the homeless. We volunteered our space for local church groups to hold services on the weekends. We provided adult basic education and literacy programs. We ran immigration clinics so that the newest members of our community would know their rights.

Like any well-intentioned soul inspired by the John Wesley quote, "Do all the good you can, by all the means you can, in all the ways you can," Roca strove to be all things for all people. Our good intentions knew no bounds.

And in the dawn of positive youth development as the social service "gold standard" for building on the strengths and skills of disconnected young people, our energetic, scrappy, and relentlessly optimistic staff recruited youth of all ages and risk levels into positive, strengths-affirming activities of all kinds. We didn't discriminate as to which youth we thought we could effectively serve, nor did we carefully select the services we would use to try to help them. We provided a long menu of engagement activities for youth to choose from and crossed our fingers that we were helping them change their lives, get out of poverty, and stay out of harm's way.

But when we began to realize that engagement alone didn't seem to be deterring them from negative behaviors and situations, we were forced to reexamine our approach. Why, we wondered, was youth violence not dropping in the community? Why were the lower-risk kids suddenly joining the most notorious local gangs? And why were the clear indicators of community poverty—rates of teen pregnancy, crime, and school failure—still on the rise?

The problem was that our model wasn't just unsustainable—it was potentially dangerous. Given the realities of the Chelsea streets and persistent youth violence, we feared that despite our own best intentions, we were running a self-esteem program for gang members: Young people who were winning Roca basketball tournaments by day were shooting at people by night.

Roca's hard-fought journey to becoming a high-performing, effective nonprofit began when we finally asked ourselves the critical, dual question, "Are we helping young people change their lives, and how do we know?"

After realizing that, despite great dedication and hard work, Roca was *not* helping young people improve their lives to a significant degree, we knew it was time to take stock and rethink what we were doing entirely.

Our young people, many of whom had grown up at Roca, deserved and needed the organization to get better at its mission so that they could, in fact, move out of harm's way and toward economic independence. To help young people change, Roca had to change first.

Over several formative years for the organization, Roca engaged in a systemic cycle of research, design, action, and use of data for continuous improvement of our model in order to deliver an intervention worthy of the young people we serve. After a series of theory-of-change processes, we narrowed our target population to the highest-risk young people, aged 17 to 24—those whom most programs give up on and whom the data showed that Roca was actually successful at helping.

Critical to the model we have today, we studied, adapted, and imple-mented evidence-based practices from behavioral health, criminal justice, community corrections and reentry, medical and mental health, and workforce development to inform and direct our approach to behavior change and skill-building for high-risk young people. Meanwhile, we deepened our capacity to collect, analyze, and use data regularly as a tool to inform our strategic and operational goals. Finally, we clarified Roca's intervention model as a single-service intervention for high-risk youth. We provide two years of intensive services (case management, life skills, education, and employment programming) and two years of less intensive services, replete with multiple opportunities along the way for young people to work on long-term behavior change through intensive relation-ships with youth workers.

In other words, we closed the community center and opened up a data-driven, targeted program worthy of serving young people in crisis—those who were in and out of jail, in gangs, had dropped out of school, and were not ready, willing, or able to reverse these destructive patterns without help. We forced ourselves to stop working with the groups we weren't helping, as painful as this was. We designed a model specifically for the high-risk young people whom we knew Roca had the means and the experience to help. We put start and end times around how long we would work with young people intensively (up to two years—any longer, and the data showed that youth began to regress). And we built program-ming to support the changes we wanted young people to learn to make: to drop their guns, stay out of jail, and learn how to go to work. Meanwhile, we built an internal culture of performance-based management to hold ourselves accountable to each other, our partners, and the young people we serve.

That meant that all of us—staff, management, partners, funders—had to learn what it means to focus on outcomes and on doing things that matter. We had to build the staff's capacity to work with our data system, read reports, and discuss what could be done differently. We had to explain, over and over, that numbers are not just numbers; they are real people, and they reflect a reality that changes (or not) for each of the young people we serve. We had to maintain our ability to have hard conversations, using peacemaking circles and other methods we have learned over the years, because when you strive to focus on what works and let go of what doesn't, hard conversations will have to happen.

We also had to develop a new type of conversation with our funders. Now that we were able to generate detailed reports about our intervention model, we also had to be accountable for what the reports showed. We learned that if we can be painfully honest with our young people and with ourselves, we can also be as honest with our funders. We learned that you can tell a funder that you used its funding to try something you thought would work, tried it, tested it, found that it doesn't work, discontinued it, and now are doing something else—all while maintaining and even increasing the funding from this funder. In fact, focusing on meaningful outcomes grew our donor base and brought us and our funders closer. Funders, too, want to do things that matter.

And we knew that if, after all was said and done, we *still* weren't effectively helping young people, then we might as well close our doors. It isn't enough to just "try" to help our young people change their lives. The stakes are too high. If we don't do our jobs well, the young people we serve remain impoverished, they continue to get arrested, and most tragically, some commit violence or die from it.

This terrible reality is Roca's call to action, and it's why our organization compulsively uses data as a companion to experience. It's why we've spent the better part of the past decade building a model that focuses on results first.

We track the performance of both young people and staff so that we can best understand the level of effort that is necessary to do this work well. We use data daily, weekly, monthly, quarterly, and annually to review how we're doing, improve the model, and compare it with other effective models. Be it a strategic conversation between a youth worker and a participant, or a participant's attendance at a pre-vocational training class, every component of Roca's model is designed to drive young people toward positive outcomes based on sustainable behavior change and skills acquisition.

Roca is proud to be one of the fortunate, few organizations that is able to track whether it's doing meaningful, measurable good on a regular and predictable basis. In fact, the data point to a robust model that is improving over time: In 2012, 90 percent of participants in the follow-up and retention phase of Roca's model had no new arrests, increasing to 93 percent in 2015; in 2012, 79 percent of participants retained employment, increasing to 92 percent in 2015.

This continual use of data has utterly transformed Roca as an organization, and the accompanying success rates of our highest-risk young people have set the stage for bringing Roca's impact to scale. In the past five years, we have become the primary service provider for our state's juvenile justice Pay for Success program, have completed two in-state program replications in Boston and Springfield, have opened a satellite office in Lynn, and are exploring national options for expansion. Today, Roca serves over 900 high-risk young people per year from over 21 communities in Massachusetts. Embarking on the journey of studying ourselves, collecting data, and driving toward meaningful outcomes was one of the most effective steps we could have taken as a youth development organization for our young people.

With governments across the country looking for more efficient, less costly ways to address the most intractable social problems, such as poverty, homelessness, and mass incarceration, performance-based funding mechanisms open the door for highly successful, results-driven organizations to differentiate themselves from the nonprofit pack. At the same time, governments are encouraged to be selective in the organizations they fund, using performance data and outcomes as the primary tool for judging a program's effectiveness. And in the face of these elevated standards, we *all* become better.

MOLLY BALDWIN *is founder and chief executive officer of Roca, a Massachusetts-based nonprofit that works to disrupt the cycle of poverty and incarceration by helping young people transform their lives. For over 40 years, Baldwin has been a tireless advocate for high-risk young people, and has led Roca to be a data-driven, effective intervention for justice-involved young adults. She is a graduate of University of Massachusetts, Amherst, holds an M.Ed from Lesley University and an honorary PhD from Salem State University and Lesley University.*

KEY CONSIDERATIONS FOR GAINING TRACTION IN MEDICAID

Allison Hamblin
Center for Health Care Strategies

An innovation will get traction only if it helps people get something that they're already doing in their lives done better.[1]

—Clayton Christensen, author of *The Innovator's Dilemma*

As the Pay for Success movement has grown throughout the United States, a broad array of intermediaries, service providers, and prospective investors have set their sights on state Medicaid programs, which serve one in five Americans, as among the most bankable beneficiaries of any number of social impact investments.[2] For example, Medicaid, a federal-state partnership that provides publicly financed health insurance for low-income individuals and people with disabilities, pays a considerable price for hospitalizations that could be avoided through more effective primary and preventive care, and by addressing the social determinants of health. Accordingly, Medicaid meets one of the key criteria for vetting potential Pay for Success end payers—namely, savings that can be monetized through social impact interventions.

However, despite all the enthusiasm directed at Medicaid from the outside, state Medicaid leaders have been slow to embrace Pay for Success—perhaps even painfully slow, depending on one's vantage point. Whereas dozens of inquiries and feasibility studies have been pursued, only the state of South Carolina has closed a Pay for Success transaction that directly leverages Medicaid funds—and not exactly in a true

---

1 Nancy Lions, "The Disruptive Start-Up: Clayton Christensen On How to Compete with the Best," *Inc. Magazine* (February 1, 2002), available at http://www.inc.com/magazine/20020201/23854.html.

2 Kaiser Family Foundation, "Medicaid Pocket Primer" (January 3, 2017), available at http://kff.org/medicaid/fact-sheet/medicaid-pocket-primer/.

end-payer capacity. The reasons for this slow take-up are many. First, the Pay for Success field arguably needs to do a better job of articulating the unique value that Pay for Success could provide to Medicaid programs. Second, the opportunity cost associated with devoting time and resources to Pay for Success implementation must be reduced. Below are suggestions for a two-pronged strategy to increase Pay for Success' traction in Medicaid, specifically: 1) honing the Medicaid-specific value proposition; and 2) addressing key limitations that are otherwise likely to remain barriers to Medicaid engagement in the near term.

REFINING THE VALUE PROPOSITION: WHAT CAN PAY FOR SUCCESS HELP MEDICAID "GET DONE BETTER?"

Fortunately, there are numerous ways that Pay for Success offers Medicaid a valuable and potentially "better-than-other-alternatives" strategy for achieving key policy objectives. Specifically, Pay for Success may provide Medicaid with an opportunity to:

Onboard investments in social determinants of health. There is growing recognition across the health care sector that social determinants play a key role in driving health outcomes and associated health care costs. Although the United States spends up to 95 percent of health care dollars on direct medical services, roughly 50 percent of preventable deaths are attributable to nonmedical indicators, including social circumstances, environmental factors, and individual behaviors.[3] Given this heightened appreciation for nonmedical factors, Medicaid programs are actively designing and implementing strategies to address beneficiaries' social determinants of health. These strategies include two primary pathways: 1) exploring options to use Medicaid funds more flexibly to pay for nonmedical services; and 2) implementing new payment incentives for providers to attend to social determinants directly.

With each of these pathways, Medicaid agencies and their contracted partners are in the early stages of a new journey—navigating new landscapes of services and service providers beyond the familiar realm of

---

3 J. Michael McGinnis, Pamela Williams-Russo, and James Knickman, "The Case for More Active Policy Attention to Health Promotion," *Health Affairs* 21 (2) (2002): 78–93; Paula Braveman and Laura Gottlieb, "The Social Determinants of Health: It's Time to Consider the Causes of the Causes," *Public Health Reports* 129 (Supplement 2) (2014): 19–31, available at http://www.publichealthreports.org/issueopen.cfm?articleID=3078.

traditional health care delivery. And understandably, many are proceeding with caution as they look to address multiple new lines of inquiry, such as assessing unmet community needs, identifying evidence-based strategies to address these needs, untangling webs of existing relationships and funding streams, identifying well-positioned partners, and, ultimately, negotiating business arrangements that satisfy mutual operational and financial needs.

In short, this is a new and heavy lift for the health care sector, and one where Pay for Success may have a valuable role to play in easing the onboarding process. In this context, Pay for Success could be viewed as a temporary financing strategy to mitigate various risks associated with navigating new terrain. Specifically, by enabling Medicaid payers or providers to pay only "if it works," and by putting tightly defined parameters around populations to be served, timeframes for implementation, and outcomes to be rewarded, Pay for Success can provide structured supports that minimize the risk and extent of stumbles and dead-ends along the way.

Scale evidence-based prevention strategies. Medicaid programs and the partners they contract with are responsible for managing the health of large populations over broad geographic regions. As an entitlement program, Medicaid is often constrained in what it can offer on a limited geographic basis, given federal requirements to offer most covered services statewide to all who could benefit. Meanwhile, in many cases, effective models of social service delivery are far more localized—specific to neighborhoods or individual communities—and not necessarily available at the capacity to adequately serve all Medicaid enrollees in a region or state.

In this context, Pay for Success may serve as a valuable financing strategy to help scale up such models to achieve the reach necessary to meet Medicaid needs. Whereas traditional models of service payment generally do not address ramp-up costs, particularly on the low margins where most social service providers operate, Pay for Success gives providers upfront access to capital, thereby supporting geographic expansion, hiring and training of new staff, and other necessary capital investments. Accordingly, Pay for Success can provide a win-win for both Medicaid stakeholders and social service providers—meeting demands of scale for Medicaid while addressing the financial and operational constraints on growth for the service providers.

Maintain clear boundaries on Medicaid-covered services. In the context of growing interest in social determinants, Medicaid has been facing new questions regarding the most cost-effective use of program funds. For example, given all the evidence around the favorable impacts of supportive housing on health care costs, there is growing interest across states to cover housing and related services for certain high-risk subsets of Medicaid enrollees.[4] However, there are also considerable countervailing pressures related to maintaining Medicaid's integrity and focus as a health insurance program, and not exposing U.S. taxpayers to an ever-broadening mandate (and associated bill) for what Medicaid could and should cover.

Pay for Success provides one mechanism that can help Medicaid achieve its goals of addressing key social determinants of health while maintaining its established boundaries as a health insurance program. Specifically, Pay for Success enables Medicaid to pay for desired health outcomes without having to amend federal coverage limitations on the underlying services that generate those outcomes. In this way, Pay for Success is similar to other allowable mechanisms that could afford Medicaid greater flexibility to use its dollars beyond the scope of the approved Medicaid benefit. Two of the other mechanisms that are gaining a lot of current attention include "*in lieu of*" and "*value-added*" services. As defined in federal regulations, *in lieu of* services allow states to contract with managed care plans to provide non-covered benefits, so long as they are demonstrated to be cost-effective alternatives; *value-added* services enable managed care plan investments in a broad array of activities that improve health care quality. With both of these mechanisms, Medicaid programs can broaden the array of services that Medicaid managed care plans can use their funds to purchase. However, whereas each of these pathways expressly expands the universe of services that Medicaid pays for, Pay for Success arguably enables the same outcomes without risking the potential creep in program scope. By enumerating the outcomes to be paid for (as opposed to the

---

4   For example: Laura Sadowski et al., "Effect of a Housing and Case Management Program on Emergency Department Visits and Hospitalizations Among Chronically Ill Homeless Adults: A Randomized Trial," *JAMA* 301(17) (2009): 1771–1778.

nonmedical services from which they originate) Medicaid may, through Pay for Success, have a greater chance at maintaining program integrity and avoiding risk or perception of runaway entitlements, as compared with these other mechanisms.

Address broader societal preference for health care over social service investment. Despite concerns at federal and state levels regarding ever-rising health care costs and their growing share of government budgets through Medicare, Medicaid, and other public coverage programs, the United States as a society continues to show a strong preference toward investing taxpayer dollars in health care, as compared with other social services. As Elizabeth Bradley and her colleagues at Yale University demonstrated, for every dollar the United States spends on health care, it spends 90 cents on social services, whereas our industrialized peers spend two dollars.[5] Notably, Bradley's findings also highlight the poorer health outcomes associated with the under-allocation of resources to social services relative to health care services. And, whereas the current policy and political climate could well lead to reductions in government health care spending, it is not likely that we will see any of these funds diverted to social service funding.

Given this uniquely American preference to spend money on health care at the expense of other social services, Pay for Success may provide one mechanism for diverting some of those health care dollars back into the social service sector. While the funds may come through the public budgeting process as health care monies, Pay for Success can allow policymakers to reroute a portion of those funds toward otherwise underfunded social services, to the extent that those services can drive desired improvements in health outcomes. To that end, Pay for Success may be an antidote to the U.S. obsession with health care—a tool to get closer to that 2:1 ratio of social service to health care spending that has been proven to drive better health outcomes.[6]

Support the health care system's broader evolution toward paying for value. Increasingly, a dominant area of focus for Medicaid and other

---

5 Elizabeth Bradley et al., "Health and Social Services Expenditures: Associations with Health Outcomes," *Quality and Safety* 20 (10) (2011), available at http://qualitysafety.bmj.com/content/20/10/826.

6 Ibid.

payers is in transitioning the health care payment system from one that rewards volume to one that rewards value. Historically, health care providers have been reimbursed on a fee-for-service basis—creating substantial incentives to increase visits and procedures, and few disincentives for unnecessary, duplicative, or potentially harmful medical care. While better known for its coverage provisions, the Affordable Care Act included a number of initiatives to stimulate broad-scale change in provider payment. Largely driven by the newly created Center for Medicare & Medicaid Innovation, value-based payment models have begun to proliferate, with lofty targets across payers for moving payments to value-based arrangements over the next three to five years. These arrangements generally fall along a continuum of fee-for-service plus bonuses tied to quality performance, shared savings/risk, and global payments, whereby providers manage the total cost of care for a defined population or suite of services, subject to quality performance benchmarks (see Figure 1).

On the one hand, Pay for Success could be viewed as an onboarding strategy for social service providers to enter into value-based payment arrangements. To date, the more advanced value-based payment arrangements—such as those including shared risk or capitation—have generally been taken on by large health care systems that are well capitalized and have the administrative infrastructure to manage that risk. By leveraging private investment, Pay for Success provides a mechanism for less-well-capitalized service providers to avoid that risk, enabling a broader universe of providers to participate in advanced payment arrangements without fears of destabilizing a fragile social service sector.

On the other hand, beyond bringing in new providers, Pay for Success can also push the envelope of how Medicaid and other health care payers think about value-based payments. While the current continuum of value-based payment arrangements presents an important shift away from fee-for-service, it arguably falls short of what Pay for Success considers outcomes-based payment. Although current value-based payment efforts better connect health care payment incentives with quality of care and hold providers accountable for managing costs, they arguably have not yet envisioned a future where providers are explicitly paid to produce, maintain, or improve health—not just as a bonus on top of fee-for-service or

Figure 1. Performance Benchmark Continuum

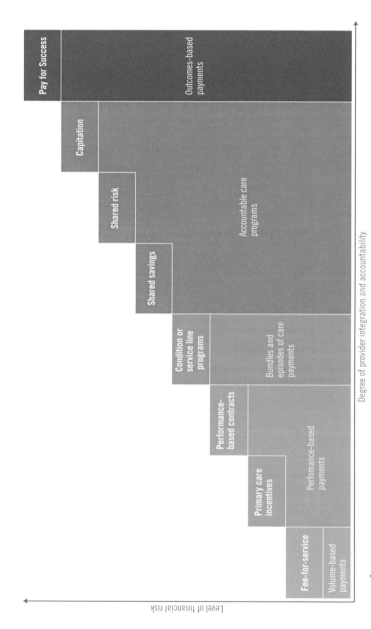

What Matters: Investing in Results to Build Strong, Vibrant Communities

as a condition for retaining profits under global budgets, but as the basis of the payment system itself. In this sense, Pay for Success or outcomes-based payment could be construed as a future state along the value-based payment continuum, or as a modified trajectory away from a focus on managing total costs to managing the production of desired outcomes. These concepts are highly related, but they have different points of emphasis that are worth noting. In this context, Pay for Success—and particularly the most recent efforts to develop rate cards that establish a fee schedule for specific outcomes—could provide important new tools for Medicaid as it and other payers further hone their approach to value-based payments over time.

Identify new financial resources in a constrained budgetary environment. Pending the outcomes of ongoing debates about the Affordable Care Act, it is possible that Medicaid could undergo significant changes in the years ahead—potentially away from its status as an open-ended entitlement program and toward some form of capped federal funding commitment through block grants or other related mechanisms. Given the commensurate interest among congressional leaders in reducing federal spending, there is considerable likelihood that any structural changes to the Medicaid program could be accompanied by federal funding cuts. For example, the Affordable Care Act and Medicaid reform bill put forth in early 2017 by Republican leadership included an $880 billion cut to federal Medicaid spending over ten years.[7]

With the prospect of fewer Medicaid resources and stronger demands on the safety net associated with losses in health care coverage, states would face new pressures to do more with less. Whereas Pay for Success might otherwise have been viewed as a modest source of discretionary capital to seed pilot projects, a new policy picture could place more of a premium on Pay for Success' ability to supplement limited public funds with private investment capital, as well as to provide a glide path for Medicaid to move over time toward paying only for what works.

---

7   Congressional Budget Office, "Cost Estimate: American Health Care Act" (March 13, 2017), available at https://www.cbo.gov/sites/default/files/115th-congress-2017-2018/costestimate/americanhealthcareact.pdf.

WHAT IT WILL TAKE TO GAIN TRACTION IN MEDICAID

As described above, Pay for Success could represent a valuable tool for Medicaid in a variety of ways. However, to gain traction, some key limitations need to be addressed:

Scale. Medicaid programs are large; for example, the median-sized program (Virginia) covers approximately one million people with a budget of more than $8 billion. Accordingly, to capture the attention and imagination of Medicaid leadership, Pay for Success needs to move beyond small, local pilots and deliver a measurable impact on cost and quality outcomes at scale. Otherwise, the requisite investment of staff time and other resources will have a hard time stacking up against other higher-priority, higher-impact initiatives.

Replicability. Medicaid leadership will want to know going into a Pay for Success transaction that, if successful, it will be straightforward to replicate the model in other regions of the state or for other targeted outcomes. Continued efforts to minimize the administrative burden associated with Pay for Success transaction structuring will be key to assuring Medicaid of the potential for replication.

State-level return on investment (ROI). Among other benefits, most states view Pay for Success as an opportunity to generate state-level Medicaid savings. The Centers for Medicare & Medicaid Services does not currently allow states to commit the federal portion of savings achieved through Pay for Success initiatives for repayment of investor capital. Simply put, this means that unless federal policy changes, Pay for Success transactions with Medicaid agencies as end payers need to have sufficient ROI that the state portion of savings alone (which is half or less, depending on the state) is sufficient to repay investors. For certain populations, such as individuals dually eligible for Medicare and Medicaid, this state share of any savings is even less.

Willingness to partner with Medicaid managed care. Many Pay for Success enthusiasts see it as a mechanism to fundamentally change the way government spends its money and are reluctant to consider the private sector as an end-payer. However, given that more than 60 percent of Medicaid enrollees receive their benefits through managed care plans, many states view their health plan partners as the entities best poised to enter into Pay for Success arrangements. The ROI equation is generally easier for the plans as well, given that the plans do not have to distinguish between state and federal dollars, and have greater flexibility to commit their combined Medicaid funds as they see fit. Given that plans are increasingly being held accountable for delivering outcomes, Pay for Success may present an attractive transaction structure for them, guaranteeing that their financial outlays are tied to outcomes that they are increasingly expected to deliver.

Alignment with the language of value-based payments. To date, Pay for Success has not adequately aligned itself with broader health care trends around value-based payments. To be embraced by Medicaid, Pay for Success needs a clearer narrative on how it relates to other efforts to transform health care payment practices—both in terms of where it fits in and what it is uniquely poised to contribute. The more Pay for Success can relate to Medicaid in terms that Medicaid understands, the easier it will be for Medicaid stakeholders to understand how and where it could be useful.

Fit within existing policy parameters. As described earlier, one clear value of Pay for Success to Medicaid is the flexibility it may provide to fund activities that are otherwise difficult for states to cover under traditional Medicaid rules. Thus, to the extent that implementing Pay for Success requires policy changes or other time-intensive administrative actions, states may prefer to devote that energy to removing the underlying barriers to the flexibility they are seeking. In other words, if Pay for Success as a "workaround" is laborious to implement, states may be better off trying to address the more fundamental policy barriers themselves.

LOOKING AHEAD

With all the large-scale changes Medicaid could be facing in the months ahead, stakeholders looking to engage Medicaid in new ideas need to closely align their pitches with the program's most pressing priorities. Fortunately, there are numerous ways in which Pay for Success can help states deliver on core strategic objectives: Transforming payment systems to reward value and addressing social determinants of health, to name two. The greater the alignment in language, the ease of execution, and the potential for scale, the more likely Pay for Success will find a ripe audience among Medicaid leaders.

––––––

ALLISON HAMBLIN *is vice president for strategic planning at the Center for Health Care Strategies (CHCS), a nonprofit policy center dedicated to improving care for low-income populations. She helps guide CHCS' program development and organizational planning activities and leads national initiatives focused on advancing and scaling integrated care models for Medicaid's highest-need beneficiaries. She also directs CHCS' work in supporting the use of Pay for Success financing for social service investments. Prior to joining CHCS, Hamblin worked at Apax Partners and Goldman Sachs, where she provided venture capital and investment banking services to companies in the health care and technology industries. She has an MSPH from the University of North Carolina at Chapel Hill, and an AB in biology from Duke University.*

STANDARDS OF EXCELLENCE CAN HELP ACCELERATE ADOPTION OF OUTCOMES-ORIENTED FUNDING IN THE PUBLIC AND PRIVATE SECTORS

David Medina
Results for America

PRIVATE-SECTOR STANDARD OF EXCELLENCE

In 2002, recognizing that there was little hope that Congress would pass a federal law prohibiting employment discrimination based on sexual orientation and gender identity any time soon, the Human Rights Campaign (HRC), our nation's largest LGBT civil rights organization, decided to promote workplace equality through a new Corporate Equality Index (CEI).

HRC believed at the time that releasing a public scorecard that high-lighted its recommended LGBT-inclusive employment policies—and ranked Fortune 500 and other large American companies based on their adoption of them—would increase the demand for equal workplace protections and benefits among America's workers while simultaneously increasing their supply among our nation's largest employers.

As an HRC national board member, I helped the organization develop its first Corporate Equality Index in 2002. This index rated 319 large U.S. companies based on seven workplace criteria and found a median score of fifty-seven percent, a score lower than I had hoped for but higher than I had expected. My experience using this public index to promote work-place equality ultimately informed my decision to use a similar strategy to promote evidence-based policy within the federal government. Inducing federal agencies to support evidence-based programs will be a linchpin in

What Matters: Investing in Results to Build Strong, Vibrant Communities

orienting funding around outcomes. A public index could be an effective tool to spur behavior change in the federal bureaucracy.

PUBLIC-SECTOR STANDARD OF EXCELLENCE

In 2012, my colleague Michele Jolin and I founded Results for America (RFA), a nonprofit organization committed to helping policymakers at all government levels build and use data and evidence to improve outcomes. We quickly discovered that there was no standard of excellence that described the "what works" infrastructure federal departments and agencies need to have in place in order to be able to use data and evidence when making budget, policy, and management decisions.

We ultimately interviewed more than 60 current and former federal government leaders and key external stakeholders, who helped us develop the data and evidence criteria in our inaugural Invest in What Works Index, which we released in June 2013. Similar to HRC's index, the primary purpose of RFA's index was to build the demand for and supply of evidence-based policymaking at the federal level.

After releasing our first four indexes in June 2013, September 2013, May 2014, and March 2015, we again worked with dozens of current and former federal policymakers and others to develop an updated index, which we released in April 2016. This index ranked seven federal departments and agencies[1] based on ten data and evidence criteria (see Figure 1).

Since 2013, our RFA team has been helping policymakers at these seven federal departments and agencies develop and implement the recommendations in our federal "standard of excellence." For example, we helped the U.S. Department of Education and bipartisan congressional leaders make several of the federal education programs highlighted in our federal index more results-driven by developing the evidence provisions in the bipartisan 2015 Every Student Succeeds Act (ESSA). These provisions could help states and school districts shift up to $2 billion toward evidence-based, results-driven solutions annually in fiscal years 2017–20. RFA's new Evidence in Education Lab is now helping states and school districts implement these ESSA evidence provisions to ensure

---

1 Results for America, "Federal Invest in What Works Index" (April 2016), available at http://2016.results4america.org/.

Figure 1: Federal Invest in What Works Index Criteria

INDEX CATEGORY	CRITERIA FOR RANKING
LEADERSHIP	Did the agency have a senior staff member(s) with the authority, staff, and budget to evaluate its major programs and inform policy decisions affecting them in FY16?
EVALUATIONS AND RESEARCH	Did the agency have an evaluation policy, an evaluation plan, and a research/learning agenda(s), and did it publicly release the findings of all completed evaluations in FY16?
RESOURCES	Did the agency invest at least one percent of program funds in evaluations in FY16?
PERFORMANCE MANAGEMENT/ CONTINUOUS IMPROVEMENT	Did the agency implement a performance management system with clear and prioritized outcome-focused goals and aligned program objectives and measures, and did it frequently collect, analyze, and use data and evidence to improve outcomes, return on investment, and other performance dimensions in FY16?
DATA	Did the agency collect, analyze, share, and use high-quality administrative and survey data — consistent with strong privacy protections — to improve (or help other entities improve) federal, state, and local programs in FY16?
COMMON EVIDENCE STANDARDS/WHAT WORKS DESIGNATIONS	Did the agency use a common evidence framework, guidelines, or standards to inform its research and funding decisions, and did it disseminate and promote the use of evidence-based interventions through a user-friendly tool in FY16?
INNOVATION	Did the agency have staff, policies, and processes in place that encouraged innovation to improve the impact of its programs in FY16?
USE OF EVIDENCE IN FIVE LARGEST COMPETITIVE GRANT PROGRAMS	Did the agency use evidence of effectiveness when allocating funds from its five largest competitive grant programs in FY16?
USE OF EVIDENCE IN FIVE LARGEST NONCOMPETITIVE GRANT PROGRAMS	Did the agency use evidence of effectiveness when allocating funds from its five largest noncompetitive grant programs in FY16?
REPURPOSE FOR RESULTS	Did the agency shift funds away from any practice, policy, or program that consistently failed to achieve desired outcomes in FY16?

that its changes in federal policy and shifts in federal funds will ultimately improve education outcomes for our nation's young people.

RFA also worked closely which the Corporation for National and Community Service which now allocates up to 12 points out of 100 to grant applicants seeking AmeriCorps funding based on their evidence of effectiveness.

At RFA, we understand that developing our federal standard of excellence was just the first step. Helping government policymakers implement its recommendations as effectively and efficiently as possible and continuing to engage and mobilize them as "what works" champions are necessary to ultimately achieve desired outcomes.

In 2016, the HRC reported that a record 407 of the nation's 851 largest businesses earned a top score of 100 percent in its fourteenth annual CEI—up from just 13 corporations in 2002. RFA's 2016 Invest in What Works Index similarly noted that the seven federal departments and agencies included in it were, on average, nearly 80 percent of the way toward meeting its ten criteria.

BUILDING ON THIS FOUNDATION

RFA's Invest in What Works Index and the HRC's Corporate Equality Index point to the potential of using standards of excellence to drive behavior change in both the public and private sectors. Similar, independent initiatives such as the LEED Green Building standards have galvanized change in other sectors. In the global development realm, Transparency International's annual Corruption Perception's Index has helped to raise public awareness of the necessity to root out corruption, and steered governments across the world to take actions to improve their rankings.

These examples indicate the potential to help accelerate progress in both the public and private sectors to evidence-based policymaking and outcomes orientation by publicly ranking organizations based on a relatively small number of objective criteria developed by a broad range of content experts. This approach can create new social norms by defining what constitutes good practice and coupling this analysis to a public campaign that celebrates early adopters and shines the light on laggards. Without waiting for legislative action, this social pressure can catalyze a healthy competition among agencies and private funders to reorient funding around outcomes. While this work is still in its early days, we are encouraged by initial progress and success of this approach in other fields, and believe this will be an important complement to other more direct actions to shift the culture and practice of social sector funding.

———

DAVID MEDINA *is co-founder and chief operating officer at Results for America. Throughout his career, Medina has also served as First Lady Michelle Obama's deputy chief of staff; the U.S. Global Leadership Campaign's government relations director; U.S. Senator John Edwards' presidential campaign political director; and the Democratic National Committee's policy director. Medina received his BA from the University of Chicago and his MPP from Harvard University's Kennedy School of Government.*

SUSTAINABLE OUTCOMES REQUIRE AN INTERDEPENDENT WEB OF STRATEGIES

Susan N. Dreyfus
Alliance for Strong Families and Communities

All of us who have been on the funding side of human services want to know that the public, private, or philanthropic dollars we spend are delivering real outcomes that help people reach their fullest potential. However, a mistake we frequently make is to think that the solutions are simply linear and technical in nature. For example, we focus on implementing a values-based payment methodology for a specific program or service, or require evidence-based interventions. Both are pieces of the puzzle, but in and of themselves won't produce the desired results. To improve the human condition is an adaptive challenge that requires adaptive solutions. For too long, we have focused our quest for outcomes solely on funding a program or service to be delivered, and not on unpacking the necessary capacities that must sit at the foundation of an organization's ability to implement its programs and services with fidelity and affect the context within which people live their daily lives. No one program or service can accomplish that alone. If we continue to make this fundamental attribution error, we will not achieve sustainable outcomes for people and communities. Adaptive challenges must be recognized and understood for their complexity, and adaptive solutions must be developed, implemented, and funded.

A great example of this is Wraparound Milwaukee. Having operated over the past 21 years, this proven evidence-based model has been implemented and replicated nationally and internationally across many different disciplines to positively change the trajectories of young people's lives and achieve measurable results. The blended, capitated, risk-sharing reimbursement and flexible payment model allows for money to follow the people being provided with services and supports "wrapped around" their needs and strengths. At the same time, the funding strategies also sustain and support the costs of the necessary infrastructure that Wraparound Milwaukee must have to ensure quality staffing, a robust and effective network of providers, innovative data systems, continuous quality improvement, and recognized community leadership and effective advocacy. The money it has saved through reduced need for institutional placements, such as unnecessary hospitalization and lower cost per recipient of services, has been reinvested back into the program to serve additional families. Wraparound Milwaukee has come to understand that achieving outcomes isn't just about effecting positive change for an individual youth and family, but about creating changes that improve the system of care for the entire community. We must seek to understand and listen to families and consumers and positively influence these factors when they are barriers to families' ability to lead safe and healthy lives. Put simply, the social determinants of health are the social determinants of life! Safe and suitable housing, transportation, employment, education, and access to integrated health care are among the areas on which Wraparound Milwaukee must focus its attention because these factors and others affect our ability to achieve positive outcomes for families and help at-risk youth move forward in their lives with greater promise, hope, and resilience.

The key to achieving outcomes-based funding models is to understand what it truly costs to realize the results we seek and equip organizations with the necessary capacities, competencies, and supports with flexibility and accountability. Often, payers do not understand the interdependent and complex web of strategies that are critical to the outcomes they claim they want to achieve. They want to fund what works, but the requirements they create resort back to the old fee-for-service, program-focused, micromanagement mindset that rigidly thwarts creativity and the ability to achieve and sustain meaningful outcomes.

If we are serious about tying funding and investment to outcomes, we need to understand that our grants and contracts must invest in the leadership and capacities of organizations. We should use our procurements to make sure that we are funding the best organizations and assessing their quality well beyond their ability to provide a specific program or service. This kind of funding would encourage experimentation and continuous quality improvement, as well as support organizations' ability to partner and effect change in external and interconnected systems. As funders, we should work alongside these organizations to understand where current policy, regulatory, or fiscal constraints are influencing their ability to be successful, and work with them to bust those barriers. Would Fortune 500 CEOs keep their jobs if they were not continuously investing in the capacities their company must have to achieve desired results? Why aren't we requiring organizations to state clearly the true cost of delivering the desired results and then comparing organizations accordingly?

I look forward to the day when an RFP comes out that requires organizations to articulate their adaptive capacities, along with the specific way they will deliver the desired program and service. Organizations should be required to clearly articulate how they are wired to authentically engage consumers; their generative governance; their capacity to use data and measurement for continuous improvement; their use of evidence and research; their staff development systems; their capacity to innovate; and their leadership, advocacy, and ability to partner deeply and effect change in the interconnected systems around them. How many more times will contracts go bad because we have not done our due diligence in differentiating between good and great organizations, or not funded great organizations for the very capacities and competencies that sit underneath and around their ability to be successful?

I learned this lesson in the late 1990s when I was administrator of children and family services for the state of Wisconsin and we implemented massive child welfare system reforms in Milwaukee County under class-action litigation. We redesigned the system to contract out by region to community-based organizations all services except child protective services and performance monitoring, which state staff continued to deliver directly. We identified the measurable goals we wanted to achieve and the child- and family-centered values on which the redesigned system was to be based. We wanted to see more children safe, able to live within their own families, and move children quickly to permanency in their lives.

But as I reflect back, I see that we implemented our contracts all wrong. We did what I continue to see government and other payers do today: We funded our contract partners for the direct-service staffing and service pattern we were expecting with little flexibility and no understanding of all the attributes of social-sector organizations we should have been leveraging. We did not understand all of the internal capacities these organizations would need to ensure quality, measurable, and sustainable outcomes over time. It's time we acknowledge that the social sector is more than just providers of program and service under contract with others. Rather, it is made up of transformative agents within communities who provide their programs and services in a values-driven way—through their leadership, capacity to innovate, agility, partnerships, and paramount responsibility to advocacy and influence within the larger community. Lester Salamon, director of the Johns Hopkins Center for Civil Society Studies, says it well when he calls this the "distinctiveness advantage" of the sector.

I have never been more hopeful as I am today that we are finally moving from program thinking to systems-change thinking as a field and across sectors. The key now is to understand the adaptive challenge we face and have the courage to invest our resources in adaptive solutions.

———

SUSAN N. DREYFUS *is president and chief executive officer of the Alliance for Strong Families and Communities, a network of more than 450 human-serving organizations nationwide working to achieve a vision of a healthy and equitable society. Prior to joining the Alliance in 2012, Dreyfus was secretary for the Washington State Department of Social and Health Services. In 1996 she was appointed to be the first administrator of the Division of Children and Family Services by the Wisconsin governor Tommy G. Thompson. The American Public Human Services Association awarded Dreyfus its Lifetime Achievement Award in 2016 for her contributions to the field of health and human services in both the public and private sectors.*

A NEW NORMAL FOR EVIDENCE BUILDING
Five Tips for Funders

Kelly Fitzsimmons
Project Evident

Twenty-five years ago, I worked for a large anti-poverty nonprofit in Boston.

We wanted to evaluate our programs—to measure what was working and improve what wasn't—but persuading foundations to fund this evaluation proved challenging. Some felt that evaluation wouldn't make a big enough difference, while others felt that the government should support such efforts.

Foundations were reluctant to pay for evidence building. However, when we asked for program funding, they demanded evidence of impact—evidence that we couldn't build without the funding they were hesitant to provide.

Twenty-five years later, although the ecosystem has grown significantly healthier, this fundamental obstacle remains.

TODAY'S CONTEXT

More and more, philanthropy and impact investors are using data and evidence to inform their funding decisions. Fully 96 percent of nonprofits report that they have at least one donor who requires impact-data reporting. Over 33 percent of foundations have a dedicated evaluation unit.[1] But the quality of impact data and evidence varies greatly.

Contrary to conventional wisdom, nonprofits want to build evidence and evaluate not because they want to meet grant requirements (only eight percent of the nonprofits we surveyed indicated this was highly important

---

1 Center for Effective Philanthropy and Center for Evaluation Innovation, "Benchmarking Foundation Evaluation Practices" (2016); Open/Impact, "The Giving Code: Silicon Valley Nonprofits and Philanthropy" (2016); Innovation Network, "The State of Evaluation 2016" (2016).

What Matters: Investing in Results to Build Strong, Vibrant Communities

to them) or to remain accountable to external stakeholders (18 percent), but to improve performance (90 percent) and to verify intended impact (96 percent).[2]

Yet, despite increased demand from all sides, the dominant approach to evaluation remains slow, expensive, and insufficient. There are many reasons for this.

Evaluations can leave nonprofits no closer to showing evidence of impact or with any more valuable organizational learning than they had in the first place. Premature and underpowered evaluations can leave otherwise effective programs with no evidence of impact. Most evaluations, regardless of findings, leave no roadmap for improvement. "Many evaluators," as one nonprofit leader we spoke to in 2016 said, "are interested in the science of program evaluation but lack the perspective of providers looking to improve impact. Sometimes they use unrealistic instruments or models."

Policymakers and funders who demand evidence tend neither to understand nonprofits' operational and financial realities, nor to use evidence consistently to set policy or award contracts. As a result, the return on evidence-building investments is not always clear to nonprofits or their boards. Funders can shift this dynamic and call for a better balance of evaluation for learning and improvement as well as impact.

Funding for evidence building (and for the infrastructure that allows it) is limited and too often in the hands of third parties. Rather than following consistent business practice, or being empowered to pursue a strategic learning agenda, nonprofits are sometimes forced into ad hoc evaluations, driven by the agendas of others versus longer-range plans guided by emerging evidence of implementation and impact.

In short, funders, evaluators, and nonprofits all have slightly different goals. Funders want proof that their money is making a difference, evaluators want answers to questions of interest to the field, and nonprofits want to improve their programs. As a result of this misalignment, the ecosystem severely limits the pipeline of evidence-based programs ready for

---

2 All data are from Project Evident's fall 2016 market survey of nonprofit organizations; 51 responses were received from 100 surveys; 80 percent of responses were from organizations with revenues greater than $5 million and serving more than 1,000 clients annually; 41 percent of the responders' organizations focus on education.

investment. Funders seek programs that "work" for investment purposes, when, in fact, they also need to seek opportunities to build the evidence and improve programs' ability to deliver outcomes to communities.

OPPORTUNITY FOR FUNDERS

Funders are in a unique position to manage conflicting incentives, hold both nonprofits and researchers accountable for learning, improvement, and proof objectives, and make sure that evaluation is in the best interest of everyone involved—nonprofits, evaluators, funders, and, most important, the communities we are all trying to serve.

Below are five ways that funders can use the resources at their disposal to create a new normal for evidence building.

Invite and Support Grantees to Lead

If philanthropy is designed to support grantees in helping their communities, it stands to reason that nonprofits desiring a bigger impact should lead their own evaluation agendas. But this is not how the current ecosystem is set up: Instead of stemming organically from organizational strategy, evidence building is usually conducted to answer questions researchers are interested in or to "prove" to funders that programs are effective. Nonprofits are too often the "caboose" of the evidence-building train; they should be part of the engine.

As an alternative, we encourage funders to support nonprofits in leading the evaluation process. We encourage a new starting point for building evidence that is based on grantees' learning agenda and priorities. Once this is established, clarity regarding prior research for the specific target population served—questions whose answers will make programs more effective—should be integrated. Finally, by using methodologies appropriate to the questions asked, the available data, and the stage of the organization, we can help nonprofits build the evidence they need to make a bigger difference in their communities. Nonprofits, rather than researchers or funders, should lead this process; it is their responsibility to know whether their program is on track, as well as what's needed to guide it toward even better performance.

A series of smaller-scale internal and external studies—to inform program implementation and impact over time—allows for a more continuous, more cost-effective, and lower-risk approach. In fact, this is how the much-lauded Nurse-Family Partnership (NFP), which provides maternity and prenatal care to poor mothers, built its evidence base. NFP was grounded in theory and epidemiology, formatively developed with a set of pilot families, and then tested in a sequential series of randomized controlled trials to examine its impact with different populations living in different contexts before it was offered for public investment.[3] At every step of this process, data on implementation and outcomes were used to refine the program model and replication process.[4]

Move From Judgment to Development

"Many funders," said one nonprofit leader, "want to fund the type of research that would lead to a third-party rigorous evaluation that 'proves' program impact. However, just as important is funding the steps leading to this type of rigorous evaluation work."[5]

There is no such thing as a one-study wonder that makes a program perfect. The road to higher impact is paved with incremental improvements.

To help grantees follow this road, funders will have to shift from a more judgmental stance to a more developmental one based on learning and organizational development in service of improvement. Our mutual goals call for joint problem-solving, rigorous experimentation, and a willingness to evolve, none of which is possible in a pure thumbs-up/thumbs-down context. By viewing evidence building not as an event but as a cycle—and supporting nonprofits to pursue rigorous, mixed methods that fit their organizational needs—we can improve outcomes not just once but continually.

Don't Stop at Research: Support Learning and Implementation

Evidence building alone will have limited utility if nonprofits don't have sufficient capability to interpret the evidence and make adjustments based on what they learn. As part of the move from judgment to development,

---

3 David L. Olds, "Prenatal and Infancy Home Visiting by Nurses: From Randomized Trials to Community Replication," *Prevention Science* 3 (3) (2002): 153–72.

4 David L. Olds, "Improving the Life Chances of Vulnerable Children and Families with Prenatal and Infancy Support of Parents: The Nurse-Family Partnership," *Psychosocial Intervention* 21 (2) (2012): 129–43.

5 From Project Evident Planning Interviews.

therefore, funders must go beyond simply supporting research studies to supporting learning, cost-benefit analyses, and implementation.

Funders can also help connect research to policy and practice, as is clear from the success of research-practice partnerships like California's Fostering Connection to Success legislation, which gave foster care youth in California the right to care until the age of 20. Philanthropy played an important role in this legislation by funding the research, as well as stakeholder engagement to connect these efforts. Legislation like this shows what is possible when multiple stakeholders come together to implement solutions using evidence connected to policy and practice.[6]

Ask For and Fund Outcomes

Too often foundations and policymakers focus on compliance over impact. This can make both funders and government seem more interested in checking boxes than in making a real difference in nonprofits' communities. Further, it can breed a thumbs-up/thumbs-down culture, at the expense of learning, which can impede the ability to understand both if and how programs work so we can focus on improvement.

This will change, however, if foundations develop a stronger understanding of different levels of evidence and what it takes to build evidence. While ensuring compliance, it will allow them to send more resources to opportunities that build and sustain stronger outcomes over time. Specifically, funders should make greater use of the following:

- Staged funding to allow for learning, failure, and adjustment over time; continuous improvement requires the resources and space for experimentation.

- Entry-evidence reviews to understand the pre-existing evidence base and best practices for a given program and to identify gaps in critical research.

- The many clearinghouses to understand the evidence for given interventions.

- Data and evidence standards aligned with one another and with federal standards to enable a more coherent and accessible ecosystem.

---

6 For more details, see Mark E. Courtney and Jennifer E. Mosley, "Partnership and the Politics of Care: Advocates' Role in Passing and Implementing California's Law to Extend Foster Care," Chapin Hall at the University of Chicago (2012).

Embrace Data and Technology

Funders have been reluctant to embrace data and technology. As a result, foundation staff struggle to gain strategic insights from evaluations, while nonprofits struggle to secure evaluations that generate useful insights. Solving these twin problems will require new capacity and investment in tools, technology, and talent, as well as a fresh approach to evaluation design predicated on questions relevant to nonprofits.

Anu Malipatil, education director at Overdeck Family Foundation, said, "As a learning organization, in the spirit of continuous improvement, we knew it was critical that we built strong data systems that would enable us to ask and answer questions about our efficiency and effectiveness on a variety of workstreams, including programmatic grantmaking, and operations. More importantly, we are making it a priority to support our grantees to be learning organizations too. We strive to model what we hope to see in the field more broadly."[7]

By building or buying evaluation and learning capacity, as well as data and technology infrastructure, for themselves and their grantees, foundations can accelerate change, reduce costs, and remain helpful to grantees in the emerging ecosystem. This is especially important as developments in big data, predictive analytics, and machine learning (among other developments) shape the world around us.

THE NEXT CHAPTER

Increasingly, nonprofits see evidence building and learning as core to their work, but the funding markets are not keeping pace. As one leader said, "Nonprofits need the runway to solve hard problems. Multi-year support is beneficial, and funding for data and evidence infrastructure would be huge!"[8] Funders play a critical role in promoting a culture of learning and evidence building in the social sector—not just for themselves, their evaluators, and their grantees, but also for the communities that will benefit from programs with stronger outcomes.

---

7   From Project Evident planning interviews.

8   Ibid.

KELLY FITZSIMMONS *is founder and managing director of Project Evident and a committed social innovator. Previously, she served as vice president/chief program and strategy officer at the Edna McConnell Clark Foundation (EMCF) where she led policy innovation, evaluation, grantmaking and the early capital aggregation pilot. Prior to EMCF, she co-founded Leadwell Partners and New Profit Inc., held senior leadership positions in nonprofit organizations and served on several foundation and social sector boards and advisory committees.*

How This Works
REASONS FOR CAUTION
AND OPTIMISM

TRULY MAKING A DIFFERENCE
The Outcome/Impact Dilemma

Gordon Berlin
MDRC

I was a young staffer at the U.S. Department of Labor years ago when the National Supported Work Demonstration findings were released.[1] I learned a critical lesson that has played out in multiple policy areas many times since: It is crucial to distinguish between *gross outcomes* (such as the percentage of program participants who enter a job or cycle off welfare) and *net impacts* (the improvement in these outcomes that was actually attributable to program participation). Failure to heed this lesson threatens to derail what can otherwise be a helpful shift now underway toward an outcome orientation to guide program improvement. Outcomes alone are often not a reliable metric for judging the effectiveness of social investments.

In the National Supported Work Demonstration, which served four subgroups of disadvantaged individuals, the data on gross outcomes and net impacts pointed in opposite directions. The most favorable net impacts on employment were found for long-term welfare recipients, the subgroup that had the *lowest* employment outcomes—meaning that the program worked best for the subgroup that had the worst absolute outcomes. Yet, there was no value added for the subgroup with the *best* employment outcomes, since a randomly assigned control group showed that its earnings would have increased just as much without the Supported Work services.

This and numerous subsequent evaluations underscore the reality that much of what is often credited as *program-produced* outcomes can be driven more by other factors, such as a strong economy or the natural progress that highly motivated participants selected for the program would have made over time anyway. Perhaps some of the confusion can be avoided if we're clear that the term "outcomes" does not apply only to

---

1 MDRC Board of Directors, "Summary and Findings of the National Supported Work Demonstration" (1980).

program participants; members of a control group (and everyone else who doesn't participate in the program) have outcomes, too.

The point is not that net impacts matter and gross outcomes do not; both measures are important, but they tell us different things that must be reconciled in the ongoing effort to build evidence on program effectiveness—and continuous improvement—under real-world conditions. As a practical matter, program operators must use gross outcomes to monitor performance and motivate staff; they typically don't have access to a control group to tell them how much their services have actually *caused* the outcomes they strive for and observe.[2] Yet, policy, funding, and program design decisions should be based more on net impacts to avoid pouring scarce resources into programs with high gross outcomes but limited, if any, value added. Excessive pressure to increase outcomes can backfire by skewing program providers' incentives, since the fastest way to show "improvement" is often to simply screen out harder-to-serve individuals—ironically, the very people who might benefit most from the services offered.

There are no easy solutions to this dilemma, but some important steps can help to identify potential distortions and at least partially overcome the risks. Other authors have explored some of the implications of the "outcome mindset,"[3] so I will elaborate briefly here on two aspects of the interplay between gross outcomes and net impacts: (1) how the characteristics of program participants can influence results; and (2) developing performance measures in the context of scaling and replicating programs.

UNDERSTANDING THE CHARACTERISTICS OF THE INDIVIDUALS BEING SERVED

It is particularly important to interpret program outcomes in light of participants' characteristics that are likely to be correlated with the intended

---

2 Even in net impact studies, evaluators need to be careful to collect accurate information on the experiences of the control group. The actual "treatment difference" between the services that programs deliver to participants and the services that members of the control group receive elsewhere is sometimes less in practice than what had been assumed, leading to disappointing (and potentially misleading) findings.

3 Patrick Lester, "The Promise and Perils of an 'Outcome Mindset'," Leland Stanford Jr. University (2015); see also Michael Bangser, "A Funder's Guide to Using Evidence of Program Effectiveness in Scale-Up Decisions," MDRC and Social Impact Exchange (2014); and Judith Gueron, "Throwing Good Money After Bad: A Common Error Misleads Foundations and Policymakers," Leland Stanford Jr. University (2005).

outcomes: for example, when a job training program enrolls participants with strong employment histories, education levels, and motivation to work; or when a preschool program mostly serves children who come from stable families and were in a similar program the year before.

Program outcomes should also be interpreted in light of how participants were recruited and the extent to which the selection process may have screened out individuals who are more difficult to serve. This can be clarified by conducting a "funnel analysis," which documents key steps in the participant recruitment and selection process (such as eligibility criteria, interviews, or testing) and the reasons why individuals fail to come forward or drop off along the way, especially if it results from decisions that the program's staff makes. A tipoff that the selection process may be whittling down enrollees to the most motivated group: programs often start the enrollment process with many times the number of potential participants who ultimately enroll.

A focus on participants' characteristics might also enhance the prospects of producing favorable net impacts. For example, a recent data analysis from the National Head Start Impact Study showed that dual-language learners and Spanish-speaking children with low early literacy and math skills when they entered Head Start had gains that doubled the average net impact for the full sample.[4] Moreover, Head Start's impacts were largely driven by children who, in the absence of Head Start, would have stayed in home-based care throughout the day.[5] Targeted outreach to ensure inclusion of these and other underserved children might help boost the program's net impacts—although perhaps not the gross outcomes.

PERFORMANCE MEASURES IN THE CONTEXT OF SCALE-UP AND REPLICATION

The pressure for accountability and an outcome orientation goes hand in hand with growing interest in expanding cost-effective interventions. Since the stakes rise as more dollars are invested and more people are served,

---

4 Howard Bloom and Christina Weiland, "Quantifying Variation in Head Start Effects on Young Children's Cognitive and Socio-Emotional Skills Using Data from the National Head Start Impact Study," MDRC (2015).

5 Avi Feller et al., "Compared to What? Variation in the Impacts of Early Childhood Education by Alternative Care-Type Settings" (January 11, 2016, draft).

substantial expansion should be guided by evidence of net impact. Indeed, there are a number of examples in both the public and philanthropic sectors that use "tiered evidence" approaches, which stimulate new model development and program improvement. However, they require that early positive outcomes be followed by more rigorous evaluations to confirm that the programs are producing a positive net impact at key stages in the development and scaling process.[6]

Although every iteration of a program with positive net impacts cannot realistically be evaluated in another round of impact evaluations, the program outcomes can be judged by asking the following questions:

1 Are the program components that drove the positive results being implemented with the same intensity and quality as in the original net impact evaluation?

2 Is the program serving a population with the same challenges, or has it enrolled an easier-to-serve group?

3 Are the same outcome measures being used as in the original evaluation?

4 How does the operating context, such as the policy environment and local economy, compare with that of the original evaluation?

These questions suggest the need for caution in assuming that the encouraging net impacts found in the original evaluation will necessarily be repeated when programs are scaled up or replicated. For example, the population being served might shift, funding constraints often force providers to sacrifice certain elements of the original program model, and it can be difficult to maintain the same level of quality when programs operate on a much larger scale or in different settings.

WHERE DO WE GO FROM HERE?

The full potential of evidence-based policy will be realized only if program operators, policymakers, and evaluators join in using the right mix of data

---

6 The federal Office of Management and Budget has been a catalyst in requiring rigorous evidence to support program scale-up. Federal initiatives, such as the Social Innovation Fund and the Investing in Innovation (I3) Fund, have enlisted private partners to match public funding in an ongoing process of evidence-building. Philanthropy-led efforts, such as the Edna McConnell Clark Foundation's investment in youth-serving organizations, calibrate funding to the level of evidence while also investing in bringing the evidence to higher levels.

on program outcomes and net impacts. Reliance on the wrong measures, lack of data on key measures, and poor-quality data can lead to faulty conclusions. Since many program providers' data systems are underfunded and data collection can be a primary driver of an evaluation's costs, public and private funders will need to support data collection infrastructure. In return, evaluators must find ways to collect, analyze, and report on the data as expeditiously as possible.

A fertile opportunity is presented by a next generation of researcher-practitioner partnerships that leverage the strengths of both entities to refine interventions. For example, one such collaboration capitalizes on a readily available database to embed predictive analytics, random assignment, and other rigorous methods to test alternative strategies for continuous improvement in a network of schools. The initial focus has been on using early warning systems to identify students who are at risk of failing to graduate and real-time data from quick-turnaround random assignment studies to test the net impact of various approaches to boosting students' attendance.

Even with such advances, bridging the distinction between program outcomes and net impacts will no doubt continue to be a struggle for the field. But if we are vigilant for potential distortions and are open to exploring promising options, such as effective researcher-practitioner partnerships, we can use both outcome and net impact measures to produce the right kind of evidence to guide policy and practice. If we are not vigilant, two key constituents — participants and taxpayers — will be the first to realize that the numbers we are touting don't actually signal any net benefit at all.

GORDON BERLIN *is president of MDRC, a nonprofit, nonpartisan research organization based in New York City and Oakland, California, that is dedicated to learning what works to improve the lives of low-income people. Before joining MDRC in 1990, he was executive deputy administrator for management, budget, and policy at the New York City Human Resources Administration. He also was deputy director of the Ford Foundation's Urban Poverty program and worked as a program analyst and project officer in the U.S. Department of Labor's Employment and Training Administration. Berlin was the founding executive director of the Social Research and Demonstration Corporation, a Canadian nonprofit social policy research organization. Berlin has authored and co-authored numerous publications, including* Learning from Experience: A Guide to Social Impact Bond Investing; Poverty and Philanthropy: Strategies for Change; Rewarding the Work of Individuals: A Counterintuitive Approach to Reducing Poverty and Strengthening Families; *and* What Works in Welfare Reform: Evidence and Lessons to Guide TANF Reauthorization.

MAKING MEASUREMENT MATTER IN HEALTH CARE

Peter Long
Blue Shield of California Foundation

Jeannette is a 37-year-old woman living with her three young children in Riverside, CA. Her husband recently returned from his third tour of duty in Afghanistan as a staff sergeant in the U.S. Air Force Reserves. Jeannette was diagnosed with type 2 diabetes three years ago and participates in the local YMCA Diabetes Prevention Program. In her most recent visit to her primary care provider, Jeannette revealed that her husband has begun to psychologically and physically abuse her and threaten their children over the past month, coinciding with a significant increase in his alcohol consumption. This situation has worsened, and she had to call 911 last week to have the police restrain him. She is feeling anxious and concerned about her and her children's safety. Her primary care doctor refers her to the local domestic violence organization for further evaluation, counseling, and support services.

Today, many organizations are collecting partial information about the health and wellbeing of Jeannette and her family related to her diabetes and family violence situation. These wide-ranging organizations include her primary care provider, her health insurance plan, the Department of Defense, the YMCA, the children's school and daycare providers, law enforcement and judicial systems, the local child welfare agency, and the domestic violence organization. No one institution has a complete picture of the family's wellbeing, and Jeannette does not have the formal training or the perspective to interpret all of the complex information on her own. Although these organizations may share fragments of information over time upon request and as legally permissible, no one is analyzing and aggregating Jeannette's overall journey to determine if there are emerging patterns. As a result, although each individual institution believes that it is doing a great job, the health care and social service system is sub-optimizing its solutions to address Jeannette's underlying concerns and help her family achieve their full potential. Jeannette's situation happens millions of times every day in communities across the United States. It provides some insights into why the United States spends significantly more on health care than any other nation while producing mediocre health outcomes. The current dysfunctional state of U.S. health outcomes measurement represents an important barrier to Jeannette's pursuit of health and wellbeing.

The two major strands of work on health outcome measurement in the United States have different goals, underlying infrastructures, and audiences. Since the Civil War, federal, state, and local governments have been regularly collecting and reporting vital health statistics, such as birth rates, infant mortality rates, and infectious disease prevalence, to monitor population health.[1] In the 1980s, the U.S. Department of Health and Human Services furthered this work when it led a collaborative process to set ten-year evidence-based, measurable national health promotion and disease prevention objectives known as the "Healthy People" series. These objectives have the potential to serve as a call to action for state and local authorities because they are issued by the federal government and are linked to national health statistics. In reality, however, assessments have often revealed a lack of progress toward many targets and a widening of health disparities in relation to many health indicators.[2] Finally, there has been a proliferation of "Healthy People" indicators and priorities over the past few decades, growing from 319 measures to more than 1,200.

Separately, for the past 50 years within the U.S. health care system, there have been systematic efforts to measure the quality of care provided, based on a conceptual framework described by Avedis Donabedian, which looks at the structure (where the care was delivered), care process (how the care was delivered), and outcomes (the effects of the care on the patient).[3] Health care outcome measures have been used to rate the quality of individual interactions and activities inside the medical care system. They also have been used to help consumers, payers, regulators, and providers assess the quality of care delivered, determine bonus payments to providers, evaluate health plan performance, and, more

1 A.M. Hetzel, "History and Organization of the Vital Statistics System," National Center for Health Statistics (1997), available at http://www.cdc.gov/nchs/data/misc/usvss.pdf.

2 L.W. Green and J. Fielding, "The US Healthy People Initiative: Its Genesis and Its Sustainability," *Annual Review of Public Health* 32 (2011): 451–470.

3 Avedis Donabedian, "Evaluating the Quality of Medical Care," *The Milbank Quarterly* 83(4) (2005): 691–729, available at http://doi.org/10.1111/j.1468–0009.2005.00397.x.

recently, inform consumer choices about certain medical procedures. A proliferation of health care measures in recent decades has significantly burdened health care providers and caused confusion among patients and frustration among other stakeholders.[4] As of February 2016, the Centers for Medicare & Medicaid Services (CMS) have approved 1,513 measures for use, the National Quality Forum (NQF) lists 615 approved measures, and 83 measures are approved for use in the National Committee for Quality Assurance's Healthcare Effectiveness Data and Information Set (HEDIS) 2015 tool.[5] These narrowly targeted health care measures are not coordinated with one another nor tied to patients' ultimate health outcome over time.[6] Further, very few health care payments are actually tied to these outcome measures.[7]

As a result, there is growing recognition in both the medical and public health fields that we need to streamline and align these two important strands of health outcomes work if we want to achieve better health outcomes as a population, lower total health care costs, and produce a better care experience, often referred to as the Triple Aim.[8] Today, important efforts are underway in both the public and private sectors to more effectively use population health measures to guide action and rationalize health care measures to focus on fewer, more meaningful indicators that use standard definitions, data sources, and calculation methods. These incremental efforts in isolation may be able to reverse the current negative trends, but they are unlikely to address the root causes of the dysfunction and significantly improve health outcomes.

---

4   Institute of Medicine, "Vital Signs: Core Metrics for Health and Health Care Progress," The National Academies Press (2015).

5   CMS Measures Inventory [Microsoft Excel]. Retrieved April 15, 2016 from https://www.cms.gov/Medicare/Quality-Initiatives-Patient-Assessment-Instruments/QualityMeasures/CMS-Measures-Inventory.html; NQF: Quality Positioning System. Retrieved April 15, 2016 from http://www.qualityforum.org/qps/; HEDIS Measures. Retrieved April 29, 2016 from http://www.ncqa.org/hedis-quality-measurement/hedis-measures.

6   Kate Bazinsky and Michael Bailit, "The Significant Lack of Alignment Across State and Regional Health Measure Sets," Bailit Health Purchasing (September 10, 2013).

7   Suzanne Delbanco, François de Brantes, and Tom Valuck, "The Payment Reform Landscape: Which Quality Measures Matter?" *Health Affairs Blog* (October 15, 2015), available at http://healthaffairs.org/blog/2015/10/15/the-payment-reform-landscape-which-quality-measures-matter/.

8   Donald M. Berwick et al., "The Triple Aim: Care, Health, And Cost," *Health Affairs* 27(3) (2008) 759–769, available at http://content.healthaffairs.org/content/27/3/759.

Effective measurement of health outcomes lies at the heart of producing good health at the individual, community, and population levels. The goals of a highly functional health outcome measurement system should be to: 1) focus the broader health system on improving the health of individuals, communities, and society, and 2) promote meaningful collaboration among health care providers and across other sectors to address complex health issues.

The fundamental cause of the misaligned, low-value, and burdensome state of U.S. health outcome measures is the lack of a clear vision for the U.S. health care system. As a nation, we have not engaged in a systematic conversation about our health care values and priorities. The recent proliferation of health care measures reflects a pervasive lack of trust among various actors in the health care system in the absence of a broader vision. Stakeholders use a multitude of narrowly focused measures to manage the behaviors of other actors.

The recently announced United Nations Sustainable Development Goals (SDG) provide a comprehensive global framework to encourage and assess progress toward sustainable human development over the next 15 years, providing tangible 2030 targets for poverty, health, employment, education, equity, and environmental issues.[9] Consistent with the goals of the SDG framework, my colleagues and I developed the 3.0 Transformation Framework to stimulate thinking and support the planning and development of the new roadmap for the next generation of the U.S. health care system.[10] Beyond medical care, it focuses on optimizing population health over the life span and suggests how the current health care system could evolve into a system designed to enhance population health.[11] With the recent release of *Vital Signs: Core Metrics for Health and Health Care Progress,* the Institute of Medicine (IOM) initiated a dialogue about possible health outcome measures consistent with a 3.0 health system in the United States. *Vital Signs* proposed 15 broad domains and corresponding measures and recommendations for their application

9 United Nations, "Sustainable Development Goals," available at https://sustainabledevelopment.un.org/sdgs.

10 Neal Halfon et al., "Applying a 3.0 Transformation Framework to Guide Large-Scale Health System Reform," *Health Affairs* 33(11) (2014) 2003–2011, available at http://dx.doi.org/10.1377/hlthaff.2014.0485.

11 Ibid.

at every level and across sectors. Ultimately, the IOM consensus committee concluded that this streamlined set of measures could provide consistent benchmarks for health progress across the nation and improve system performance in the highest-priority areas.[12]

Beyond the lack of a clear vision, there is also a lack of a national infrastructure to support a health outcome measurement system. Significant progress has been made over the past two decades with the widespread adoption of electronic health records, the development of health information exchanges, and a national focus on interoperability.[13] Despite these ongoing efforts in the public and private sectors, it appears that we are building a measurement system that resembles the Winchester Mystery House in San Jose, CA, which contains hundreds of rooms, designed individually without relation to one another, and many staircases that lead to dead ends. Building the digital health infrastructure to support an effective learning health care system requires a shared vision derived from multiple competing perspectives.[14] Without a robust infrastructure, outcome measurement generates a tremendous amount of work but produces very little value.

Here the United States can learn from other countries to develop the basic infrastructure for outcome measurements, such as standardized definitions, agreement on data sources, common assessment, and evaluation approaches. For example, Cuba's robust health information infrastructure is key to its positive population health status relative to income and health care spending. The infrastructure creates the capacity to demonstrate how advances in community health status are central to distributing financial incentives to providers who successfully reduce costs and improve population health outcomes.[15]

---

12 Institute of Medicine, *Vital Signs: Core Metrics for Health and Health Care Progress*, The National Academies Press (2015).

13 David Blumenthal and John Glaser, "Information Technology Comes to Medicine," *New England Journal of Medicine* 356:24 (June 14, 2007).

14 Institute of Medicine, Digital Infrastructure for the Learning Health System: The Foundation for Continuous Improvement in Health and Health Care: Workshop Series Summary, Washington, DC: The National Academies Press (2011), available at https://www.nap.edu/catalog/12912/digital-infrastructure-for-the-learning-health-system-the-foundation-for.

15 C. William Keck and Gail A. Reed, "The Curious Case of Cuba," *American Journal of Public Health*, 102(8) (2012), available at doi:10.2105/ajph.2012.300822.

Once outcome measures are identified and data infrastructure are developed, additional work will be needed to meet the additional population health assessment, improvement, and innovation requirements of a 3.0 health system that promotes health. To optimize population health, an information system will need to measure population health trajectories and calculate the health impacts of investments to health, social, community, and economic outcomes. It will need to link outcomes over time to measure the impact of longitudinal integration on health trajectories and to measure how multisector interventions affect health determinants. Finally, it must link individual, population, and systems measures to gauge overall system progress and performance.[16]

Nothing less than a fundamental rethinking of our approach to health outcome measurement is required to produce substantially better results. Streamlining the existing approaches alone or focusing only on technical fixes will limit the potential to improve health outcomes while reducing health care spending. In the current political environment, however, it will be incredibly challenging to have a candid conversation about our national health values and priorities. Despite the inherent risks and challenges, now is the moment to summon our courage to ask and answer these critical questions. If we are successful, Jeannette, her husband, and their children will receive the information, support, and services they need to manage her diabetes, stop the violence and address substance use and trauma so that they can all be healthy and safe. Further, the various institutions and systems that support them will learn what works and what doesn't so they can they improve the health of the entire community over time. That is a vision worth pursuing.

——

PETER LONG *is president and chief executive officer of Blue Shield of California Foundation. In addition to his philanthropic background, Dr. Long has extensive experience working on health policy issues at the state, national, and global levels. Prior to serving in leadership roles at the Henry J. Kaiser Family Foundation and the California Endowment, Dr. Long was executive director of the Indian Health Center of Santa Clara Valley, and earlier, a legislative analyst for the Progressive Primary Health Care Network in Cape Town, South Africa during the country's transition to democracy. He currently serves on the boards of*

16 Halfon, "Applying a 3.0 Transformation Framework" (2014).

Grantmakers for Effective Organizations and Grantmakers in Health, and is a member of the National Academy of Medicine's Leadership Consortium for Value & Science-Driven Health Care.

THE ETHICS OF OUTCOMES-BASED FUNDING MODELS

Jodi Halpern
University of California, Berkeley

Douglas Jutte
Build Healthy Places Network

Combating the high costs of asthma — the most common chronic disease of childhood — seems an obvious win. But how to go about it? Heavy doses of steroids would be effective but can stunt growth. Preventing asthma attacks by taking away family pets and moving families into featureless cement homes would also be effective, but at what human cost? Keeping children permanently inside, away from pollution and inciting pollen and dust would have their own consequences: decreased activity, resulting obesity, social isolation. Given the long-term expense of poor mental health, type 2 diabetes, and cardiovascular disease, perhaps a focus only on the specific, measurable outcome of reduced costs for asthma is misplaced. If instead, the short-term but expensive medical treatment of childhood asthma were continued — allowing children to stay in their homes and play outside in the pollen and puppy-filled world — perhaps better long-term health and even bigger healthcare savings could be achieved.

While the idea of promoting any improved health outcome with associated cost savings sounds good on its face, implementing outcomes-based funding requires isolating an outcome more narrowly than may make sense for long-term benefits. This is because applying outcomes-based funding requires delineating clear, measurable goals to demonstrate success. And of course there are very good reasons to focus on specific societal aims in an accountable way. However, what matters ethically is not just the value of a stated goal in the abstract, but the specific pathways to meeting these goals. And, as the childhood asthma example suggests, there is the opportunity cost of choosing a lesser goal over other more important goals. Which leads us to argue that we need an ethical framework for choosing specific goals and setting programmatic priorities. Specifically, insofar as the outcomes-based strategies considered in this book are presumed to be meeting societal goals, it is necessary to prioritize projects according to the priorities of society.

This analysis stands as a challenge to the status quo in policy making which is to presume that finding a way to improve any positive outcome while expending fewer resources would seem to represent a good choice. Given economic scarcity to meet social goals, why wouldn't any efficiency be good in and of itself? The idea that under conditions of scarcity, efficiency alone will properly inform the ranking of goals already presupposes a particular ethical approach, that of utilitarianism. The utilitarian framework is often the default approach for policymakers, particularly those influenced by economists. As a result, absent explicit attention to values, the application of outcomes-based funding approaches is likely to be implicitly utilitarian.

The core utilitarian ethic is to maximize the ratio of benefit to cost—which is the definition of efficiency. When all relevant outcomes can be measured according to a homogenous unit of "benefit," this approach makes the most sense. It makes less sense when the outcomes have disparate social value and there is no single type of "benefit." In such cases, simply seeking to get more of any given benefit does not ensure the value of that benefit vis-à-vis other potential goals. In commonsense terms, doing relatively less important things at a bargain rate is poor policy when it leaves more important things undone.

Our main point is that efficiency itself has no normative or ethical value. Of course it is morally preferable to do "more good" overall by doing each thing efficiently, but what counts as "more good" still has to be established in some independent way. Rather than treating efficiency as a noun (seeking to create "efficiencies") we ought to treat it as an adverb—seeking to reduce, for example, illiteracy or depression efficiently. While this may seem obvious, it entails something less apparent: we need to decide what problems to address and how to select outcomes to measure according to societal values that are *independent of the dollars a project might offset*. Lacking this perspective, an outcomes-based approach regresses into taking efficiency itself as its fundamental value.

The error of attributing ethical value to efficiency alone is made repeatedly in social policies. The most common error is to equate equity or justice with the most efficient use of a limited resource, but to do so without any independent ethical rationale. For example, during the early stages of managed health care, an influential health policy leader, David Eddy, made this error in an important article in *JAMA* on how to ration health care.[1] He literally defined equity in terms of efficiency, stating:

> In the context of health care, a preferable definition of *equitable* is that services should be used in such a way that the services received by each individual should provide them with approximately equal amounts of benefit per unit of resource consumed. Thus, an equitable distribution means equal yield or, more colloquially, equal "bang for the buck."

We disagree with this definition of *equitable*. Eddy's approach does not necessarily consider people or their needs equally; instead, it treats the benefits per dollar equally. People vary in the complexity of their health problems. Thus, they will vary in which medical interventions they need, and how much cost is involved, to address their medical conditions. Consider, for example, two people with cardiac disease who are both good candidates for treatment that can return them to equally productive lives and good health. However, while one can be treated with an inexpensive, noninvasive catheterization, the other—because of a quirk in blood vessel anatomy—will require expensive open-heart surgery. Using an "equal benefit per dollar spent" approach would prioritize the inexpensive treatment, yet this may not be equitable. What if the person needing the more expensive treatment was 20 years old and the other person was 70? The fact that the 20-year-old would likely gain many more years of life from the surgery could be factored into a more complex measure of efficiency. However, the trigger to make the measure more complex comes from outside the value of efficiency itself. Rather, it concerns each person's right to a decent life trajectory. And concerns about the fair treatment of each person cannot be simply reduced to dollars spent, the number of years of life gained, or even one homogenous measure of quality of life.

A version of this essay appeared in the *Community Development Investment Review*, Federal Reserve Bank of San Francisco (vol 9, issue 1: 2013).

1   David Eddy, "The Individual vs. Society: Resolving the Conflict," *JAMA*, 265 (18) (1991): 2399–2401, 2405–2406.

Thus, this relatively simple scenario poses questions of equity or fairness that an "equal benefit per dollar spent" approach alone cannot resolve.

In *A Theory of Justice*, John Rawls developed an alternative conception of distributive justice, rejecting utilitarianism and arguing that, rather, an impartial approach to justice would prioritize helping the least well off first.[2] In the Rawlsian tradition, Amartya Sen and Norman Daniels have pointed out difficult policy dilemmas that can arise between equity and efficiency.[3] People at greater health and societal disadvantage may be more expensive to bring to the same outcome as people who are better off. It cannot be fair to exclude those most in need because of this. For example, in the case of microcredit loans in developing countries, it was more difficult for loan recipients who were worse off to begin with to achieve the same benefits as others who started with more resources.[4] Note that there is no inherent reason that efficiency should disadvantage those most in need—the point is just that efficiency and equity (or justice) can conflict.

ETHICAL CONSIDERATIONS FOR EVALUATING OUTCOMES-BASED FUNDING

So how can an outcomes-based approach incorporate ethical goals such as promoting equity? And how can other ethical goals—regarding societal priorities and the equal treatment of individuals and communities—be addressed in the design of such interventions? Given that the emphasis on outcomes and efficiency is already, as it were, baked in, we suggest the following ethical framework for analyzing new outcomes-based policies. Address three fundamental ethical questions: (1) Is there a hidden human toll? (2) Are we aiming for the easy money rather than doing what is more important? and (3) Are we using problematic means to achieve a desired end?

Is There a Hidden Human Toll?

In the case of health care, abundant evidence demonstrates that for-profit organizations targeting efficiencies for measured outcomes may provide

---

2 John Rawls, *A Theory of Justice* (Cambridge: Harvard University Press, 1971).

3 Amartya Sen, "Why Health Equity?" *Health Economics* 11 (8) (2002): 659–666; Norman Daniels, *Just Health, Meeting Health Needs Fairly* (New York: Cambridge University Press, 2008); Norman Daniels, "Four Unsolved Rationing Problems: A Challenge," *Hastings Center Report* 24 (4) (1994): 27–29.

4 Paul Mosley and David Hulme, "Microenterprise Finance: Is There a Conflict between Growth and Poverty Alleviation?" *World Development* 26 (5) (1998): 783–790.

lower than previously offered quality care for outcomes that are not being measured. This result could even extend to providing no care to more vulnerable patients or those requiring expensive treatment for problems that are not being evaluated. We call this the hidden human toll when there is a close relationship between reorganizing services to produce a certain outcome and neglecting or even harming others in need.

For example, while health maintenance organizations (HMOs) originally claimed that they would improve care for entire populations by eliminating inappropriate care, studies show that many HMOs have actually excluded sicker and/or vulnerable patients to contain costs. They may be providing more efficient care to their selected patients, but at what cost to the population as a whole? In "Health Care and Profits: A Poor Mix," *The New York Times* reporter Eduardo Porter gives multiple examples of for-profit health organizations that routinely underserve vulnerable populations.[5] He writes:

> Our track record suggests that handing over responsibility for social goals to private enterprise is providing us with social goods of lower quality, distributed more inequitably and at a higher cost than if government delivered or paid for them directly.

We do not believe that there is an intrinsic conflict between seeking profit or savings and seeking quality, but our point is that the incentives need to reflect both aims.

Are We Aiming for the Easy Money Rather Than Doing What Is More Important?

We need to begin with the question: are we addressing the more fundamental human needs first? Selecting a certain social goal and a specific intervention always entails opportunity costs. What goals or approaches were *not* selected? Attention is needed to ensure that more ethically important endeavors are not passed over because they may not save as much money or result in savings as quickly. Again, saving societal dollars can be a goal in and of itself, but then that goal should be explicit and not cloaked as addressing high priority societal goals. If the goal is to provide important health and social benefits, then those proposing an intervention

---

5 Eduardo Porter, "Health Care and Profits: A Poor Mix," *The New York Times* (January 8, 2013), available at http://www.nytimes.com/2013/01/09/business/health-care-and-pursuit-of-profit-make-a-poor-mix.html.

should assess whether the outcomes targeted reflect the higher priority needs of the population.

Again, while this may seem obvious, we have seen health policies shipwreck over this issue. When policymakers sought to set priorities to ration Medicaid in Oregon, they faced such a problem. Through a democratic process they established rankings for health care treatments by calculating the number of quality-adjusted life years (QALYs) gained from a treatment divided by the cost. They then set population priorities according to the resulting aggregate value. This utilitarian approach resulted in ranking vasectomies higher than mobility-preserving hip repair surgeries and placing tooth capping higher on the list than lifesaving appendectomies. This "aggregation problem" arises whenever an intervention provides an inexpensive but relatively less important benefit for a large number of people.[6] We suggest that those designing outcomes-based interventions keep this issue in mind. The most valuable or most important outcome may not be the one that saves the most money or benefits the largest number of individuals.

Are We Using Problematic Means to Produce a Given End?

This is the old moral problem that the ends do not necessarily justify the means. In a public school setting, an outcome of value might be reducing the cost of expensive special education classes. Improving preschool quality or initiating earlier screening for developmental delays or reading disabilities could potentially accomplish that goal. Blocking children with educational difficulties from enrolling in the school or hiring cheaper, less qualified teachers for the special education classrooms would also reduce expenses, but at what moral cost?

In another example from the health care setting, Porter reports that when nursing homes transition from not-for-profit to for-profit status, their quality of care plummets. For example, one study showed that patients were given four times the dosage of sedatives in the for-profit condition as they were given in the not-for-profit condition. Porter quotes economist Burton Weisbrod, who states that sedatives are "less expensive than, say,

---

6 Daniels, "Four Unsolved Rationing Problems" (1994).

giving special attention to more active patients who need to be kept busy."[7] Efficiency-focused child care facilities could use equally problematic means—such as television for children rather than stimulating, interactive play—to create cost-savings. While outcomes-based approaches like those described in this book would presumably avoid a focus purely on efficiency, the desired outcomes would still have to be carefully chosen and monitored to avoid problematic means of reaching those goals.

Thus, using an appropriate ethical framework—beyond just efficiency—to identify the "true" societal goals of an intervention should be an important component of funding any outcomes-based approach. And the measures of success should incorporate these goals in addition to assessing the efficiencies gained as a result of a successful intervention.

CASE DISCUSSION

Consider, for example, the first social impact bond intervention, at HM Prison Peterborough (HMPP) in the United Kingdom. In this example of outcomes-based funding, the local community wanted to reduce the rate of re-incarceration among short-term prisoners held at HMPP, 60 percent of whom re-offended within a year of release. With a control group as comparison, the Ministry of Justice signed a contract agreeing to repay investors in full if the recidivism rate was lowered by 7.5 percent over a six-year period as well as pay out an additional percentage of the cost savings for any reduction beyond 7.5 percent. While we lack firsthand knowledge of how the project actually changed the lives of those involved (the program has since been discontinued as a result of a larger criminal justice policy change and we base our discussion here on an initial summary description),[8] we might apply the three ethical questions to assessing such a project as follows.

Is There a Hidden Human Toll?

It is easy to imagine how a recidivism intervention whose singular aim was to keep former inmates out of prison might have other noxious effects. Imagine, for example, an intervention that instructed police to

---

7 Burton Weisbrod, *The Nonprofit Economy* (Cambridge: Harvard University Press, 1988), quoted in Porter, "Health Care and Profits" (2013).

8 Social Finance, "Peterborough Social Impact Bond" (2011), available at www.socialfinance.org.uk/sites/default/files/SF_Peterborough_SIB.pdf.

make fewer arrests, just as a for-profit HMO might limit access to health care. This could lead to worse crime rates in the community. Or an intervention might reduce social services for prisoners and families (decreased scrutiny might lead to decreased arrests), resulting in increased domestic violence and strife.

Fortunately, in the actual case of HMPP, the interventions appear to have been designed to achieve the goal of reducing recidivism by improving the individual and family wellbeing of the people released from prison, not by other noxious means such as ignoring crime and making fewer arrests. At the early formative stages of the project, the input of prisoners, their families, and community social workers was elicited regarding their needs for a successful transition out of prison. These needs appear to have guided the design of the intervention:

> Experienced social sector organisations, such as St Giles Trust and Ormiston Children and Families Trust, provide intensive support to prisoners and their families, both inside prison and after release, to help them resettle into the community.[9]

Are We Aiming for the Easy Money Rather Than Doing What Is More Important?

The HMPP intervention appears to be meeting an important societal goal. The targeted population—prisoners serving short-term sentences—lacked social services to assist them upon returning to their families and communities. The released individuals and their families have important unmet needs, so this does not appear to be a case of simply taking the easy money.

However, to fully address the question of importance involves learning more about the other social ills present in this community. Is preventing recidivism as important for this community as, say, improving the local schools, reducing the frequency of premature births, or increasing the availability of well-paying jobs? This intervention has an easily monetized marker of success—dollars not spent on re-incarcerated former inmates. Were other important opportunities for more complicated yet still measurable outcomes passed over? Given limited resources, choosing one outcome to focus on may leave other goals untouched.

---

9   Ibid.

Are We Using Problematic Means to Produce a Given End?

In the case of HMPP, the means of preventing recidivism involved addressing the unmet needs of the released inmates and their families through the use of experienced social service agencies. This is hardly problematic. However, consider if, instead, recidivism were kept down by evicting the former inmates and their families and driving them out of the neighborhood, or by forcing them to take sedatives that made them too weak and tired to commit crimes. The latter may sound implausible, but it is not too far a stretch from prescribing four times the normal dosage of sedatives to elders in nursing homes to keep costs down.

CONCLUSION

An outcomes-based approach has clear societal value when it inspires innovation to find more efficient means to reach important goals. This utilitarian approach to achieving societal goals is practical but not in and of itself ethical. We suggest a framework for assessing proposed outcomes-based funding projects: consider its hidden ethical costs, its relative human importance, and the appropriateness of the means used to achieve the given outcome.

The HMPP project provides an inspiring example for addressing these ethical concerns in future interventions. Notably, the outcomes-based model used by HMPP was funded by philanthropic donors who were already committed to meeting community needs. We are concerned that investors whose overriding aims are financial might not address such concerns unless an explicit ethical standard is developed. The basis for this concern is some observations regarding the early history of HMOs. Policymakers initially conceived of HMOs as improving efficiency by eliminating excessive treatment previously incentivized by the fee-for-service system. In particular, health leaders argued that patient care would improve as costs were reduced. Because of this expectation, little attention was paid to developing explicit safeguards for threats to quality posed by cost containment. In retrospect, those threats are now all too clear. We recommend that those working in the still-nascent outcomes-based funding field learn from the shortsightedness of the health services sector and get ahead of such challenges by developing explicit ethical standards.

JODI HALPERN *is a professor of bioethics at the University of California, Berkeley. Dr. Halpern is the author of* From Detached Concern to Empathy: Humanizing Medical Practice *(Oxford University Press, paperback 2011). She received her BA from Yale College, MD from Yale School of Medicine, a PhD in philosophy from Yale University and completed a psychiatry residency at UCLA and a post-doctoral fellowship through the RWJF Clinical Scholars program at the University of California, Los Angeles.*

DOUGLAS JUTTE *is executive director of the Build Healthy Places Network, a national organization that works to catalyze and support collaboration across the community development and health sectors. He is also a pediatrician and associate professor at the University of California, Berkeley School of Public Health. Dr. Jutte graduated from Cornell University, Harvard Medical School, and University of California, Berkeley's School of Public Health, and completed a pediatric residency at Stanford University and a post-doctoral fellowship through the RWJF Health & Society Scholars program at the University of California, San Francisco.*

THE PROMISE AND REALITY OF SOCIAL IMPACT BONDS

Richard McGahey
Institute for New Economic Thinking

Mark Willis
New York University

I n March of 2015, The Rockefeller Foundation announced "tangible success" for a social impact bond supporting a program designed to reduce recidivism in Peterborough in the United Kingdom. The program resulted in a four percent reconviction differential between experimental and control groups of released prisoners. The foundation said the Peterborough experiment "launched global excitement about the social impact bond model."[1] But since the initial rush of excitement, appropriate caution and skepticism has grown about social impact bonds as a tool to produce innovation and to get significant amounts of private capital dedicated to solving difficult social problems.

Social impact bonds, or "Pay for Success" investments, continue to draw much attention and hope in the philanthropic, social services, and public sectors. Social impact bonds are designed to link private, for-profit capital with social- and public-sector innovation, stimulating program innovation and providing a new source of risk-taking capital for the resource-starved public sector. Muhammad Yunus, founder of the Grameen Bank, and Judith Rodin, former president of The Rockefeller Foundation, summarized this dual attraction succinctly in an article entitled "Save the World, Turn a Profit."[2]

But in practice, social impact bonds are showing limited results. Although some advocates argue that early stage social impact bonds will work

---

1   The Rockefeller Foundation, "Peterborough Social Impact Bond Reduces Reoffending by 8.4%: Investors on Course for Payment in 2016" (March 16, 2015), available at https://www.rockefellerfoundation.org/report/peterborough-social-impact-bond-reduces-reoffending-by-8-4-investors-on-course-for-payment-in-2016/.

2   Muhammad Yunus and Judith Rodin, "Save the World, Turn a Profit," *Bloomberg View* (September 25, 2015), available at https://www.bloomberg.com/view/articles/2015-09-25/save-the-world-turn-a-profit.

through their initial challenges,[3] we think the limited results to date suggest more basic flaws. We are concerned that many advocates for social impact bonds misdiagnose why the public sector is slow to support innovation, and they also misunderstand how for-profit capital seeks a balance of risk and return. We worry, too, that sincere social impact bond advocates are diverting attention, resources, and creative talent that could better address the pressing social problems they care about.

THE GROWTH OF SOCIAL IMPACT BONDS: RHETORIC AND REALITY

The attention paid to social impact bonds has grown dramatically since their first successful deployment in the Peterborough anti-recidivism program. In the past few years, McKinsey, Accenture, Deloitte, the Brookings Institution, Goldman Sachs, the Wharton School, the Conference Board, the Stanford Business School, New York University, and many others have issued favorable reports on social impact bonds. The United Kingdom established a Cabinet Office of Social Impact Bonds, the Obama administration endorsed what it called Pay for Success, and there have been congressional hearings that advocate for legislation. There are annual conferences and panels that focus on social impact bonds, and scholars, advocates, foundation staff, and private investors have written papers on the subject.

But although there are many advocates, there seem to be relatively few deals, with existing ones highly concentrated in the United Kingdom and to a lesser extent in the United States.[4] And it is not clear how many of these deals really are just standard pay-for-performance contracts with nonprofits or government agencies.[5]

---

3 Kenneth Dodge, "Why Social Impact Bonds Still Have Promise," *The New York Times* (November 13, 2015), available at http://www.nytimes.com/2015/11/14/business/dealbook/why-social-impact-bonds-still-have-promise.html.

4 It is difficult to get a consistent count of how many social impact bonds are in existence, due to a combination of varying definitions of what qualifies, whether to count a large fund as one social impact bond or count each locality using that fund as a separate social impact bond, whether the count contains only active projects or also those in development, etc.

5 Some social impact bond advocates now argue that calling them "bonds" is misleading, because of variable and risky returns that make the investments more like equity: Lindsay Beck et al., "Social Impact Bonds: What's in a Name?" *Stanford Social Innovation Review* (October 12, 2016), available at https://ssir.org/articles/entry/social_impact_bonds_whats_in_a_name. But the vehicle—whatever it is called—still is intended to get significant amounts of profit-seeking capital into social innovation.

Given the excitement around social impact bonds, observers might not realize that they rest on a very small evidence base of programmatic success. The iconic social impact bond case is the Peterborough, England, recidivism reduction program, which initially reduced recidivism by 8.4 percent relative to a control group. However, the program had targeted a ten percent reduction in order to pay investors immediately, although the program was on track to reach its average 7.5 percent reduction over time. But the United Kingdom phased out the program in 2015 due to larger changes in rehabilitation policy.

In the United States, Goldman Sachs invested in a program at New York City's Rikers Island jail, making a $9.6 million loan to fund targeted therapy for 16- to 18-year-olds, with Bloomberg Philanthropies guaranteeing 83 percent of Goldman Sachs' investment against losses. The program was rigorously evaluated against a goal of reducing recidivism by at least ten percent. When the young people going through the program showed no significant reductions in recidivism it was canceled. Although there was no direct budgetary cost to New York City, there were operating disruptions from introducing the program, and costs born by the Bloomberg Foundation's $6 million guarantee of over 80 percent of Goldman Sach's investment.

Goldman Sachs, along with the Pritzker Family Foundation, also invested in a Utah early childhood education program often cited as a success based on an unusually high finding that 109 of 110 participants were successfully diverted from future expensive special education. This finding is far out of line with other similar programs for poor children.[6] Yet this triggered an initial payment to Goldman Sachs, with a rate of return estimated between five and seven percent.[7]

---

6 The best known programs for low-income children that have been rigorously studied are the High/Scope Perry Preschool, Abecedarian, and Child Parent Center (CPC) programs. None of them, or others, found effects anywhere close to those reported for the Utah program. See the review in W. Steven Barnett, "Preschool Education and Its Lasting Effects: Research and Policy Implications," National Institute for Early Education Research at Rutgers University (September 2008), available http://nepc.colorado.edu/files/PB-Barnett-EARLY-ED_FINAL.pdf.

7 The evaluation also was not done with a random assignment methodology, and used diagnostic instruments that some researchers claim could have resulted in very large misclassifications of children's potential entry into special education: Nathaniel Popper, "Success Metrics Questioned in School Program Funded by Goldman," *The New York Times* (November 3, 2015), available http://www.nytimes.com/2015/11/04/business/dealbook/did-goldman-make-the-grade.html?_r=0.

WHAT PROBLEMS ARE SOCIAL IMPACT BONDS TRYING TO SOLVE?

Social impact bond advocates seek progress on four major issues. They believe that social impact bonds can:

1 **Spur program innovation.** Advocates argue that social impact bonds will encourage greater exploration of existing or potential social innovations. Using private investment to incentivize nonprofits and governments will allow new innovations to be tested and then scaled up, as they are in the private market.

But private-sector innovations funded by venture capital mostly fail, at rates ranging from 65 to 90 percent.[8] Faced with that reality, some social impact bond advocates now argue that the investment risk should be reduced by relying on some earlier "proof of concept" by a nonprofit, often funded by philanthropy. That is an appropriate role for foundations, but it isn't clear why for-profit social impact bonds then are necessary for governments to scale up early program success.

Some advocates argue that foundations are taking on the risky venture capital role by funding this first stage, but that undercuts the claim that social impact bonds can bring significant risk-tolerating private capital into the social innovation space. If deals cannot be structured to attract private capital to take high risk for high returns, the social impact bond model is not scalable.

2 **Improve nonprofit and government operating performance.** By bringing in private capital, advocates argue that nonprofits and government agencies will perform better because of market discipline and oversight.

Complaints about governmental lack of innovation are longstanding and, in our generation, go back at least to the "Reinventing Government" movement driven by then-Vice President Al Gore, which sought to adapt "best practices" from the private sector. But

---

8　See among others: CB Insights, "The Venture Capital Funnel: Your Chances of Raising Follow-Ons, Existing, and Becoming a Unicorn" (December 9, 2015); Deborah Gage, "The Venture Capital Secret: 3 Out of 4 Start-Ups Fail," *The Wall Street Journal* (September 20, 2012), available at https://www.wsj.com/articles/SB10000872396390443720204578004980476429190.

government is not a private business, and there are questions as to what extent government can or should operate like a private firm. Government can learn from private firms (and vice versa), but we should be well past the day when we invoke private-market efficiency as a simple, broad solution to public management problems.

3 **Attract private capital.** Advocates see social impact bonds as a way to get profit-seeking private capital into public and nonprofit work, arguing that this will increase resources in a time of public austerity. But critics argue that social impact bonds work at a very small financial scale, so there is no significant overall budget relief. And private-sector investors seek to minimize risk and uncertainty, not create or embrace it. As in the Rikers Island case, investors will seek guarantees or other risk-minimizing practices such as introducing more complex and differentiated payment tranches to protect their investment, cutting against the social impact bond argument that private capital will increase government's risk tolerance.[9]

Operationally, social impact bonds demand a lot of administrative attention, added expenses for monitoring and evaluation, and budgeting for contingent liabilities created by promises of future repayments to investors. Adding them into a regular government program and budgeting structure can create real disruptions while getting the benefits of only a very small additional investment.

4 **Use rigorous evaluation methods.** Social impact bond advocates often promise a strong evidence base in the form of rigorous random assignment evaluations, where demonstrated success is required before investors are paid. But high-quality rigorous evaluations are expensive and take a long time to yield results. And the methodology militates against changing program models during the evaluation, which paradoxically means that social-impact-bond-funded programs threaten the rigor of their evidence if they try to learn and improve their operations.

---

9 McKinsey & Company, "Taking Off: A Hybrid Investment Fund to Unlock the Growth Potential of Social Enterprises in Germany" (December 2016), available at https://www.mckinsey.de/files/170109_report_impact_investment_hybrid_fund.pdf; Liz Farmer, "New 'Pay for Success' Model Offers Money-Back Guarantee," *Government Technology* (March 25, 2016), available at http://www.govtech.com/budget-finance/Pay-for-Success-Programs-Success-or-Your-Money-Back.html.

Government programs, especially new innovations, need flexibility in the early stages. The Rikers Island program was based on scaling up a program for 16- to 18-year-olds. However, not enough participants could be found in those age groups, so older youth were added, and the program that was delivered differed significantly from the original "proof of concept" version. While these changes may have been sensible adaptations to the operational reality at Rikers, they challenged the evaluation design and success benchmarks. Some advocates claim that the Rikers program was unlike other programs so program problems and evaluation difficulties stemmed from its novelty, but there is a body of evaluation literature on such programs in a variety of contexts that undercuts that claim.[10]

And faced with the pressure to produce findings, evaluation rigor can easily slip as investors seek repayment and program advocates want to claim success. The Utah early childhood program payouts to Goldman Sachs were based on problematic assessments claiming success far beyond any impacts ever found for similar programs, and also were not based on the type of rigorous evaluation that social impact bond advocates often endorse.

While we would not insist on RCT evaluations (because of their cost and how they impose a lack of flexibility on programs), the claim of 99 percent success should have raised a caution flag and been examined more critically. Advocates for the Utah program generally do not discuss how such an extraordinary success level (99 percent) was achieved. Nor do they compare their very high level of reported success to other rigorous evaluations of how early childhood programs for low-income children reduce later referrals to special education. There are a number of rigorous studies that find a positive impact, but at much lower magnitudes than the Utah program reports.

---

10 Nana A. Landenberger and Mark W. Lipsey, "The Positive Effects Of Cognitive-Behavioral Programs For Offenders: A Meta-Analysis Of Factors Associated With Effective Treatment," *Journal of Experimental Criminology* 1(4) December 2005: 451–476; On moral reconation therapy in particular, see L.M. Ferguson and J.S. Wormith, "A Meta-Analysis of Moral Reconation Therapy," *International Journal of Offender Therapy and Comparative Criminology* 57(9) 2013: 1076–1106.

SOCIAL IMPACT BONDS: SOLUTION OR DISTRACTION?

We strongly agree with social impact bond advocates that more program innovation, improved government and nonprofit operational performance, increased funding, and better assessment are necessary to address major social problems. But we believe each of those goals can be addressed through other means, and that trying to find one "magic bullet" solution through social impact bonds may actually weaken results for all four goals.

First, philanthropy can and should continue to encourage and test innovative program ideas. But these can be financed through grants, or in the case of programs with a revenue stream, recoverable grants or program-related investments (PRIs). Putting private-equity investors or banks into this space may well weaken innovation instead of encourage it, as for-profit investors generally seek some assurance of positive financial returns and discourage risk in the absence of high expected returns.

Second, government and nonprofit agencies do need improved performance. But that may be better done through encouraging "better practices" in public management, or through such models as The Robin Hood Foundation, where grantees are provided with a high level of technical assistance and deep managerial engagement to improve operations. Technical assistance to grantees, or changed public management practices, will not suddenly appear or be implemented because of social impact bonds. And any additional costs for technical assistance will increase total program expenditures, raising the per capita costs and lowering the return on investment.

Finally, we strongly agree that increased funding is needed for testing innovations and bringing them to scale. But the testing can be done by philanthropy, and scaling should come through government's existing ability to tax, spend, and evaluate. Money being spent on the mechanics of social impact bonds might better be spent on advocacy for appropriate levels of taxation to meet our social needs rather than trying to leverage for-profit capital into difficult non-market problems.

And we see some worrisome signs about social impact bonds. For example, there is no justification for exploiting philanthropy's tax-advantaged status to guarantee private profits, as in the Rikers Island case, where Bloomberg Philanthropies (itself already benefiting from its tax-free status) guaranteed around 75 percent of Goldman Sachs' investment returns.[11] Using public tax expenditures in that way wastes scarce resources and reduces accountability.

Perhaps our biggest concern is that social impact bonds and other Pay for Success approaches are drawing too much philanthropic, governmental, and nonprofit talent and creativity at the cost of other support for social innovation. Philanthropy, government, and nonprofits need to keep at the difficult but necessary work of improving program outcomes in fields like criminal justice and education, and support the advocacy and coalition work needed to increase funding for public programs. There is no private-sector-based magic that will solve these critical needs, and the money, talent, and energy devoted to social impact bonds might better be directed elsewhere.

—————

RICHARD MCGAHEY *is the vice president of programs at the Institute for New Economic Thinking. He was formerly the director of impact assessment at the Ford Foundation, assistant secretary for policy at the U.S. Department of Labor, and a managing vice president at Abt Associates.*

MARK A. WILLIS *is senior policy fellow at the New York University Furman Center for Real Estate and Public Policy. His career has included serving as a visiting scholar at the Ford Foundation, executive vice president for community development at JPMorgan Chase, deputy commissioner for development at New York City's Department of Housing Preservation and Development, and senior economist on the regional economics staff of the Federal Reserve Bank of New York. He writes and teaches on a range of urban topics including affordable housing, housing finance, and the Community Reinvestment Act.*

---

11 Goldman Sachs then wrote off the nonguaranteed part of the investment, presumably also deducting those losses from its tax bill. So there are significant tax subsidies undergirding all of the Goldman Sachs investment, which seems to be another hidden cost not accounted for when calculating the total cost of social impact bonds.

PERFORMANCE-BASED CONTRACTING IN NYC
Progressive Practice or Punitive Pursuit?

Jaclyn Kelly and Margaret Ross-Martin
Nonprofit Finance Fund

We made a conscious decision to serve families as long as they needed us. We did get cuts to our [New York City] contract for this. This is a concern because we're dealing with real live human beings and [instead] we're looking at numbers.

— NYC human services nonprofit staff member (NFF focus group, 2016)

Does the above scenario sound dire? Consider it in the larger context of nonprofits' experience in recent years: In 2015, 84 percent of human services nonprofits (HSNs) surveyed in New York State reported an increase in demand for services over the previous year. At the same time, more than half (58 percent) reported being unable to meet that demand.[1]

While New York City HSNs continually struggle to meet the public's growing need for their life-saving programs, they are often faced with an additional challenge: reconciling the needs of their clients with the mandates of city-generated, performance-based contracts, which tie

Many thanks to the Human Services Council (HSC) and Jina Paik of Nonprofit Finance Fund for their collaboration, insight, and many excellent jokes during this research. In addition, we would like to thank Professor L.L. Martin of the University of Central Florida for lending us his resources and sharing his expertise on performance-based contracting. Finally, thanks to Professor Christa Altenstetter of the CUNY Graduate Center for her guidance, mentorship, and intellect on this project among many over the years.

1 Nonprofit Finance Fund, "State of the Nonprofit Sector Survey" (2015), available by request.

payments to measurable outcomes.[2] These contracts are part of a larger trend in procurement practices that began at the federal level as an effort to improve the efficiency and quality of service delivery. In recent years, performance-based contracting has become an increasingly preferred method for state and local government contracting as well.[3] New York City has been a pioneer in implementing performance measurement standards at the local level, and in the context of New York City's human services sector, performance-based contracts are intended to orient government and providers around the shared goal of offering the best outcomes for New Yorkers in need. Ironically, these contracts, which exist specifically to provide critical financial support to HSNs and incentivize outcomes-based practices, can also significantly interfere with that goal.

This chapter draws on data, input, and recommendations gathered from HSNs and other city stakeholders to examine this tension. In 2016, Nonprofit Finance Fund (NFF) disseminated two surveys about city performance-based contracts, and conducted a complementary set of four focus groups with HSNs, local government agencies, and researchers. Survey #1 is an in-depth survey that explored how HSNs' organizational characteristics affect their ability to successfully compete for and manage performance-based contracts.[4] Survey #2 solicited input from HSNs and city stakeholders on a set of 15 possible modifications to city performance-based contracts, generated from the previous survey's findings and the focus groups.[5] It is our hope that the feedback we received from our surveys and focus groups can serve not only as a bridge to effective collaboration within New York City, but also as a guide to other

---

2 There is no universal definition of performance-based contracts. We used the following definition, which is a synthesis of a series of working definitions written by various government agencies and associations: "A performance-based contract can be defined as one that focuses on the outputs, quality, and outcomes of a service provision and may tie at least a portion of a contractor's payment as well as any contract extension or renewal to their achievement," as defined in Lawrence L. Martin, "Performance Contracting: Extending Performance Measurement to Another Level," *Public Administration Times* 22(1) (1999): 1 & 2.

3 Lawrence L. Martin, "Performance-Based Contracting," *Government Contracting: A Public Solutions Handbook*, ed. Robert A. Shick (New York: Routledge, 2016).

4 A total of 53 nonprofit employees participated in Survey #1 in April and May of 2016. Survey #2, disseminated in August 2016 based on findings from Survey #1, received a total of 45 responses. These employees represent organizations throughout New York City that varied in terms of size, budget, and current and anticipated use of performance-based contracts.

5 A total of 45 employees from nonprofits, city agencies, funding agencies, and advocacy organizations completed Survey #2.

communities and sectors embarking on their own outcomes-based funding efforts.

DEFINING SUCCESS

Consider the two statements below and the deep divide in institutional perspectives that they reflect:

Government is best at setting outcomes, designing policy and overseeing and supervising performance.[6]

—Mark Hoover, former first deputy commissioner, NYC Human Resources Administration

Most benchmarks are developed [by the city] without input from providers, or in spite of it, and often do not reflect the complexity of the work nonprofits do, particularly with marginalized communities.

—HSN service provider comment (NFF survey, August 2016)

The most innovative element of a performance-based contract is its focus on defining programmatic outcomes, rather than programmatic process. This shift is intended to provide HSNs significant freedom in implementation, encouraging creativity and use of their applied expertise. However, because the city unilaterally defines the ultimate objectives of the performance-based contract—its outcomes—as well as the benchmarks and milestones that demonstrate progress toward the contract's objective, disconnects like the one in the statements above can emerge. While performance-based contracts do provide substantial flexibility in process, the funder-mandated outcomes may result in significantly different opinions between governments and service providers regarding valid indicators of success.

By virtue of their role in administration and governance, city agencies may focus on cost-benefit analyses and budgeting constraints when developing service contracts. By contrast, HSNs are embedded in the communities that they serve and invested in meeting the specific needs of their individual clients. This divergence can be particularly pronounced

---

6 Bryna M. Sanger, *The Welfare Marketplace: Privatization and Welfare Reform*, Brookings Institution Press (2003).

and problematic in the context of performance-based contracts, in which the achievement of city agency-dictated outcomes determines HSNs' reimbursement. Practices that appear cost-efficient and economical to a city agency may be at cross-purposes with an HSN's goal of high-quality, client-driven services. This is especially true when the nonprofit serves clients who are members of marginalized communities. These service providers are less likely to have had a platform to voice their community's needs, challenges, and experiences to their government funders.[7]

An additional consideration that should factor into performance-based contract benchmarks is accommodating the potentially profound effects that external factors wield on HSN program implementation. Because these factors are often both unexpected and beyond the control of HSNs, the performance-based contract structure is useful only insofar as it is able to adapt and respond to fluctuations in the need and context for services. As an HSN professional described, "We recently had to write an appeal to [our funding agency] because...performance-based contracts don't take into account external variables that affect our ability to manage these contracts" (NFF focus group, 2016).

From previous conversations with HSNs, we have heard that these externalities can include shifts in the political climate or unexpected events, such as Hurricane Sandy in 2012 and the sudden disintegration of the Federation Employment & Guidance Service (FEGS) in 2015. Our survey findings confirm the importance of giving service provider organizations a larger role in determining appropriate outcomes and milestones for performance-based contracts, not only at the outset of the contract but also throughout the duration of the contracting relationship.

Recommendation: We recommend that government contract managers collaborate quite closely with HSNs who are expert in the communities that they serve, especially when those clients are members of groups who may have significant historical reason to distrust traditional authority figures like government officials. This collaboration should not only inform the initial content and structure of performance-based contracts, but also should remain part of the process of contract fulfillment, with contract managers and HSNs continuing to be in close communication.

---

7 For an excellent exploration of how certain communities and beneficiaries have been classified as more deserving of investment and resources than others, see Anne L. Schneider, Helen Ingram, and Peter Deleon, "Democratic Policy Design: Social Construction of Target Populations," *Theories of the Policy Process* (3rd Edition, 2014: 105–149).

MEASURING SUCCESS

In addition to defining success, *measuring* success is also an integral element of engaging in performance-based contracts. For an HSN to measure its performance, it must have the capacity for data collection and evaluation. It is rare for any type of government contract to cover a provider's full cost of services, but performance-based contracts put providers in a particular double-bind: They require HSNs to collect data and report on performance but typically fail to fund these resource-intensive activities.

This unfunded element of performance-based contracts creates bias in the awarding of contracts. Specifically, organizations that are large and well-funded enough to invest in data collection and evaluation capacities are able to pay for the cost of demonstrating performance and outcomes, rendering organizations without this capacity or budget flexibility—often smaller, newer, or possibly serving especially vulnerable and high-poverty communities—unable to compete for performance-based contracts.

These smaller organizations' limited resources are likely to be consumed by client service delivery, without available funding for specialized administrative roles or data management systems. Indeed, data from Survey #1 demonstrated that larger organizations (as defined by budget size) were more likely to have made successful bids for performance-based contracts, arguably because they have staff and resources allocated toward packaging successful applications.

On the other hand, findings from Survey #1 revealed an exception to this trend: Organizations with "specialized staff" (e.g., staff roles that include data management, strategy development, or grant writing) were more likely to have successfully bid for a performance-based contract than organizations without specialized staff, regardless of organization size.

Recommendation: A critical component of ensuring that performance-based contracts can function effectively is providing support for all of their activities. In this case, that includes not only providing funding for client-focused services, but also adequate financial support for HSNs to engage in data collection and report on the required client outcomes. We recommend that cities adopt performance-based contracting practices that compensate HSNs for data collection and reporting activities. This will ensure that highly qualified service providers are not excluded because they are too small or not well-resourced enough to have the budgetary flexibility to absorb the costs associated with data collection. This is an especially important consideration if communities are invested in ensuring that contracts are awarded to HSNs who are truly providing the highest quality services to clients, not only those who have the budget flexibility to cover the costs of outcomes management.

HSNs feel the strain of having to bear the cost of collecting and providing the outcomes data required of performance-based contracts. In Survey #2, HSNs expressed a uniform plea that performance-based contracts cover both the complete cost of providing high-quality service delivery as well as indirect costs. These include costs associated with running high-quality organizations, such as administration, facilities, and outcomes measurement. Interestingly — and perhaps not surprisingly — in their survey responses, city stakeholders and contract managers assigned notably less importance to funding modifications that addressed indirect costs. This highlights a disconnect between HSNs and city stakeholders in their perspectives regarding funding practices, and therefore an opportunity for city agencies to hear why covering full costs, including outcomes measurement, is key for HSNs' success.[8]

COLLABORATING FOR SUCCESS

We posted a concept paper for feedback and only one person responded. And that person was in Thailand!

—NYC agency staff member (NFF focus group, 2016)

---

8 The survey options "Incorporate full cost of services into payment tiers" and "Incorporate indirect cost of services into payment tiers" received average scores above 9 on a 10-point scale (9.5 and 9.3 respectively, with 10 being "extremely helpful"). Also notable, not a single HSN respondent assigned either option a score below 6. This demonstrates that the average level of support for these modifications is not only exceptionally high, it is also uniform across the entire group of HSNs. By contrast, city stakeholders and contract managers assigned notably lower scores to these two possible modifications, yielding average scores of 6.8 and 6.2, respectively.

Before publishing a formal request for proposal to solicit HSNs' applications for service contracts, the city distributes a "concept paper" that invites feedback on the proposed intervention and service model. As expressed in the quote above, from the city's perspective, opportunities for collaboration on contract development do exist, but HSNs do not engage them. This stance appeared at odds with the one held by HSNs, who consistently reported a strong desire for a much greater role in the process of creating contracts' structure and content. However, a closer examination of the data and input from both groups reveals a more complex dynamic.

Surveys #1 and #2 yielded consistent feedback from HSNs. For example, in Survey #1, when asked to select the single practice that would be most helpful in building capacity to meet the demands of performance-based contracts, the most frequently selected option was, "Give service provider organizations a larger role in defining the structural elements of performance-based contracts" (40 percent). The second most frequently selected option was, "Give service provider organizations a larger role in determining appropriate outcomes and milestones/benchmarks for performance-based contracts" (26 percent).[9] When pressed to reconcile this strong desire to participate in contract creation with their unresponsiveness to city-generated concept papers, HSN focus group participants revealed dissatisfaction and disengagement with the current concept paper input process. They proposed the following modifications to how the city gathers HSN feedback on contracts:

1 Develop a system in which concept papers are published in a central location for a period of time that is predictable and adequate for submitting feedback. This would enable HSNs to be aware of all concept papers relevant to the communities they serve and have sufficient time to respond and contribute their content expertise.

2 Expand the scope of concept papers. Many are limited to somewhat theoretical content and omit elements of the contract, such as progress milestones or payment structure.

---

9 In Survey #2, HSNs were presented with a list of 15 possible modifications to performance-based contracts—including the same two options so heavily favored in Survey #1. Their responses yielded an average score of greater than 9 on a 10-point scale (9.1 and 9.3, respectively, with 10 being "extremely helpful").

3　Improve the feedback review process for concept papers. Currently, HSNs' input and suggestions are not acknowledged in any way. The city should acknowledge feedback and outline which recommendations were included and excluded in the final contract, as well as the basis for these decisions. Such feedback would be good progress toward facilitating a dialogue between the city and its human services sector.

Interestingly, when we reported these recommendations back to city representatives, we learned that strict procurement standards—created with the intention of preventing bias or conflicts of interest—can, in fact, inhibit interaction and a meaningful feedback loop between city agencies and HSNs. As one city representative expressed during a focus group: "Procurement considerations that were set up to create fairness and openness are prohibiting real and meaningful conversations" (NFF focus group, 2016). This concern was echoed in stakeholders' responses to Survey #2. From a list of 15 possible refinements to performance-based contracts, "Adjust procurement rules so that city agencies may solicit input from nonprofits without concerns of appearing biased" scored the highest among city stakeholders (excluding HSNs), with a median score of 10 out of 10 (i.e., "extremely helpful") and an average score of 8.[10]

Recommendation: We recommend that government officials consider modifying procurement policies, adding systematic opportunities for significant and meaningful interaction between contract managers and HSNs, while still ensuring neutrality in the processes of shaping performance-based contract outcomes. In addition, we suggest that communities interested in employing performance-based contracts create a single online clearinghouse for concept papers, and ensure that they are available for a consistent amount of time, such that HSNs are able to review and thoughtfully respond to them. This clearinghouse should also include a function for publicly listing feedback from HSNs on concept papers, and specifying decisions on whether to incorporate that feedback.

CONCLUSION

The objective of this research was to develop an understanding of how performance-based contracts affect New York City HSNs, and to use those insights to make a series of practical recommendations to cities and communities across the country. Two surveys and several focus groups later, we feel that we've gained insight into the challenges that HSNs face when they engage performance-based contracts; we've also learned about

---

10　City stakeholders include employees of city agencies, funding agencies, and advocacy organizations.

some of the challenges faced by city agencies that make it difficult to resolve those issues within the complex and fluctuating ecosystem of New York City. We hope this will spark discussion and provide some useful input as city government and HSNs work together to achieve strong outcomes for New Yorkers and communities beyond.

──────

JACLYN KELLY *is associate director of impact at Nonprofit Finance Fund (NFF), where she spearheads NFF's strategies and implementation of impact measurement. Kelly is a doctoral candidate at the City University of New York (CUNY) Graduate Center in Political Science, and was a 2015 Global Social Innovation Fellow at the Sanford School of Public Policy at Duke University. She sits on the board of Inner-City Enlightenment (ICE), a Brooklyn-based nonprofit, and is an adjunct faculty member at The City College of New York and Long Island University, where she teaches classes on applied research methods and policy analysis.*

MARGARET ROSS-MARTIN *is an associate at Nonprofit Finance Fund (NFF), where she supports the organization's Social Innovation Fund Pay for Success Program. Before joining NFF, Ross-Martin lived in New Orleans and consulted with a diverse range of corporate, nonprofit, and municipal clients committed to rebuilding and protecting the Gulf Coast post-Katrina. Ross-Martin received her BA in politics from Whitman College in 2012.*

A FOCUS ON COST SAVINGS MAY UNDERMINE THE INFLUENCE OF OUTCOMES-BASED FUNDING MECHANISMS

Megan Golden
Mission: Cure Pancreatitis

Jitinder Kohli and Samantha Mignotte
Monitor Deloitte

Think of a world where the only things you did were the things that saved you money—not the things that helped you succeed in life, not the things that helped others, just the things with quantifiable cash savings. Now imagine if governments did the same, meaning they wouldn't pay for roads or support early childhood development programs if the monetary costs outweighed savings to the budget.

That might sound outrageous because we all know that the value to society of roads and early childhood development go well beyond just budget savings. However, when governments determine whether or not to fund outcomes-based projects, such as Pay for Success projects, they routinely require that these projects produce real, "cashable" savings in government budgets. This assumed need for cashable savings thus poses a direct risk to the success of Pay for Success—and more broadly outcomes-based funding—as a means for promoting change.

THE RISKS OF ALLOWING COST SAVINGS TO DRIVE DECISIONS ABOUT OUTCOMES-BASED PROJECTS

A Pay for Success project—also called a social impact bond—is an outcomes-based funding mechanism where one or more government entities agrees to pay a set amount for specific outcomes. The government's promise of payment allows organizations to raise money to bring programs to the people who need them to achieve these agreed-upon outcomes. Governments, foundations, intermediaries, banks, and service providers around the world are exploring and using Pay for Success to address pressing problems, including homelessness, crime, education, and health disparities.

In our experience monitoring and assisting with Pay for Success projects across the United States, identifying a source to pay for outcomes is a key bottleneck preventing Pay for Success from reaching its potential. This is because many mistakenly believe that a government should pay for outcomes only if they save money in that government's budget that can then be used as the main funding source. Why is this belief so widespread? Because when Pay for Success was first introduced in the United States, advocates—including the authors of this piece—presented it that way. At the core of the original pitch for Pay for Success was the idea that outcomes could be paid for out of cashable savings—the amount that an agency would save from the reduced need for costly remedial services.[1] Governments could therefore achieve outcomes without committing any new funds and might even "make money" off the project by paying out less than it saved.

We have learned, however, that using savings as the sole basis for determining whether and how much government should pay for outcomes poses two important risks. First, it can lead to missed opportunities to fund programs that can solve some of our nation's most pressing problems. Second, it risks enshrining the status quo rather than shifting government resources to more effective programs.

Missed Opportunities to Fund Effective Programs

Government agencies make decisions about what to fund every single day—such as patching a road or operating parks. Governments allocate billions of dollars to social services every year. In each of these areas, governments invest because they believe that there are gains to society as a result of the spending (although some commentators find scant evidence

---

1 Jitinder Kohli, Douglas J. Besharov, and Kristina Costa, "Fact Sheet: Social Impact Bonds-A Brief Introduction to a New Financing Tool for Social Programs," Center for American Progress (April 12, 2012), available at https://www.americanprogress.org/issues/general/news/2012/04/12/11406/fact-sheet-social-impact-bonds/.

of effectiveness for many programs).[2] In none of these areas, does government only invest when there are cashable savings. Yet they tend to focus on cashable savings only when contracting for social outcomes.

This emphasis on cashable savings makes it harder to fund social impact outcomes than to fund most other government services. Many projects that provide support to domestic violence survivors, for example, would not be funded if they had to meet the cashable savings standard. Underinvestment may also occur if the savings from outcomes-based projects accrue to another agency or level of government than the one directly undertaking the contract (which some have referred to as the "wrong pockets" problem).[3] For instance, if cost savings for asthma prevention accrue to state and federal health care programs, a local housing agency would be less likely to fund cutting-edge ways of reducing home-based environmental health hazards that can provide a healthier environment for its residents.[4]

Sustaining the Status Quo

In addition to underfunding programs that make a documented impact, basing funding decisions on cashable savings alone makes it difficult to shift funds from less effective programs to new, more effective approaches. If new initiatives cannot be undertaken unless offset by savings, current funding allocations will remain in place as the default, even if these programs are not the most effective way to achieve the government's ends.

ALTERNATIVE SOURCES OF OUTCOMES FUNDING THAT DON'T RELY (SOLELY) ON SAVINGS

The belief that government budgets are too tight to fund outcomes-based projects without cashable savings incorrectly assumes that government funding allocations cannot and do not change. There is, however,

---

2 John Bridgeland and Peter Orszag, "Can Government Play Moneyball," *The Atlantic* (July/August 2013), available at https://www.theatlantic.com/magazine/archive/2013/07/can-government-play-moneyball/309389/.

3 For more information on the "wrong pockets" problem, see John K. Roman, "Solving the wrong pockets problem: How Pay for Success promotes investment in evidence-based best practices," Urban Institute (September 2015), available at http://www.urban.org/sites/default/files/alfresco/publication-pdfs/2000427-Solving-the-Wrong-Pockets-Problem.pdf.

4 For more information on the Green and Healthy Homes Initiative in Salt Lake City, see http://www.greenandhealthyhomes.org/get-help/pay-success.

flexibility within budgets that offers alternative ways for governments to find the funds to pay for outcomes beyond just cashable savings.

Almost all city, state, and federal budgets include discretionary funds for political priorities or emerging needs. If paying for outcomes is set as a priority, discretionary funding could also be used to support it. Some jurisdictions have already found ways to use discretionary funds to support outcomes-based projects. Massachusetts, for example, created a Social Innovation Financing Trust Fund that the state uses to support Pay for Success projects funded through annual appropriations.[5] Utah, similarly, created a School Readiness Restricted Account, composed primarily of funds appropriated by the state legislature, which pays for the outcomes of its preschool Pay for Success project.[6]

In addition, government could pay for outcomes by repurposing existing programmatic budgets. Agencies responsible for social outcomes typically have budgets to fund specific types of services to achieve those outcomes. As these programs scale down, end, or are found to be less effective, there may be opportunities to shift some funding to outcomes-based contracts. To do this, an agency could allocate a portion of a programmatic budget to outcomes-based contracts and then issue a solicitation for projects to achieve an outcome for a particular population, instead of issuing a solicitation for a specific type of service. The U.S. Department of Labor, for example, created a Workforce Innovation Fund that allocated $24 million for outcomes as a test of a more effective way to accomplish the agency's mandate.[7] Its solicitation for grant applications called on state and local governments, service providers, and intermediaries across the country to design outcomes-based projects that would improve employment outcomes for high-risk groups in measurable, verifiable ways. As a result, Department of Labor funds will pay for outcomes for both the

---

5 Mass. Gen. Laws Chapter 10, § Section 35VV, available at https://malegislature.gov/Laws/GeneralLaws/PartI/TitleII/Chapter10/Section35VV.

6 U.S. Government Accountability Office, "Pay for Success: Collaboration Among Federal Agencies Would be Helpful as Governments Explore New Financing Mechanisms" (September 2015), available at http://www.gao.gov/assets/680/672363.pdf.

7 For more, visit: U.S. Department of Labor, "What Is the Workforce Innovation Fund," available at https://www.doleta.gov/workforce_innovation/; See also, U.S. Department of Labor, "The Pay for Success Solicitation," available at https://www.doleta.gov/workforce_innovation/success.cfm.

New York State and the Massachusetts recidivism reduction and employment Pay for Success projects.[8]

Economic development funds, which often exist even for small cities and counties with limited budgets and areas of government responsibility, offer another possible source of outcome funding. Projects such as those focused on early childhood development often bring jobs and revenue to the community, thus contributing to economic development goals. These economic impacts are often not included in the cost-benefit analyses of social programs that underlie Pay for Success efforts as indirect benefits can be difficult to quantify. The Institute for Child Success, in its work around the country, has seen interest in using economic development funds to pay for outcomes of effective early childhood programs.[9]

Yet another source of funding for outcomes, especially for local governments, is sales taxes or other assessments. Government officials have told the Institute for Child Success that such taxes are a viable option for funding outcomes.

Though the applicability of these methods may vary, what they show is that cashable savings are not the only way to fund Pay for Success programs, even for cash-strapped governments. Given these alternatives and the risks posed by focusing only on cashable savings, governments should begin exploring alternative ways of determining whether and how much funding to allocate for Pay for Success initiatives.

A BETTER STANDARD FOR DECIDING WHETHER TO COMMIT GOVERNMENT FUNDS TO AN OUTCOMES-BASED PROJECT

In our 2015 paper for the Center for American Progress, we recommend that governments consider three factors in determining how much funding to commit for a Pay for Success initiative:[10]

---

8 U.S. Government Accountability Office, "Pay for Success: Collaboration" (September 2015).

9 Kelly O'Donnell, "More than just Pre-K: The Positive Economic Impact of Preschool in Los Angeles County," Institute for Child Success (March 2016), available at https://www.instituteforchildsuccess.org/publication/just-pre-k-positive-economic-impact-preschool-los-angeles-county-brief/.

10 Jitinder Kohli et al., "From Cashable Savings to Public Value: Pricing Program Outcomes in Pay for Success," Center for American Progress (September 1, 2015), available at https://www.americanprogress.org/issues/economy/report/2015/09/01/120300/from-cashable-savings-to-public-value/.

1 **Wellbeing benefits.** To what extent does the outcome lead to improvements for individuals and communities?

The full benefits of outcome based projects include much more than monetary savings to taxpayers. They also include improvements for individuals and the community at large. The price of outcome payments should thus reflect the value of these broader benefits in all instances where they can be quantified and measured.

2 **Public willingness to pay.** Is the outcome important enough to the community that additional public dollars should be allocated to achieving it?

In some instances, the public may assign additional value to an outcome based on factors beyond wellbeing or savings. The price of an outcome should therefore include public willingness-to-pay for outcomes that reflect their values (such as preventing domestic violence), pressing priorities (such as finding a vaccine for the Zika virus), or moral obligations (such as supporting veterans).

3 **Cashable savings.** Will government achieve cashable savings by investing in this initiative?

Despite its potential drawbacks, the amount that government is likely to save should be one of the key factors in determining the price of outcomes, however, it should not be considered in a vacuum.

The goal of this approach is to present key factors that together capture the true value of an outcome to government, individuals, and society as a whole—and, therefore, a better sense of the right price to assign it. New York State's "Increasing Employment and Improving Public Safety" project did exactly this. It based outcome payments on both estimated savings from reduced prison expenses and the value of benefits to society from reduced crime.[11] This combination of factors presents a more holistic, and realistic, approach to valuing Pay for Success outcomes.

While a holistic approach offers many potential benefits, there are still challenges to using it in practice. For instance, wellbeing benefits and

---

11 U.S. Government Accountability Office, "Pay for Success: Collaboration" (September 2015).

public willingness to pay are often difficult to accurately quantify, as noted previously with the example of the economic impacts of early childhood development programs. However, there are good examples of ways to overcome this challenge. The Washington State Institute for Public Policy has developed a rigorous approach to valuing benefits and costs of an intervention over time.[12] When analyzing a crime intervention, for example, the institute looks both at the savings to government as a result of a reduction in future crime as well as benefits to potential victims of crime and the improved labor market benefits for participants with improved rates of graduation.

Proxies can also be used to overcome challenges related to the accuracy of public willingness-to-pay. One of the easiest proxies to use is the willingness of legislature or executive branch leaders as their choices often reflect the priorities of their constituents.

Getting better at valuing outcomes is important not only for Pay for Success initiatives, but also for the multitude of outcomes-focused funding strategies spreading across the nation, such as performance-based contracts, evidence-based budgeting,[13] and outcomes-based bonuses (to name a few).[14] As we shift our thinking from basing funding on cashable savings to a more holistic understanding of outcome value, we can unlock funding for strategies worth far more to society than just the things that save us money.

---

12 Washington State Institute for Public Policy, "Benefit-Cost Technical Documentation," Washington State Institute for Public Policy (June 2016), available at http://www.wsipp.wa.gov/TechnicalDocumentation/WsippBenefitCostTechnicalDocumentation.pdf.

13 Policymakers are integrating evidence of results into the budget process. For example, since 2015, the Mississippi Legislature has required agencies seeking funding for new programs to answer questions indicating whether it is evidence- or research-based, and detailing how measures will be monitored and measured. For more information, see Pew-MacArthur Results First Initiative, "A Guide to Evidence-Based Budget Development: How to Use Research to Inform Program Funding Decisions," Pew Charitable Trusts (July 6, 2016), available at http://www.pewtrusts.org/en/research-and-analysis/issue-briefs/2016/07/a-guide-to-evidence-based-budget-development.

14 In Tennessee, outcomes-based bonuses have been used to further improve child welfare outcomes by providing additional rewards to providers that exceeded set performance targets. For more information, see Beeck Center for Social Impact and Innovation, "Funding for Results: How Governments Can Pay for Outcomes," Georgetown University (May 2015), available at http://beeckcenter.georgetown.edu/wp-content/uploads/2016/06/Funding-for-Results_BeeckCenter.pdf.

MEGAN GOLDEN *is the co-founder of Mission: Cure Pancreatitis, which is using outcome-based financing and impact investing to develop effective treatments for a devastating chronic illness, demonstrating a new model for curing disease. Until recently, Golden led the Institute for Child Success' national Pay for Success work. She conducted ICS' feasibility study on Pay for Success financing for the Nurse-Family Partnership in South Carolina, which resulted in a $30 million expansion that will serve thousands of low-income first-time mothers. She has a BA in political science from Brown University and a JD, magna cum laude, from New York University School of Law.*

JITINDER KOHLI *is a director at Monitor Deloitte, where he leads the firm's Pay for Success work. He also currently serves as a senior fellow at the Center for American Progress, a progressive U.S. think tank, where he specializes in outcomes-based design and financing. Kohli has advised a wide range of agencies on outcomes-based financing and published widely on the issue. He has spoken at over 50 events globally on Pay for Success to nonprofit, investor, and governmental audiences, including the White House. A native of the U.K., Kohli spent 15 years as a senior official in British government, including time at the British Treasury, Cabinet Office, and Business Department. He studied at Oxford University, Southampton University, and the Wharton School at the University of Pennsylvania.*

SAMANTHA MIGNOTTE *is a consultant in Monitor Deloitte's federal practice where she works with government agencies on enterprise strategy, performance management, and program evaluation. Prior to Monitor Deloitte, Mignotte worked with the World Bank's Independent Evaluation Group, where she worked on project and program level evaluations on poverty alleviation initiatives. She has also served as a research associate for the Small Planet Institute. Mignotte holds a master's degree in public affairs and international development from Princeton University, and BA in economics and political science from Vassar College.*

INVESTING IN WHAT IT TRULY TAKES TO DELIVER OUTCOMES
Approaching Collective Challenges with Collective Responses

Kristin Giantris and Jessica LaBarbera
Nonprofit Finance Fund

The year is 2030. Social funding has evolved to consist primarily of performance-oriented contracts, which has been a difficult transition for many organizations that have not been able to mobilize the resources needed to invest in capacity to measure their outcomes per contract requirements.

WorkingHands is one of nine local human services organizations in Anytown, a low-income community suffering from economic stagnation, philanthropic neglect, and environmental pollution. WorkingHands helps people coming out of jail find jobs and is the only local workforce development agency.

WorkingHands has been undercapitalized for decades, lacking enough staff to provide the high-touch support that Anytown residents need. Its largest contracts now require outcomes performance reporting in order to get paid, and WorkingHands struggles to collect and process the data necessary for sharing its outcomes. The executive director knows she needs to invest in infrastructure but does not have the money for it. The other eight organizations in Anytown face similar challenges; collectively, they barely provide a skeleton safety net for Anytown's people. The local government and foundations are focused on paying for performance but haven't supported the capacity building and investment needed for service providers to be able to measure results. These organizations are caught in a vicious cycle: Insufficient resources mean they can't report effectively on outcomes, which leads to reduced payments—and even fewer resources for needed services. In the end, it is the Anytown residents who pay the biggest price.

Creating positive outcomes in our communities is a widely shared goal. The challenge lies in how we get there. Outcomes enthusiasts believe orienting our funding around results that can be proven through external evaluation will lead to better strategies to deliver effective services. And, in an era of limited resources, we must direct resources more efficiently and weed out unsuccessful programs and organizations. Outcomes skeptics remind us that not every human service has outcomes that can easily be measured, and, for those that do, measuring and attributing social outcomes accurately is difficult, costly, and requires investment and time to realize. And many skeptics worry about the true motivation and unintended consequences of an increased drive to measure and fund outcomes, where prioritizing efficiency and scale overrides culturally competent and community-based responses, possibly resulting in a "race to the bottom" for human services across the country.

Both sides raise valid points. So instead of asking, "Should we move to an outcomes-oriented system?" we need to consider how we reorient our system around outcomes in a responsible way—one that avoids this bleak future for Anytown. This responsible path requires us to address two additional questions:

1 How do we determine whether organizations fail to demonstrate outcomes because they are truly ineffective and incapable of change or because they haven't had the resources to invest in tracking and demonstrating outcomes?

2 And how do we reward well-resourced, high-performing organizations while not punishing those less prepared to adapt to outcomes-oriented funding, all while ensuring that the neediest communities are served?

If we do not address these questions, our efforts to reorient our sector around outcomes could yield positive, short-term results in very narrow circumstances for some people, but leave many others more disenfranchised than they are today.

CREATING A (REALISTIC) PATH TOWARD READINESS

We believe the shift to an outcomes-oriented system is necessary, and it cannot succeed without human services organizations capable of operating with outcomes-based funding. Yet we have collectively underinvested in our social sector for decades, primarily funding direct programs and ignoring infrastructure needs, including organizations' ability to measure outcomes.

Current efforts have focused on finding and scaling those nonprofit "unicorns," the rare organizations that deliver great services with the capacity to prove their outcomes. These organizations certainly deserve support, but we cannot expect that a handful of elite organizations will meet all social needs and continue to deliver with optimal fidelity to their program models. The country is too big, and our social needs are too complex. The elite "winners" are not always best placed to work in all local settings; the "losers" will disproportionately be under-resourced organizations from vulnerable communities, where positive outcomes and strong community-based organizations are needed most.

If we truly desire a systemic shift, we need to invest in organizations' ability to make the initial transition and to continue to measure their outcomes on an ongoing basis. Instead of focusing on who is already "ready," we will need thousands of organizations to move up a continuum of readiness. This will not happen without dedicated investment, particularly in anchor institutions in underinvested communities who are serving the hardest-to-reach populations. We must fund this transition to an outcomes focus with widespread efforts to enhance the adaptive capacity of nonprofits to:

1 Build human capital, information technology (IT), and organizational culture to capture and analyze program data, and use these data for performance management, continuous improvement, and reporting.

2 Decide on meaningful and, where possible, measurable metrics of success.

3 Understand programs and drivers that will result in improved results, as well as the costs required to deliver such services.

4 Understand, articulate, and demand the full cost required to deliver outcomes.

5 Jointly craft funding arrangements, such as a mix of grants, fee-for-service contracts, and possibly loans with various payers, funders, and investors.

Government funders, private donors, corporate partners, and impact investors who want to enjoy the benefits of an outcomes-oriented system will need to make significant upfront investments to enable service delivery agencies to undertake this work.

BUILDING THE BRIDGE TO OUTCOMES: CONDITIONS FOR SUCCESS

Beyond funding investment in adaptation for specific organizations, the shift to an outcomes orientation requires coordinated change across the social system. We cannot shift the system if we do not overcome current confusion about the different motivations of various stakeholders and assumptions about who is responsible for making this system work.

The concept of orienting around outcomes is gaining momentum partly because it appeals to different people for different reasons. But what are the different motivations for focusing on outcomes? They cover a spectrum of intent:

- Make meaningful impact on intractable problems in communities.

- Ensure quality services are being delivered.

- Guarantee funds are being used effectively.

- Provide a means by which to justify funding cuts.

- Create a fig leaf of acceptability for an agenda to withdraw from the commitment of collective responsibility to care for all communities.

The complex partnerships necessary to pull off outcomes-oriented work are hard to initiate and maintain when motivations are unclear. All participants must understand their own motivation and share it openly with partners. We can come together for different reasons, but lack of clarity and obfuscation sow debilitating distrust. And trust is fundamental to establishing a new set of relationships and contracts based on aligning stakeholders and resources around shared goals and performance.

Beyond clarifying motivations, a healthy shift to outcomes will require systemic change that all stakeholders must undertake together. No one part of our system can be responsible for leading a shift that requires everyone to work in different ways. Government and private donors cannot build the new system by simply changing funding rules. Human services agencies cannot unilaterally decide to orient around outcomes when their funders still focus on compliance with activity-focused contracts. And the communities we serve cannot, on their own, insist that the service providers in their neighborhoods orient around outcomes.

But they can work together effectively if we recognize that all of the above are necessary and jointly responsible to make the system work. We have to change the blame game that dominates today's outcomes discussion, where government and private donors insist that service providers must, on their own, improve their ability to measure outcomes; service providers insist on maintaining the status quo just to keep their doors open day to day; and community members become largely disempowered from participating in this conversation and thus do not demand change. The promise in outcomes is in a collective response. There is a role for everyone to play in this transition—service providers, industry groups, local and federal government, private sector actors, and, more broadly, communities. Each social issue likely will require a different set of partners to establish the right formula for moving toward outcomes in that field. For example, ensuring the best health outcomes will require a new set of partnerships between health systems and community-based organizations, which will look inherently different from how local communities plan for and achieve high-quality early childhood care and education. But we need to recognize that we are all collectively responsible to build and maintain a social system that reaffirms our commitment to each other, while acknowledging the history of under-investment in poor communities and our social system in general.

Creating new ways of working together is difficult, but the explosion of recent innovation points to both its possibility and importance. Public-private partnerships, collective impact approaches, performance partnership pilots, and Pay for Success contracts offer new models for such collaboration. These early efforts are time-consuming and resource-intensive, as new partners learn to speak each other's language, integrate data and platforms, and devise strategies for bridging silos and ensuring responses that include the community. The high upfront costs of such systems transitions are partly driven by the need to correct for historic underinvestment in data, systems, and collaboration, which could be a barrier to the broader uptake of these models. Programs like the Social Innovation Fund have offered one means of funding the required transitions and overcoming barriers to systems change. To maintain this momentum, government, philanthropy, and the private sector will need to expand support for this adaptation.

So, what could this mean for the residents of Anytown?

What if the county board supervisor, a regional foundation, investors committed to the community, the leaders of WorkingHands and their peers, and the clients they serve had all joined together almost 20 years earlier to agree on what they wanted to achieve for their community and collaborated to make it happen? What if they had suspended their suspicion of each other long enough to see the complementarity of their motivations and the common ground in their collective aspirations? And what if they had mobilized the political will to make the investments necessary to enable all participants to thrive in a new outcomes-oriented system? This could spark a new way of working together—a virtuous circle, instead of a vicious one—in which better results build trust and buy-in across stakeholders and deepen their collaborative commitment. And we know from our work in communities across the country that this this not an impossible dream. But it will take clarity, honesty, and an appreciation of how far we need to go to make this our waking reality.

To achieve better outcomes for the communities we all care about, we must approach collective challenges with collective responses. We will reach our best results by taking a system-wide approach, investing in many organizations' ability to adapt and capture outcomes, rather than focusing on the few who are ready or near-ready now. Nor can we expect to transition to an outcomes-oriented social sector by investing in organizations one-by-one. We must move the system together. There is a role for everyone in this new paradigm—one built on trust, partnership, and catalytic investment by those social impact investors willing to be this era's innovators and builders.

———

KRISTIN GIANTRIS *is a managing director at Nonprofit Finance Fund (NFF) and directs NFF's national advisory services practice. She leads the design of innovative funding and financing initiatives, oversees the development and delivery of consulting products and services for NFF's nonprofit clients, and manages business development and relationships with a number of strategic, national partners. Giantris's professional experience combines over 20 years of economic development and debt financing in both the nonprofit and for-profit sectors. Prior to joining NFF, Giantris was a vice president at Citigroup Global Markets in debt origination. She came to Citigroup after an initial career in the nonprofit sector,* where she managed technical assistance programs supporting agriculture and agribusiness development for an international nonprofit organization, Volunteers in Overseas Cooperative Assistance. Giantris earned an MPA from the School of International and Public Affairs at Columbia University and a BA in political science from Kenyon College.

JESSICA LABARBERA is a vice president of strategic innovation at Nonprofit Finance Fund (NFF). Since 2010, she has spearheaded NFF's work in the Pay for Success arena, including federal and statewide programs to direct over $10 million to the development of Pay for Success projects; oversight of the Pay for Success Learning Hub (www.payforsuccess.org) and "Pay for Success: The First Generation," a comparative analysis of the first ten Pay for Success projects in the United States; creation of curriculum to ready service providers for participation in Pay for Success arrangements; and acquisition of over $1 million in CDFI funds to leverage in Pay for Success investments. She has spoken prolifically on Pay for Success, including testifying to the California State Legislature and facilitating convenings presented in partnership with the White House Office of Social Innovation. She holds an MPA in nonprofit management from Columbia University's School of International and Public Affairs and a BA in sociology from the University of Virginia.

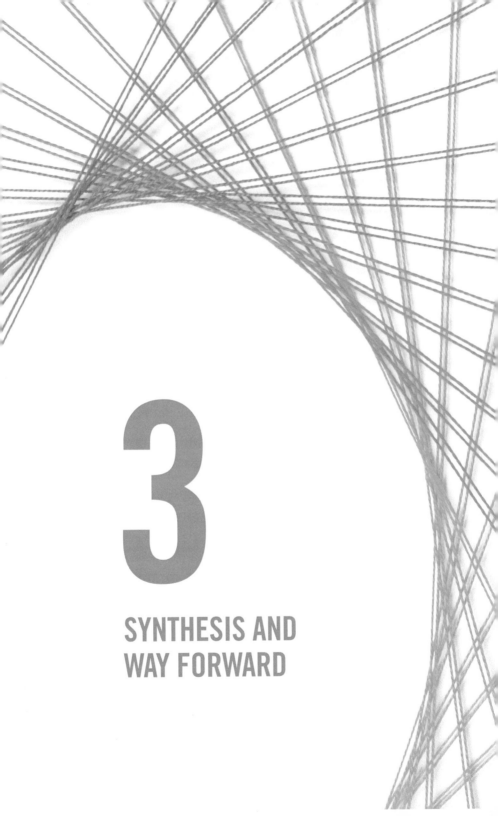

3

SYNTHESIS AND
WAY FORWARD

THE MEASURES OF A MOVEMENT
Investing for Results Now and Tomorrow

Andrea Levere
Prosperity Now

What *Matters* is the fourth volume in a remarkable series imagined and published by the Federal Reserve Bank of San Francisco and its nonprofit partners, the Low Income Investment Fund, Urban Institute, Prosperity Now (formerly CFED), and Nonprofit Finance Fund. Although each book in the series shares the word "What" prominently in its title, the subjects addressed in *What Works*, *What Counts*, *What It's Worth*, and *What Matters* range from community development, to the application of evidence and data, to advancing financial wellbeing, to the use of outcomes-based funding.

What Matters is unique among its literary companions in being both the most focused and the most broad-ranging in its content. Its central idea seems narrow: to convert how we structure, finance, operate, and evaluate the delivery of social services to an outcomes-based approach to achieve better results, maximize efficiencies, leverage new sources of capital, and achieve unprecedented levels of scale. Yet its scope becomes as wide as human experience, as this approach is applied through 15 different tools to the work underway in at least a dozen sectors or specialties.

Despite their differences, the four books are all grounded in a common pursuit to identify and advance policies and practices that strengthen this nation's ability to create a better life for all Americans, with a special focus on those who are most vulnerable or disadvantaged. Each volume affirms that effective solutions are uniformly grounded in collaboration across pre-existing silos and the necessity of taking a collective approach. And the mission is framed as a work in process, almost always outlining what has already been accomplished as a prelude to what still needs to be done.

The authors of the essays in *What Matters* often write as if they have just started their exploration of how service delivery can be transformed by an outcomes approach. Few have more than a few years of experience behind them. They acknowledge how challenging it is to change systems, culture, and rewards. But they are united in their belief that this is the right direction. As Governor Deval Patrick states in his foreword: "This is not the easiest path forward. But the examples in this book point to its potential… Reorienting our social system around outcomes could finally honor the generosity of donors and the effort of nonprofit workers with the results they deserve and that our communities sorely need." And Antony Bugg-Levine, of Nonprofit Finance Fund, adds in his introduction, "Realizing this potential will require all of us to honestly acknowledge how many of our cherished practices and assumptions are accommodations to a broken system rather than necessary or beneficial."

AN OVERNIGHT SUCCESS THAT TOOK 50 YEARS

What Matters begins the story of how investing in results began by taking the reader back more than half of a century. David Erickson, of the Federal Reserve Bank of San Francisco, traces the modern community development industry back to the first community development corporations of the mid-1960s. "The idea was to fund local corporations that were rooted in and rooting for struggling communities….CDCs were nonprofit but subject to market discipline in pursuit of better local social outcomes and a stronger local economy." This appeal to market discipline is the procurer of today's outcomes-based funding movement, according to Erickson, and the basis of future community development expansions into new fields, particularly health. In her chapter, Emily Gustafsson-Wright, of the Brookings Institution, provides a detailed history, complete with timeline, that tracks how responsibility for service delivery moved from the public sector to nonprofit agencies. She also explores how the structure of this relationship evolved from paying for time and materials to rewarding specific outcomes tied to goals and programs funded or services delivered. Jaclyn Kelly and Margaret Ross-Martin, of Nonprofit Finance Fund, offer a helpful case study from New York City that outlines the opportunities and pitfalls associated with this evolution.

Daniel Barker, John Cassidy, and Winny Chen, of Monitor Deloitte, expand on this history with a vivid example of how and why

Tennessee used outcomes-based contracts to reinvent its child welfare system—saving money and improving results to document "the challenges of traditional funding models and how results-based funding improves on that model." They are the first, but not nearly the last, authors to describe the flaws in our current funding model, which too often fails not only to achieve the intended purpose but also "does not lend itself to knowing which programs work and which do not."

These authors present typologies of how the practice of outcomes-based funding has developed. Gustafsson-Wright explores how the scope of what counted as performance varied considerably "from statements of work based on performance outputs, to contract renewal based on outcomes, to a payment scale tied to degrees of performance." Performance-based contracts have evolved into new products that link financial rewards to outcomes, such as social impact bonds.

Barker, Cassidy, and Chen build on this by sharing three options for delivering rewards: incentive prizes and challenges; outcomes-based grants or contracts; and Pay for Success financing. They recommend that the mechanism chosen match the "social policy objective" by applying four criteria: nature of the problem; knowledge of the solution (how much do we know about what works?); time frame to achieve outcomes/make payments; and level of external resources and partners.

Annie Donovan, of the CDFI Fund of the U.S. Treasury, makes a crucial distinction between the role of funding—which requires no repayment—and financing—which requires repayment. In a typical Pay for Success transaction, "the money is loaned to the service provider for the period of service provision. The outcomes-based investor is then repaid by the government funder when the agreed-upon outcomes are delivered." For an investor to take this risk, there must be a reasonable chance of success based on demonstrated results to date. Donovan concludes that this type of financing "is not likely to be used to *create* social innovation, but rather to *scale* it." She cites community development financial institutions (CDFIs) as essential partners in promoting the innovation on which outcomes-based financing must depend.

The authors set the stage for the next section by affirming the superiority of investing for results over other approaches. In Gustafsson-Wright's view: "Outcomes-based funding has enormous potential to help achieve equitable access to quality social services. The greater focus on outcomes can lead to flexibility, innovation, and adaptive learning in service delivery, and an emphasis on evaluation can enhance transparency in social spending and facilitate funding what works." Barker, Cassidy, and Chen remind us what is necessary to realize this potential: "An important step to leveraging this growing body of evidence will be to develop a common language in describing outcomes and measuring performance."

WHY RESULTS MATTER

Authors from multiple sectors and disciplines share their opinions on why outcomes-based funding is important and what difference it can or does make in the design and delivery of programs. Michael Weinstein, of ImpactMeasures, and Jacob Harold, of GuideStar, ground their arguments in the power of data themselves to build knowledge and improve practice. Weinstein describes how The Robin Hood Foundation's entire philanthropic practice is shaped to measure the outcomes produced by grantees that aim to reduce poverty and that by "assigning a dollar value to 'monetize' each outcome," the foundation finds "that it makes judgments explicit." Harold eloquently captures the unspoken power of data to shape our world: "How we organize information matters for how we understand the world, and how we act on it. Nowhere is this truer than in the work of social good."

How data and evidence inform public policy is championed by many, including President Obama, as David Wilkinson, who led the White House Office of Social Innovation, recounts in his description of both the rationale and methodology deployed by his office. "Results-driven, collaborative, person-centered approaches are all part of what we've referred to as social innovation" in the eight years in which the Obama administration invested millions of public dollars in workforce development and educational programs to advance an outcomes approach. Wilkinson believes that today the field has "achieved proof of concept," a perspective echoed by Erica Brown, Kathy Stack, and Josh McGee, of the Laura and John Arnold Foundation, in their description of the game-changing approach embodied in the Investing in Education Initiative at the U.S. Department of Education (DOE).

In short, this program made a twofold commitment to both use and produce evidence of how to close the achievement gap for disadvantaged students to make progress in this decades-long struggle at a faster rate than ever achieved before. The DOE began by structuring partnerships between the research/evaluation team and the program staff. The design of projects mirrored this partnership, with evidence used to inform design and evaluation charged with creating new knowledge to inform the next iteration of program design. Brown, Stack, and McGee believe that evidence-based policymaking is a "dynamic, long-term pursuit of outcomes that requires sustained focus on using data and evaluation to learn and continuously improve approaches to addressing important problems."

But just because it is important doesn't mean that it is easy or that structural and systemic changes aren't still necessary to take this approach to scale. Tamar Bauer and Roxane White, of the Nurse-Family Partnership, mince no words when they pronounce that "Pay for Success may be the most grueling growth strategy we will someday celebrate." Even though the Nurse-Family Partnership was a program designed to measure metrics from the start, with a commitment to building evidence every step of the way, it still found that it "had to put its performance management 'on steroids' to meet the requirements of Pay for Success projects."

Molly Baldwin, of Roca, describes the soul-searching and organizational transformations that were necessary for her youth development organization to actually achieve the mission for which it was founded. This required "a systemic cycle of research, design, action, and use of data for the continuous improvement" of its model, which involved integrating "evidence-based practices from behavioral health, criminal justice, community corrections and reentry, medical and mental health, and workforce development." The rigor and sustained focus on data led her organization to participate in a Pay for Success program for juvenile justice, which is now considering a national expansion. Again, a process not for the faint of heart.

Andy McMahon and Stephanie Mercier, of CSH, use their experience to explain how the Pay for Success model solves one of the most vexing quandaries in social services: the "wrong pockets" problem. Given the complexity of how problems are solved, services delivered, and costs incurred in the social service sector, it is often true that "the entity investing the resources in an intervention is not the sole—or even primary—beneficiary of the program's success." This dilemma has profound implications for the behavior and priorities of institutions and programs in terms of collaboration, budgeting, and service delivery, and often works against the very outcomes the agencies aspire to achieve.

At the heart of this solution is the fact that Pay for Success offers "a mechanism through which the comprehensive needs and costs of a particular target population are assessed and budget allocations agreed prior to implementing an intervention." Yet McMahon and Mercier also raise challenges to success, including structural barriers created by historic funding patterns and the lack of data to track outcomes.

Kerry Sullivan, of the Bank of America Charitable Foundation, urges us to challenge these historic patterns by funding outcomes measurement and supporting nonprofit leaders to make the changes necessary to be able to track meaningful data. She recognizes that nonprofits cannot bear the cost of this transformation alone: "Monitoring and evaluation are at the very heart of an outcome-focused approach, and nonprofits can ask to be compensated to cover this work."

Wilkinson outlines the structural reasons why these projects are so challenging: the lack of incentives to reward outcomes in our existing systems; the barriers created by our categorical approach to funding and compliance; and the lack of capacity among both public-sector and nonprofit staff to manage the data, evaluation, and outcome measurement that this approach requires. He proposes specific actions to address each factor to produce "an enabling infrastructure" that ties funding to outcomes, promotes cross-program/-sector collaboration, and provides training and technical assistance in the skills necessary to succeed. Capacity-building is endorsed by Sullivan: "(V)aluing and investing in nonprofit leadership is critical to the success of the sector and how we will make the shift to focusing on outcomes."

Caroline Whistler, Third Sector Capital Partners, Inc., and Matt Gee, BrightHive, cut to the core of the structural challenges by stating that if the government wants to invest for results, "it needs to solve the dual problem of how it procures information technology (IT) and how it contracts for services." They agree with Gustafsson-Wright and Barker, Cassidy, and Chen that these changes enable governments to purchase value in place of a focus on managing costs or tracking compliance. They make the powerful connection that IT systems must mirror the service integration of providers by bridging data silos if they are to deliver the information necessary to truly track and assess effectiveness and impact.

Zia Khan, of The Rockefeller Foundation, deepens this analysis by underscoring the complex interplay between the "rules" of the game and the "underlying rituals" that so often determine the fate of any change effort. When assessing the difficulty of changing systems, he accords necessary importance to "whether the emotional dynamics of what it takes for people to change behaviors are factored into the change strategy." If we believe in the wise words of Peter Drucker that "culture eats strategy for lunch," we should listen to Khan's advice to ensure that existing rituals "can be channeled to drive the change instead of being a barrier," such as sharing stories of impact to motivate people to change the way they do business. He brings us back to Barker, Cassidy, and Chen's recommendation for a shared language earlier in the book when he states: "What's also needed is the informal sense of shared values, common language, and trust in others' intentions to tackle the issues and problems that emerge."

What about the end game? Wilkinson states: "These tools and approaches can help us build a country that is more just, a society that is more equal, and communities that are stronger." Bauer and White concur: "If a provider delivers on the promise of Pay for Success and meets outcome metrics, government should make success payments and also commit to sustaining services going forward. That would be truly transformative." Whistler and Gee add: "There is a structural inertia that makes a culture of innovation both elusive and incredibly scalable if we are able to drive that inertia toward outcomes for the largest organization in service of humanity.... We have the opportunity to ignite a public-sector innovation revolution in our lifetime."

HOW DO I MEASURE AND FINANCE SUCCESS? LET ME COUNT THE WAYS!

The process that led to the focus on investing in results for the delivery of services and the investment in building evidence and data infrastructure to capture outcomes has led to multiple innovations in philanthropy, public and private financial products, and capital market opportunities. Tracy Palandjian, of Social Finance Inc., opens this section by describing how social impact bonds launched the tide of financial innovation in this country after importing the model from the United Kingdom. She highlighted the impact of their design: "Social impact bonds are predicated on aligned incentives for all involved stakeholders. They allow governments to focus on preventive services, nonprofits to scale, and investors an opportunity to make an impact."

Yet Palandjian echoes the constructive criticism of Bauer and White and Baldwin that the social impact bond, as currently implemented, is too complex to scale efficiently. In response, three variations on the structure of social impact bonds are recommended: the social impact guarantee, outcomes rate cards, and the impact security. George Overholser, of Third Sector Capital Partners, Inc., advocates that we flip the social impact bond so that the government provides funding at the start of the project and private investors provide funding—if necessary—at the end, thereby turning the tool from a financing instrument into a form of insurance. While the social impact guarantee has yet to be tried, Overholser believes that it deserves investment to "simplify the contracting process, lower project costs for governments, and tap into the immense world of mainstream insurance."

Metcalf and Levitt present another British tool known as outcomes rate cards. Skipping the capital markets completely, service providers can use these cards to collect payments based on reimbursement rates, or prices, set by public agencies in return for achieving specific outcomes. Lindsay Beck and Catarina Schwab, of NPX, and Anna Pinedo, of Morrison & Foerster, recommend a replacement for the social impact bond known as the "Impact Security" which is "a novel financial product that explicitly links financial returns with social and environmental impact" targeted to social investors. This product is designed to keep the focus on outcomes but offers a simpler, easier structure that can be sold publicly as a standard debt instrument with repayments linked to achievement of results.

Other financial innovators are adapting the structure of social impact bonds to the needs of specific sectors. Beth Bafford, of the Calvert

Foundation, Mark Kim, of DC Water, and Eric Letsinger, of Quantified Ventures, tell the Story of DC Water's environmental impact bond, issued last September, which is not only the first environmental impact bond but the largest Pay for Success transaction done to date in the United States. The environmental impact bond's unique structure transfers the risk from issuer to investor by embedding a "two-way contingent payment feature into the bond itself, the first time a tax-exempt municipal security explicitly tied financial payments to measurable outcomes." The implications of this innovative structure are potentially profound in the way that it "can support public officials in their embrace of innovation when the status quo is proven but the alternative has the potential to deliver better long-term results."

Several articles describe and analyze the role of prize competitions to advance efforts to finance outcomes while also modeling new methods of philanthropy and public-sector procurement practices in service of big social goals. Prizes are hosted by philanthropists, governments, and entrepreneurs and differ according to three models: resource prizes, incentive prizes, and recognition prizes, with incentive prizes often getting the most attention. Reyna Reed Wasson, of the Children's Prize, reflects on their impact: "Resource and incentive prizes have enormous potential for addressing the problems that vulnerable populations face…and can shine a spotlight on problems that have plagued humanity forever, but are not very sexy."

Experience to date has shown that prizes bring new human capital into the task of solving social problems by disrupting how the government does business and leveraging capital that wouldn't normally engage with government. Jennifer Bravo, Christopher Frangione, and Stephanie Wander, of the XPRIZE Foundation, explain that prizes involve "small teams of innovators…creating breakthroughs that touch the lives of billions, tackling challenges and solving problems once thought to be solely the domain of governments." Prize advocates freely admit that they don't work for every issue, with clean energy, education, and public health being the areas of highest promise.

Prizes also have some unexpected benefits. Jenn Gustetic, of NASA, says "the increased use of prizes within the government is also encouraging broad discussions of outcome-driven procurement approaches." Finally, Ruth Levine, of Hewlett, offers a variation on the idea of prizes with advance market commitments, which create financial incentives for companies to conduct research and development and manufacture "products where the social value exceeds the perceived willingness to pay." Proven effective in developing economies, advance market commitments offer a price guarantee to create a positive net present value for firms while providing protections to keep the price affordable in the long term.

Four articles explore innovations to existing capital market and impact investing products. Terri Ludwig, of Enterprise Community Partners, Inc., urges us to build on the successes achieved by leveraging the tax code through the Low Income Housing Tax Credit and New Markets Tax Credit now used to develop the built environment for social services. She advocates adding "bonus credits" for achieving outcomes related to financial security, health, or education tailored to community needs and the interests of social investors.

Maggie Super Church, of CLF Ventures, affirms Ludwig's use of a "creatively assembled capital stack of tax credit equity, multi-sector partnerships, and local support" with her description of the Healthy Neighborhoods Equity Fund's investments in projects that aim to integrate multiple uses to achieve transformative outcomes. She measures over 50 outcomes for each investment and believes that "the concept of a blended capital stack can be replicated nearly anywhere. Individual and institutional investors, including bank, hospitals, and health systems, can bring new resources to the table, bolstered by first-loss capital from the public and philanthropic sectors."

Nancy Andrews, of the Low Income Investment Fund, proposes a new financing product, Equity with a Twist, to empower "community quarterbacks" with operational flexibility. "At the highest level, [it] is intended to demonstrate that integrative, outcomes driven approaches can alleviate poverty." Appealingly, it is also "meant to be much more user friendly than current outcomes based capital tools like social impact bonds or Pay for Success structures."

Kimberlee Cornett, of The Kresge Foundation, outlines the origins and appeal of the Strong Families Fund, "a Kresge–led, multi-partner effort to fund up to 10 years of resident service coordination in Low Income Housing Tax Credit (LIHTC)–financed family housing through a pay-for-performance, incentivized loan structure." The fund has been a work-in-progress but offers a larger lesson for those interested in pursuing the strategies in the book: "New products and fund structures take much longer to be accepted in the marketplace" than we might expect.

LET MANY FLOWERS GROW THEIR IMPACT

The essays that chronicle the progress among practitioners in adopting an "investing for results" approach affirm that most of the field is still in the startup stage of this work. The application of outcomes-based tools varies by sector, with success tied to the ability to customize the structure and measures of success. Practitioners affirm the benefits of data analysis and a knowledge of what works, both on internal operations and how they are regarded in the marketplace, as strong outcomes drive program expansion and access to capital. However, the impact of outcomes is much less certain in terms of influencing policy change.

The evidence is clear and compelling that the big prize is in the health care sector. Five essays address different elements related to health outcomes. Tyler Norris of the Well Being Trust and Jme McLean, of Mesu Strategies document the financial stakes of an industry that spent $3.2 trillion in 2014 with a consensus that only 20 percent of health status results from access to medical care. They add: "The primary factors that shape health outcomes are the same ones that drive economic opportunity: equitable access to education, housing, transportation, and healthy foods, reducing stress, and improving public safety." Thus, a multi-sectoral strategy that addresses all the factors affecting health is the only way to achieve meaningful improvements while addressing cost. To achieve this, Norris and McLean call for "building a market for health outcomes that complements the existing marketplace for health care services. A marketplace for health outcomes would supply community members with the social and economic opportunities that are upstream from health."

Peter Long, of Blue Shield of California Foundation, builds on this essay with a call to radically improve the nation's capacity to measure health outcomes in a way that incorporates all we know about the broader social determinants and "promotes meaningful collaboration among health care providers and across other sectors to address complex health issues." When it comes to funding this broader approach to realizing health outcomes, Allison Hamblin, of the Center for Health Care Strategies, cites "state Medicaid programs as among the most bankable beneficiaries of any number of social impact investments." She recommends the use of Pay for Success as the onramp to leverage Medicaid funding and align with a growing trend in health care to tie payments to the delivery of value in health outcomes. She also speaks directly to service providers when she says: "Given this uniquely American preference to spend money on health care at the expense of other social services, Pay for Success may provide one mechanism for diverting some of those health care dollars back into the social service sector." The potential of Pay for Success is even raised as a solution to the opioid crisis by Katherine Klem, of the Institute for Child Success.

Early childhood education, child welfare, criminal justice, workforce development, and supportive housing are all sectors that have been early adopters of outcomes-based research and funding strategies. Janis Dubno, of the Sorensen Impact Center, describes a Pay for Success project in Salt Lake City that influenced the state legislature to increase its funding by $33 million over three years to help low-income children attend preschool. The child welfare field has worked with performance-based contracts over the years and is engaged in several social impact bond projects. Susan Snyder, of Georgia State University, believes that "social impact bonds could effectively support the widespread use of preventive interventions."

Carrie McKellogg and Carla Javits, of REDF, advocate for the power of social enterprise to achieve significant outcomes to accelerate effective workforce development programs. And Louis Chicoine, of Adobe Services, details the travails of negotiating a Pay for Success project for permanent supportive housing and candidly outlines both the strengths and weaknesses of the deal.

Kate Howard, of the city and county of San Francisco, and Fred Blackwell, of the San Francisco Foundation, describe HOPE SF as "the first initiative that marries the multi-strategy, cross-sector approach of collective impact and the Pay for Success model." The project, which focuses on disconnected youth aged 16–24, parallels the commitment demonstrated in the health sector to create a structure that aligns all the systems that must work together to make a meaningful change in their lives. This ambitious commitment and vision is shared by Prabhjot Singh and Anna Stapleton, of the Arnhold Institute for Global Health, who predict that the switch from health to health outcomes "will require a massive cultural shift within both medicine and the social service sector, away from old thinking that segregated clinical and social needs and into a new understanding of the human whole."

PUTTING RESULTS IN THEIR RIGHTFUL PLACE

All of us whose careers are dedicated to expanding social and economic justice and opportunity in this nation would agree that we are all better off when we know "what works" best to achieve our missions. We also realize the essential role of all types of data—organized in ways that enlighten, rather than obscure—in revealing "what counts" in determining our effectiveness and, ultimately, our impact. As Kelly Fitzsimmons, of Project Evident, reports from a 2016 market survey of nonprofits: "Contrary to conventional wisdom, nonprofits want to build evidence and evaluate, not...to meet grant requirements (eight percent) or to remain accountable to external stakeholders (18 percent)...but to improve performance (90 percent) and to verify intended impact (96 percent)."

Over the past decade, virtually every sector or field has come to understand that their outcomes rely in part or almost entirely on factors out of their direct control—an insight that is captured by the social determinants of health. This truth is eloquently shared by Susan Dreyfus, of the Alliance for Strong Families and Communities: "The social determinants of health are the social determinants of life."

What Matters tackles the looming question of how we embed an "investing for results" mindset and tools that are necessary to structure, finance, and assess this type of service integration into all our institutions. These essays are both aspirational and constructively critical, as they frame out the opportunities and the barriers to achieving this transformation in practice, policy, and culture. They all begin with the assumption, best captured by Jeremy Keele and Sara Peters, of the Sorenson Impact Center, that "outcomes provide a common language with which state and local governments and the nonprofit, private, philanthropic, and academic sectors can communicate their shared and competing visions and expectations of public programs and services." Carol Naughton, of Purpose Built Communities, offers a compelling outcomes-based strategy that uses this common language to marshal the many partners and resources needed to tackle concentrated poverty in neighborhoods across the country.

At the same time, many of the writers are candid that outcomes are not the sole metric for designing and evaluating programs and policies. Gordon Berlin, of MDRC, draws upon his nearly four decades of evaluation experience: "Outcomes alone are often not a reliable metric for judging the effectiveness of social investments." He draws careful distinctions between the "gross outcomes" and "net impacts" of evaluations, where the latter provide the data that determine if the intervention actually drove the outcomes or if they resulted from multiple other factors. Yet this level of rigor is commonly unrealistic for the majority of service providers, who lack the data infrastructure and analytic capacity needed to conduct it.

Jodi Halpern, of the University of California, Berkeley, and Douglas Jutte, of the Build Healthy Places Network, caution that adhering to outcomes metrics isn't enough. The moral and ethical implications of how those metrics are defined and delivered should be part of the conversation as well. "What matters ethically is not just the value of a stated goal in the abstract, but the specific pathways to meeting these goals." Building on that point, Megan Golden of Mission: Cure Pancreatitis, and Jitinder Kohli and Samantha Mignotte, of Monitor Deloitte, warn against conflating cost savings with value. Making that mistake "can lead to missed opportunities to fund programs that can solve some of our nation's most pressing problems [and]...risks enshrining the status quo rather than shifting government resources to more effective programs."

This gap between aspirations and reality is most consistently articulated in the multiple essays that are devoted in whole or in part to social impact bonds. Several articles in earlier sections of the book outlined the pros and cons of specific transactions—the Nurse-Family Partnership in South Carolina, child welfare programs in Connecticut and Tennessee, supportive housing to address homelessness, and a collective impact model for opportunity youth in San Francisco. Four articles consider social impact bonds and other outcomes-based funding models on a more systemic basis and reach some dramatically different conclusions.

David Merriman, of Cuyahoga Job and Family Services, recounts how his agency pioneered the application of the Pay for Success model at the county level. Although they encountered logistical, political, and staffing challenges along the way, Merriman is convinced that these models "make us more responsive to the needs of our clients and communities" and offer the platforms to "focus on impact over compliance, develop meaningful goals instead of achievable outputs, and commit the time and resources to work through decades of failed policies."

Keele and Peters underscore how the dramatic improvements in access to data and analytical tools provide the foundation for today's focus on outcomes and are the major drivers of outcomes-based funding tools. Although "outcomes have the potential to transform our relationship with state and local government," there are major and significant weaknesses inherent in relying on outcomes that range from "who owns them" to the lack of data infrastructure in most state and local governments. They remind us that "this field is still in its infancy; transforming the public sector into something more results-focused and measured is going to take many iterations."

The most comprehensive critique of social impact bonds is delivered by Richard McGahey, of the Institute for New Economic Thinking, and Mark Willis, of the Furman Center for Real Estate and Urban Policy at New York University. Although social impact bonds are clearly the hottest social impact fad since their introduction five years ago, there are fewer than 50 projects to date, and many are not meeting expectations. McGahey and Willis agree with the need for the stated benefits of social impact bonds—innovation, performance improvement, new funding sources, and high-quality evaluation. However, they believe that "social impact bonds and other Pay for Success approaches are drawing too much philanthropic, governmental, and nonprofit talent and creativity at the cost of other support for social innovation."

If we aspire to a future filled with scaled programs and policies with demonstrated effectiveness and results, we all have a role to play. Fitzsimmons outlines a new philanthropic agenda that puts the grantees at the center of program design and evaluation, practices patience and long-term investments, and is based on the belief that "the road to higher impact is paved with incremental improvements." Muzzy Rosenblatt, of the BRC, challenges the nonprofit sector to "manage with data, not to it" in ways that are forever in search of the results that "improve the lives of those we serve, consistent with our missions." Both the private and public sectors can achieve "standards of excellence" by implementing data and evaluation practices and policies outlined in the type of indexes created by Results for America co-founder David Medina.

It is the essay by Kristin Giantris and Jessica LaBarbera, of Nonprofit Finance Fund, that succeeds in bringing all these threads together to present a balanced and realistic path forward to "reorient our system around outcomes in a responsible way." They acknowledge the cumulative impact of the lack of investment in the social sector over decades, and how this compromises its ability to measure outcomes. They start with an inclusive assumption: "Instead of focusing on who is already 'ready,' we will need thousands of organizations to move up the continuum of readiness." They agree that all sectors need to do their part to advance "coordinated change across the social system" and welcome multiple models for making this transition.

This book is a giant step forward in advancing a movement that puts results at the heart of how we promote social and economic justice and opportunity in this nation.

———

ANDREA LEVERE *is president of Prosperity Now (formerly CFED), a private nonprofit organization with the mission of building assets and expanding economic opportunity for low-income people and disadvantaged communities through financial inclusion and capability, matched savings, entrepreneurship, and affordable housing. In 2013, President Obama appointed Levere to the National Cooperative Bank's (NCB) board of directors to represent the interests of low-income consumers. Levere holds a BA from Brown University and an MBA from Yale University. In 2001, she received the Alumni Recognition Award from the Yale School of Management and in 2008 was named to the inaugural class of its Donaldson Fellows Program, which recognizes alumni who help educate business and society leaders.*

FROM FUNDING ACTIVITIES TO INVESTING IN RESULTS
How Do We Get from Here to There?

Antony Bugg-Levine
Nonprofit Finance Fund

We can orient around outcomes, as a growing set of examples across geography and sectors are demonstrating. We can put funding in the hands of capable organizations, hold them accountable for making a positive difference, free them from the red tape of project compliance, and generate better long-term results. And we can reinvigorate our collective dedication to social-sector spending by providing taxpayers with the assurance that their resources are generating strong results.

To sustain a movement that can ultimately shift the system of social spending from outputs to outcomes will require much more than an increase in the pace of new examples. Outcomes arise from complex interactions that can never be under the control of any one organization. Whether a former prisoner in an anti-recidivism program stays out of jail will depend not only on the quality of the training he receives in the program, but also on whether political winds blow toward a more or less punitive court system, how economic shocks affect the job market, how demographics affect the housing market, and how public policies concentrate health hazards in his neighborhood, etc. Innovations in government contracting, financial engineering, and impact measurement are all necessary but insufficient to build an outcomes-oriented system. The only foundation that can sustain an outcomes-oriented system is a collective, actionable commitment to being accountable for what happens to all people in all communities.

WHAT CHANGE WILL THE SHIFT TO OUTCOMES REQUIRE?

What will it take to build that collective commitment and expand take-up of outcomes-oriented solutions? Our current way of organizing people and resources to solve social problems creates frustration and inefficiency. But it is familiar, well intentioned, and entrenched. Government agencies, nonprofit organizations, philanthropic donors, and investors have all built structures and rules and career paths that perpetuate it.

For outcomes orientation to go from inspirational anecdotes to a systemic shift will require overcoming the resistance to change. We know that complex social and environmental problems — ending chronic homelessness, reducing prison recidivism, building climate change resilience—will not be solved through one program, one intervention, or one agency. We need many people on board. And we cannot hope to recruit these people and their institutions, or to enlist them to the cause of addressing complex social challenges, if we do not understand what we are asking them to do.

Although we will all be called to support an outcomes-oriented system, the most important players will be the service providers, government funders, private donors, investors, and the people this system is organized to support. Understanding what the shift from an output- to outcomes-based system will entail for them is a crucial first step in figuring out how we can all work together to support this transition.

Service Providers: From "Do What You're Told" to "Show Us What You Can Do"

Our current social services system prizes delivering services at minimum cost and ensuring timely and accurate filing of the paperwork that proves the work got done. In an outcomes-oriented system, service delivery organizations instead are freed to innovate, finding the right interventions that will most likely support their clients' long-term success. The homeless shelter operator who understands clients' unique psychological needs could invest in mental health professionals to help clients leave homelessness, just as the early childcare operator could invest in anger-management training if she believes it can improve a child's readiness to learn. And importantly, this approach aligns how funding flows with the ultimate motivation that brings most social service professionals to work in the first place—to see long-term improvements in their clients' lives.

Such freedom to innovate brings a reliance on others that can be unnerving. In our current system, the homeless shelter and early childcare center operators largely control the variables that determine their success. They will be paid as long as they keep their facilities filled and follow the actions they committed to undertake. In contrast, outcomes are rarely within any one institution's control. A tight rental market that drives up the cost of affordable housing can curtail the ability to place homeless-shelter residents in permanent housing, just as instability in the job market can make it harder for parents of preschoolers to support the early child care center in preparing their children for kindergarten. Outcomes-oriented approaches risk shining a potentially damaging light on an organization for a perceived "failure" that's due to external forces.

The outcomes approach also requires service providers to transform how they operate internally. They will need to be able to measure and communicate the results of their work. This could require investments in data-tracking software, professional staff with impact measurement skills, and a longer-term relationship with their clients that is often difficult to sustain. They may also need to shift their internal culture to become more of a learning organization that can constantly experiment, assess, and implement what works. All this while operating in the current system where they must maintain the traditional compliance function, they lack operating reserves to cushion against potential failure, and where most funding does not cover costs. It's a tall order.

Government: From Control to Collaboration

In our existing system, government funds organizations that provide services for the lowest cost and monitors them to ensure taxpayer money is spent on specific activities agreed to in advance. In an outcomes-oriented system, government will instead focus on setting clear and measurable outcomes targets (e.g., reducing homelessness by a certain percentage or increasing the rate of children who complete an early childhood education program ready to learn in kindergarten) and provide flexible, full-cost funding to organizations who will decide on their own how best to achieve the predetermined goals.

Often outcomes will defy bureaucratic silos. For example, reducing foster care placement rates often requires collaboration between the housing department, the emergency shelter system, the education department, and the police and courts. We are already seeing that interventions organized around outcomes generate unexpected collaboration between institutions and agencies. After government and nonprofit leaders in Denver oriented around the outcome of ending chronic homelessness, police officers walking the beat now carry cards identifying known homeless residents so they can connect them to the local organization that can help them leave the streets. Prison department officials in New York are now proactively informing a local organization about prisoners poised for release to ensure their enrollment in a program aimed at reducing recidivism. In Los Angeles, the health department has shifted resources to invest in supportive housing after advocates generated evidence that "housing first" approaches save more in healthcare costs than they require in rental subsidy.

Government agencies also will need to invest in impact measurement capabilities. They will need to disclose data, and to strike the right balance between respecting individual privacy and sharing data on individual and community outcomes necessary to set targets and know if they've been met. And government will have to provide funding to help service providers to develop the internal capacity to use data to improve their programs and prove their results. Many service providers are already using new technologies and data, helping them to identify high-need clients more effectively, solicit real-time client feedback, and collaborate. These innovations require resources that cost-recovery contracts do not sustain.

Given these challenges, people outside government will need to back politicians and agency heads who take a stand for an outcomes-oriented system. These officials will need supporters who push for more flexible funding despite skepticism from the public and the media who are conditioned to highlight when taxpayer money pays for activities not prescribed in a government contract.

Private Donors: From Project Buyer to Capacity Builder

Like government funders, most private donors primarily provide project-based grants with detailed reporting requirements to ensure an organization did what it said it would. In a healthy outcomes-oriented system, these donors will provide flexible support that covers grantees' full costs, enabling them to invest in management teams, research, and impact measurement and monitoring, and to build up the operating reserves and fixed assets necessary to implement outcomes-based programs.

Private donors will help convene community discussions that identify goals and bring together the range of players necessary to reach them.

They will write funding contracts that focus on setting clear results targets and will release their funding based on outcomes milestones rather than activities or time. They will be an advocate for their grantees in a collective effort to bring together the private- and public-sector partners necessary to reach these goals. And they will take advantage of the flexibility that comes from operating without the glare that government agencies face to support grantee innovation, program development, and the investments in provider capacity that will be necessary but not always easy to defend politically.

Social Service Clients: From Input to Purpose

Our current output-based funding system treats the recipients of social services as units of output or activity—the filler of a bed in a shelter or a seat in a school. Funders pay organizations to provide services for these people, families, and communities. In an outcomes-based system, the activity is a means to the ultimate end. Success is measured not by what was done to a person or family but by what positive change occurred in their lives.

This has transformational implications. In our current system, many service providers know clients need tailored approaches, but their contracts prevent them from offering them. Instead, the recipients of a service are only guaranteed to receive as much attention from service providers as is mandated in a contract. In an outcomes-based system, they receive as much care and attention as is necessary to create the opportunity for better outcomes. In our current system, many people cycle through programs that do not comprehensively address the root cause of their problems. To succeed in an outcomes system, social service providers will need to coordinate to address root causes.

More people will be better off because of this shift, but for the person who is thrust into the center of an outcomes-based system, the collective investment in data tracking of his or her success could be disorienting and intrusive. To ensure clients thrive in this new system will require incorporating into program design and implementation the perspective of people whose lives social programs must ultimately impact. We will have to support people to sustain their engagement in programs that may take longer and require deep, trusting relationships. And, finally, we must guard privacy at the same time as track progress.

Investors: From Financing Operations to Financing Progress

In an output-oriented system, many contracts are paid at least partly upfront, so organizations that have adequate funding often do not require an investor to finance upfront costs. Where financing is necessary, private investors finance the service providers and are paid when the service provider completes the activities a contract mandates. A loan to a homeless-shelter operator to build a new shelter will be repaid as long as the shelter stays full, the operator runs it efficiently, and government honors its contract to pay for each night a bed was used. In this world, debt, often secured with real-estate collateral, is the primary way that investors finance interventions.

Investors will have a more important role to play in an outcomes-oriented world, but they will need new capabilities to play it. Finance becomes centrally important because funding will typically not flow to the provider until after the service has been delivered and the result assessed. Providers will need upfront capital to implement programs before they are paid based on their outcomes contracts. In the case of the investor in the homeless shelter, the provider will not be paid, or the investor repaid, unless the people who come through the shelter escape homelessness long-term. So, the investor now needs to understand how the activities the shelter operator plans to undertake will actually help the clients transition out of homelessness. This requires insight into the social science research about whether the proposed activities will lead to positive results. Investors will need to partner with those well versed in social science insights on the wide range of issues to which outcomes-oriented financing could be applied.

Investors will also need greater comfort with the uncertainty and risk inherent in striving for outcomes. And they will have an opportunity to develop new investment products that not only provide upfront financing for social services but also help service providers manage the new risk that comes with outcomes-based contracts.

LOOKING AHEAD

This essay is just a start to encourage the empathy necessary to support the different players who will need to embrace a new way of working if we want outcomes-oriented solutions to become more than islands in a sea of output-constrained activity. If you identify with one of the actors outlined above, imagining the changes required in your own organization is likely daunting. Fortunately, you are not alone. Across the country, extraordinary leaders are overcoming the status quo, making change happen in their communities, and pushing through the challenges highlighted here. But, relying on extraordinary people to find a way to overcome the existing system is not a formula for widespread success. Instead, we must create new norms so that the vast majority can comfortably embrace this new way of working.

To do so, we need a new narrative centered in a moral commitment that our society will do better for the poorest and most vulnerable people among us, and we need to organize this new narrative around that success. Social service providers want this; that is why they got into their work/field in the first place. Government and taxpayers want this. Donors and investors want it, too. And, of course, the recipients of social services want it for themselves.

This narrative must recognize that we are embarking on a generation-long journey and must help to sustain political support for work whose results will come after current election cycles end. We must draw motivation from the opportunity to address social challenges in the long term rather than to save money in the short term. This new narrative must confront the status quo while recognizing the discomfort that change creates for many people. It must be co-created by the people and the organizations that work most closely with them. We must reject calls for defunding programs that cannot prove their results before the providers of those programs have been given the investments and trust they need to do so. And, ultimately, we must recognize that achieving the outcomes we all seek is our collective responsibility.

ANTONY BUGG-LEVINE *is chief executive officer of Nonprofit Finance Fund (NFF), a national nonprofit and financial intermediary that advances missions and social progress through financing, consulting, partnerships, and knowledge-sharing that empowers leaders, organizations, and ideas. A leading community development financial institution (CDFI), NFF has $250 million in assets under management and has provided $620 million in financing and access to additional capital in support of over $2.3 billion in projects for thousands of organizations nationwide. Bugg-Levine is the co-author of* Impact Investing: Transforming How We Make Money While Making a Difference. *Prior to joining NFF in 2011, he designed and led The Rockefeller Foundation's impact investing initiative and oversaw its program-related investments portfolio. He was the founding board chair of the Global Impact Investing Network and convened the 2007 meeting that coined the phrase "impact investing." A former consultant with McKinsey & Company, he also taught at Columbia Business School.*

ROUTINIZING LEADERSHIP
Creating a Market for What Works

Ian Galloway

Federal Reserve Bank of San Francisco

By the late 1980s, acid rain had become a global scourge. Man-made emissions of sulfur dioxide and nitrogen oxides, byproducts of burning fuel for electricity generation and other industrial uses, were alarmingly high. Congress responded by passing the Clean Air Act, a multi-pronged policy to address pollution, which included a cap-and-trade program specifically targeting acid rain. This novel program incentivized power companies to find creative solutions to lower their own emissions, leading to a 76 percent reduction since 1990.[1] "The brilliance of the scheme," according to The New York Times *columnist Joe Nocera, was "that while [cap-and-trade] set emissions targets, it did not tell power companies how to meet those targets, allowing them a great deal of flexibility."[2] That flexibility led to industry-wide innovation and, ultimately, a solution at scale: near-elimination of acid rain in the United States.*

In the mid-1990s, getting to space meant booking a seat on the NASA shuttle. Sensing an opportunity, Peter Diamandis traveled to Missouri in honor of Orteig-Prize-winner Charles Lindbergh's Spirit of St. Louis solo transcontinental flight from New York to Paris and proposed something bold: a $10 million prize for the first company to send three people 100 kilometers above the Earth twice in two weeks (and bring them back alive).[3] Eight years later, the Ansari XPRIZE was claimed by SpaceShipOne, a spaceplane designed by aerospace engineer Burt Rutan and financed by Microsoft co-founder Paul Allen (see Bravo/Frangione/Wander in this volume). This was, by all accounts, an enormous scientific breakthrough in a relatively short period of time. But the Ansari XPRIZE paid dividends beyond SpaceShipOne. While competing to win the $10 million prize, 26 companies from

---

Thanks to my Federal Reserve colleagues David Erickson and Joselyn Cousins for their assistance with this chapter. The views expressed are my own and may not reflect those of the Federal Reserve Bank of San Francisco or the Federal Reserve System.

1   U.S. Environmental Protection Agency, "National Air Quality: Status and Trends of Key Air Pollutants" (last updated September 15, 2016), available at https://www.epa.gov/air-trends.

2   Joe Nocera, "Obama's Flexible Fix to Climate Change," *The New York Times* (August 4, 2015), available at https://www.nytimes.com/2015/08/04/opinion/joe-nocera-obamas-flexible-fix-to-climate-change.html.

3   XPRIZE Foundation, "Mojave Aerospace Ventures Wins the Competition that Started it All," available at http://ansari.xprize.org/teams.

around the world spent a combined $100 million developing new space technology. That collective investment now forms the foundation of today's $2 billion private space industry.[4]

At the turn of the century, pneumococcal infections were killing half a million children annually worldwide.[5] There was no viable market for vaccine development to prevent these infections, which primarily afflicted children in developing countries. At the same time, in 2000, the Global Alliance for Vaccines and Immunization (GAVI) was formed by the Bill & Melinda Gates Foundation in partnership with the United States, United Kingdom, Norway, and several other large donors to bring expensive vaccines to impoverished countries. However, this wasn't enough to get pharmaceutical companies to create new vaccines specifically for use in the developing world, given the limited market potential for low-cost treatments. So GAVI took a different tack, making an advance market commitment to buy, at a pre-specified cost, a certain volume of vaccine doses should a company choose to produce one (see Levine). This $1.5 billion commitment led directly to the creation of a new vaccine, which now protects children from pneumococcal infections in 54 countries around the world.

These examples showcase inspired leadership: Congress aggressively tackling acid rain; Diamandis launching a modern-day space race; GAVI saving millions of lives. But what makes their leadership notable is actually what they *didn't* do. Congress didn't reflexively mothball power plants. Diamandis didn't hire engineers to build him a spaceship. GAVI didn't directly fund vaccine research and development. They knew that their challenges were too hard to solve alone and that the solutions they needed were largely unknown. They understood that trying to "pick winners" from among any number of proposals at hand would likely fail. So they created an incentive to unleash creativity, a reward for outside-the-box thinking. And they insisted on results.

GETTING TO THE ROOT OF THE PROBLEM: PERFORMANCE RISK

Some 400,000 mission-driven nonprofits provide critical services to people in crisis every year in the United States.[6] Serving these communities effectively—e.g., the homeless, mentally ill, abused, and neglected—is

---

4 Ibid.

5 Ruth Levine, Michael Kremer, and Alice Albright, "Making Markets for Vaccines: Ideas to Action," Center for Global Development Advance Market Commitment Working Group (2005).

6 Defined as social safety net nonprofits. Lester M. Salamon, *America's Nonprofit Sector: A Primer*, 3rd edition (New York: Foundation Center, 2012).

incredibly hard and a clear moral imperative. Yet, even as we routinely talk about exceptional social programs that work (and we published a book predicated on that idea),[7] there are very few genuinely "evidence-based" programs from which funders can choose.[8] "In many areas of public policy, we simply don't know much about what works, for whom, and under what circumstances," according to Erica Brown, Josh McGee, and Kathy Stack.[9] Many programs, while promising, are ultimately unproven. In other words, they can be risky bets.

This risk matters. Funders, both government and philanthropic, don't want to invest in programs that don't work. But their ability to assess the likelihood that a program will succeed is limited. Social challenges are dynamic: Something that once worked, in a different place, with a different set of people, may not work again. Programs are dynamic, too: Fidelity to the model isn't just a matter of following a recipe; the people following the recipe matter, too. Put the two together and it's easy to see that any social program, however well-studied or replicated, entails taking a risk.

Predictably, in light of this risk, nonprofit reporting and program monitoring requirements have gotten more onerous (see Gustafsson-Wright). Funders want to know that their investments are performing as promised. But that isn't enough to guarantee results, so they also tend to fund programs at their base cost.[10] This may be rational (if you don't know if something's going to work, invest sparingly), but it's pernicious in practice. The consequences are familiar and widespread: administrative functions are underfunded and undervalued; innovation is discouraged because it threatens lean program budgets; and nonprofits are frequently treated like commodities, competing primarily on price, not performance. Paying nonprofits on a cost-of-service basis, and not a value-creation basis,

---

7 Nancy O. Andrews and David J. Erickson eds., *Investing in What Works for America's Communities* (San Francisco: Federal Reserve Bank of San Francisco and Low Income Investment Fund, 2012).

8 Steven Goldberg, "Scale Finance: Industrial Strength Social Impact Bonds for Mainstream Investors," Federal Reserve Bank of San Francisco (April 2017), available at http://www.frbsf.org/community-development/publications/special/scale-finance-social-impact-bonds-for-mainstream-investors-pay-for-success/.

9 Uncited quotations in this essay refer to *What Matters* book chapters.

10 Claire Knowlton, "Why Funding Overhead is Not the Real Issue: The Case to Cover Full Costs," *Nonprofit Quarterly* (January 25, 2016), available at https://nonprofitquarterly.org/2016/01/25/why-funding-overhead-is-not-the-real-issue-the-case-to-cover-full-costs/.

makes it very difficult for them to build organizational capacity.[11] As Kelly Fitzsimmons observed, "Foundations were reluctant to pay for evidence building. However, when...asked for program funding, they demanded evidence of impact—evidence that we couldn't build without the funding they were hesitant to provide." This reluctance to fund organizational capacity leads to an endless cycle of resource scarcity which, tragically, is reinforced by the continuing lack of capacity needed to prove program effectiveness, which would otherwise limit funder risk and break the cycle of scarcity.

PAYING FOR OUTCOMES INSTEAD OF PICKING WINNERS

The way out of this performance-risk trap is for funders to stop gambling on individual programs and take an adaptive, program-agnostic approach that mirrors the breakthrough examples at the start of this essay. There's actually precedent for this in the social sector: the Low Income Housing Tax Credit (LIHTC). LIHTC is the primary subsidy source for multifamily affordable-housing construction and rehabilitation (see Ludwig). To date, the LIHTC program has produced over three million affordable housing units nationwide (see Erickson), while leaving nearly all the risky design, construction, and financing details up to the project developer.

LIHTC works like a tax coupon that raises money for affordable housing. State housing finance agencies award the credits to housing developers, who sell them to investors with tax liability—usually through a syndicator—and then use the proceeds to lower the overall project cost. This, in turn, allows developers to take out a smaller mortgage to cover the remainder of their expenses. A more manageable mortgage allows them to charge lower rents, effectively transferring the project subsidy to the individual tenants living in the building. As long as rents stay low, the investors who bought the credits get to keep them. However, if rents go up beyond a certain threshold, the IRS recaptures the credits, and the investors lose their money.

Critics of LIHTC's complexity call for the government to simply award subsidies directly to affordable housing developers, cutting out the syndicators, investors, reporting requirements, and consultants. But there's a

---

11 Ibid.

good reason for the complexity: It buys the government a performance guarantee. If an affordable housing project can't maintain affordable rents for a minimum of 15 years, the government gets its money back. This performance guarantee—effectively an adaptive, program-agnostic feature—is widely considered to be an improvement over the largely maligned top-down, federally funded public housing projects of the past.[12]

The LIHTC program recognizes that affordable housing needs will be different in different places. In some cases, affordable housing should be blended with market-rate housing to create mixed-income communities; in others, it should be anchored by a health clinic or grocery store. One community may need senior housing; another, housing for foster care families. Low-income renters have different needs and preferences. It's difficult for the federal government alone to properly assess these and craft an affordable housing solution to meet them. Instead, LIHTC allows the government to buy what it really wants—housing affordability—and leaves the community customization to the housing developer.

Much like the federal government's role in LIHTC projects, the prototypes highlighted in this book suggest a new role for nonprofit funders. Instead of investing in programs, funders would purchase outcomes and leave the program specifics to the provider. Funders could buy these outcomes any number of ways—through a rate card, an advance market commitment, a loan modification covenant, an impact insurance policy, a Pay for Success contract, or even a prize—but they wouldn't need to become program experts to do so. By shifting out of their traditional investor role, which depends on correctly identifying winners, funders would be funding what works, at the price they agreed to, without taking any risk. This is how an adaptive, program-agnostic social sector could function. Getting there successfully, though, will depend on whether we can define and deliver outcomes that matter.

DEFINING WHAT MATTERS

In an adaptable, program-agnostic world, the party paying for the outcome generally decides "what matters" based on its own set of preferences. A hospital system, for example, may care deeply about reducing

---

12 David Erickson, *The Housing Policy Revolution: Networks and Neighborhoods* (Washington, DC: Urban Institute Press, 2009), pp. 90–91.

health disparities in its local community (see Norris/McLean) or fear a financial penalty from its state health authority for failing to deliver on a particular health measure (see Long). In either case, the hospital would be the party deciding the outcome it would be willing to pay for.

Projected cost savings can also drive outcomes-based funding projects. A program that promises to reduce unnecessary incarceration, for example, may be selected over a program that increases child literacy on purely a cost-savings basis. This is a controversial aspect of outcomes-based funding, and the moral, ethical, and political implications of prioritizing cost savings are discussed at length in this volume (see Golden/Kohli/Mignotte and Halpern/Jutte). But the fact remains: The virtuous cycle of prevention leading to less treatment is financially compelling. This may prove short-sighted, however, in cases where the cost of producing a particularly valuable social outcome (ending homelessness, for example) exceeds the current cost of treating it or in cases where a successful outcome leads to greater use of a different, more expensive, service. Cost savings, while instructive, shouldn't be the sole basis on which outcomes are decided.

Outcomes-based funding tools also require a high degree of nonprofit capacity. An outcomes rate card may be an efficient way to deliver social programs at scale (see Metcalf/Levette), but its success will depend on whether nonprofits are prepared to use it. Capacity is a significant predictor of what types of projects receive outcomes-based funding. Nancy Andrews argues in her chapter that we need an onramp (what she calls "Equity with a Twist") to outcomes-based funding that allows nonprofits to build capacity around measurement and program administration. Kerry Sullivan argues for the same. Without sufficient capacity-building, the field will be limited by the relatively small universe of evidence-based providers that can take advantage of these tools. "If we truly desire a systemic shift, we need to invest in organizations' ability to make the initial transition, and to continue to measure their outcomes on an ongoing basis," note Kristin Giantris and Jessica LaBarbera. Another reason to invest in capacity building: Existing high-capacity providers may influence how the outcomes-based funding field evolves to their advantage, potentially freezing out peer organizations that could one day participate.

The maxim "you get what you measure" applies doubly here. Getting the measurement piece right is critical to defining outcomes. "Reliance on the wrong measures, lack of data on key measures, or poor-quality data can lead to faulty conclusions," warns Gordon Berlin. If we're serious about funding outcomes, we need absolute confidence that we're measuring them correctly. This means being scientific about enrollment processes, intervention tracking metrics, and "compared to what?" counterfactuals. Good information technology solutions (see Whistler/Gee) will be crucial.

Data availability plays an important role as well. At root, outcomes-based funding models depend on data to prove that an outcome has been achieved (or not). Acquiring useful data is critical to the success of any outcomes-based funding project. But in some cases, what we track may be less a function of what matters and more a function of what data we can collect. This is immensely limiting and risks moving the field toward outcomes that happen to be easy to track and away from outcomes that may be more valuable but aren't currently measured. "We cannot allow [information] availability bias to determine how we understand organizations," according to Jacob Harold. This caution should also extend to outcomes. If we allow existing data to define what's valuable, simply because we can measure it, we may end up celebrating statistically significant outcomes but not meaningful ones.

DELIVERING WHAT MATTERS

An adaptable, program-agnostic approach is not a good fit for every social challenge, nor is it a good fit for every nonprofit. Right-sizing the intervention to the outcome is crucial. A preschool provider shouldn't be held accountable for high-school graduation rates. Likewise, a job training provider shouldn't be held accountable for reducing homelessness, even if a job is a critical factor in housing stability. Outcomes-based funding is better used in cases where there is a clear and direct relationship between a given program intervention and the desired outcome: For example, reducing foster-care placements by addressing family substance abuse (see Merriman) or increasing post-release employment for former prisoners with in-prison computer coding classes (see Beck/Schwab/Pinedo). Holding nonprofits accountable for outcomes outside of their direct purview is unfair to them and unlikely to succeed.

Moreover, meaningful social change can take a long time. We know that high-quality early childhood education increases the chances of graduating from high school and leads to higher rates of adult employment, lower rates of criminal behavior, and greater family stability.[13] But these outcomes don't appear for years—and, in some cases, decades—after early childhood. This makes structuring outcomes-based contracts for interventions like early childhood education more difficult. Someday, it may be possible to link outcomes-based funding projects, with each delivering a component piece of the outcome "value chain." For instance, there are certain intermediate markers throughout childhood—healthy birth, third-grade reading scores, pro-social behavior development, high-school graduation, etc.—that could be standalone links in that chain but, put together, lead to a longer-term "stretch goal,"[14] such as avoiding teenage pregnancy or graduating from college. Each successful link would trigger an outcomes payment, which could be valued based on its relative importance in the chain.

Another promising approach is comprehensive, place-based development that targets an entire neighborhood with services over a sustained period of time. Melody Barnes, former director of the White House Domestic Policy Council, made the observation at a 2010 Federal Reserve conference that low-income people don't have a housing day, then a transportation day, then a job day, then a fresh food day—every day is an everything day.[15] Put another way, interrupting the cycle of intergenerational poverty requires a complex set of effective interventions. Maggie Super Church makes the case in this volume that investment funds can be structured to capture an array of health benefits based on a successful neighborhood investment strategy. Similarly, Kate Howard and Fred Blackwell are piloting an outcomes-oriented collective impact approach to transform four low-opportunity neighborhoods in San Francisco. These

---

13 James Heckman, "Invest in Early Childhood Development: Reduce Deficits, Strengthen the Economy," The Heckman Equation (July 2013), available at https://heckmanequation.org/assets/2013/07/F_HeckmanDeficitPieceCUSTOM-Generic_052714-3-1.pdf.

14 The term "stretch goal" refers to a difficult-to-achieve outcome, as described in James Radner and Jack Shonkoff's essay "Mobilizing Science to Reduce Concentrated Poverty," *Investing in What Works* (2012), available at http://www.whatworksforamerica.org/ideas/mobilizing-science-to-reduce-intergenerational-poverty/.

15 Melody Barnes, Remarks at Federal Reserve Healthy Communities Conference (Washington, DC: Federal Reserve Board of Governors, 2010).

examples offer proof of concept that neighborhood-scale, place-based developments, augmented by effective social programming, can deliver meaningful outcomes for whole communities.

Looking ahead, there's an untapped opportunity to build on these early success stories. Purpose Built Communities (see Naughton) has pioneered a place-based model in Atlanta—now replicated nationwide—that integrates mixed-income housing, a pre-K-through-college education pipeline, and wellness programs ranging from physical fitness, to job training, to financial literacy. Importantly, these supports aren't offered in isolation; They're carefully coordinated by a "community quarterback" that senses and responds to changing needs on the ground. In the future, organizations like community quarterbacks could be funded for achieving a set of stretch goals related to health, education, employment, and crime that are achievable only through large-scale neighborhood coordination.

Regardless of the intervention, these projects must deliver on their core promises to be successful. If you commit to getting kids ready for kindergarten, you have to actually prepare them for kindergarten (see Dubno). If you commit to reducing opioid use disorders (see Klem), you're on the hook to reduce opioid use disorders. In the end, delivering the outcome is what matters most.

ROUTINIZING LEADERSHIP

When my colleagues and I wrote "Routinizing the Extraordinary" in the first book of this series, most of our focus was on the nonprofits themselves: BakerRipley (formerly Neighborhood Centers Inc.) in Houston; Harlem Children's Zone in New York City; Purpose Built Communities in Atlanta.[16] They were all producing astonishing results in health, education, housing, and employment for their communities. They also tended to be entrepreneurial in nature, fundamentally cross-sectoral, and data-driven, and they deployed a careful blend of human services and place-based interventions.[17] We wanted to highlight these examples so they could be replicated in the field.

---

16 David Erickson, Ian Galloway, and Naomi Cytron, "Routinizing the Extraordinary," *Investing in What Works* (2012), available at http://www.whatworksforamerica.org/ideas/routinizing-the-extraordinary.

17 Ibid, p. 378.

But replicating transformational community change is hard. Not every nonprofit can become the Harlem Children's Zone. The better solution, we thought, was to routinize the key elements. Make it easy for anyone, anywhere to do this work. It would also depend on a certain kind of leadership "able to promote a compelling vision of success for an entire community, marshal the necessary resources, and lead people in an integrated way."[18] Routinizing extraordinary results meant routinizing extraordinary nonprofit leadership as well.

A new kind of institution was needed to coordinate community development activity that anyone would deploy, which we termed a community quarterback. The quarterback could take on any number of forms depending on community needs; it would be empowered by real-time data and sophisticated data systems; it would deploy a mix of people- and place-based strategies; and it would be held accountable for results. And, ideally, those results would be carefully tracked and rewarded through an investment tax credit, a social impact bond, or another outcomes-based funding tool.

But in our rush to routinize nonprofit leadership, we failed to account for something else: Just as we can't "rely on saints"[19] to produce outcomes, we can't rely on saints to pay for them. Ben McAdams and Armond Budish are rare.[20] The Bill & Melinda Gates and XPRIZE foundations are rare.[21] And as the outcomes-based funding field has matured, this over-reliance on extraordinary funder leadership has been laid bare. It's not enough to deliver better outcomes for Medicaid-eligible patients, or foster children, or the chronically homeless if someone isn't willing to pay for them. Routinizing nonprofit leadership will fall short if we don't routinize funder leadership as well.

---

18 Ibid, p. 382.

19 A reference to Langley Keyes' book *Strategies and Saints: Fighting Drugs in Subsidized Housing*, as cited in Erickson, Galloway, and Cytron, "Routinizing the Extraordinary," *Investing in What Works* (2012).

20 Ben McAdams, Salt Lake County (see Keele/Peters); Armond Budish, Cuyahoga County (see Merriman). There are other outcomes funders that deserve recognition for their leadership but space precludes naming them here.

21 Bill & Melinda Gates Foundation (see Levine); XPRIZE Foundation (see Bravo, Frangione, and Wander).

A MARKET FOR SOCIAL OUTCOMES

At the beginning of this book, David Erickson imagines a future market for social outcomes that will "permit problem-solving ideas to come from every direction." This market would be "inherently anti-monopoly, pro-local, and community-empowering." It would also be adaptive and program-agnostic, like the three examples highlighted at the outset of this essay. By intentionally not picking winners, Congress, Diamandis, and GAVI were able to achieve their goals without gambling on the wrong solution. Their leadership was the act of handing over program-selection control to a market that selects on their behalf. They understood that markets can be useful tools when you aren't sure if something is going to work.

Framing the solution to poverty in market terms may seem counter-intuitive. After all, the market economy created many of the challenges we're trying to address in this book. These concerns also extend to "privatizing" the social safety net. "There is no private-sector-based magic that will solve these critical needs," cautioned Richard McGahey and Mark Willis at the conclusion of their chapter. This common view is rooted in a long history of neighborhood disinvestment and the economic marginalization of low-income communities by the private sector. But it also misses the mark.

The social safety net was privatized long ago. The 400,000 service nonprofits that currently comprise the social sector are nongovernmental.[22] The real issue, I suspect, isn't the privatization of the sector but more broadly a fear of the "private prison" scenario. Private prisons represent, for many people, the open-and-shut case for why we shouldn't hand crucial government services over to the private sector. But the comparison fails to account for two significant distinctions: First, the private prison system is largely comprised of profit-driven companies, not mission-driven nonprofits; and second, it probably fingers the wrong culprit. Most private prison operators are paid based on how many beds they fill.[23] But what if they were paid for reducing recidivism rates instead? Prison operators may focus more on rehabilitation and skill building. Prisoners may reenter their communities better prepared to succeed, leading to fewer

---

22 Salamon, *America's Nonprofit Sector: A Primer* (2012).

23 In the Public Interest, "Criminal: How Lockup Quotas and Low-Crime Taxes Guarantee Profits for Private Prison Companies" (September 2013), http://www.njjn.org/uploads/digital-library/Criminal-Lockup-Quota,-In-the-Public-Interest,-9.13.pdf.

reoffences. Long-term criminal justice outcomes may actually improve. The private sector isn't inherently better or worse at delivering important services provided we're mindful of the incentives that drive it.

Another commonly voiced concern about market-based solutions to poverty is the role financial institutions play. Peter Nadosy, the chairman of the Ford Foundation's investment committee, echoed this recently in *The New York Times*: "Not to malign Wall Street, but when they smell a profit opportunity, you have to be careful."[24] Nevertheless, financing is often a necessary component of outcomes-based funding. In order to pay staff, run programs, and otherwise "keep the lights on," nonprofits may have to appeal to a financial institution for up-front working capital. That financing may come from a private philanthropy like Ford, an impact investor, a community development financial institution, or even a bank. While outcomes-based financing is relatively new, it's a natural extension of 40 years of community development lending and investing, which has produced millions of affordable housing units, in addition to thousands of health clinics, community centers, and schools, all located in historically underinvested neighborhoods.[25]

Still, for many people, financing social services just *feels* different from other types of financing. But it's a distinction without a difference. The mortgage attached to an affordable housing building, for example, is paid back based on how well the housing performs: Unrented apartments, or unexpectedly low rents, and the project won't generate enough cash flow to repay the loan. Outcomes-based financing, likewise, is repaid based on the nonprofit's performance: Failure to deliver the specified outcome(s) and the nonprofit won't be able to pay back its investor. In both cases, the financing is tied to how well the project serves its intended beneficiaries. Whether that's through a real estate development or a social program should be immaterial.

---

24 James B. Stewart, "Ford Foundation Is an Unlikely Convert to 'Impact' Investing," *The New York Times* (April 13, 2017), available at https://www.nytimes.com/2017/04/13/business/ford-foundation-mission-investment.html.

25 Erickson, *The Housing Policy Revolution* (2009), pp xii-xv.

Despite a veneer of efficiency, there is also a worry that markets can create unnecessary complexity and waste. This seems to be borne out in our early experience with Pay for Success: Projects take a long time, involve many partners, and cost more than a conventional service contract. Tamar Bauer and Roxane White's observation, "If parenthood is the toughest job you will ever love, then Pay for Success may be the most grueling growth strategy we will someday celebrate," seems to confirm this worry. But as LIHTC has proven, the complexity can be worth it. A performance-based guarantee allows for maximum provider flexibility and minimal funder risk. It can be a good tradeoff in cases of performance uncertainty. Likewise, the added expense of transaction structuring, evaluation, and cross-sector data management serves a purpose, which is to ensure a higher level of measurement and implementation rigor.

That said, for all the attention successful programs receive in an outcomes-funding context, less is paid to the program "losers" that have innovated and failed. It's fair to ask: Shouldn't the net benefit of a successful outcome factor in the cost of all the programs that tried but ultimately didn't work? Given the potentially net-negative cost of producing a positive outcome, it can be tempting to first test promising programs with grants before going to scale. The flaw with this kind of accounting is that program-related innovations that fail aren't sunk costs. The $100 million collectively spent competing for the Ansari XPRIZE wasn't wasted. It became the foundation of a $2 billion private space industry. Contrast that with the substantial time and resources required to respond to grant requests from funders. That energy produces fundraising innovation, not program innovation. And if the grant isn't secured, the effort that went into the grant application often becomes a sunk cost that doesn't grow the organization or contribute to the field.

The biggest concern of all, though, is probably trust. Why should we trust a market mechanism to deliver better results than funders who are disciplined, evidence-based, and in tune with the needs of the communities they care about? This is the central question of this book. In my view, we depend too much on the leadership of funders—both government and philanthropic—to direct resources. Nonprofits shouldn't have to convince funders that their programs are valuable in order to be funded. If the value is self-evident then their funding should be routine. A market for social outcomes—deployed through all the tools highlighted in this book—would be an adaptable, program-agnostic method of distributing resources based on value. But it requires that funders give up control over program selection. If they resist that role, a market for social outcomes will never materialize.

Eighty authors contributed to this volume, offering a range of perspectives on outcomes-based funding. Through all the diversity of opinion, one thing is clear: The sector's shift to outcomes is as much a cultural departure as it is a technical one. "A paradigm shift toward results-based funding is a major analytical breakthrough. But its benefits can be realized only if we look at the number of rituals that need to change and make sure we balance strategy with culture in thinking about how to make those changes," predicts Zia Khan.

The hardest part of this cultural transition will be getting comfortable with a different kind of leadership, both from nonprofits and their funders. In a market that values social outcomes, leadership will be routinized by a set of market conditions that identifies and rewards results. To skeptics, this may seem like letting the fox guard the henhouse. But a market is just a tool, a social compact that steers resources on behalf of society—an invisible hand attached to the body politic, so to speak.[26] A market that values social outcomes would be no different, steering resources based on results. Those results may be guided by a market mechanism but what matters will still be up to us.

———

IAN GALLOWAY *is director of the Center for Community Development Investments at the Federal Reserve Bank of San Francisco. He is a co-editor of this book and the first book in this series,* Investing in What Works for America's Communities *(2012). He received an MPP from the University of Chicago and a BA in political science and philosophy from Colgate University.*

———

26 Gary Gutting, "Why Conservatives Should Reread Milton Friedman," *The New York Times* (September 26, 2013), available at https://opinionator.blogs.nytimes.com/2013/09/26/why-conservatives-should-reread-milton-friedman/.